THE DEMOGRAPHIC T
OF CITIZENSHIP

The Demographic Transformations of Citizenship examines how attempts by contemporary states to govern demographic anxieties are shaping ideas about citizenship both as a boundary-maintaining mechanism and as an ideal of equal membership. These anxieties, while most often centred upon immigration, also stem from other demographic changes unfolding in contemporary states – most notably, the longstanding trend towards lower birth rates and consequent population ageing. With attention to such topics as control over borders, national identity, gender roles, family life and changing stages of life, Askola examines the impact of demographic changes, including but not limited to immigration. Drawing from a variety of disciplines, including law, demography and sociology, this book discusses how efforts to manage demographic anxieties are profoundly altering ideas about citizenship and belonging.

DR HELI ASKOLA's background as an international migrant informs both her research and her teaching. Having left her native Finland in 2001, Dr Askola has since worked for several years in Italy, the United Kingdom and, currently, Australia. Her central research theme is the study of migrant-receiving states' management of international migration, from an interdisciplinary and comparative perspective. Her main research interests are in the areas of immigration and citizenship, trafficking in human beings, EU law, gender equality, human rights and multiculturalism. She is the author of a number of publications, including a book on the European Union's role in combating trafficking in human beings. She has taught courses in many countries, including Canada, Italy and Malaysia. She has also done consulting work for the International Organization for Migration, the European Commission and the European Parliament on areas such as trafficking in human beings, EU citizenship, hate speech and children's rights.

CAMBRIDGE STUDIES IN LAW AND SOCIETY

Cambridge Studies in Law and Society aims to publish the best scholarly work on legal discourse and practice in its social and institutional contexts, combining theoretical insights and empirical research.

The fields that it covers are: studies of law in action; the sociology of law; the anthropology of law; cultural studies of law, including the role of legal discourses in social formations; law and economics; law and politics; and studies of governance. The books consider all forms of legal discourse across societies, rather than being limited to lawyers' discourses alone.

The series editors come from a range of disciplines: academic law; socio-legal studies; sociology; and anthropology. All have been actively involved in teaching and writing about law in context.

Series Editors

Chris Arup *Monash University, Victoria*

Sally Engle Merry *New York University*

Susan Silbey *Massachusetts Institute of Technology*

A list of books in the series can be found at the back of this book.

THE DEMOGRAPHIC TRANSFORMATIONS OF CITIZENSHIP

Heli Askola
Monash University Faculty of Law
Victoria, Australia

CAMBRIDGE UNIVERSITY PRESS

CAMBRIDGE
UNIVERSITY PRESS

University Printing House, Cambridge CB2 8BS, United Kingdom

One Liberty Plaza, 20th Floor, New York, NY 10006, USA

477 Williamstown Road, Port Melbourne, VIC 3207, Australia

314-321, 3rd Floor, Plot 3, Splendor Forum, Jasola District Centre, New Delhi - 110025, India

79 Anson Road, #06-04/06, Singapore 079906

Cambridge University Press is part of the University of Cambridge.

It furthers the University's mission by disseminating knowledge in the pursuit of education, learning and research at the highest international levels of excellence.

www.cambridge.org
Information on this title: www.cambridge.org/9781316506172

© Heli Askola 2016

This publication is in copyright. Subject to statutory exception and to the provisions of relevant collective licensing agreements, no reproduction of any part may take place without the written permission of Cambridge University Press.

First published 2016
First paperback edition 2018

A catalogue record for this publication is available from the British Library

ISBN 978-1-107-14079-0 Hardback
ISBN 978-1-316-50617-2 Paperback

Cambridge University Press has no responsibility for the persistence or accuracy of URLs for external or third-party internet websites referred to in this publication, and does not guarantee that any content on such websites is, or will remain, accurate or appropriate.

CONTENTS

Acknowledgements	*page* vii

1	Introduction	1
	Demographic Transformations	4
	Demographic Governance?	12
	Demographic Governance and Citizenship	18
	The Structure of the Book	23
2	Missing Citizens? Birth Rates and the Making of New Citizens	28
	Italy: La morte di un popolo?	31
	Two Demographic Revolutions	31
	To Govern or Not to Govern National Reproduction?	39
	Variations on a Theme? Finnish, British and Australian Trajectories	45
	Citizenship and the Governance of National Reproduction	55
	Final Remarks	66
3	Misguided Citizens? Transitions into Adulthood and the Management of Diversity	67
	The United Kingdom: Shaping the Choices of the Young	70
	Troubled Youth? De-standardised Transitions to Adulthood	70
	Governing Misguided Young Citizens	76
	Variations on a Theme? Australian, Italian and Finnish Trajectories	85
	Citizenship and the Quality of the Future Citizenry	96
	Final Remarks	105
4	Casual Citizens? The Desirable Labour Migrant and Conditional Citizenship	107
	Australia: Welcome and Wanted (Conditions Apply)	110
	From Nation-Building to Misgivings about Immigration	110
	Quality or Quantity, Immigrants or Migrants?	116
	Variations on a Theme? British, Italian and Finnish Trajectories	125

CONTENTS

	Citizenship and the Governance of Labour Migration	137
	Final Remarks	145
5	Depleting Citizens? Ageing Populations, Care and Migration	147
	Finland: Walled or Weakened Welfare?	150
	Ageing Pains of a Welfare State?	150
	The Turn Towards Familialism – But 'Why Can't Granny Stay'?	157
	Variations on a Theme? Italian, British and Australian Trajectories	167
	Citizenship and the Management of Ageing Populations	177
	Final Remarks	186
6	Conclusion	188
Bibliography		193
Index		247

ACKNOWLEDGEMENTS

I started work on this book while on sabbatical from the Faculty of Law at Monash University in 2012. I am grateful for the financial support of Monash University and for the help of my colleagues and friends in the Faculty of Law. I am also indebted to the British Institute of International and Comparative Law in London, where the early part of this research was conducted.

I have given papers and presentations which have explored different aspects of this research at various international fora, including at Izmir University (Turkey), the University of Roehampton, the European University Institute in Florence and Cardiff Law School. I have benefited greatly from the constructive comments and questions received on these occasions. I am also grateful to Finola O'Sullivan and the anonymous readers for Cambridge University Press for their support for the project.

Finally, it has been said that authors should dedicate their books to the person who had to suffer most while they were writing. In that spirit, this book is dedicated to Michael Debenham.

CHAPTER ONE

INTRODUCTION

This book examines the ways in which demographic anxieties and attempts to govern them are shaping ideas about citizenship. Demographic anxieties are often expressed regarding immigration but also arise in relation to other demographic changes unfolding in the contemporary 'Global North'[1] – most notably, the longstanding trend towards lower birth rates and consequent population ageing. With particular attention to changing gender roles and life courses, the book examines how unfolding demographic transformations, including *but not limited to* immigration, and efforts to manage these changes are interacting and transforming ideas about citizenship.

Citizenship is, of course, a multi-functional and multi-dimensional concept – it is used to describe both a formal legal status as a member of a bounded political community and an ideal of equal membership, with associated rights and duties and political participation. A voluminous body of literature has emerged in the last decades around the ways in which international migration challenges states' right, ability and willingness to control who enters and stays in their territory, as well as the assumed cultural and religious uniformity of the (nation) state. Such analyses, often focusing on the legal regulation of immigration and

---

[1] The term 'Global North' is often used as a shorthand to distinguish between 'developed' states (that is, states with high human development: industrialised, politically and economically stable, with high levels of human health) and other states (the 'Global South'). This is a rough divide based on socioeconomic and political factors rather than geography – not all of these states are located in the Northern Hemisphere (Australia and New Zealand are the most obvious examples of states located in the Southern Hemisphere which are part of the Global North).

citizenship, capture part of the picture of the ways in which immigration shapes ideas about citizenship. However, they typically leave out or only cursorily refer to the remarkable demographic changes which stimulate and underpin continuing immigration, knowledge of which is driving states to encourage or at least tolerate further immigration, albeit with considerable anxiety and constant efforts to minimise those impacts of international mobility that they consider most detrimental. These changes have to do with the trend towards lower birth rates and consequent population ageing, and they include dramatic shifts in gender and family dynamics, as well as changes in age structures and adaptations of the life course. When immigration is viewed with attention to these demographic transformations, which form the context for continuing immigration, a more nuanced picture of the manifold challenges to citizenship emerges. The topic then raises issues around not just sovereignty, control over borders and national identity but gender roles, reproduction, intergenerational responsibilities and family life and relationships.

This book tries to connect the dots between some of the many debates about and struggles over citizenship and immigration, by drawing attention to the changes in demographic background and attempts to govern or manage these changes based on demographic knowledge. In particular, it emphasises the shifting role of gender relations and a time dimension, both of which are important for understanding the current set of anxieties around citizenship and immigration and for getting a fuller picture of states' attempts at managing demographic change. With special attention to four late-modern societies – Italy, the United Kingdom, Australia and Finland – the book argues that efforts to manage demographic changes that seek to sustain a (nation) state are bound up with contestations regarding gender relations, the family form and intergenerational compacts, as well as transformations in the role of the state in relation to its population. The book discusses both the legal rules on immigration and citizenship and other areas of policy which shape citizenship, such as aspects of economic and social policy and the welfare state, family law and employment regulation. It uses insights from the social sciences (sociology, legal anthropology and, of course, demography) to investigate how demographic trends, and knowledge and fears related to them, are shaping states' approaches to citizenship, as well as to examine what these demographic contestations reveal about the interconnections between national and biological reproduction.

INTRODUCTION

Investigating efforts to manage population changes, or 'demographic governance' (see later) – for instance, through measures aimed at raising the birth rate or at altering immigration patterns – involves venturing into an area that used to be called 'population policy'.[2] As Jacques Vallin has noted, 'the desire to influence the size or composition of the population is an ancient one',[3] and modern states' ongoing interest in their populations is explained by the absolute indispensability of the latter as a condition for their existence.[4] Talking about population policies, however, immediately raises the spectre of the many attempts, often repugnant, to control the lives of populations and subpopulations in the not so remote past. These include, most obviously, Nazi Germany, where racially motivated extermination of subpopulations was undertaken along with eugenic research to improve 'population quality', but also the neo-Malthusian[5] 'global population control' movement which became associated with the promotion of coercive means to reduce childbearing in the Global South.[6] It is of course the rejection of ideas associated with eugenics and coercion that has led to the extension of personal freedoms, and indeed the rise of human rights that largely keeps democratic states in the Global North away from explicit population policies. However, this book argues that just because liberal states' direct and explicit control over population developments is more circumscribed, this does not mean they have lost interest in the current and future resource their populations represent, nor the threats segments of them may pose. The fact that states continue to shape their populations is most evident with regard to immigration, but extends beyond it.

Rather than demonising demographic governance through references to its sinister past, this book examines the attempt to manage demographic trends and anxieties as something that deserves attention

---

[2] May, *World Population Policies*, 2, defines population policies as 'actions taken explicitly or implicitly by public authorities, in order to prevent, delay, or address imbalances between demographic changes, on the one hand, and social, economic, and political goals, on the other'.
[3] Vallin, 'Population policy', 1. See also McIntosh, *Population Policy*, 28, who characterises the link between population and power as a persistent theme of population policy.
[4] The Montevideo Convention on the Rights and Duties of States defines a state as an entity that has 'a permanent population, a defined territory, government and capacity to enter into relations with the other states' (Art. 1).
[5] For Malthus's original essay, see Malthus, *Essay on the Principle of Population*.
[6] These include forced sterilisations in India and the infamous one-child policy in China. On the population control movement and its discontents, see e.g. Connelly, *Fatal Misconception*; Eager, *Global Population Policy*; Hartmann, *Reproductive Rights and Wrongs*. On the Chinese one-child policy as a form of demographic governance, see Greenhalgh and Winckler, *Governing China's Population*.

3

INTRODUCTION

because of its implications for scholars interested in the regulation of citizenship and immigration, as well as gender equality. In fact, much of what can be characterised as population policy in the contemporary Global North is mundane and takes place every day, under the agency of a range of actors.[7] Governments plan for the future and use various forms of demographic knowledge, for instance censuses and demographic projections, uncertain as they are,[8] to plan long-term strategies around the labour market and health care systems. This sort of management, though not necessarily innocuous, is typically considered both rational and benign. However, what makes it important are the ways in which the governance of populations is connected to the changing concept of citizenship. This book argues that ideas about citizenship, the rights and duties that membership entails for citizens (men and women) and the conditions under which migrants are allowed to join politico-legal communities are embedded in demographic histories and rationales. Decisions about managing demographic changes in contemporary states involve political and legal choices that carry real consequences for citizens and non-citizens alike. As one demographer admits, 'the question of equity is most often absent from demographic thinking, though central in terms of political action.'[9] What is therefore of interest is precisely the nexus between demographic thinking and political action, as a site of inclusion and exclusion, contestations and resistance.

The rest of this chapter introduces the demographic background that will be explored in the book, outlining the most important demographic trends that are creating (sometimes contradictory) anxieties. It then discusses states' efforts at managing demographic changes ('demographic governance') and outlines some of the many implications of these efforts for citizenship. Finally, it sets out the structure of the book.

DEMOGRAPHIC TRANSFORMATIONS

Current issues related to citizenship and immigration are connected to global, regional and national population trends, as well as increased awareness of and anxiety over them. The broad and increasingly global

[7] Livi-Bacci, 'Population policy', 192.
[8] Demographic projections are not *predictions* – they extrapolate based on past trends and do not take into account changes in policy parameters but assume that the trends will continue to operate in the future.
[9] Toulemon, 'Should governments in Europe', 188. On demographers' lack of sensitivity to gender equality, see Presser, 'Demography, feminism'.

trend, though not unfolding in the same way in every place, involves a slow shift from high birth and death rates to low birth and death rates, as countries develop from pre-industrial to industrial and post-industrial societies. This transformation started in Europe and is sometimes described as being part of a complex worldwide process known as the 'demographic transition'.[10] Demographers and social scientists are still debating the origin and theoretical interpretation of this shift,[11] but the idea of a demographic transition is a useful shorthand for describing broad demographic developments that have taken in place in the last couple of centuries. The argument goes as follows: improvements in health, sanitation, nutrition and medical science led/lead to lower mortality and longer lifespans, which in turn led/lead (initially) to population increase. This growth, together with factors like improving contraception and societal and cultural changes (e.g. urbanisation, which reduces the value of children's agricultural work; women's increasing education; attitudinal change), is linked with women adjusting their birth rates downwards, thus leading to 'reproductive efficiency'.[12] This modernisation of demographic behaviour is arguably underway, but progressing at uneven pace around the globe.[13] Once started, this gradual process tends to become an ongoing and long-lasting transformation that takes centuries to complete and brings with it societal, economic and political upheavals, thus playing 'a fundamental role in the creation of the modern world'.[14]

A period of population growth is part of this process of demographic change in most societies. Globally, population has been growing for some centuries, but this growth accelerated in the 1800s, as mortality started to decline but fertility decline had not yet begun in most countries. As is well known, world population growth in recent decades has been remarkable: world population was estimated at one billion in 1800, two billion in 1927, three billion in 1960 and reached six billion by 1999 and seven billion in 2011.[15] As one commentator aptly

---

[10] See Livi-Bacci, *A Concise History*, ch. 4.
[11] As Kirk, 'Demographic transition theory', 384, points out, 'it has not been resolved whether the demographic transition is a theory, a generalisation, a framework for analysis, or merely an "idea"'.
[12] For a sample of discussions around the theory, see Chesnais, *The Demographic Transition*; Dyson, *Population and Development*; Kirk, 'Demographic transition theory'; Lee, 'The demographic transition'; Reher, 'Towards long-term population decline', 'Economic and social implications'.
[13] For a discussion of alleged exceptions and whether they constitute exceptions, see e.g. Chesnais, *The Demographic Transition*.
[14] Dyson, *Population and Development*, ix.
[15] The 7 billion mark was generally greeted with alarmist headlines – see e.g. the *Guardian*, 'Why current population growth is costing us the Earth', 24 October 2011.

remarked, seven billion is four times the world population existing just a century earlier.[16] The acceleration of population growth is due to still relatively high birth rates at the global level, especially in parts of the Global South; though global fertility is now declining all over the world, the rates vary greatly (and growth remains strong in areas like Sub-Saharan Africa).[17] Despite the overall decline in birth rates, the momentum of large age cohorts of women reaching childbearing age is projected to keep global population growing for some decades. While exact population forecasting is a complex task, the latest United Nations (UN) projections show a continued increase of world population – but a decline in the population growth rate – with the global population projected to reach between 8.4 and 8.6 billion persons in 2030.[18] Regional distribution of population is shifting more towards Asia: it now accounts for over sixty per cent of the world population, and China and India together have about thirty-seven per cent of the world's population.[19]

Global population growth is starting to slow down, though the changes will take decades to filter through, if they do at all (the predictive force of the demographic transition 'theory' is not strong[20]). Concerns over global population increase and, in particular, the sustainability of societies experiencing strong population growth – even slowing growth – in parts of the Global South, along with associated urbanisation, have been connected to climate change and other environmental and resource concerns, as changes in population size, rate of growth and distribution have an impact on both the natural environment and development prospects. Though studies show there is little association between nations with rapid population growth and nations with high emissions,[21] it is at present very common to hear environmentalists express the sentiment that the 'growth in human numbers

---

[16] Pearce, *Peoplequake*, 3.
[17] May, *World Population Policies*, ch. 2. On demographic patterns in the Global South, see Livi-Bacci, *A Concise History*, ch. 5.
[18] United Nations, 'World population prospects'. On the uncertainties involved in the UN and other demographic projections, see O'Neill et al., 'Global population projections'.
[19] In both of these states, the sex ratio is skewed due to modern technology being used to enforce son preference – see Sen's influential article that estimated that 100 million women were 'missing' worldwide: Sen, 'Missing women'; on China, see Hvistendahl, *Unnatural Selection*.
[20] This issue with the demographic transition theory highlights a general issue regarding demography, which, as Kirk, 'Demographic Transition Theory', 361, puts it, is 'a science short on theory, but rich in quantification'.
[21] Satterthwaite, 'The implications of population growth'.

is frightening'.[22] At the same time, it is clear that it is the populations of the Global North, not the poorer, still growing populations of Africa and Asia, who use the vast majority of the world's limited resources and emit most greenhouse gases.[23] Moreover, the most prosperous states are not likely to see the worst effects of environmental degradation and climate change (food and water scarcity are typically seen in places with limited financial means and inadequate political and managerial resources). How to build a sustainable and globally fair system of dealing with the human impact on the environment, including climate change, is both the big moral question of our time and the urgent practical one in many states. While these matters are largely beyond the scope of this book, they form the broader background against which the global sustainability and sensibility of states' policies ultimately need to be evaluated.

In the meantime, the local populations of most states in the Global North, where the transition started in the 1800s, have largely completed it.[24] Women in these societies have significantly fewer children, and many of the populations of late-modern states ceased to grow some decades ago, owing to longstanding low mortality and birth rates that stay barely at or, in most cases, below those required for the replacement of generations (hence, this is often referred to as 'below-replacement fertility'). The total fertility rate (TFR, as in births per woman) has been below the replacement level (1.05 per woman, or 2.1 per couple) in practically all industrialised states for some time;[25] so-called 'lowest-low' fertility states in Europe and East Asia have persistent TFRs below 1.3.[26] Sustained low birth rates in the 'developed' (and increasingly the 'developing') world are often stressed to be 'new' and considered a historically unprecedented shift.[27] Lesthaeghe, with van de

---

[22] David Attenborough, on joining the Optimum Population Trust; see BBC, 'Attenborough warns on population', 13 April 2009.
[23] And even in the Global North, argue Angus and Butler, *Too Many People?*, most resources are not consumed by individuals or households, but by mines, factories and power plants run by corporations.
[24] Dyson, *Population and Development*, 64. Note that population ageing, the last stage, is still ongoing: Lee, 'The demographic transition'. Taking the long, long view, Caldwell, 'Demographic theory', 311, argues that the world is still in the early stages of moving from a society based on agriculture to one structured by industrial production.
[25] If there were no mortality in the female population until the end of the childbearing years then the replacement level of TFR would be very close to 2.0. The replacement fertility rate is roughly 2.1 births per woman for most industrialised states.
[26] Kohler et al., 'Emergence of lowest-low fertility'.
[27] Douglass et al., 'Introduction', 5; Kramer, *The Other Population Crisis*, 1.

Kaa, calls the sustained and persistent below-replacement birth rates of many northern states a 'second demographic transition' – a new and unpredictable stage in demographic history, associated with trends towards later marriage, increase in cohabitation, fertility postponement and childlessness.[28] Demographers have struggled to explain this development (which is often linked to societal trends such as secularisation, rising individual autonomy and women's emancipation), let alone predict how birth rates may develop in the future.[29] In practice, however, the significant shifts in birth rates that have already unfolded mean that without continuing and, in some cases, higher levels of immigration, contemporary states face the prospect of population decline, and markedly so if projected trends continue.[30] Many states would be in population decline already but for continuing immigration, and indeed, even with immigration, Japan and some states in Europe are likely to encounter negative population growth soon.

The 'second demographic transition' has many enduring consequences. One of the most notable, apart from the prospect of population decline, is rapid population ageing. Population ageing – a shift in the population towards older age groups – is part of the transition to lower birth rates and higher life expectancy, and it is inevitable that the proportion of the population above a certain age rises as part of that transition.[31] However, sustained low birth rates speed up this process. The shift in the distribution of a population towards older ages, crudely encapsulated by the concept of a changing dependency ratio – the age-dependent ratio of those in the labour force, paying taxes, and of those typically outside it (retired and children) – shapes all facets of late-modern societies. Most notably, ageing affects pay-as-you-go pension systems and the provision of health and social care for the growing older cohorts (especially with the increasing numbers of the frail very elderly), but it also has implications for economic growth, labour

---

[28] Lesthaeghe, 'The unfolding story'. The idea of a second transition was originally raised in Lesthaeghe and van de Kaa, 'Twee demografische transities?'. See also Chesnais, 'Below-replacement fertility'. Reher, 'Towards long-term population decline', considers long-term decline a 'virtual certainty' for Europe and a possibility for some of the other regions still at the earlier stages of the transition.

[29] E.g. Chesnais, 'A march toward population recession'; Lutz and Skirbekk, 'Low fertility'. Most demographers predicted that birth rates would stop falling when they reached the replacement rate, but instead they kept falling – very much so, in some countries.

[30] E.g. Coleman, 'Europe's demographic future'; Demeny and McNicoll, 'Political demography'; Frejka and Sobotka, 'Overview chapter 1'; Reher, 'Towards long-term population decline'.

[31] Another arguably inevitable consequence of the demographic transition is urbanisation – see Dyson, *Population and Development*.

markets, taxation, living arrangements and housing.[32] Similarly, a decline in the proportion of the population composed of children and increasing diversity in the younger age cohorts will have significant long-term impacts, testing intergenerational loyalty, commitments to universal entitlements of citizenship and social cohesion. While environmental reasons might persuade states to accept ageing and eventual population decline as inevitable or even welcome, the challenges of low birth rates make ageing 'too quickly' an alarming prospect for many states.[33] Globally, demographic decline will also involve readjustments in political weight, for instance in the international political arena.[34] Hence, the contradictory ways in which the prospect of a declining population is considered both a 'threat'[35] (an economic and social one) and 'very good news indeed'[36] (from the standpoint of natural resources and the environment).

Deeming the demographic threat to be more crucial has led many contemporary states to seek strategies to deal with the challenges of ageing — most notably, immigration. Practically all late-modern states consider (though sometimes reluctantly) immigrants as necessary for filling, at least in part, the perceived demographic gap in their workforce and society.[37] However, many states would have to import what they consider to be 'unsustainable' numbers of immigrants to prevent population ageing altogether.[38] Welcoming more immigrants has thus not been the only answer. Some states have adopted family policies to induce citizens (couples, but in particular women) to produce more future workers and tax payers.[39] The relationship between birth rates and migration, in both ideological and practical policy terms, is one

---

[32] European Commission, 'The 2012 Ageing Report'; see also Tremmel, *Demographic Change and Intergenerational Justice*.
[33] On alarmist discourse around population ageing, see Katz, 'Alarmist demography'; Messerschmidt, 'Garbled demography'.
[34] See Demeny, 'Population policy dilemmas'. In 1950, six of the ten most populous states were in the 'developed' world, four of them in Europe; by 2020, only the United States will remain in the top ten. Livi-Bacci, *A Concise History*, 219.
[35] Demeny and McNicoll, 'Political demography', 269.
[36] Reher, 'Towards long-term population decline', 200.
[37] As Livi-Bacci, *A Concise History*, 233 puts it, 'migration gives a substantive contribution ... to the rich countries' renewal'.
[38] See e.g. Coleman, 'Immigration and ethnic change', 'Demographic effects', 'Divergent patterns' on how even current immigration numbers involve, in the long run, substantial alteration of the composition of the European population. Note also, however, the ahistorical tendency to treat immigration and resulting population change as 'new' phenomena, especially in Europe, despite immigration having been an integral part of European history for centuries; see Sassen, *Guests and Aliens*.
[39] See Chapter 2.

that is frequently remarked upon but little analysed from the point of view of its policy consequences (and is one of the topics that will be examines in this book). Increased migration and higher birth rates are often argued to be mutually reinforcing elements in a population policy that seeks to mitigate, if not remove, the impact of the demographic transition: for instance, both are argued to be necessary for European states' responses to population decline.[40] A more ethno-nationalistic view, less frequently stated outright, frames higher birth rates and migration as *alternatives* in the management of demographic challenges:

> Federal Opposition Leader [later Prime Minister] Tony Abbott wants Australians to have more babies and let fewer migrants into the country. Mr Abbott today said the Coalition would cut the annual immigration intake to 170 000 places, compared to a peak of 300 000 two years ago, if elected. The Coalition wanted to make immigration more sustainable because many people thought it was 'out of control', he said.
> But Mr Abbott is keen for Australians to have more babies, echoing an instruction from former Liberal treasurer Peter Costello who called on them to have three children – one for mum, one for dad and one for the country. 'I would like to see our birth rate improve because even now, despite the uptick in the birth rate over the last few years, it's still significantly below replacement level,' Mr Abbott said.[41]

Quantitatively speaking, birth rate levels are decisive for future population size and structure – and it is because of women having fewer children that many contemporary states are headed for decline, while some less wealthy ones are still heading in the opposite direction (with many intermediate states too now headed in the direction of lower birth rates).

However, in wealthier states, more attention has focused on the (far smaller) variable of immigration. As a demographic process, immigration is 'volatile'[42] – while in a state-centred world order, immigration is more easily controllable by states than are the family decisions of citizens (at least in liberal states), it is also prone to alter the make-up of the receiving states, especially those with low birth rates, contributing to a host of anxieties about new entrants (whether justified or not).[43] As

---

[40] European Commission, 'Green Paper'.
[41] The *Australian*, 'Tony Abbott says we should have more babies and let fewer people into the country', 25 July 2010.
[42] Van Nimwegen and van der Erf, 'Europe at the crossroads', 1367.
[43] Winter and Teitelbaum, *Global Spread of Fertility Decline*.

Koslowski puts it, 'the policy impact of migration is often out of proportion to the actual size of migratory flows because of public perceptions in the host country that migrants increase employment competition, challenge religious, cultural or ethnic homogeneity or pose threats to national security'.[44] Promoting immigration from regions that have a population 'surplus' (and high birth rates), while in some ways logical in abstracto,[45] thus taps into already high anxieties over immigration, ethnic minorities and 'second-generation'[46] immigrant-citizens in receiving states. Fears over the preservation of cultural (and, implicitly, religious and ethnic) homogeneity and social solidarity loom ever larger in many states that were unprepared for the irreversibility of this demographic change, which some demographers have called the 'third demographic transition'.[47] This change is not about the size of the population but about the *kind* of population that is being reproduced. Unsurprisingly, there is disagreement over whether (and what kind of) migrants are in fact 'needed' to solve the economic and social issues caused by ageing.[48] Even where the case is accepted for some migration, the size of the potential pool of immigrants created by global population growth has made states in the Global North ever keener to admit only a select few, chosen on the basis of skills and suitability – the overall trend is towards 'more control, restriction, and selection'.[49]

In summary, various trends around birth rates, concerns over immigration and environmental fears are fuelling complex and often contradictory demographic anxieties about reproduction, membership, social cohesion and intergenerational relationships. As one commentator puts it, 'not since the panic of the 1930s has demographic change been such a live political issue.'[50] Some of those particularly concerned about

---

[44] Koslowski, Migrants and Citizens, 2. For a historical perspective, see Sassen, Guests and Aliens.
[45] Logical in the sense that it allows them to release the pressures of population growth, as European states once did by sending immigrants to all corners of the world, to populate e.g. North America and Australia. See Chesnais, The Demographic Transition, ch. 6; Livi-Bacci, A Concise History, 132–7. However, it may also cause 'brain drain', which can have detrimental consequences for sending societies. See Docquier and Rapoport, 'Globalization, brain drain'.
[46] Talking about second- (or 1.5-, or third-) generation 'immigrants' is problematic (and telling) in that calling someone who is born in a certain country (and has not immigrated) a second-generation immigrant assumes migrants' descendants remain outsiders even when citizens. See further Chapter 3.
[47] See Coleman, 'Immigration and Ethnic Change', 'Demographic effects', 'Divergent patterns' for a discussion of how immigration is irreversibly changing European societies. See also Teitelbaum and Winter, A Question of Numbers; Weiner and Teitelbaum, Political Demography, ch. 8.
[48] Demeny and McNicoll, 'Political demography', 260, argue that migration is often used as the 'easy' solution to avoid serious thinking about how to raise fertility rates.
[49] Livi-Bacci, A Concise History, 227.   [50] Hampshire, Citizenship and Belonging, 185.

INTRODUCTION

the urgency of environmental decline condemn all attempts to take measures to increase the populations of wealthy states as 'deck chair arranging', given the current environmental footprint of such states:

> there are already over a hundred countries whose combination of numbers and affluence have already pushed them *past* the sustainable level. They include almost all developed countries. The UK is one of the worst. There the aim should be to reduce over time both the consumption of natural resources per person and the number of people – while, needless to say, using the best technology to help maintain living standards. It is tragic that the only current population policies in developed countries are, perversely, attempting to increase their birth-rate in order to look after the growing number of old people. The notion of ever more old people needing ever more young people, who will in turn grow old and need even more young people and so on ad infinitum is an obvious ecological Ponzi scheme.[51]

From this point of view, declining birth rates and the prospect of population decline should be welcomed and encouraged everywhere (most benignly, through strengthening the commitment to women's reproductive rights, which is believed to result in a low birth rate), and South–North immigration should be discouraged (as it tends to lead to higher consumption and environmental footprint for the migrants). Whether global environmental problems are predominantly or even partly due to population numbers is, however, fiercely disputed.[52] Forecasting what will happen to birth rates globally or regionally is similarly a very complex and highly uncertain task.[53] And changes in immigration and citizenship policy are perhaps most controversial of all.

DEMOGRAPHIC GOVERNANCE?

The quote from Tony Abbott in the previous section suggests a perception that the population situation, especially regarding international migration, is 'out of control' – stressing the challenge that international mobility, encouraged by the processes of globalisation, has posed to states' capacity to control who enters and resides in their territories.[54]

[51] Attenborough, 'People and planet'.
[52] See Angus and Butler, *Too Many People?*, who argue that a focus on human numbers mischaracterises the causes of environmental problems.
[53] Booth, 'Demographic forecasting'.
[54] E.g. Castles and Davidson, *Citizenship and Migration*; Hollifield et al., *Controlling Immigration*; Jacobson, *Rights Across Borders*; Joppke, *Challenge to the Nation-State*; Sassen, *Losing Control?*.

Undeniably, the presence of irregular migrants and the famous guest workers who became permanent are examples of how the declared aims of liberal states' immigration policies may conflict with the unfolding reality.[55] Similarly, as will be discussed later in this book, in liberal democracies, where direct government intervention in individuals' lives is avoided, it has proved difficult to increase the national birth rate or enforce the workforce participation of older people. It is thus true that demographic challenges are unlikely to dissipate and that the total control over demographic variables (most notably, international migration) that is desired by some politicians is impossible, at least in liberal states. Though there may be gaps between the stated aims of immigration policy and the actual outcomes, however, states are 'deeply involved in organizing and regulating migration'.[56] Globalisation has undoubtedly put states under pressure regarding immigration flows, but it would be ahistorical to claim that states were ever sealed off and inaccurate to maintain that late-modern states lack the means to influence the population changes facing them. Contemporary states have many ways to respond to the demographic challenges they are facing – indeed, immigration policies exemplify continuing state engagement with the shaping of their populations. As Brubaker puts it, 'far from escaping the control of the state, migration is subjected to ever-more sophisticated technologies of regulation and control'.[57]

The ways in which states continue to use their laws and policies to control their borders and manage their populations have been described as 'demographic governance'. Hampshire, evoking Foucault, uses this term to mean:

> the way in which modern states regulate and manage their populations using a variety of governmental techniques. These techniques include tools and methods to monitor, gather information and create knowledge about population trends... as well as interventionist policies designed to effect changes in the size or composition of a population.[58]

Unsurprisingly, considering the controversial history of population policies and the current diversity of views and priorities on population matters (among them, economic, social and environmental), rarely is demographic governance explicitly framed in terms of a 'population

---

[55] Freeman, 'Modes of immigration politics'; Joppke, 'Why liberal states accept'.
[56] On this gap, see Hollifield et al, 'The dilemmas of migration control', 26.
[57] Brubaker, 'Migration, membership', 77. [58] Hampshire, *Citizenship and Belonging*, 2–3.

policy'.[59] Yet contemporary states do have population policies – in the form of myriad laws, policies and practices that either actively define or, perhaps even more commonly, implicitly form the parameters of demographic governance.[60] Active demographic governance is most evident in immigration and citizenship policy, which set criteria for immigrant admission, residence and naturalisation, but as Hampshire points out, 'any state that wishes to exercise even a modicum of control over its population must attend to inflows and outflows of people as well as to those who are settled.'[61] Demographic governance of 'insiders' – citizens and residents – takes a great number of forms, many of them indirect, but examples such as the collection and use of official statistics, welfare policies, policies regulating work and retirement and rules on the permissibility and availability of family planning and abortion can all be understood as incorporating elements of demographic governance or population management.[62]

Demographic governance is underpinned by the persistent idea that the 'people' constitute a closed system (apart from carefully controlled immigration), typically based on implicit demographic assumptions of the legitimacy and indeed the 'naturalness' of the (nation-) state.[63] While this notion matches the prevalent approach to contemporary states, especially 'nation-states', as bounded units, the concept of a population is of course 'neither neutral, nor natural'.[64] As Koslowski, among others, has argued, (European) nation-states are a historically specific development, built on population growth, expulsion and emigration.[65] The constructed nature of demography's foundational concept explains why it is a constant source of anxiety that has to be monitored and guarded. The processes through which the modern state constructs its population and, through a range of mechanisms, begins to treat its subjects as amenable to calculated transformation were most famously traced by Foucault.[66] He employed the

---

[59] In Europe, the eugenics legacy has especially prevented Italy and Germany from openly wording their demographic policies as population policies. The few states that have an explicit population policy keep it rather vague. See e.g. Commonwealth of Australia, 'Sustainable Australia'. On the challenges involved in the development of population policies, see May, 'Population policy'.

[60] As Jones, 'The dangers of muddling through', 142, puts it, 'in practice, every nation has its own population policy. The existential choice is whether it is to be explicit (transparent, open to debate) or implicit (the incremental outcome of short-term pragmatic decisions).'

[61] Hampshire, *Citizenship and Belonging*, 3.   [62] Livi-Bacci, 'Population policy', 192.

[63] E.g. May, *World Population Policies*, 43.   [64] Messerschmidt, 'Garbled demography', 305.

[65] Koslowski, *Migrants and Citizens*, esp. ch. 3.

[66] Foucault, *History of Sexuality*, esp. pt 5; see also Foucault, *Society Must Be Defended*, *The Birth of Biopolitics*.

notion of biopower to describe how the state disciplines and regulates human beings in its territory through institutions, using both anatomo-political techniques aimed at the individual body (including its sexual and reproductive functions) and biopolitical techniques aimed at the collective or social body: the population.[67] Biopower thus involves both individualisation (targeting individuals and their bodies) and totalisation (treating individuals as a collectivity). It makes use of truth discourses, including demographic knowledge and assumptions, articulated by authorities (experts in demography, economy, statistics, public health, welfare and so on) to implement beneficial interventions on populations, while also seeking to make individuals work on themselves in appropriate ways.[68] The mechanisms of biopower constitute, in Foucaultian terms, techniques of 'governmentality' or governmentalisation of population.[69]

In the context of biopower, governmentalisation entails calculation and strategies to manage the collective life and health of the population through interventions aimed at securing the population's prosperity and security.[70] Some of this activity directly implicates law as a characteristic instrument of sovereignty (though this is not what is of most interest to Foucault himself).[71] This is most obvious with regard to persisting state powers over international migration, which involves crossing boundaries between sovereign states as spaces where populations are governed. As Hampshire argues, law and policy on citizenship and migration have become central to demographic governance, because anxieties related to increased international mobility between states have propelled states to refine their strategies to maintain stable borders and populations.[72] Laws regulating immigration and citizenship as a formal legal status are thus crucially implicated in efforts to limit, control and monitor entry based on criteria regarding the desirable characteristics of immigrants (based on which, some are channelled towards permanent residency and citizenship and others denied entry). However, legal mechanisms are of course also implicated in the management of the populations inside states (for instance, via the mechanisms

---

[67] Foucault, *History of Sexuality*, 139–41.   [68] Rabinow and Rose, 'Biopower today'.
[69] Dean, *Governmentality*; Lemke, 'The birth of bio-politics'; Rose and Miller, 'Political power beyond the state'.
[70] Rabinow and Rose, 'Biopower today'.
[71] Rose and Valverde, 'Governed by law?', 542; see also Macleod and Durrheim, 'Foucauldian feminism'. For a survey of Foucault's relevance for law and legal theory, see Golder and Fitzpatrick, *Foucault's Law*.
[72] Hampshire, *Citizenship and Belonging*, 8.

of family law), with law operating increasingly to maintain norms for the regulation of conduct.[73] At the same time, legal configurations can be said to be intermixed and to interact with extra-legal processes and practices of governance.[74] A good example of this intertwining is the governance of reproduction: as Yuval-Davis points out, decisions over reproduction are not characterised by a 'laissez-faire' situation 'even in the most permissive societies',[75] and while laws regulating the permissibility of abortion directly intervene in individual behaviour, control over reproduction is often exercised in indirect ways (involving, for instance, the medical profession as experts).[76]

Indeed, many techniques of governmentality in liberal democracies are indirect and seek to turn individual subjects into 'responsible' or rational populations and to produce optimal citizens and collectivities best suited to fulfil governments' policies.[77] An essential element of biopower is that where possible, individuals are persuaded to work on themselves 'in the name of their own health or life'.[78] Some argue these modes of governing individuals are increasingly informed by neoliberal reason, seeking to enhance the quality of citizens in order to allow national populations to gain a competitive advantage in the global marketplace, while limiting states' direct responsibility for them.[79] Economic liberalisation (corporatisation, privatisation and deregulation) is certainly relevant to the ongoing transformation of individual–state relations and the way in which the boundaries between state and non-state action are being recast.[80] Though such approaches to governing populations are also evident in an immigration policy context (such as initiatives to 'responsibilise' new immigrants to integrate into society as economic actors and 'good' immigrant-citizens), most discussion of such mechanisms has been in terms of how they target states' 'insider' populations and subpopulations 'at a distance', seeking increasingly to steer them towards appropriate life choices throughout the life course, from the cradle to the grave.[81] For instance, the indirect governance of reproduction, an enduring site of population anxiety, entails techniques to persuade women – as the reproducers of the nation – to procreate

---

[73] Dean, *Governmentality*, esp. ch. 6.   [74] Rose and Valverde, 'Governed by law?', 546.
[75] Yuval-Davis, 'Gender and nation', 629.   [76] E.g. Sheldon, *Beyond Control*.
[77] Inda, *Targeting Immigrants*; Lemke, 'The birth of bio-politics'; Rose, 'Governing liberty'; Rose and Miller, 'Political power beyond the state'.
[78] Rabinow and Rose, 'Biopower today', 197.
[79] Ong, *Neoliberalism as Exception*. See also Lemke, 'The birth of bio-politics'; Rose and Miller, 'Political power beyond the state'.
[80] Brown, *Undoing the Demos*.   [81] Rose, 'Government and control', 324.

appropriately through self-regulation, encouraged by various medical and welfare discourses (for instance, advice on how to maintain fertility).[82] At the other end of the lifespan, older people are encouraged to save and plan in order to be self-sufficient at the end of their life.[83]

Demographic governance is closely tied up with demographic anxieties; that is, ideas about the risk posed to and by populations and subpopulations, in both quantitative and qualitative terms. Much has been written about the paradoxical yet heightened role of risk and fear in contemporary societies.[84] In terms of governmentality, expert knowledge and discourses shape understandings of risk and identify where its boundaries lie, facilitating the identification, management and disciplining of vulnerable/at-risk individuals and groups using various techniques of surveillance (surveillance is, of course, often mentioned as a key attribute of modern states).[85] Demographic governance, involving efforts to govern demographic risks and uncertainties on the basis of demographic knowledge, is particularly implicated in constructing understandings of risk that seek to regulate individuals and groups on the basis of their demographic characteristics in circumstances characterised by lack of trust and a sense of insecurity. Such efforts involve political discourses that promote self-management of various risks to individuals but are also evident in the identification of 'suspect populations' (such as 'criminals', 'single mothers' or 'welfare-recipients'). 'Suspect populations', constructed on the basis of demographic knowledge and assumptions, are those identified as posing particular threats (and are often simultaneously at-risk because of their marginalisation) and are therefore singled out for special attention, surveillance and discipline.[86] Though the images of otherness may attach to deviant insiders, in an age where the boundaries of states are a site of increasing anxiety, protecting external boundaries from the threat of dangerous non-citizens ('illegal immigrants' and 'fake asylum-seekers') and managing the behaviour of certain groups of outsiders-on-the-inside ('homegrown terrorists') both have heightened importance.[87]

---

[82] Inda, *Targeting Immigrants*; Macleod and Durrheim, 'Foucauldian feminism'; Rose, 'Government and control'. See also Chapter 2.
[83] See Chapter 5.
[84] For influential discussions, see Beck, *Risk Society, World Risk Society*; Dean, *Governmentality*; Furedi, *Culture of Fear*; Giddens, *Consequences of Modernity, Runaway World*; O'Malley, *Risk, Uncertainty*. For a recent summary of some of these debates, see Walklate and Mythen, 'Agency, reflexivity and risk'.
[85] See Foucault, *Discipline and Punish*. [86] Rose, 'Government and control'.
[87] See e.g. Inda, *Targeting Immigrants*; Mythen and Walklate, 'Criminology and terrorism'.

'Taking charge of life' is a project that 'needs continuous regulatory and corrective mechanisms'.[88] Demographic governance thus involves an ongoing set of processes, techniques and practices that create knowledge, identify problems and seek to govern conduct, steering individuals and managing populations. Moreover, the state itself should be treated 'not as a political singularity but as an ever shifting assemblage of planning, operations and tactics'.[89] In other words, rather than involving a single master plan, much of what could be characterised as demographic governance, for instance in the arena of reproduction, is conducted by a variety of actors, and the results can also be in some ways coincidental, stemming from a complex interaction of implicit messages sent by various sets of policies and actors, rather than from a single coherent and explicitly framed demographic rationale.[90] States, in other words, are both agents of change and actors reacting to that change. Therefore, demographic governance does not always constitute a coherent or effective set of policies – and indeed, sometimes it may involve a set of contradictory policies that, for instance, reflect conflicting sets of anxieties and actually encourage migration even while attempting to limit it (or result in fewer births despite official pro-child rhetoric). The state-centred assumption of states as closed systems also allows, for instance, states in the Global North to subscribe to the seemingly conflicting aims of reducing world population yet increasing population in the Global North. As a related matter, demographic governance involves contestation and struggle, due to the coexistence of power and resistance.[91] Again, this is particularly obvious regarding immigration, where states' assumption of control is often resisted by individuals or groups who devise strategies to overcome and subvert policies that try to impede them.

DEMOGRAPHIC GOVERNANCE AND CITIZENSHIP

As stated earlier, this book examines demographic governance (attempts to manage demographic change, based on assumptions and knowledge about demographic trends) and its relationship with understandings of citizenship. It seeks to understand how demographic issues – not just immigration but lower birth rates and consequent population ageing, and related changes in individual and gender roles and

---

[88] Foucault, *History of Sexuality*, 144.   [89] Ong, *Neoliberalism as Exception*, 99.
[90] Heitlinger, 'Pronatalism and women's equality', 350.
[91] Macleod and Durrheim, 'Foucauldian feminism', 55.

family relationships – have been framed as targets for government in the last few decades, as well as how the responses to the perceived problems of demographic change – whether deliberate and evidence-based or rash and ill-judged – are affecting citizenship. In other words, it is interested in citizenship as a tool and target of demographic governance. Population dynamics, perceptions about demographic change and attempts to adjust demographic patterns (as well as to adjust to them) are often ignored or only briefly mentioned as a background issue by those interested in immigration and citizenship, whether they be citizenship theorists concerned with citizenship as a democratic ideal of equality and participation or scholars interested in it as the legal bond between states and their citizens (with the concomitant exclusion of outsiders).[92] Insofar as this is because past population policies are recognised as a terrible historical mistake associated with a brutal history, this unwillingness makes much sense – however, it is the contention of this book that paying explicit attention to the unfolding demographic transformations and the growing anxieties around them offers a way to critically evaluate how various citizens and non-citizens are included, managed or excluded in contemporary states.

At one level, this book is therefore yet another addition to the vast body of literature that has emerged in the last two decades about citizenship, and especially the challenges that continuing immigration poses for citizenship as membership. The complex nature of citizenship as a concept and the multitude of issues involved in these challenges means scholars have often focused on either citizenship in the 'thin', legal sense that relates to the maintenance of international borders or citizenship in the 'thick' sense of belonging and rights of citizens. Immigration scholars have analysed and critiqued citizenship in the former sense as an exclusive principle, a 'filing mechanism'[93] that allocates people into territorial units, often on a biological basis.[94] This aspect of citizenship as a form of closure, founded on state sovereignty and sanctioned by liberalism on grounds of democratic representation, allows states to manage the number and composition of non-citizens who enter and reside in their territory; at the same time, this control, while a taken-for-granted foundation of the international legal order, is also contested by the forces of globalisation, most notably increased

---

[92] See e.g. Joppke, 'Comparative citizenship', 1–2.
[93] Joppke, 'How immigration is changing citizenship', 629.
[94] Rose and Novas, 'Biological citizenship', 443.

international mobility between states.[95] Much, if not more, has also been written about citizenship (in the thicker, inward-looking sense) as the link between citizens and the state. This scholarship has discussed, among other things, the challenges that increasing social and cultural pluralism are posing to the established ideas of membership, rights and belonging in liberal democracies.[96] These issues interconnect with other pressures on citizenship prompted by structural economic shifts and globalisation processes, such as questions regarding the fiscal sustainability of the welfare state, the social rights of citizenship[97] and the gendered organisation of citizenship inside contemporary states.[98]

In examining demographic governance, this book examines aspects of both the thin and thick notions of citizenship together. In that sense, it follows Linda Bosniak[99] and other authors who follow her,[100] holding that the 'boundary-conscious' and 'inward-looking' aspects of citizenship inform each other and have to be examined together. Bosniak is, in her work, particularly interested in the citizenship (in the thick sense) of 'aliens' (non-citizens) and how their presence and work in the national territory is linked with (and facilitates) the full (thick) citizenship of some citizens.[101] However, there are arguably also reasons to speak of the non-citizenship (in the thick sense) of some who are formally citizens (in the thin sense). Such 'alien citizens' may enjoy the formal membership of a state, but their belonging is suspect (often for reasons to do with ethnic background, culture and religion) and they may not be treated as full citizens.[102] Individuals who are formally citizens may also become vulnerable to exclusionary practices because they fail to live up to changing expectations of good

---

[95] For a selection of some of the debates, see e.g. Anderson, *Us and Them?*; Bauböck et al., *Citizenship Policies in the New Europe*; Benhabib, *The Rights of Others*; Brubaker, *Citizenship and Nationhood*; Dauvergne, *Making People Illegal*; Jacobson, *Rights Across Borders*; Joppke, *Challenge to the Nation-State, Citizenship and Immigration*; Shachar, *The Birthright Lottery*. For an overview of these debates, see Bloemraad et al., 'Citizenship and immigration'.
[96] For a selection, see Kymlicka, *Multicultural Citizenship*, *Politics in the Vernacular*; Kymlicka and Normann, 'Return of the citizen'; Mouffe, *Dimensions of Radical Democracy*; Okin, *Is Multiculturalism Bad for Women?*; Parekh, *Rethinking Multiculturalism*.
[97] Roche, *Rethinking Citizenship*; Schierup et al., *Migration, Citizenship*; Somers, *Genealogies of Citizenship*.
[98] Lister, *Citizenship: Feminist Perspectives*; Lister et al., *Gendering Citizenship*; Orloff, 'Gender and the social rights'; Sainsbury, *Gender, Equality and Welfare States*; Siim, *Gender and Citizenship*.
[99] Bosniak, *The Citizen and the Alien*, 2.   [100] See e.g. Raissiguier, *Reinventing the Republic*.
[101] See Bosniak, 'Universal citizenship', *The Citizen and the Alien*, 'Making sense of citizenship'.
[102] Ngai, *Impossible Subjects*; Volpp, 'Impossible subjects'. See also Somers, *Genealogies of Citizenship*.

membership, for instance by lacking 'neoliberal potential' in terms of economic expectations.[103] This book adds to analyses of the way in which the two sides of citizenship are inextricably linked by incorporating a perspective that brings understandings of citizens' – and, in particular, women's – changing roles as reproducers of the nation and the reality of demographic ageing together with analyses of the governance of increasing immigration and minority formation. It is underpinned by the idea that in order to understand and critique states' immigration policies, especially in their global context – for instance, their possible unfairness or counter-productiveness – it is essential to have the full picture of how these policies fit in with and indeed stem from states' attempts to manage demographic change.

Another sense in which this book builds on the work of Bosniak is that it takes seriously the role of gender as a central aspect of discussions about citizenship, again in both its thin and its thick senses. Citizenship in contemporary states of the Global North is now, in theory, a demographically inclusive status that incorporates women, who have historically been marginalised as citizens. In practice, however, citizenship is a notion that remains highly gendered; as feminist work on women's citizenship has demonstrated through discussions over paid and unpaid work, women's and men's roles as citizens have never been the same, and the ways in which power over the human body and (classed and racialised) populations is exercised are highly gender-specific.[104]

Women's bodily difference and ability to create new citizens[105] raise questions about their emancipation as full citizens, their continuing responsibility for managing the consequences of human dependency, the restructuring of the welfare state and the desire to oversee and regulate the direction of national reproduction. In a similar fashion, immigrant and minority women's reproduction links citizenship with concerns over the governance of migrant families, social cohesion and the intergenerational continuity of the state.[106]

This book pays attention to how the demographic governance of women's bodily capacities and their reproductive and caregiving roles, based on the division between private and public, continue to have implications for their citizenship. At the same time, however, it

[103] Ong, *Neoliberalism as Exception*, 6–7, 16.
[104] Bussemaker and Voet, 'Citizenship and gender'; Halsaa et al., *Remaking Citizenship*; Walby, 'Is citizenship gendered?'; Yuval-Davis, 'Gender and nation', 'Women and the biological reproduction', *Gender and Nation*, esp. ch. 4.
[105] (Biological) sex is, of course, a central demographic variable. Poston, 'Age and sex', 19.
[106] Raissiguier, *Reinventing the Republic*, 12. See also Halsaa et al., *Remaking Citizenship*.

explores the many consequences of the feminisation of international migration, including the implications of gendered migration trajectories in labour migration and associations between international migration and caregiving.[107]

Citizenship is typically examined as a spatial concept, being tied to a particular territory and political community. Indeed, demographic governance is based on this fundamental assumption that connects states and populations, just as much of demographic anxiety stems from uncertainties over whether this assumption is tenable. However, a perspective that centres demographic changes also draws attention to the need to consider the temporal aspects of citizenship.[108] As Balibar has argued, it is an essential aspect of nations that they configure time by instituting the connection between generations.[109] This necessitates a closer examination of the time-related aspects of citizenship – such as the long-term dimension of national reproduction, or the time periods that are required and expected to create bonds of belonging, as well as the changing nature of the human life course and the intergenerational relationships that shape individuals' roles as citizens at different stages in their lives. Age is also an aspect of social stratification that has traditionally been under-explored.[110] Citizens' life courses in advanced societies are directly and indirectly governed in many ways, with the modernised life cycle being characterised by a division into separate life stages and age group-based trajectories (education in youth, paid work/reproduction during adulthood, retirement in old age).[111] The growing field of life course research maps how patterns of family formation, childbearing, education, employment and retirement are changing.[112] Based on such insights, many have suggested that contemporary societies are moving towards more flexible and individualised (as well as less gendered) life courses, away from the tripartite approach, which means that investigations into citizenship need to adjust accordingly.[113] The present challenges to citizenship are thus

[107] Benhabib and Resnik, *Migrations and Mobilities*; Brettel, 'Gender, family, and migration'; Kofman et al., *Gender and International Migration*; Kraler et al., *Gender, Generations and the Family*.
[108] Demographers are always interested in age (age at marriage, at reproduction, at retirement, etc.), and age is the other central demographic variable alongside sex. Poston, 'Age and sex', 19.
[109] Balibar, *We, the People of Europe*, 17. [110] Turner, 'Ageing, status politics', 589.
[111] Mayer and Schoepflin, 'The state and the life course', 195–6. For an overview of states' government of the life course, see Leisering, 'Government and the life course'; Settersten, 'Age structuring'.
[112] Mayer, 'New directions'.
[113] Bussemaker, 'Citizenship and changes in life courses'; Furstenberg, 'Reflections on the future'; Settersten, 'Age structuring'.

also temporal, raising questions about the relevance of existing models of age differentiation and the extent to which the taken-for-grated patterns of citizenship hold force for both men and women. Citizenship thus also needs to be examined from a perspective that pays attention to time and runs from infancy to old age.

In short, this book, by combining discussions regarding low birth rates and demographic ageing with analyses of immigration, seeks to add a new perspective to the debates about the meaning and regulation of citizenship in contemporary states. It draws from interdisciplinary insights, in particular from research into demography, which, with its long-term perspective, offers insights into both past and future patterns of citizenship. It also utilises works by authors from other disciplines – social and political scientists, economists, sociologists and anthropologists – who have examined demographic trends, most notably the long-term implications of low birth rates[114] and global population ageing.[115] These bodies of literature do also discuss immigration, but often without singling it out quite in the same way as much legal scholarship on citizenship (in the thin sense) often does, usually emphasising instead the remarkable changes that have occurred in family structures and societal dynamics in contemporary societies. Their perspectives on demographic change can thus offer new insights that help fill gaps in more legal investigations of citizenship and immigration policy.[116] The regulation of immigration can then be examined as one element in the overall puzzle of how ideas about citizenship are changing in terms not just of external boundary maintenance but also of gender roles (especially regarding reproduction, but also paid work), family relationships (for example who counts as kin) and family responsibilities (particularly regarding care of the young and the very old).

THE STRUCTURE OF THE BOOK

This book, in studying the demographic management strategies of contemporary states, has an ambitious breadth. Constraints of time and space mean it cannot be a comprehensive account of all possible aspects

---

[114] Buchanan and Rotkirch, *Fertility Rates and Population Decline*; Douglass, *Barren States*; Teitelbaum and Winter, *The Fear of Population Decline, A Question of Numbers*; Winter and Teitelbaum, *Global Spread of Fertility Decline*.
[115] Goerres, *The Political Participation*; McDaniel and Zimmer, *Global Ageing*; Vincent, *Inequality and Old Age*.
[116] They are thus ideal 'auxiliary disciplines' for this research. See van Klink and Taekema, 'On the border', 11.

INTRODUCTION

of demographic governance but has to be rather selective in its coverage. Chapters 2 to 5, therefore, examine four areas, chosen on the basis of what they illustrate about ongoing demographic change, with the aim of providing four snapshots of late-modern states' governance of their demographic transitions. These chapters take an approach that goes from the cradle to the grave, starting with the generation of new citizens (Chapter 2) and finishing with issues related to the care of old citizens in ageing societies (Chapter 5). The book is limited to citizenship in the contemporary Global North, leaving the Global South outside its scope. The situation faced by the states in the Global North today, characterised by persistently low birth rates and consequent transformations that will take decades to unfold, is demographically unique and previously unseen in history. In this sense, these states, and European ones in particular, are frontrunners in dealing with demographic change that will affect other regions in due course, albeit in slightly different ways.[117] In the future, the unfolding demographic transformation – decline in numbers of children born, population shifts from rural areas to cities, increasing migration – is going to make the rest of the world look a lot more like Europe (moreover, other states will have to deal with such changes in a much shorter time frame).[118]

There is great variety between states in the Global North in terms of their approach to demographic governance: few have an explicit population strategy (and where they exist, they are often very generally phrased[119]), and in some, for reasons to do with history, demographic issues such as birth rate and population composition have been largely taboo (e.g. Germany[120]). Some states are considered to be in serious demographic decline (Japan, Russia[121]), while others, though experiencing below-replacement-level fertility, are closer to or at the level of maintaining their populations (most notably, France and the United States[122]). Regarding immigration, states range from established states of immigration to ones not accustomed to dealing with immigration (parts of continental Europe) to ones largely rejecting immigration (Japan, South Korea). The primary jurisdictions chosen for the sample studies in this book are Italy, the United Kingdom, Australia and Finland – these share many of the experiences of the demographic

[117] Reher, 'Towards long-term population decline'.
[118] Reher, 'Economic and social implications'.
[119] See Commonwealth of Australia, 'Sustainable Australia'. [120] See Dorbritz, 'Germany'.
[121] On Japan, see Rosenbluth, *Japan's Low Fertility*; on Russia, Perelli-Harris and Isupova, 'Crisis and control'.
[122] On France, see Toulemon et al., 'France'; on the United States, Cherlin, 'Demographic trends'.

THE STRUCTURE OF THE BOOK

transformation process, as well as an acceptance that some international migration is essential for their demographic future. However, they display significant differences in terms of colonial history, cultural background, welfare systems, geography and policy approaches to international migration and multiculturalism. Three of them are in the European Union, which has significant implications for their immigration policy.[123] For reasons which will be explored in this section, these states represent a selection that illustrates the complex and variable nature of domestic contexts. Each chapter starts with a case study from one state, chosen to emphasise issues that are relevant in a number of jurisdictions, as well as national specificities.

Chapter 2, 'Missing Citizens? Birth Rates and the Making of New Citizens', discusses the perception that too few new citizens are born in late-modern societies of the Global North. It is also a stepping stone for the subsequent chapters, in that it argues that as production of new citizens is an essential part of nation-making, the longstanding trend of low birth rates is at the heart of contemporary population anxieties in late-modern states, including those related to women's citizenship and continuing immigration. The chapter starts with a case study on Italy: the country's very low birth rates present an apparent paradox in a relatively family-focused society, and its recent yet rapid transformation into a country of immigration (where large numbers of migrants, often from outside the European Union, perform much of the care and domestic work that Italian women are not able to) makes it an ideal place to examine the connections between low birth rates, gendered citizenship and the ways in which policies around immigration and citizenship construct and interact with these anxieties. After the case study, the chapter examines the trajectories in the other three jurisdictions and then, more broadly, the common issues around low birth rates, including the debates on the effectiveness of and rationale for policies that encourage more births and immigrant inclusion in these attempts. The chapter critically reflects on pronatalist policy aspirations against a background where, historically, women's reproductive capacity has been used to exclude them from full citizenship.

Chapter 3, 'Misguided Citizens? Transitions into Adulthood and the Management of Diversity', analyses fears that many of the formal legal citizens growing up in contemporary states are not developing into or

---

[123] Though this book includes discussion of EU law, where relevant, it does not examine demographic governance in the EU context.

acting like proper citizens, especially if they are of immigrant origin. It argues that amid resurging concerns about young people's trajectories, new means of controlling the transition to adulthood have been developed to manage teenagers and young adults. The chapter starts with a case study on the United Kingdom. In the wake of a host of anxieties about young people and several incidents involving troublesome 'second-generation' young people, the United Kingdom has increased control over migration and fused it with integration measures, 'youth management' and gender policies. The example of family formation migration involving young people is used to shed light on the interconnections between the treatment of young people of immigrant background and the management of migration. The chapter argues that concerns over both the economic and the cultural integration of the 'second generation' are used to single out individuals wishing to marry someone from the country of their parents' birth. After the case study, the chapter examines the ways in which the citizenship of young people of immigrant origin is changing in the other three national contexts. The chapter concludes with a discussion of how young people are seen as a future resource that needs to be encouraged to be responsible and the ways in which young people of migrant background and their families are managed in an effort to ensure the quality of the future citizenry.

Chapter 4, 'Casual Citizens? The Desirable Labour Migrant and Conditional Citizenship', is about labour migration and the issues around selecting and admitting the 'right' immigrants and turning some of them into citizens. As a case study, the chapter starts by examining Australia, which is often considered to be a model of how to attract desirable immigrants (even though Australia's unique conditions and circumstances are not easily emulated by other contemporary states). It argues that new means of temporariness and conditional citizenship have been introduced in Australian immigration and citizenship law, which in some ways mirror the increasing precariousness of segments of the Australian population working as 'casuals' in the Australian labour market. After the case study, the chapter considers other states' efforts at managing labour migration. It analyses the trend towards prioritising and preferring skilled migration, which nonetheless coexists with continuing flows of less skilled migration (it also briefly considers the way in which EU law fits in with this picture). It analyses the trend to direct many migrants, even those who have been actively recruited for labour migration, towards increasingly conditional trajectories that emphasise usefulness and self-sufficiency as conditions for permanent residence and citizenship. The chapter concludes with a discussion regarding the tensions that exist in these approaches, whereby most contemporary states consider labour migration essential for dealing with the many challenges brought on by low birth rates (and prefer it over family migration), yet have reservations about turning those recruited into citizens, thus impeding their efforts to achieve their own goals.

Finally, Chapter 5, 'Depleting Citizens? Ageing Populations, Care and Migration', links the three preceding discussions to the much-lamented realities of population ageing, a relative growth in the share of people in older age groups. Population ageing is caused by both high life expectancy and low birth rates, and its implications for the citizenship of older people, especially in the context of providing them with necessary care, are now becoming clear.

As a case study, the chapter examines Finland, which is particularly interesting because its 65-years-and-older age group is growing more rapidly than that in any other EU Member State. Its old age dependency ratio will be the highest of all EU states in 2025, making Finland a frontrunner in dealing with pressures on citizenship.

The case study also examines the controversy over the situation where adult immigrants who have settled in Finland wish to bring elderly dependent relatives, usually their mothers, to join them in order to care for them in their old age. The chapter then examines the trajectories in the other three contexts and addresses the common policy issues around demographic ageing, including the increasing practice of importing care workers and the outsourcing of care to private actors and families. The chapter concludes with an analysis of the changes in citizenship that anxieties over the future costs of ageing populations are causing, which are manifesting internally but are also present in rules on immigration, which see older migrants as making no contribution to the receiving society.

CHAPTER TWO

MISSING CITIZENS? BIRTH RATES AND THE MAKING OF NEW CITIZENS

Despite the growth in immigration and naturalisation, the majority of us are, as Bryan Turner puts it, 'born into citizenship'.[1] As outlined in Chapter 1, a longstanding transformation towards lower birth rates – the so-called 'demographic transition' – has been taking place in most late-modern states (and, increasingly, elsewhere) over the last few centuries. It was for a long time assumed that birth rates would stabilise around replacement level. However, in the last four decades it has become clear to most states in the Global North that this demographic shift entails a further development – sustained below-replacement birth rates – referred to (especially by demographers) as the 'second demographic transition'. This pattern is associated with delayed and reduced childbearing, owing to changed economic, societal and cultural circumstances. Knowledge of declining birth rates has prompted longstanding general concern in many states over the last century, giving rise to attempts to restore higher birth rates (especially before the Second World War). In the wake of growing awareness of the below-replacement birth rates that have taken hold since the 1970s, these anxieties about population decline have begun to be revisited. The spectre of population ageing and its economic consequences are highlighting the seemingly unavoidable prospect of continuing and/or increasing immigration to ameliorate the consequences of below-replacement birth rates. The issues around why continuing immigration is perceived both as indispensable, yet in some ways lamentable, are thus rooted in

---

[1] Turner, 'Citizenship, reproduction and the state', 45.

the longstanding anxieties surrounding birth rates. The perception of demographic decline, based on demographic awareness that 'too few' citizens, or at least not enough citizens of a particular kind, are born to renew the nation is at the heart of contemporary demographic governance in the West, linking issues around women's citizenship with the regulation and consequences of immigration.

This chapter first examines a case study on Italy, a state where demographic anxieties related to the birth rate are particularly acute. Italy, along with states like Germany, Poland and Japan, has experienced so-called 'lowest-low' fertility;[2] that is, TFR at or below 1.3, with recent rises to levels just below 1.5. This Italian phenomenon of *denatalità* ('lacking births') is rapidly shifting Italy's demographic profile towards older age groups. These changes thus involve significant population ageing and, without immigration on a massive scale, even a prospect of population decline, both of which are much discussed and analysed by demographers as an existential threat. Thanks to the Italian media's alarmist reporting, the apparently impending 'population implosion'[3] is something of which Italians, including policy-makers, are keenly aware. For various reasons, Italy has also recently started a rapid transformation into a country of immigration. Though it began to experience large-scale inflows much later than many other states, it now has one of the highest net migration rates in the Global North. A large part of these migration flows is made up of immigrant women, who perform much of the domestic and care work that Italian women are not able to perform because of the increasing expectations of commitment to paid work. This background makes Italy an ideal starting point from which to examine how the enduring pattern of low birth rates has re-emerged as a target for concern and how the efforts to manage the issues raised interweave the regulation of reproduction with that of immigration and minority formation, with implications for gendered citizenship and incorporation of immigrants.

The example of Italy is in many ways specific, because it is more extreme than that of most other countries, but it also draws attention to issues that many contemporary states have in common regarding the links between the governance of reproduction and that of international migration. In order to explore the similarities and variations between different national contexts, the chapter next discusses how

---

[2] A term coined by Kohler et al., 'The emergence of lowest-low fertility', 641.
[3] Krause, 'Toys and perfumes', 159.

issues around the demographic transition and low birth rates are framed in other late-modern societies and outlines the responses adopted in the Finnish, UK and Australian contexts. These states experienced a temporary 'baby boom' after the Second World War (though with differences in terms of timing and duration), but have returned to declining birth rates since, with TFRs plunging in the 1970s and stabilising slightly under the replacement rate in the last few decades. The Italian case study shows that perceptions of and government responses to low birth rates and immigration are not always coherent, nor logical, but take place in a specific historic and social context and reflect longstanding historical trajectories and constraints. The responses to birth-rate trends in Finland, the United Kingdom and Australia similarly reflect specific national experiences and controversies around national reproduction, conflicting views over women's roles as citizens and concerns about the incorporation of immigrant 'others' and their descendants. At the same time, in all three states, awareness of the inevitable consequences of low birth rates is creating controversy about the available options and their long-term implications.

The chapter pulls together the themes raised in the national contexts and links them to issues around deep and longstanding contestations regarding national reproduction, challenges to the gendered reproductive roles of citizenship and the integration of immigrant others in societies characterised by low birth rates. Some of the frequently suggested measures to influence demographic change, most notably state support for gender-equality measures or work–family balancing with an eye to pronatalist gains, are assumed to be unproblematic for women's citizenship or, in some contexts, even welcomed as advantageous for the overall project of creating a more gender-equal society. However, given women's reproductive capacity has historically been used to exclude them from full citizenship, pronatalist governance (which is seeking to encourage (some) women to perform the 'reproductive duties of citizenship') raises questions about the framing of national reproduction and the creation of new citizens as a duty to the state or nation. Furthermore, it also raises questions about who is deemed suitable for producing new citizens, in terms of both local and global considerations involving class and race. In other words, as pronatalist governance does not target all citizens equally, and indeed as an antinatal agenda is arguably applied to those women who, for various reasons, are not seen to be good mothers or good citizens, the determination of appropriate and desirable reproducers invites further questions.

ITALY: LA MORTE DI UN POPOLO?

Two Demographic Revolutions

Italy is undergoing large demographic shifts. The first of these, the slowly unfolding transition to enduring low birth rates, has been called a 'quiet revolution'.[4] The broad shape of Italy's birth-rate transformation is, however, in many ways, broadly consistent with general trends associated with the demographic transition.[5] The birth rate started declining at the end of the nineteenth century (somewhat later than in Northern Europe) and concerns over the trend, especially in central and northern Italy, as well as over the loss of citizens through emigration, prompted the fascist dictatorship to adopt a series of pronatalist measures in the 1920s and 1930s.[6] The birth rate was still well over replacement level after the Second World War and even rose slightly in the 1960s.[7] Considering the relatively high starting level, this cannot quite be called a 'baby boom', and the downward trend continued from the late 1960s onwards, with the birth rate reaching below-replacement rates (2.1) in the 1970s.[8] Once the birth rate dropped below replacement level in the 1970s, it remained low, with levels below 1.5 since the 1980s. The all-time minimum of 1.18 was reached in 1995, during a twelve-year period of lowest-low fertility (birth rates at or below 1.3[9]), though recent rises have lifted the level back above 1.3.[10] The overall rate hides large regional differences in birth rates, and in particular a south/north division, which persists to this day: northern Italy experienced earlier declines but now has higher birth rates, while the birth rates in the south were slower to start to decline but once low, they remained low.[11] The total Italian fertility rates are still very much on the low side (1.39 in 2013 and 2014[12]), but some demographers have interpreted the recent uptick as evidence that the birth-rate gap with the rest of Europe is narrowing slightly.[13]

---

[4] Krause, 'Empty cradles', 577; see also Krause, *A Crisis of Births*, 22.
[5] Livi-Bacci, *A History of Italian Fertility*, 284.
[6] Forcucci, 'Battle for births'. On Italy's history of long history of emigration from 1815 onwards, see Bertagna and Maccari-Clayton, 'Italy: migration 1815'.
[7] Livi-Bacci, 'Modernization and tradition'.
[8] Frejka and Calot, 'Cohort reproductive patterns'. See also Livi-Bacci, *A History of Italian Fertility*.
[9] Kohler et al., 'The emergence of lowest-low fertility'.
[10] Goldstein et al., 'The end of "lowest-low" fertility', 669.
[11] Caltabiano et al., 'Lowest-low fertility'. For a historical overview of regional differences, see Livi-Bacci, *A History of Italian Fertility*.
[12] Istat, 'Indicatori demografici'.
[13] Castiglioni and Dalla Zuanna, 'Marital and reproductive behavior'.

This phenomenon of *denatalità* since the 1970s has been much discussed and analysed by demographers, especially since its permanence became evident.[14] Demographers generally link the transition to below-replacement rates to the economic, social and cultural dynamics of the first and, subsequently, second demographic transitions – the shift in both mortality and fertility from high and fluctuating levels to low and relatively stable ones.[15] This adjustment of birth rates, involving greater 'reproductive efficiency',[16] was reinforced by various developments, such as better birth control, mass education, cultural change and urbanisation.[17] It freed women from life-long reproductive roles, enabling greater female emancipation, education and labour-force participation, and entailed delayed family formation and increased investments in the health and welfare of a smaller number of children.[18] Economic models showing the 'opportunity costs' of childbearing and the subsequent long-term financial consequences of motherhood as disincentives for motherhood have been put forward as mechanisms that cause women to delay motherhood and limit the number of children they have.[19] In sociological terms, the trend towards later and more limited childbearing can also be considered in light of theories of reflexive modernisation, in particular focusing on the role of social liberalisation (freedom of individuals, and particularly women, from both state and religious control over their personal lives) and new capitalism (economic deregulation that increases uncertainty and puts a premium on individual solutions, such as participating in higher education and securing stable employment before childbearing).[20] This modern subjectivity, while bringing individual and economic benefits in modern societies, thus also changes individuals' and in particular women's life cycles and encourages caution in terms of family formation, giving rise to the so-called 'second demographic transition', characterised by sub-replacement fertility.[21]

Though the Italian patterns may be consistent with general trends towards low birth rates across the Global North, the persistence of very

---

[14] See, for instance, Caltabiano et al., 'Lowest-low fertility'; Castiglioni and Dalla Zuanna, 'Innovation and tradition'; Castiglioni et al., 'Planned and unplanned births'; Dalla Zuanna, 'Population replacement'; Dalla Zuanna and Micheli, *Strong Family and Low Fertility*; De Rose et al. 'Italy: delayed adaptation'; Mencarini and Tanturri, 'High fertility or childlessness'; Santarelli, 'Economic resources'.
[15] See Chapter 1.   [16] See Reher, 'Towards long-term population decline'.
[17] Dyson, *Population and Development*.   [18] Lee, 'The demographic transition'.
[19] Reher, 'Towards long-term population decline'.
[20] See in particular Beck, *Risk Society*; Beck and Beck-Gernsheim, *Individualization*.
[21] McDonald, 'Low fertility and the state'.

low birth rates has been constructed as paradoxical, challenging the stereotypes of the large Italian family and of a Catholic country.[22] While some demographers have simply treated Italian women's 'refusal' to have children as 'irrational',[23] Peter McDonald has argued in an influential work that very low birth rates in places like Italy are the result of a tension between growing gender equity in individual-orientated institutions (education, employment) and low gender equity in institutions that deal with families.[24] Due to social emancipation and greater legal equality, women are at present provided with opportunities that are nearly equivalent to those of men in education and market employment (and encouraged to grasp them), but these opportunities are severely curtailed by having children, especially where the ideals of the family and family-orientated institutions are based on a male-breadwinner model (one that assumes a strong gendered division of labour in terms of parenthood and involves only limited support for working mothers, such as childcare).[25] In such circumstances, women, especially women who have spent much time on their education, will postpone family-formation and restrict the number of children they have. States which are easing this conflict through family policies that allow women to combine family and work (for instance, the Nordic states) have higher birth rates than ones that do not.[26] That states with high female educational attainment and employment have higher birth rates than states like Italy suggests, in other words, that the previously negative relationships between fertility and labour-market modernity can be overcome.[27]

---

[22] Krause, *A Crisis of Births*, xiii; Dalla Zuanna and Micheli, *Strong Family and Low Fertility*. See also Castles, 'The world turned upside down'.

[23] Krause, 'Empty cradles', 586.

[24] McDonald, 'Gender equity, social institutions'. The argument is inspired by Nancy Fraser's work on gender equity; see Fraser, 'After the family wage'. See also Hochschild with Machung, *The Second Shift*.

[25] McDonald, 'Gender equity, social institutions'. See also Chesnais, 'Fertility, family, and social policy'; McDonald, 'Gender equity in theories'.

[26] On the complexity of family policies, see Neyer and Andersson, 'Consequences of family policies'. These authors argue that family policy includes a variety of different policies – on maternity leave, parental leave, childcare entitlements, family law and, more indirectly, health care, housing, education, social security and welfare, taxation and civil law. See also Brewster and Rindfuss, 'Fertility and women's employment'; Neyer, 'Welfare states'; Neyer et al., 'Gender equality'.

[27] Castles, 'The world turned upside down'. On the effects of family policies, see also Gauthier, 'The impact of family policies', 'Family policy and fertility'; McDonald, 'Low fertility and the state'; Neyer and Andersson, 'Consequences of family policies'. See also Esping-Andersen, *The Incomplete Revolution*, for an argument about the role of the state in mitigating this tension.

Though confirming such a hypothesis about a positive correlation between supportive family policies and higher birth rates involves difficult empirical questions (causality being very complex in modern welfare systems), in the Italian context such explanations have some appeal. It is a truism that family has a special place in Italy – and idealisation of motherhood even more so, thanks to the longstanding legacy of fascism and the tenacity of Catholicism's teachings on marriage and gender roles.[28] Though equality in education between men and women has consistently risen and Italian women increasingly work outside the home,[29] gender inequality in the family – including in childrearing, household chores and care for older relatives – has remained a significant feature of Italian society.[30] Most crucially, the Italian family-policy model relies strongly on kinship solidarity, with few formal services and little support for families and working mothers – either from the state or from the market.[31] In cultural terms, the model is highly gendered in that it is women who are expected to fulfil most of the caring and domestic roles as mothers, daughters and grandmothers.[32] In addition to economic and social policy factors, Krause, in her anthropological research into birth rates in Italy, also locates reasons for this in the intense cultural expectations of motherhood in Italy (tied to class, race and ethnicity).[33] Moreover, the Italian welfare system is skewed towards old people (e.g. via generous pensions) and does not pay attention to young women, children and the compatibility of parenthood with education and work.[34] Despite a strong tradition of intergenerational solidarity and transfers between generations in the family, the high uncertainty faced by young adults, in terms of labour-market and economic stability, leads to the general delay of all events characterising

---

[28] Caldwell, 'Women as the family'.
[29] Addis, 'Gender in the reform'; Saraceno, *Mutamenti della famiglia*.
[30] Bimbi, 'The family paradigm'; Cooke, 'Gender equity and fertility'.
[31] Naldini, *The Family*; Saraceno, *Mutamenti della famiglia*; Saraceno and Naldini, 'Social and family policies in Italy'. Under Esping-Andersen's three-way model of welfare states in *The Three Worlds*, Italy can be classed as part of the conservative–corporatist model, but some, like Ferrera, 'The "southern model"', have also treated the Mediterranean countries as a separate group, characterised by a Catholic imprint and a strong familialism.
[32] Fargion, 'Children, gender and families', 105; Naldini, *The Family*. Women of the 'sandwich generation' are expected to provide care and support to both the preceding and the following generations.
[33] Krause, 'Toys and perfumes', 163, *A Crisis of Births*.
[34] Ballarino et al., 'Italy'; Fargion, 'Children, gender and families'; Sciortino, 'Immigration in a Mediterranean welfare state', 113.

the transition to adulthood, from forming their own household to getting married and having children.[35]

All these factors can be argued to be inimical to early family formation and larger family size in contemporary society, suggesting that the apparent 'paradox'[36] that is lowest-low fertility in Italy is not such an enigma after all. It is plausible that *denatalità* has to do with the lack of adaptation of the institutional and cultural framework (involving state, church and family) to changes in economic and social conditions, regarding women's increasingly important economic roles and the devaluation of care work, especially when related to reproduction.[37] The recent trend towards slightly higher birth rates in the north of Italy seems to support this insofar as it is linked to social and cultural patterns, family arrangements and value changes that are connected to higher birth rates elsewhere in Europe: increased cohabitation, births out of wedlock, secularisation, local and regional measures to support working parents and increasing gender equality in the home.[38] Indeed, the modest signs of recovery are above all evident among the youngest generations of women in northern Italy, who have the highest levels of education, while birth rates in the south and among less-educated women remain depressed.[39] This is consistent with the growing amount of local attention that has been dedicated to improving institutions and policies which promote the balance between work and family. Caltabiano, Castiglioni and Rosina note that women with higher levels of education also tend to have greater resources, which are needed to pay for services in the private sector, such as childcare and assistance for their parents.[40]

This last issue – the need for resources to pay for care services in order to feel able to have children – links with the issue of immigration and Italy's second demographic revolution. Italy has in the last few decades started a relatively rapid transformation into a country of

---

[35] Billari and Rosina, 'Italian "latest-late" transition'; also Livi-Bacci, 'Too few children'. On transitions to adulthood, see Chapter 3.
[36] Dalla Zuanna and Micheli, *Strong Family and Low Fertility*.
[37] Unsurprisingly, the large number of childless women in Italy is typically characterised by higher education. See Mencarini and Tanturri, 'High fertility or childlessness'; Tanturri and Mencarini, 'Childless or childfree?'.
[38] Castiglioni and Dalla Zuanna, 'Marital and reproductive behavior'. See also Cooke, 'Gender equity and fertility'.
[39] Caltabiano et al., 'Lowest-low fertility'. Women in the north also have a much higher employment rate – see Ballarino et al., 'Italy'.
[40] Caltabiano et al., 'Lowest-low fertility'.

immigration.[41] Some demographers have argued that higher levels of labour migration 'make up for' lost births; that is, that the entry of migrants replaces, at least in the demographic short run, the 'missing births'.[42] Immigrants arguably also facilitate Italian women's childbearing, assisting in particular middle-class working women to have the (few) children that they do have.[43] This is because immigrant workers, often women from poorer countries, increasingly fill some of the care and domestic work deficit created by Italian women's economic participation, which is preventing them from fulfilling their traditional role of caring for children and ageing parents.[44] Some have argued this has led to a transition from a 'family' to a 'migrant in the family' model of care, where the state is supporting care (especially care for older relatives) through monetary benefits, which can be and are being used to recruit migrant women to replace the unpaid care that Italian women are no longer able to provide.[45] Through this flow of increasingly feminised migration for care work, a new division of labour is emerging between the family, the market and the state, one that combines the continued privatisation of care issues with the development of an unregulated globalised care market.[46] Van Hooren argues the Italian state is, because of the apparently desperate need for immigrant carers, taking a special approach to immigrant domestic workers, facilitating their entry even where the immigration context is generally characterised by anti-immigration sentiment.[47]

Immigration for the purposes of care and domestic work is part of Italy's swift transition from an emigration country[48] to an immigration

---

[41] For an overview, see Fondazione ISMU, 'Ventesimo rapporto'.
[42] Dalla Zuanna, 'Population replacement', 189.
[43] Marchesi, 'Reproducing Italians', 181. There remains a large gap between desired and actual fertility rate in Italy: see d'Addio and d'Ercole, 'Trends and determinants'.
[44] Anthias and Lazaridis, *Gender and Migration*; Calavita, *Immigrants at the Margins*; Da Roit, 'Changing intergenerational solidarities'. As Ambrosini, 'Immigration in Italy', 185 puts it: 'Italian women's emancipation and their entry into the labor market have been fostered and accompanied by their substitution, in household tasks and care, by foreign women (and men).' See also Chapter 5.
[45] Bettio et al., 'Change in care regimes', 272. On the gender, race and class dimensions of such work, see Andall, 'Organizing domestic workers'.
[46] Bettio et al., 'Change in care regimes'. See also Da Roit and Sabatinelli, 'Nothing on the move'; Fargion, 'Italy'; Sciortino, 'Immigration in a Mediterranean welfare state'.
[47] van Hooren, 'When families need immigrants'.
[48] The age of massive Italian overseas emigration lasted from 1815 to the 1970s (see Bertagna and Maccari-Clayton, 'Italy: migration 1815'), though Italians still emigrate. (Young and educated Italians, in particular, are increasingly seeking economic opportunities abroad, especially since the recent economic crisis.)

destination with 'highest-high' levels of immigration.[49] This transformation started in the 1970s and is driven by structural demand, but it has taken place in an uncoordinated way,[50] involving significant irregular labour migration for low-paid, precarious work.[51] It has been argued that 'economic emancipation is the factor driving the behaviour of both Italian women and female immigrants'.[52] The high reliance on care by non-citizens allows Italian women to alleviate the tension between their family and paid work obligations – not completely, but to some degree. For immigrant workers, their employment is an example of Hochschild's famous 'care chains', where migrant women from poorer regions of the world migrate to take up paid work as carers of children and older people; though their countries are also increasingly characterised by lower birth rates, migrant women often leave behind a gap with regard to their own care responsibilities towards their children.[53] As well as separation from their own children (often cared for by other female family members in their country of origin), immigrant women doing care and domestic work in Italian families typically experience situations of irregularity.[54] Indeed, Italian social and migration policies have tolerated and favoured the irregular and informal nature of care and domestic work.[55] This state of informality keeps migrant workers a flexible and economical option for Italian families, but it also means it is often impossible for migrant workers (and also impracticable for live-in carers) to seek family reunion with their own existing children until they have managed to secure legal residency; indeed, despite frequent regularisations, immigration law makes it difficult and slow for

---

[49] Billari, 'Lowest-low fertility', 8. See also Chapter 4.

[50] Governmental policies to deal with the legacy of the early 'open-door' policy that persisted until the 1980s have been overdue and incomplete. The first systematic Italian migration law was the so-called Turco-Napolitano law (Act 40/1998, then consolidated Act 286/1998). Several regularisation programmes have been used to deal with irregular migration. For overviews, see Zanfrini, 'Immigration and labour market'; Zincone, 'The case of Italy'.

[51] On the underground economy in Italy and migrants' roles in it, see Reyneri, 'Underground economy'; see also Ambrosini, 'The role of immigrants'. On the demand factors in the Italian welfare state, see Sciortino, 'Immigration in a Mediterranean welfare state'. On female migrants, see Andall, 'Organizing domestic workers'; Chell-Robinson, 'Female migrants in Italy'; Orsini-Jones and Gattullo, 'Migrant women in Italy'.

[52] Bettio et al., 'Change in care regimes', 274. [53] Hochschild, 'Global care chains', 131.

[54] Irregularity is an endemic feature of immigrant involvement in the Italian welfare system, rooted in the desire to prevent immigrant workers from acquiring rights that would be costly to the state and/or the families employing them. See Sciortino, 'Immigration in a Mediterranean welfare state'; van Hooren, 'When families need immigrants'.

[55] Triandafyllidou and Ambrosini, 'Irregular immigration control'; van Hooren, 'When families need immigrants'.

even legal residents to get a status that would allow for family reunification.[56]

For those women who migrate in order to perform care and domestic work, typically from Eastern Europe and the Philippines, the nature of the work (often involving living with the employer) and lack of childcare services (and family members in Italy) means they themselves have low birth rates, like Italian women.[57] However, overall, immigrants to Italy replace the 'missing citizens' not just by filling in gaps in the workforce, but also by having children themselves. Though care workers have low birth rates, the growing number of immigrants in Italy means immigrant women's fertility has become relevant to the birth rate. In fact, despite all the alarm over the last few decades, Italy's total population is currently still growing, in part because immigrants are giving a minor but positive contribution to the TFR through a combination of higher population share and higher birth rate.[58] How immigration affects childbearing patterns has become contentious and has been the subject of increasing monitoring – while in time migrants' birth rates tend to assimilate to local patterns (and often are lower than those of their countries of origin), this depends on many variables.[59] In the Italian context, noting that 'without the contribution of migrants, Italy would still be experiencing lowest-low fertility', demographers have found great differences between various groups of migrants.[60] Immigrants' profiles differ from those of natives due to their personal histories (for instance, their education and marriage histories).[61] Unsurprisingly, those who migrate for family reasons (most typically, to join a spouse) and come from a country of origin where birth rates are relatively high have a higher rate of fertility than those who migrate for employment and come from low-fertility countries – hence high birth rates for Moroccans and low for Romanian women.[62]

---

[56] Ambrosini, 'Parenting from a distance'; Basa et al., 'Remittances and transnational families'. On the Consolidated Law on Immigration, Legislative Decree No. 286/1998 and amendments to it, see Favilli, *Migration Law in Italy*. See also Chapter 3.
[57] Farina and Ortensi, 'When low fertility affects'.
[58] Goldstein et al., 'The end of "lowest-low" fertility', 681. See also Billari, 'Lowest-low fertility'; Sobotka, 'Overview chapter 7'. See Istat, 'Indicatori demografici' for the latest figures, which show a birth rate of 1.31 for Italian women and 1.97 for non-Italian women (2014).
[59] Sobotka, 'Overview chapter 7'.
[60] Mussino and Strozza, 'The delayed school progress', 102.
[61] Mussino and Van Raalte, 'Immigrant fertility'.
[62] Farina and Ortensi, 'When low fertility affects'; Mussino and Strozza, 'Does citizenship still matter?', 'The fertility of immigrants'.

To Govern or Not to Govern National Reproduction?

The relatively rapid pace of immigration and longstanding awareness of birth-rate patterns have together revived Italian debates and controversies around national reproduction and identity. In popular media, Italian women's low birth rates are discussed in apocalyptic terms, with talk of the demise of the Italian race, which is also linked to fears of immigration and population change.[63] This concern has also been taken up by political parties – in particular by the right-wing Legal Nord, which has framed the low birth rate as an issue in ethno-populist terms as 'a threat to survival of Italian culture and ethnicity in the face of immigration'.[64] At the same time, widespread demographic alarm has finally opened space for discussion of issues around family and gender relations, the cost of having children and the care needs of both children and older people, issues which were for long taboo because of the legacy of fascism. The fascist dictatorship of the 1920s and 1930s was terrified of population decline and imposed various pronatalist measures, which included a tax on bachelors, fiscal inducements for large families, fertility prizes and medals, criminalisation of abortion and a ban on contraceptives (the fascist regime also sought to restrain women's emancipation in general and to discourage emigration).[65] This history of repressive state measures that directly intervened with Italian families has precluded discussion of many of the family policy measures, like supporting working parents, which have been more openly discussed in other states for some time.[66] Since the 1990s, however, this has started to change.[67]

In terms of governance, ideas about the role of existing institutions and policies as brakes to higher birth rates have opened discursive space for debating policy interventions seeking to ease women's 'dilemma': that 'they perceive their future family role as inconsistent with their aspirations as individuals'.[68] This argument rests on an interpretation of low birth rates that emphasises that women act rationally by limiting the number of children they have when their greater presence in the workplace has not been accompanied by adequate services to allow them to combine work and family. Thanks to legislative reforms in the 1960s and 1970s, pushed through by the second wave of feminism –

---

[63] Krause, 'Empty cradles', 595. [64] Naldini and Saraceno, 'Social and family policies', 735.
[65] Albanese, *Mothers of the Nation*, ch. 3; Forcucci, 'Battle for births'. Albanese, at 54, notes Mussolini and the Fascists were 'consumed by demographic statistics'.
[66] Albanese, *Mothers of the Nation*, 151; Naldini and Saraceno, 'Social and family policies', 735.
[67] Naldini and Saraceno, 'Social and family policies', 735.
[68] McDonald, 'Gender equity in theories', 437.

which included the legalisation of abortion and divorce and equal-opportunities legislation – Italian women now have greater control of their lives and their trajectories, yet the reform project stalled, leaving the direction of family policy ambiguous and uncertain.[69] Despite much chatter about the need to accept that women's lives have changed permanently, comprehensive reform has proved elusive, partly as a result of stretched finances, and work/family reconciliation has not been supported by the measures needed to address gender imbalances and gaps in support for families, most notably in terms of childcare.[70] Commenting on recent measures to deal with Italy's 'dismal record in gender equity, financial support to families, childcare services and child poverty',[71] Fargion notes that recent governments, regardless of political orientation, have not been able to redesign the welfare system.[72] Thus, the actual message Italian policies send to Italian women is still that reasonable women do not have more children than they can deal with within their care system (that is, kin and/or migrant carer support). Even in the presence of comprehensive family-policy reforms, change would of course be slow, and it would require a broader shift in personal and political culture, most notably regarding gender roles and the expectations of employers.[73]

As in-depth structural changes have been difficult to push through, more symbolic and short-term pronatalist attempts have caught the attention of politicians, ushering in an era of 'overt and urgent pronatalism'.[74] This has involved the introduction of various ad hoc measures seeking to steer women towards appropriate reproductive paths, such as 'baby bonuses' (lump sums paid to mothers), which are largely symbolic as the sums involved are often insufficient to offset (even remotely) the costs involved in having a child. Often, these initiatives have been local or regional: for instance, Milan offered pronatalist incentives for those who had lived there for 15 years.[75] In 2003, the Berlusconi government managed to pass the first post-war baby-bonus law, which offered a one-off payment of 1000 euros for mothers who had a second child born between 1 December 2003 and

---

[69] Bimbi, 'The family paradigm'.
[70] Fargion, 'Children, gender and families'; Naldini and Saraceno, 'Social and family policies'. Reasons for this have to do both with economic and political factors, as well as resistance by powerful actors such as the Catholic Church.
[71] Fargion, 'Children, gender and families', 105.
[72] Fargion, 'Children, gender and families', 'Italy'.
[73] Neyer and Andersson, 'Consequences of family policies'.
[74] Krause and Marchesi, 'Fertility politics', 350.   [75] Krause, 'Empty cradles', 598.

31 December 2004.[76] Though the national scheme was a one-off, some Italian regions (responsible for much of social care and social assistance) give similar 'incentives' under family-assistance schemes. For instance, Friuli Venezia Giulia (a region in the north-east of Italy) started to offer a similar baby bonus in 2000, initially €3000 for second births and €4600 for subsequent ones (the amount has since been reduced, due to economic pressures: for 2014, it was €600 per child, regardless of birth order). Such measures are a small step towards recognising the sacrifices made by women, but they tend to have a limited effect, which depends on the socioeconomic profile of the recipient. In Friuli Venezia Giulia, the early bonus, while larger than most such schemes, had an impact mostly on low-educated women with two or more children – and the low number of such women meant the bonus had a small impact overall.[77] It is rather optimistic to assume such bonuses would make a large difference in the absence of other reforms.

Moreover, baby bonuses were introduced amid continued controversy over women's roles as citizens and renewed rhetorical appeals asking women to sacrifice themselves for the state and family. In the context of Italy's 2004 law reform on in vitro fertilisation (IVF),[78] Hanafin has identified a desire to return to a traditionalist conception of Italian national identity, based on hetero-patriarchal family formation.[79] This was supported not just by some political actors but in particular by the power of the Church, which, though no longer commanding the same privilege as it once did,[80] is still able to exert influence over moral questions.[81] Something similar can be identified in the context of baby bonuses. They were introduced amid a discourse that suggested citizens, especially married Italian women, needed to be woken up from their selfishness to do their duty. The hope was that a symbolic show

---

[76] Krause and Marchesi, 'Fertility politics'.   [77] Boccuzzo et al., 'The impact of the bonus'.
[78] Italy's law 40/2004 is very strict. As Benegiano and Gianaroli, 'The new Italian IVF legislation', 117 put it, it was 'inspired by the desire to protect every newly produced embryo'. It allows only heterosexual couples access to IVF and bans the use of donor gametes and pre-implantation genetic diagnosis; the latter was held to be incompatible with Article 8 of the European Convention of Human Rights in *Costa and Pavan v Italy* (Application 54270/10, judgment 28 August 2012).
[79] Hanafin, 'Gender, citizenship'. See also Fenton, 'Catholic doctrine'; Metzler, 'Nationalizing embryos'.
[80] The turning point in the role of the Catholic Church came in the 1970s, when abortion was legalised and divorce law liberalised. See Caldwell, *Italian Family Matters*.
[81] This is clear regarding abortion, for example – though abortion is legal, the Catholic Church has encouraged doctors to exercise their right to conscientious objection, with the result that it is difficult to access in some areas. *La Repubblica*, 'Aborto: in Italia è ancora un percorso a ostacoli', 10 November 2014; Hanafin, *Conceiving Life*, ch. 3.

of appreciation, even in the absence of practical help with reconciliation, might jolt Italian women out of their refusal to have the children wanted by both religious and secular authorities. As Krause points out, whereas high fertility was seen as irrational and 'backward' in the past, this kind of discourse now seeks to represent low fertility as irrational and amoral behaviour on the part of Italian women.[82] In this context, and in the absence of structural reform, baby bonuses seek to reinforce old notions of family, trusting that symbolic and rhetorical gestures will persuade women to stop abusing their freedom and resume normal levels of reproductive service. Where the IVF law took power out of the hands of citizens and doctors and 'nationalised embryos', integrating them 'into the community of "citizen subjects"',[83] the baby bonus seeks to 'bribe' women into doing their duty as reproductive citizens[84] and to produce the 'babies who refuse to be born.'[85]

What is also notable about baby-bonus schemes is the manifest desire to place limits on these arrangements, allowing only specific groups to access them: the national bonus given by the Berlusconi government was limited to mothers who were Italians or EU citizens (and, in fact, the Alleanza Nazionale party sought to limit it further, to Italian citizens only[86]). The Friuli Venezia Giulia bonus was initially similarly limited to Italian/EU citizens, who, furthermore, had to be married (the limits were subsequently relaxed to cover also cohabitees and non-EU citizens who had been resident for at least five years).[87] In other words, while Italian (and European) women, especially married ones, are targeted for their very low birth rates, the schemes explicitly try to exclude other women, most notably migrants who are non-EU citizens. This is consistent with a trend of scrutinising migrants and racial- and ethnic-minority women over their 'excessive' fertility (and, interestingly, also abortion) rates.[88] The birth rate of Italians and immigrants are frequently crudely contrasted:

> Italians don't produce babies anymore, the idiots. For decades they have had and still have the lowest birth-rate in the West. Our "foreign workers", instead, breed and multiply gloriously. At least half of the Moslem

---

[82] Krause, 'Empty cradles', 584–6; Marchesi, 'Reproducing Italians'. See also Krause, 'Toys and perfumes'.
[83] Metzler, 'Nationalizing embryos', 414–15.   [84] Fenton, 'Catholic doctrine', 9.
[85] Krause and Marchesi, 'Fertility politics', 353.
[86] Krause and Marchesi, 'Fertility politics', 356.
[87] Boccuzzo et al., 'The impact of the bonus', 127.   [88] Marchesi, 'Reproducing Italians'.

women you see in our streets are pregnant or surrounded by streams of children.[89]

Limiting the baby bonus to certain (predominantly white) groups makes it clear that certain kinds of migrant reproduction – the reference to Muslim women in the quote is particularly telling – are considered inherently problematic for the reproduction of the Italian nation. Interestingly, a similar antinatalist discourse has been applied to southern Italian women in the not-so-remote past, and indeed the discourse over immigrants versus Italians now masks the heterogeneity of Italian reproduction and conflicting attitudes towards these internal trends.[90] The difficulty of boundary-drawing is further underlined by European women, who had to be included as EU citizens to avoid legal challenges.

The overt anxiety over immigrant reproduction is connected to Italy's general (un)preparedness to tackle the social impacts of immigration and unresolved questions about whether immigrants have the right to produce the next generation of Italian citizens. This anxiety over the children of resident immigrants is complemented by demographers carefully scrutinising 'second generation' children in terms of their integration, analysing them by nationality, family background and language.[91] Italy's legal framework has continued to be characterised by a persistent gap between the norms on labour migration and the actual processes for immigrant inclusion.[92] One of the issues that has remained unresolved is the citizenship status of second-generation children as members of the national community. Italy, traditionally an emigration country and a latecomer in terms of state formation, last reformed its citizenship regime in 1992.[93] This regime was built on a strong tradition of *jus sanguinis*, according to which citizenship is not determined by place of birth – *jus soli* – but parentage: by having one or both parents who are citizens.[94] Despite Italy's growth as a country of immigration, the 1992 citizenship law prioritised citizenship via the idea of 'Italian blood' and

---

[89] Fallaci, *The Rage and the Pride*, 137–8.
[90] Krause, 'Empty cradles'. For interdisciplinary analyses of the racialised divisions between southern and northern Italy, see Schneider, *Italy's 'Southern Question'*.
[91] See e.g. Gabrielli et al., 'Just a matter of time?'; Paterno and Gabrielli, 'Two years later'; Chapter 3.
[92] Zanfrini, 'Immigration and labour market'.
[93] The 1992 law restricted reform of the previous law, passed in 1912. For an overview, see Arena et al., 'Italy'. See also Zincone, 'The case of Italy'.
[94] Statute 91/92; Zincone and Basili, 'Country report: Italy', 1. See Koslowski, *Migrants and Citizens*, on this arguably anomalous inclination. On how both principles are, despite their differences, forms of sustaining citizenship as a bounded exclusive concept, see Shachar, *The Birthright Lottery*.

did not envisage the presence of a large 'second generation'.[95] Italian nationality by descent was made easy to maintain, even when families had long emigrated from Italy and acquired other nationalities; in contrast, Italian nationality is difficult to obtain for those who do not have a connection with the country through Italian blood.[96] Though a limited *jus soli* path to naturalisation was created in 1992, it is quite restrictive – moreover, it is easier to achieve for people of Italian descent and EU citizens than for non-EU immigrants.[97]

In practice, this has meant that children born and raised in Italy do not automatically become Italian citizens – when they turn 18, children of non-Italian parents can acquire Italian nationality by proving uninterrupted residence (living in Italy for 18 consecutive years) and requesting citizenship within one year of becoming an adult.[98] Moreover, this path is not open to children who were not born in Italy (but who have, for instance, joined their immigrant parents later, as is the case for children of many women who work in the care sector).[99] Thus, descendants of expatriates are able to keep Italian citizenship through generations, while it has been very difficult for immigrants and their children to acquire citizenship status, especially if they have maintained links with their countries of origin. Recent years have, at last, seen a concerted campaign – *L'Italia sono anch'io* ('I, too, am Italy') – to move the rules of citizenship acquisition in a more generous direction in order to facilitate the integration and path to citizenship of immigrants and their children.[100] As a result of this push, the bill making it easier for migrants' children to obtain Italian citizenship cleared the Lower House in October 2015.[101] If passed by the Senate, children born in Italy of foreign parents could become citizens if at least one of the parents has a long-term permit of stay. Children born in Italy or who enter Italy before their twelfth birthday would also be allowed to apply for citizenship once they had attended Italian schools for at least five years. The

---

[95] Pastore, 'A community out of balance'.
[96] Pastore, 'A community out of balance'; Zincone, 'The case of Italy'; Zincone and Basili, 'Country report: Italy'.
[97] With Italian descent, citizenship can be acquired in three years. Other European citizens can request citizenship after a residency period of four years, while non-EU immigrants must reside in the state for ten years before they can apply for citizenship. Zincone and Basili, 'Country report: Italy'.
[98] Circulars have softened some of the hardship in these requirements, but they are not law and can be changed easily.
[99] Zincone and Basili, 'Country report: Italy'.
[100] On the campaign, see e.g. Ambrosini, 'Acting for immigrants' rights'.
[101] *La Repubblica*, 'Cittadinanza: sì della Camera allo ius soli', 13 October 2015.

proposed changes would constitute a step towards accepting that Italy has become a country of immigration, but for this reason they are causing considerable political and societal anxiety in a state that has been politically, bureaucratically, psychologically and culturally unprepared for the change.[102]

VARIATIONS ON A THEME? FINNISH, BRITISH AND AUSTRALIAN TRAJECTORIES

Many of the issues around Italy's lowest-low birth rate are similar to those experienced in other states with very low birth rates.[103] This section outlines how birth rates have re-emerged as a target for government attention in Finland, the United Kingdom and Australia. It argues that though their demographic trends are less acutely framed as a crisis, the situations in these states are different in degree but not in kind to those experienced by lowest-low fertility states. As already stated, the last few decades have been a period of prolonged below-replacement birth rates in the Global North. Amid a general pattern of declining birth rates, Finland, the United Kingdom and Australia experienced a 'baby boom' after the Second World War (though with differences in terms of timing and duration[104]), but returned to declining rates in the 1970s. In Finland, the birth rate started to fall in the 1950s, reached a bottom (TFR of 1.5) in 1972 and then recovered slightly; the latest trend is downwards from 1.87 in 2010 to 1.71 in 2014.[105] In England and Wales, the TFR fell below replacement in the mid-1970s, then recovered somewhat and stabilised; in the 1990s it remained mostly below 1.80, falling to a record low of 1.63 in 2001 but increasing to 1.96 in 2008. In 2014, the TFR decreased to 1.83 children per woman, from 1.94 in 2012.[106] In Australia, birth rates fell below replacement level in 1976, and the lowest level (1.73) was recorded in 2001.[107] In 2014, Australia's TFR was 1.80, after a brief high of 2.02, which was reached in 2008.[108] As

---

[102] Ambrosini, 'Acting for immigrants' rights'; Zincone and Basili, 'Country report: Italy'.
[103] For instance, Italy shares many issues related to the Catholic Church with states like Poland. See Mishtal, 'Irrational non-reproduction?'. On Japan, see Rosenbluth, *Japan's Low Fertility*.
[104] For a comparative overview, see van Bavel and Reher, 'The baby boom'.
[105] Tilastokeskus, 'Syntyneiden määrä'.
[106] Office of National Statistics, 'Birth summary tables'. For statistics on Scottish birth rates – slightly lower than in England and Wales – see General Register Office for Scotland, 'Vital events'; for Northern Ireland – slightly higher than in England and Wales – see Registrar General Northern Ireland, 'Annual report 2014'. For a summary of the variety inside the United Kingdom, see Office of National Statistics, 'Fertility summary'.
[107] Gray et al., 'Fertility and family policy', 2.
[108] Australian Bureau of Statistics, 'Births, Australia'.

in Italy, these governments are keeping a close eye on birth rates, but how, when and why the issue of birth rates is framed as a problem for governance varies.

In Finland, as in Italy, (de)population fears were first raised a century ago and family and child policies were introduced in the 1930s, partly for pronatalist reasons.[109] As in Italy, after the Second World War it became difficult to articulate policy measures as having to do with population per se, in this case because of the Finnish collaboration with the Nazis (and forced sterilisations of disabled persons, even after the war[110]).[111] Instead, population policy came to be embedded in Finland's strong family policies, which were reframed as part of the welfare state, aiming at universal services and equality (largely following the Swedish example, which seeks to make it easier for women to combine work and family[112]).[113] Finland provides a contrast with Italy's 'dismal record'[114] on gender equality and support for families and children, with a range of family benefits, leave policies and subsidised family services (such as childcare and early education), and correlation between work and motherhood is strong.[115] In further contrast with Italy, where both religious and secular authorities sometimes blame women for their 'irrational' refusal to have children, Finnish government policy officially recognises that explanations behind below-replacement birth rates, such as postponement, are often based on 'rational' grounds, such as uncertainty over economic prospects.[116] However, the social-democratic welfare model, while arguably supporting the higher birth rates that are present in Italy, has not been able to lift the birth rate to replacement level; moreover, family policies are considered expensive and even traditionally well-funded welfare societies are under pressure to reduce family benefits.[117] These pressures, especially after the financial crisis, have recently resulted in governments also cutting traditionally well-funded policies supporting children.[118]

---

[109] Patosalmi, *The Politics and Policies*, 63. This concern eventually led to the establishment of Väestöliitto (Family Federation of Finland) in 1941, an influential organisation that produces and disseminates information about the size and structure of the population and advocates for improving families' life circumstances.
[110] Broberg and Roll-Hansen, *Eugenics and the Welfare State*. [111] Isola, 'Fertility concern'.
[112] Kramer, *The Other Population Crisis*, ch. 1. [113] Patosalmi, *The Politics and Policies*, 64.
[114] Fargion, 'Children, gender and families', 105. [115] Ferrarini, *Families, States*.
[116] Valtioneuvoston kanslia, 'Hyvä yhteiskunta kaikenikäisille'.
[117] Schleutker, 'Women's career strategy choices'. For an overview of the current state of and pressures on the Finnish welfare system, see Blomgren et al., 'Finland: growing inequality'.
[118] Yle, 'Näin lapsilisät pienenevät leikkausten jälkeen', 27 March 2014.

Fertility concern has remained an important topic in Finnish population discussions, cropping up regularly despite comparatively high birth rates. The prevalent discourse is now framed in terms of an 'ageing nation', worsening dependency ratios and the desire to maintain economic competitiveness, and is explicitly linked to the advanced stage of demographic ageing in Finland (see further Chapter 5).[119] In the last decade, raising fertility, even slightly, has been explicitly framed as a partial answer to these issues. Stronger voices have been heard advocating for a proper population policy (including that of Prime Minister Matti Vanhanen in 2003 and 2004[120]), but Finland has so far refrained from articulating clear pronatalist goals (and the emphasis on reproductive rights remains strong).[121] At the same time, some policy documents, such as the 2004 Governmental Report on the Future, increasingly mention ideas that aim to increase the number of families with many children.[122] In this regard, there is some evidence suggesting that having children has become more polarised – a growing number of women have no children and those who decide to have children, have more children than before – and such demographic knowledge has become an essential element in identifying families which might be encouraged to have children through adjustments in the welfare system; adjustments of family policy facilitating this have been much analysed and debated.[123] Some commentators have argued it would be sensible to encourage additional childbearing among those families where women stay outside the labour market for longer periods of time and which already have at least three children.[124] In contrast with this view, which accepts the separation of women into those who should have children and those who should work (controversial in the Finnish context), other actors, like the Finnish Business and Policy Forum EVA (a pro-market think tank), adopt a view that more highly

---

[119] Isola, 'Fertility concern', 'Hyviä työntekijöitä', 335.
[120] Patosalmi, *The Politics and Policies*, 66–7.
[121] The Government Programme for 2011 mentioned 'raising fertility' as one of the ways of increasing the sustainability of the state, but did not elaborate. Valtioneuvoston kanslia, Pääministeri Jyrki Kataisen, 7.
[122] See Valtioneuvoston kanslia, 'Hyvä yhteiskunta kaikenikäisille', 'Väestökehitykseen vaikuttaminen'. For commentary, see Isola, 'Fertility concern'.
[123] See e.g. Hiilamo and Kangas, 'Trap for women'; Repo, 'Finnish child home care'; Schleutker, 'Women's career strategy choices'; Vikat, 'Women's labor force attachment'. Much discussion has focused on the effects of the so-called 'child home care allowance', which involves an extra income transfer to allow parents (usually women) to stay home until their child is three years old. The Home Care Allowance Act was introduced in 1985.
[124] Väestöliitto, 'Väestöpoliittinen ohjelma'.

educated and self-sufficient individuals should be supported to have more children.[125]

Part of the appeal of raising birth rates is that it would limit the need for future immigration, which is perceived as a problem. Finland, like Italy, was traditionally a country of emigration, but increasing immigration since the 1990s has challenged the prevalent perception of Finland as homogeneous (though the proportion of immigrants is still comparatively low).[126] Labour migration is officially accepted as necessary to resolve problems associated with a rapidly ageing population.[127] However, a number of issues with existing immigration flows have created reservations about actively encouraging immigration. These have to do with concerns over immigrant integration, xenophobia and high unemployment among many immigrant groups (a significant proportion of the entrants in the 1990s were refugees, return migrants and family migrants).[128] In contrast with Italy, which has rapidly transitioned to a country with large labour migration flows, including irregular streams, Finland's approach to labour migration has been more tightly managed and labour migration numbers have been low.[129] As in Italy, the Finnish citizenship regime is largely based on *jus sanguinis*, but *jus soli* is an available avenue for children born or raised in Finland.[130] Since 2007, the majority of the population increase has been a result of immigration, but the proportion of immigrant births is not yet significant enough to prompt mainstream concern.[131] However, the political anti-immigrant right has called for further measures to raise the Finnish birth rate through family policies (which allegedly would prevent abortions) instead of further immigration, which suggests there will be scope in Finland for further debates about who exactly is reproducing the nation.[132]

---

[125] EVA, 'Tuomitut vähenemään'. See also Isola, 'Hyviä työntekijöitä'.
[126] The start of these changes is connected to the collapse of the Soviet Union in 1991 and the arrival of the Ingrians and other ethnic Finns. Salmio, 'Kylmän sodan loppuminen'. For an overview of immigrants in Finland, see Tilastokeskus, 'Ulkomaalaiset'.
[127] Valtioneuvoston kanslia, 'Hyvä yhteiskunta kaikenikäisille'.
[128] Keskinen et al., *En ole rasisti*; Valtonen, 'Cracking monopoly'. See further Chapter 4.
[129] For an exploration of the reasons for this, see Bartram, 'Conspicuous by their absence'.
[130] Nationality Act 2003 (as amended in 2011), s. 28. For an overview of the current Finnish citizenship regime, see Fagerlund and Brander, 'Country report: Finland'. For the historical background, see Fagerlund, 'Finland'.
[131] The statistics show that the average birth rate for foreigners is higher than for Finnish women (e.g. persons from Iraq, Somalia and Kosovo have much higher rates). Söderling, 'Suomen väestökysymys'. Many women from these states tend to stay at home and take care of their families rather than work outside the home.
[132] Niikko, 'Syntyvyyden lisääminen'.

If in Finland and Italy the question of immigration in the context of the reproduction of the nation is recent, in the United Kingdom, characterised by the legacy of the British Empire and longstanding colonial emigration (and, importantly, also colonial immigration since the Second World War), debates about the links between birth-rate trends and migration go further back. As in Italy and Finland, the birth-rate decline, consistent with European trends, was framed as a concern in the 1920s, with heightened anxiety in the 1930s (though the proposed pronatalist programme was never implemented and the post-war baby boom rendered the threat less immediate).[133] During the population panic of the 1930s and 1940s, immigration from the colonies was discussed as a possible solution to the problems of the low birth rate but ultimately rejected as undesirable; after the Second World War, immigration controls were directed primarily at colonial immigrants in an (ultimately futile) effort to prevent, limit and manage immigration from the former colonies amid concerns over the assimilation of non-white immigrants and, later, their families.[134] The United Kingdom is also where Malthusian[135] arguments about the threat of over- rather than (or as well as) under-population were first made and popularised, and indeed they have often been raised there since, creating a counter-narrative to the story of declining birth rates as a risk to the nation.[136] The population panic of the 1930s was not only quantitative but qualitative and eugenistically informed: disquiet was particularly expressed over the availability of birth control, preventing reproduction of the 'socially responsible'.[137] In that vein, a *high* birth rate was also a problem to be governed, when it involved 'irresponsible' reproduction by those who produced children they could not support, placing a burden on society (a narrative with a strong class dimension).[138]

This background also helps to explain the traditional lack of family support in the British liberal welfare-regime context – the UK government's official position is that it takes no stance on birth rates and that citizens will make their own choices as a private matter, based

---

[133] Hampshire, *Citizenship and Belonging*, ch. 3. On the eugenic assumptions of this era, see Soloway, *Demography and Degeneration*.
[134] Hampshire, *Citizenship and Belonging*, 45. See also Joppke, *Immigration and the Nation-State*.
[135] Malthus introduced his influential principle of population in his *Essay on the Principle of Population*.
[136] Coole, 'Population stories'. [137] Hampshire, *Citizenship and Belonging*.
[138] Coole, 'Population stories'. Malthus criticised the Poor Laws on grounds that they encouraged the poor to have more children than they could support. Malthus, *Essay on the Principle of Population*.

on their own resources.[139] Yet, despite this liberal approach to reproduction, which has been hesitant to venture deep into (what it sees as) the private world of work/family reconciliation and gender roles,[140] birth rates are only moderately below replacement, with a recent trend upwards close to replacement level. Though this seemingly contradicts arguments about the need to support families to raise the birth rate presented in the Italian context, McDonald and Moyle explain it partly in terms of cultural reasons and value orientation (high work participation of mothers is a fundamental feature in English-speaking countries) and partly as a result of a recent development in services.[141] The higher birth rate is also due to highly differentiated patterns in childbearing: higher-earning women, who find work and motherhood difficult to combine in the absence of supportive family policies, have low birth rates, whereas women with lower occupational status and weak attachment to the labour market have more children (often at young ages).[142] The birth rates of highly educated women, particularly those in managerial positions, remain low relative to those of other women, and the social and economic policies of the Labour government (1997–2010) aimed at providing support to families with children were more targeted at families on the lower end of the income scale.[143] Thus, the costs of reproduction appear to be falling disproportionately on population groups with fewer economic opportunities and lower stability. In short: 'high fertility depends on high levels of inequality... High fertility is also likely to be accompanied by relatively high rates of child poverty and all of its related social problems.'[144]

Just as awareness of the class dimension of this trend has led to a focus on the decline of the middle classes, awareness of its ethnic and racial component is linked to renewed debates about the reproduction of the nation and the impact of continued and increasing immigration since the 1990s.[145] Though 10 years ago the United Kingdom was in

---

[139] Dunnell, 'Policy responses'. Then opposition leader (now prime minister) David Cameron did argue in 2007 that the United Kingdom needed a 'coherent long-term population strategy' – but his focus was on immigration and he repeated the government would not interfere in decisions on reproduction. BBC News, 'In full: Cameron on population', 29 October 2007.
[140] See Lewis and Campbell, 'UK work/family balance'.
[141] McDonald and Moyle, 'Why do English-speaking countries'.
[142] Hansen et al., 'The timing of motherhood'; Sigle-Rushton, 'England and Wales', 'Fertility'; Smith and Ratcliffe, 'Women's education'. For a discussion of the significance of class, see Crompton, 'Class and family', who finds that working-class girls are most pro-motherhood. On the class dimensions of lone motherhood, see Rowlingson and McKay, 'Lone motherhood'.
[143] Sigle-Rushton, 'England and Wales'. See also Brewer et al. 'Does welfare reform'.
[144] Sigle-Rushton, 'Fertility', 36. [145] Brown and Ferree, 'Close your eyes'.

the grip of demographic gloom over the decline in the birth rate, the current discussions over immigration and immigrant reproduction are again taking a Malthusian direction amid projections that the UK population is set to grow to 70 million by the early 2030s.[146] In terms of birth rates, over a quarter of births in England and Wales in 2013 were to mothers born outside the United Kingdom, with a birth rate for UK-born women of 1.79 and that for non-UK-born women 2.19 (Poland, Pakistan and India were the most common countries of birth for non-UK mothers).[147] Though immigration is seen as an economic necessity by economic elites, British demographers have warned about the consequences of long-term ethnic change (driven by both immigration and differential birth rates).[148] Recent discussions over restricting immigration, both from the new EU Member States (especially Poland) and from other countries, can be situated in the context of earlier attempts to stem immigration from former colonies in the Caribbean and South Asia.[149] These attempts failed to prevent the transformation of Britain into a diverse society, but culminated in the elimination of *jus soli* citizenship in 1981. The British Nationality Act (1981) dealt with the colonial legacy by redefining British citizenship in terms of descent (*jus sanguinis*), as is typical in continental Europe.[150] The current immigration trends have reawakened questions about how to govern immigrant integration and social cohesion in an increasingly multi-ethnic society (for a further discussion of these issues, see Chapter 3).

In Australia, a vast settlement state built on immigration, concerns about the birth rate and its implications for efforts to 'populate the country'[151] can be traced back well over a century. In 1904, a Royal Commission was established to seek reasons for the dramatic fall in the birth rate in New South Wales.[152] Concerns over white women's

---

[146] Coole, 'Population stories'.
[147] Office of National Statistics, 'Births in England and Wales'. On the fertility trends of ethnic minorities, see Coleman and Dubuc, 'The fertility of ethnic minorities'.
[148] Coleman, 'Immigration and ethnic change'.
[149] Hampshire, *Citizenship and Belonging*, 179 notes the continuities between contemporary debates on immigration and the period of colonial immigration.
[150] Though the regime, which is a mix of *jus sanguinis* and *jus soli*, is still relatively generous (especially compared to continental European countries), Sawyer and Wray, 'Country report: United Kingdom', 1, call the move away from *jus soli* a 'fundamental shift', as even UK-born people can be legally foreigners (only children of settled parents will be born British citizens). For background, see Anderson, *Us and Them?*, ch. 2; Dummett, 'United Kingdom'.
[151] Australia has, of course, been populated for tens of thousands of years, but the white colonisers considered it an 'empty' continent. On modern Australia's founding through the convict transportation system, see Hughes, *The Fatal Shore*.
[152] For more on the Royal Commission on the Decline of the Birth-Rate and on the Mortality of Infants in New South Wales, see Siedlecky and Wyndham, *Populate and Perish*, 17. Concerns

fertility – indigenous people were officially excluded from 'the Australian population' until the 1960s[153] – were revisited in the decades afterwards, and pronatalist policies were attempted (without success) before the Second World War.[154] The Japanese attack in early 1942 and Australia's inability to defend itself made it a priority for post-war governments to increase the nation's population ('populate or perish'[155]), and it was accepted that the previous ineffectual attempts to promote births should be abandoned in favour of an emphasis on immigration, which was accepted as the primary solution for the defence and security issues posed by Australia's location and geography.[156] However, immigration was to be of the right kind – hence the (in)famous White Australia policy, which was maintained to keep the Australian state white (and based on British culture). Restrictions on non-white immigration had first been introduced in the nineteenth century (to limit, for instance, Chinese immigration),[157] but after the war Australia rapidly shifted towards soliciting and incorporating huge numbers of immigrants – white settlers from English-speaking countries were preferred, but Southern European immigrants and displaced persons were also admitted. However, non-white Asians were prevented from immigrating.[158] The White Australia policy was formally abandoned in the 1970s, after having been eroded to some degree already, and since then, Australia has rapidly transformed into one of the most multi-ethnic states in the world (for a discussion of Australia's current immigration programme, see Chapter 4).[159]

After a period of absence from public discourse, below-replacement birth rates became a focus of attention again in the late 1990s, when the conservative Howard government began to reassert the importance of families and to take an active interest in the birth rate, adopting the view that it was 'too low'.[160] As in Finland, this renewed interest was connected to demographic knowledge and warnings about ageing and

were particularly acute over the low birth rates of educated women; see Mackinnon, 'From one fin de siècle'.
[153] Clarke and Galligan, 'Protecting the citizen body'.
[154] Mackinnon, 'From one fin de siècle'. For a historical overview, see Mackinnon, 'Bringing the unclothed'.
[155] Calwell, *How Many Australians*. For discussion, see Jupp, *From White Australia*, 11–14.
[156] Mackinnon, 'Bringing the unclothed'. [157] Rubenstein, 'Citizenship and the centenary'.
[158] On the White Australia policy, see Joppke, *Selecting by Origin*, ch. 2; Tavan, *The Long, Slow Death*.
[159] For an overview of this transition, see Jupp, *From White Australia*, ch. 2.
[160] In 1994, fertility had still been considered beyond the scope of government intervention, with immigration the only tool for influencing population direction. Heard, 'Pronatalism under Howard', 12–13.

dependency rates.[161] Though Australia shares many features with other English-speaking states, like the United Kingdom (work-orientated culture, large educational differences in birth rates),[162] it now has an array of support policies that are aimed at alleviating the cost to parents of raising children.[163] What it has in common with Italy is that in addition to measures not directly touted as pronatalist, such as tax benefits for families with children, recent conservative governments have simultaneously employed more symbolic pronatalist messages pushing women towards motherhood. This is particularly evident in the context of the maternity payment (soon dubbed 'baby bonus') introduced under the Howard government in 2004.[164] The baby bonus was modest in value (with yearly amounts ranging between AU$3000 and AU$5000), but its effects – possibly real, but also imaginary – have been much analysed.[165] As in Italy, the maternity bonus was connected to a discourse of 'procreate and cherish',[166] sending a pro-motherhood message to Australian women – and as in Italy, though in a less overt fashion, political anxiety was expressed about whether the message was heard by the wrong recipients.[167] Heard has concluded that despite the conservative government's rhetoric about facilitating a balance between work and family, in reality the baby bonus was not accompanied by measures promoting this (and sometimes it seemed to promote the reverse).[168] Indeed, the government's policies were largely ambivalent about facilitating mothers' workforce participation.[169]

---

[161] For a summary of these, see Jackson and Casey, 'Procreate and cherish'.
[162] Fertility differentials between ethnic groups do not have the same resonance as in Britain, perhaps because migrants come from a diverse range of countries and no single origin country is sufficiently large to make a difference to the fertility rate. McDonald and Moyle, 'Why do English-speaking countries', 259.
[163] See e.g. McDonald and Moyle, 'Why do English-speaking countries'.
[164] On the history and details of the bonus, see Jackson and Casey, 'Procreate and cherish'. The bonus was initially continued under the Labour government, but later modified (e.g. to introduce means-testing). It was scrapped in 2014.
[165] Small rises occurred, but to what extent they are due to the bonus is unclear – alternative explanations include a change in the timing of births and overall economic prosperity. The strongest increase occurred among women from lower-income households. See e.g. Heard, 'Pronatalism under Howard'; Lain et al., 'The impact of the baby bonus'; Parr and Guest, 'The contribution'; Risse, '... And one for the country'.
[166] Jackson and Casey, 'Procreate and cherish', 155.
[167] This anxiety was expressed over teenagers and indigenous women. Cover, 'Biopolitics and the baby bonus', 441; Jackson and Casey, 'Procreate and cherish', 138. Note that the baby bonus a century earlier (1912) was only paid to white women, not indigenous or Asian women. See Grimshaw et al., *Creating a Nation*, 206.
[168] Heard, 'Pronatalism under Howard'. See also Jackson, 'When is a baby boom', 11, who calls pronatalism an 'ad hoc tack-on'.
[169] Brennan, 'Babies, budgets, and birthrates'.

The attempts to manage the birth rate were also connected to the other partial 'solution' to population ageing; that is, immigration.[170] Australia's immigration policy is no longer racially based, but this does not mean that immigration and the demographic changes to national identity it entails have ceased to cause anxiety among the Anglo-Australian majority.[171] The multi-ethnicity created by immigration rapidly challenged conceptions of belonging and citizenship built on British heritage. Australia's citizenship law (only introduced in 1948),[172] based on favouring British immigrants and requiring cultural assimilation, was moved in a more uniform direction in 1986; it is now a combination of *jus soli* and *jus sanguinis* (though *jus soli* is typical for states built on immigration, in Australia it was always tempered by the British connection, and one of the changes in 1986 involved a move towards a more limited idea of *jus soli*).[173] The official transformation of Australia into a multicultural state that successfully incorporates large numbers of migrants did not prevent a discourse around the time of the introduction of the baby bonus that suggested further immigration was, at best, cautiously welcomed. The Federal Minister for Immigration and Multicultural and Indigenous Affairs said she favoured encouraging an increased birth rate, to which Australia could then add immigration 'with the right people in the right place at the right time'.[174] The idea of a tightly controlled immigration programme that welcomes (only) the 'right' immigrants (based on skills and economic need) is accompanied by governments' eagerness – regardless of political side – to demonstrate they can effectively control all forms of immigration. Since 2001, asylum policy has emerged as the focal point for fears over unwanted ('illegal') migrants,[175] but the population numbers of the regular immigration

---

[170] On the longstanding connections between women as the reproducers of the nation and immigration, see de Lepervanche, 'Breeders for Australia'. Baird, 'Maternity, whiteness', 206 argues that increased fertility among 'Australian' women has always been the preferred method for national reproduction, with implications for both abortion and immigration.

[171] Joppke, *Selecting by Origin*, ch. 2.

[172] Until the Nationality and Citizenship Act (1948) was passed, Australians were British subjects.

[173] A person born in Australia is only a citizen if one of their parents is an Australian citizen or a permanent resident at the time of birth; or if the child has lived in Australia for ten years from the time of birth. The 1986 decision to limit *jus soli* was the result of the desire to prevent challenges by 'illegal immigrants' who attempted to 'use' their children to stay in the country. Zappalà and Castles, 'Citizenship and immigration', 43. For a historical analysis, see Rubenstein, 'Citizenship and the centenary'.

[174] Vanstone, 'Federal government perspective', 39.

[175] On the role of the Tampa incident, see Dauvergne, *Making People Illegal*, ch. 4; McNevin, 'The liberal paradox'.

programme – involving large numbers, but also large fluctuations – have also caused anxiety amid population projections showing strong growth as a result of immigration (see further Chapter 4).[176]

CITIZENSHIP AND THE GOVERNANCE OF NATIONAL REPRODUCTION

This last section discusses the patterns of 'reproductive governance'[177] that emerge from these examples and their implications in light of gendered citizenship and immigrant inclusion. The way the story has been framed so far matches the typical way in which birth-rate debates tend to be presented in all of the countries discussed. The birth rate is understood as a public-policy problem related to the numbers of missing citizens that would be needed to keep up the vitality of the state, with some anxiety also over who exactly is producing (or not producing) the next generation of citizens. There is an overwhelming focus on numbers and the size of the future population, and a prevalent assumption even in states with relatively high – if still below-replacement – fertility that at the very least, a close eye needs to be kept on the trends.[178] The need for policy intervention that would encourage appropriate reproduction comes up frequently, but concerns over raising birth rates are not easily translated into policy consensus, let alone successful measures. Immigration features in these discussions as the somewhat disconcerting but effectively unavoidable fallback option, which, because of expected future problems associated with it, needs to be carefully managed even in established countries of immigration. Together, knowledge of both birth rates and immigration patterns contributes to a sense of anxiety about the reproduction of the national body. This section elaborates on two aspects of this dominant framing. First, it discusses the way these debates collectively present women as citizens, (re)asserting

---

[176] Australian Bureau of Statistics, 'Population projections', projects an increase to between 36.8 and 48.3 million people by 2061. In 2009, then Prime Minister Kevin Rudd controversially stated he was in favour of a 'big Australia'. His successor, Julia Gillard, moved away from that position to argue for a 'sustainable Australia'. On the sustainability argument in the Australian context, see Lowe, *Bigger or Better?*.

[177] A term borrowed from Morgan and Roberts, 'Reproductive governance'.

[178] In contrast, it could be argued, and has been argued by some, that fertility levels slightly below replacement do not justify policies intended to increase the birth rate, considering such rates still make population decline very slow and easy to adjust to. See e.g. Guest, 'The baby bonus'; Neyer, 'Should governments'. As to whether even population decline is necessarily harmful, see e.g. Coleman and Rowthorn, 'Who's afraid of population decline'.

female citizens' role as predominantly that of reproducers of 'national stocks'.[179] Second, it analyses how some individuals, including immigrant others but also non-conforming insiders, are singled out as problematic reproducers.

Responses to low birth rates frame women as reproductive citizens who are failing at their traditional role either through sheer immorality (Italy) or, in demographers' dominant framing regarding family policy reform, because they need support to fulfil their appropriate reproductive function. The dominant argument (presented especially by Peter McDonald) is that the state can no longer abstain from action but must intervene to ease the tensions between women's dual roles as modern worker-citizens and good reproductive citizens.[180] Such efforts should seek to resolve the demographic-transition paradox – that is, adapt policy to the fact that contemporary society is putting a premium on education, building a career and self-sufficiency and thus changing women's life cycles to delay or prevent childbearing. This aim also appeals to feminist critiques of social citizenship, which often revolve around the importance of care and women's equality in the labour market. Heitlinger argued over 20 years ago that though one might assume that promoting gender equality and attempting to raise birth rates are incompatible, there need not be an 'antagonistic relationship'.[181] As is often noted, women's childbearing ideal in late-modern states is, on average, over two children per woman.[182] This seems to suggest there is a place for policies seeking to facilitate women having these 'missing' children. It is now accepted, at least in terms of official discourse in many states, that policy options that would support families with children, in particular mothers who work, have to be explored.[183] Considering the strong role of the state this solution envisages, it is not surprising that Nordic countries have taken these ideas furthest, but it is increasingly advocated as a model of reproductive governance more generally.[184] As the European Commission sums it up, 'families must

---

[179] Yuval-Davis, 'Gender and nation', 629.
[180] McDonald, 'Gender equity, social institutions', 'An assessment of policies'.
[181] Heitlinger, 'Pronatalism and women's equality', 344.
[182] d'Addio and d'Ercole, 'Trends and determinants'. Note, however, that family *ideals* may be far removed from actual desires and practical intentions, let alone outcomes. See Gauthier, 'Family policy and fertility', 272–4 on the reliability of surveys of fertility desires.
[183] Castles, 'The world turned upside down'; Esping-Andersen, *The Incomplete Revolution*; Gauthier, 'The impact of family policies'; McDonald, 'Gender equity, social institutions'; Neyer and Andersson, 'Consequences of family policies'.
[184] See in particular Esping-Andersen, *The Incomplete Revolution*.

be further encouraged by public policies that allow women and men to reconcile family life and work.'[185]

By focusing attention on the detrimental economic, demographic and social consequences of *not* adapting to women's new life cycles, including their roles in working life, this pronatalist discourse is strongly reinforcing feminist arguments about women's citizenship being tied to the recognition of the realities of caregiving and household work and the importance of working towards a sustainable work–life balance for both men and women.[186] An extensive demographic literature has emerged analysing different family policies, often in a comparative context, seeking to find which levers states can pull in their welfare systems in order to regain their ability to encourage national reproduction.[187] Demographic knowledge regarding the seriousness of decline, costs of ageing and risks to social cohesion point in the direction in which states must seek to remedy women's partial inclusion as citizens, even when it means going against the desire to contain the expenditure associated with the welfare state:

> Increasingly, wealthy governments will take steps to reduce the conflict women experience between work and children. This move will probably come about in part as a deliberate means to raise fertility, but more out of fairness to women, and mostly out of fairness to children... These measures will be at odds with recent attempts to weaken the welfare state in industrialized countries. Indeed, they may reduce the rate of economic growth. But such measures are almost certain to be preferred to a demographic path that seems to point to national extinction.[188]

Insofar as furthering gender equity in contemporary welfare states is a steep challenge requiring the deconstruction of the many gendered expectations that now marginalise women as both workers and carers, demographic warnings of 'extinction' have provided powerful backing for feminist arguments about the need to change contemporary welfare states to support both women's and men's changing roles as citizens.[189]

---

[185] European Commission, 'Green Paper'. For critical commentary on the European Union's position, see Repo, 'The governance of fertility'.
[186] Bussemaker and Voet, 'Citizenship and gender'; Orloff, 'Gender and the social rights'; Shaver, 'Gender, social policy regimes'. On the economic consequences of low fertility, see Bloom et al., 'The cost of low fertility'; Lee and Mason, 'Fertility, human capital'.
[187] For just some of the recent analyses, see Castles, 'The world turned upside down'; Gauthier, 'The impact of family policies'; Neyer et al., 'Gender equality'; Thévenon and Gauthier, 'Family policies'.
[188] Caldwell, 'Demographic theory', 312.   [189] Fraser, 'After the family wage'.

In a sense, they seek to co-opt the anxieties over missing citizens to support more gender-equal notions of citizenship.

However, at the same time, this renewed interest in more overtly governing reproduction raises a number of red flags for women's citizenship, autonomy and choice. There is a strong instrumentalist undercurrent which sees women's changing roles not so much as a positive sign of recognition of women as equal citizens but as an imbalance that has to be rectified because it is economically inefficient.[190] The focus on numbers and on women as the biological group that collectively produces new citizens reasserts women's citizenship as predominantly linked to maternity and the reproduction of the nation.[191] It frames women (or some groups of women) as both the problem and the solution – the problem, because some (too many) of them are 'abusing their freedom' from the constraints of more restrictive gender roles and failing to do their reproductive duties, and the solution, because they can (perhaps when given the appropriate support) fix the problem of the birth rate by reproducing appropriately. This maternal discourse on women's citizenship assumes a homogenised desire for children, especially regarding married (and, more broadly, coupled) women and, conversely, implies that there is something wrong with women who do *not* wish to reproduce, especially if all the right factors (partner, employment, etc.) are in place.[192] This argument especially relates to middle-class, educated, relatively well-off women who 'could afford to have children' but are having 'too few children' for the good of the nation or are failing to have children altogether.[193] Voluntary childlessness, especially when the economic conditions are right, becomes a particularly difficult choice to accept in this framing, yet the ability to choose not to have children is crucial for women's equal citizenship.[194] More broadly, being largely economically inspired, this approach has only a very hazy idea about the importance of non-economic factors, such as values, attitudes and social context, that create a continuum between voluntary and involuntary childlessness.[195]

---

[190] See e.g. Esping-Andersen, *The Incomplete Revolution*.
[191] Yuval-Davis, 'Gender and nation'. On this in the Finnish context, see Anttonen, 'Vocabularies of citizenship'.
[192] Valtioneuvoston kanslia, 'Hyvä yhteiskunta kaikenikäisille', is a good example of such assumptions.
[193] Kligman, 'A reflection', 250.   [194] Meyers, 'The rush to motherhood'.
[195] Holton et al., 'To have or not to have?' argue (in the Australian context) the barriers to maternity include diverse biological, psychological and social factors.

Moreover, the biopolitical focus on women as those who produce (or do not produce) the actual number of babies born obscures men as reproductive citizens, while at the same time the context of these analyses is invariably the monogamous, heterosexual, two-parent unit. While women are defined through their (potential) motherhood, men are merely implicit in much of the discussion around the birth rate.[196] Demographic experts in the Finnish context, for instance, view 'motherhood as a societal duty, and fatherhood as personal and elective'.[197] Consequently, men's childbearing behaviour has been much less studied and men's roles and attitudes are only beginning to be canvassed.[198] This is, of course, consistent with longstanding ideas of men as worker-citizens, free to decide about their roles as fathers without their contribution to society being defined by fatherhood.[199] Yet, most decisions on childbearing are taken by couples, and it remains important for partnered women that any child is wanted by both partners.[200] Though men cannot directly enforce their fertility desires, male power and privilege have not disappeared. Men continue to have influence on reproduction, and their attitudes (not just their economic contributions) are relevant (men may, for instance, reduce births by 'being a drag on the process of forming partnerships and parenting with women'[201]). Moreover, the rise of alternative family structures raises issues to do with increasing divorce and step-parenting, which have not been much researched with regard to men's reproductive citizenship, even though the increasing diversification of family life seems an essential element in understanding childbearing decisions in contemporary societies. On a similar note, demographic discussions invariably assume that the main place of reproduction is a biological, two-parent, heterosexual, monogamous nuclear unit.[202] While this can be defended in purely numerical terms, it again ignores the potential implications of increasing diversity (for instance, blended families) in family formation and reproductive decisions.

---

[196] See Esping-Andersen, *The Incomplete Revolution*, ch. 3.   [197] Vuori, 'Men's choices'.
[198] For recent work, see Goldscheider et al., 'Reconciling studies'; Neyer et al., 'Gender equality'; Puur et al., 'Men's childbearing desires'; Westoff and Higgins, 'Relationships between'. For discussions on why men have been neglected, see Greene and Biddlecom, 'Absent and problematic men'.
[199] Hobson, *Making Men into Fathers*.
[200] According to Gauthier, 'Family policy and fertility', 274, men have a lower desire for children than do women in almost all European states.
[201] Jamieson et al., 'Fertility and social change', 482.
[202] On the family in demography, focused on the married couple, see Waite, 'Marriage and family'.

Perhaps the most significant issue with seeking to govern births through adjusting institutional support is that low birth rates may, in fact, be emblematic of modernity.[203] The evidence for the proposition that gender equity and higher fertility go hand in hand is not conclusive, as the links are complex and difficult to measure empirically.[204] Moreover, adjusting family policies is both expensive and slow: it requires deep cultural change and involves a tension between the desire for more state involvement and the diminishing state role in supporting citizens, who are often expected to support their families with less, not more, assistance. Many countries, including the Nordic countries, with traditionally large social expenditure, have seen a trend towards privatisation of financial responsibility away from the state and towards families (on Finland, see Chapter 5). Even with generous family-friendly policies, birth rates remain below replacement, implying that larger families are still difficult to sustain.[205] Demographers recognise that most contemporary societies are not likely to return to replacement rates. As Höhn puts it:

> Allowing for childless and one-child couples, replacement of generations cannot be attained unless about 40% of families are willing and able to have three children. Pronatalist policies can perhaps maintain a final family size of 1.8 to 1.9 children, but they seem unlikely to be able to achieve the 2.1 necessary for replacement.[206]

Even contemporary states are still at the *early* stages of the transition to a postmodern economy and society, which involves substantial rearrangement of women's position in society, and in time alarm over demographic realities may subside.[207] Some have argued, however, that if higher levels of fertility are truly desired, the value of childbearing, childrearing and caregiving – not merely their reproductive products – must be much more fundamentally recognised.[208] Fraser argues this requires redistributing care responsibilities so that both men and women both

---

[203] As Jackson, 'When is a baby boom', 10, puts it, 'if women's emancipation is one of the pillars of modernity... low fertility is its plinth'. See also Goldstein et al., 'The end of "lowest-low" fertility'; Lutz et al., 'The low fertility trap'.
[204] Neyer and Anderson, 'Consequences of family policies'. See also Brewster and Rindfuss, 'Fertility and women's employment'.
[205] France and Sweden, the states with the most longstanding and active family policies, are also below replacement. On their policies, see Kramer, *The Other Population Crisis*.
[206] Höhn, 'Population policies', 476. See also Demeny, 'Population policy and the demographic transition', 268.
[207] See e.g. Caldwell, 'Demographic theory'.   [208] Jackson, 'When is a baby boom'.

care and work, supported by appropriate institutional design – a project she is the first to admit is utopian.[209]

In contrast with such visions, some demographers, recognising the possible impact of and economic strains created by the low-birth-rate trend in the long run, warn of future scenarios involving, at worst, 'aggressive public policies, social and political conflict, and the progressive abandonment of the social, economic and political achievements of the past two centuries'.[210] These far more sinister visions of more direct biopolitical interventions mean that there is an inherent contingency in the convergence of interests between policy-makers worried about low birth rates and those keen to advance the cause of equal citizenship. Some of those keen on 'improving' birth rates *now*, rather than at some point in the distant future, may conclude that the current model of trying to co-opt gender-equality policy for demographic ends is not fast enough or that it involves undesirable social change. The temptation may thus be – as evident in the intermittent arguments about the benefits of bringing back housewifery of the baby-boom era – to try to reassert control more directly and to reinforce the 'full-scale breadwinner model of the 1950s'.[211] Policy suggestions with such illiberal underpinnings are never far from the surface, as the Italian example makes clear.[212] Arguments about the precarious right of women to their own bodies have been revived amid struggles over abortion in countries like the United States and, recently, Spain.[213] The abortion debate is never far from the surface in any of the countries examined in this chapter.[214] Considering the long and contested trajectory towards women's reproductive agency in law and practice and the revitalisation of maternal citizenship, which defines women's values through motherhood, tensions will continue to exist over the growth of female autonomy and its consequences, as evident in the push to make women's citizenship more contingent on their continued fulfilment of their 'reproductive

---

[209] Fraser, 'After the family wage', 610.
[210] Reher, 'Towards long-term population decline', 204.
[211] McDonald, 'Gender equity, social institutions', 10.
[212] Regarding similar issues in Australia, see Summers, 'Women and the birth rate', 239, who argues the Australian baby bonus and other conservative government policies to support families were introduced by a prime minister who 'yearns for the 1950s'.
[213] On Spain, see Astudillo, 'Protests grow'.
[214] Though the issue is rather muted in Finland, where rhetoric concerning reproductive rights is strong (Isola, 'Fertility concern') and attempts to politicise current abortion practices have been few and unsuccessful. On Australia, see Baird, 'Maternity, whiteness'. On Italy, see Hanafin, *Conceiving Life*, ch. 3.

duties'. Reproductive rights (especially the right *not* to have children) are therefore likely to remain a site of ongoing tensions.[215]

The second issue regarding this reproductive governance relates to how some individuals are framed as particularly problematic reproductive citizens, in a different way than women who postpone or forgo motherhood because of education and employment. These are, for instance, women who have children when the conditions are *not* right. Pronatalism for some women has often in history been combined with (strong) antinatalism for others.[216] In extremis, like in Italy, racially motivated exclusion has lifted its head, but overall the picture involves more than just crude racism. The female citizen whose sufficient reproduction states are most keen to facilitate is the one they are most proud of as a Western achievement: the independent, educated working woman.[217] This woman, as part of a middle-class dual-worker self-sufficient couple, is now the reproductive ideal, for both migrants and citizens. The flipside of this picture is made up of those who embrace the call to have children too enthusiastically (or when they should not at all). Though single, lesbian and unemployed women are having children in practice, they are socially constructed as 'others'.[218] Non-conforming women – typically women who are young, single and/or economically and socially disadvantaged – have children despite the many signals that they should not risk it until they are partnered and ready to support them in the ways expected. However, for some women, that time may never arrive, and for others, circumstances may cease to be 'right' (hence the rise in single parenthood). In many place, most notably Britain, there is a strong class aspect to the disapproval of those who opt to have children early (especially in teenage pregnancy).[219] Some current demographic work is genuinely concerned about the poor intergenerational outcomes associated with youthful childbearing,[220] but in other contexts the concern uncomfortably echoes arguments

---

[215] Hodgson, 'Abortion, family planning', 513, argues that globally, the reproductive-rights movement coincided with many states' desire for lower birth rates, and that 'there will be much greater potential for direct conflict' once states frame low fertility as a problem.

[216] Heitlinger, 'Pronatalism and women's equality', 345; see also Yuval-Davis, 'Women and the biological reproduction'; Zarkovic Bookman, *The Demographic Struggle*, esp. ch. 4.

[217] As Phillips, 'Provocative women', 599–600, puts it, 'In the modern nation-state, then, women's emancipation, or, more specifically, women's status as political subjects, is of central importance for how that modern nation-state defines itself as modern. However, women's emancipation is expected to go hand in hand with the containment of women within certain parameters so that the "natural" reproduction of the nation may be ensured.'

[218] Kligman, 'A reflection', 252.   [219] Crompton, 'Class and family'.

[220] Jackson, 'When is a baby boom'.

about the 'wrong women' having children, associated with the more eugenic discourse about irresponsible reproducers.

From the point of view of citizenship, it is significant that a gap is emerging and, in some cases, growing between those women who are primarily in paid work, with no or few children, and those who are primarily having children, yet are often treated as problematic reproductive citizens (especially because of youthful childbearing and lack of attachment to the labour market).[221] In both the Italian and the Australian context, the (not very large) baby bonus turned out to have the most significant impact on the birth decisions of women who were economically most vulnerable, with limited attachment to the labour market.[222] Considering this was in the context of a pronatalist discourse that simultaneously idealised motherhood as a higher calling, Meyers's rhetorical question, 'Is it any wonder that historically subordinated, devalued women seize the opportunity to become mothers?',[223] resonates strongly.[224] As Lutz and Skirbekk point out, such divisions of labour in national reproduction connect the issue of intergenerational justice to the issue of intragenerational justice.[225] Insofar as being able to work and being able to form a family are both aspects of citizenship that citizens should be able to take part in if they so desire, this division of labour appears to carry fundamental consequences for both women's and men's equality as citizens, as well as for the stability of a national reproductive system and intergenerational outcomes. Some of these trends associated with higher birth rates among certain groups are highly correlated with negative prospects for the next generation, such as childhood poverty and educational disadvantage.[226] When, however, these trends are also the result of policies that deny opportunities to some groups and individuals, especially based on class and race, the stigma of excessive reproduction masks questions about why citizens are so differently placed in terms of their contribution towards societal continuation (see further Chapter 3).

---

[221] See also Esping-Andersen, *The Incomplete Revolution*, who is worried about social polarisation (caused by marital homogamy), whereby privileged/high-educated parents pass on privilege to their children, while low-paid/low-educated parents do not.

[222] See notes 77 and 165 in this chapter.

[223] Meyers, 'The rush to motherhood', 761.

[224] On the British context, see Lee et al., 'A matter of choice?'. In the Finnish context, see Vikat, 'Women's labor force attachment', 203, who writes: 'Women with little education and poor prospects in the labor market may seek uncertainty reduction in motherhood, which brings order and stability to the life course, whereas other women may reduce uncertainty through their work career.'

[225] Lutz and Skirbekk, 'Low fertility', 18.   [226] Jackson, 'When is a baby boom'.

Ideas about problematic reproductive citizens are also closely related to anxieties about and governance of immigration and multi-ethnicity. Immigrant workers filling labour shortages have become an essential part of the economies of contemporary states (see Chapter 4) and immigration has become the driving force behind demographic change. The proportion of the total population that is of foreign origin is set to grow in the future, because of both entry of immigrants and childbearing by those of immigrant origin. The fact that some groups of immigrant women from the Global South, especially those outside the formal labour market, tend to have higher fertility than 'native' women, particularly shortly after arrival, is much discussed and analysed in terms of what this tendency, if it continues, means for the future of national reproduction in these states.[227] Sobotka has concluded that immigrants contribute substantially to the total number of births in the Global North and that their share of total births has increased.[228] Coleman has warned about a prospective 'third demographic transition', whereby the ethnic composition of the population of the developed world will come to resemble that of the developing world (but not conversely).[229] He expresses the common concern about social cohesion that 'with larger numbers, populations of foreign origin may feel less need to adapt to local norms, instead becoming more confident in extending their own values, language, or laws in a wider society'.[230] This kind of demographic of analysis, even when treating arguments about 'ethnic replacement' with care, has the tendency to provoke alarmist press coverage that implies countries are being overcrowded and swamped by immigrants:

> Britain's population is growing at more than twice the European average. The number living in the UK soared by 400 000 last year – almost a third of the increase across all 27 EU countries. The rise is underpinned by high levels of migration and a baby boom itself brought about mainly by immigrants.[231]

Fears over demographic change add to pressures to manage both reproduction and immigration more forcefully, lest the rights of newcomers

---

[227] Frejka et al., 'Summary'. See also Abbasi-Shavazi and McDonald, 'Fertility and multiculturalism'; Coleman and Dubuc, 'The fertility of ethnic minorities'; Milewski, 'First child of immigrant workers'.
[228] Sobotka, 'Overview chapter 7'.
[229] Coleman, 'Immigration and ethnic change'; see also Coleman, 'Divergent patterns'.
[230] Coleman, 'Immigration and ethnic change', 426.
[231] *Daily Mail*, 'UK population grows at twice EU average: migrant baby boom fuels 400 000 rise in one year', 17 August 2011.

trump the 'rights of natives to conserve their own way of life, language, laws, neighborhoods and communities, and prior privileges'.[232] The low birth rate of the dominant group is then emphasised as a sign of loss of power and privilege.[233]

Babies born to immigrants in particular straddle the boundary between immigrants and citizens. In contexts where stereotypes may portray some groups of immigrant women, typically those who have recently migrated, as hyper-fertile baby machines,[234] the role of citizenship rules in terms of defining who is able to produce new citizens becomes central. Fears of 'too high' birth rates among 'others', be they immigrant workers, family migrants, naturalised citizens or indeed marginalised insiders, are linked to fears of challenges to existing national, class, racial and gendered interests.[235] The trends on citizenship attribution in the Global North, which readjust the line between belonging based on birth and inclusion based on later incorporation, are fundamentally a part of the governance of national belonging.[236] As Shachar has argued, both *jus sanguinis* and *jus soli* principles limit the possible pool of future citizens.[237] States are modifying their citizenship policies in response to two conflicting desires – on the one hand, to incorporate children who will grow up in their territory as citizens, and, on the other, to exclude those who are not seen to properly belong to the national community. The successful integration of the children of immigrants is now among the foremost policy challenges for Europe, and demographic knowledge about the opportunities and life trajectories of children born to immigrants features prominently in these debates. The questions that then arise are not just about the numbers of citizens missing or present, but also about what kinds of future citizens are being produced. The alleged lack of integration of some immigrant communities is seen to be persisting to the extent that the failure of multiculturalism has been announced in some countries. As Coleman states, 'much depends on the origins of the immigrant populations, their desire to integrate or otherwise, and the policies put in place on integration and immigration.'[238] These issues will be examined in more detail in Chapter 3.

---

[232] Coleman, 'Immigration and ethnic change', 427.   [233] Douglass et al., 'Introduction', 6.
[234] Chavez, *The Latino Threat*.   [235] Kligman, 'A reflection', 253.
[236] For an update on changing citizenship law trends, including the trend of convergence between states with *jus soli* and *jus sanguinis* traditions, see Vink and de Groot, 'Citizenship attribution'.
[237] Shachar, *The Birthright Lottery*.
[238] Coleman, 'Divergent patterns', 473.

FINAL REMARKS

Anxieties about population decline and attempts to steer national reproduction to produce 'missing citizens' underline the interconnections between the governance of reproduction on the one hand and the governance of immigration on the other. The main stream of citizenship into the Global North is made up of people born into citizenship (citizenship as birthright being 'the river that sustains a citizenry'[239]), but the entry of immigrants and the fact that many of the newcomers eventually also have children are creating and feeding anxieties about what long-term trends of demographic change mean for the future of increasingly multi-ethnic states. There are many similarities between the various national debates on the rationale for and effectiveness of policies to encourage more births and their relationship with immigration, integration and social cohesion. All reflect deep controversies around national reproduction, belonging and women's roles as citizens, even though they do not play out in exactly the same way everywhere. Given the history of population policy towards various groups of women and the history of women's struggle for equal citizenship, the current developments in reproductive governance cannot simply be welcomed as good for all women, men and children. If the official commitment to gender equality turns out to be contingent on women 'doing their part' (that is, breeding for the good of the narrowly defined nation), then a lot of the current policy discourse is going to be potentially dangerous for women's citizenship and for the inclusion of newcomers into developed societies.

[239] Mayton, 'Birthright citizenship', 221.

CHAPTER THREE

MISGUIDED CITIZENS? TRANSITIONS INTO ADULTHOOD AND THE MANAGEMENT OF DIVERSITY

As Cruikshank has noted, 'citizens are not born; they are made'.[1] Because of persistent birth-rate patterns as well as continuing and diversifying immigration, the next generations of citizens in the Global North are both smaller and more diverse. Concerns have therefore been expressed not just about the numbers of children being born, but about how well these 'provisional citizens'[2] are transitioning into adulthood and whether they are growing up to embrace their roles as responsible and productive citizens. In modern states, youth has emerged as an important developmental period during which central demographic events that shape the future trajectories of citizens take place, but also one that is characterised by many possible risk factors, possibly compromising normative ideas about transitions into adulthood. In the context of economic globalisation and insecurity and more ethnic, cultural and religious diversity, longstanding yet mutating anxieties over teenagers and young adults as emerging citizens are meshing with fears over the integration of newcomers, the inevitability of cultural change and future risks to social cohesion. For the citizenship of young people of immigrant background, concerns are raised over both their age and also their immigrant origin, underscoring their status as 'second-generation immigrants' (citizens born to immigrant parents).[3]

---

[1] Cruikshank, *The Will to Empower*, 3. In her work, she investigated how self-governing citizens are made through small-scale and everyday practices in voluntary associations, reform movements and social-service programmes.
[2] Brysk, 'Children across borders', 156.
[3] The term 'second-generation immigrant' is still commonly used despite it having attracted much criticism (for one discussion, see Thomassen, 'Second generation immigrants', 25–30).

Near-adults and young adults of immigrant background are thus located at the intersection of two sets of ambiguities about their readiness for adult citizenship – some related to their age, maturity and transition to adulthood and others associated with questions over their cultural belonging and loyalty, drawing attention to their transnational ties.

As a case study, this chapter starts with a jurisdiction that has seen one of the largest panics regarding the 'integration' of 'second-generation' young people and consequent efforts to reshape their paths as citizens (even as these young people's transitions into the labour market and adult citizenship are (again) shadowed by the risks of unemployment and precariousness). Reinforced by events such as the urban disturbances of 2001 (as well as the September 11 attacks) and the 2005 London bombings, demographic unease over young British Muslim citizens, especially of Pakistani and Bangladeshi origin, has been channelled into policies that fuse immigration control, criminal justice, integration measures and gender policies in an effort to steer young people of immigrant origin towards appropriate citizenship values and life trajectories. Imperfect but powerful demographic knowledge and assumptions about appropriate transitions to adulthood play a role in singling out some groups of 'second-generation' citizens for special attention. Attempts at shaping their life transitions implicate the aim of optimising minority youth for the nation's economic advantage, the management of future national reproduction and the desire to exercise control over the conditions of entry of newcomers, as is shown by the example of family-formation migration, involving young people wishing to marry someone from the country of their parents' birth. Though much has been written about the increasing concerns over family migration,[4] seen as a problematic channel for 'less desirable' migrants with social and cultural practices taken to be at odds with prevailing norms, less attention has focused on what the efforts to restrict family migration say about the contributing role of demographic and economic anxieties.

It implies that children born of immigrant parents remain immigrants despite not having migrated themselves and/or in spite of being born as citizens; it also lumps together people who may not belong to the same generation, creating false illusions of simultaneity. The prevalence of the term means it is impossible to avoid using it altogether, but the problematic assumptions about migrants' descendants as not proper citizens are precisely what this chapter is about.

[4] Kofman, 'Family-related migration' distinguishes a number of types of family migration, including family-formation migration (bringing marriage partners from the country of origin), family-reunification migration (bringing members of the immediate family), marriage migration (bringing partners met while abroad) and family migration (when all members migrate simultaneously). This chapter particularly focuses on family-formation migration. On family reunification, see also Chapter 5.

After the case study, the chapter examines youth transitions and the ways in which young people of immigrant origins are governed in the other three national settings, all characterised by apprehensions regarding young people's insertion into changing labour markets, as well as the long-term effects of immigration. As young people of immigrant descent are growing up and asserting themselves, these concerns are revealed also in attempts to modify citizenship requirements and immigration policy in order to ensure the 'integration' of young people and the quality of any further entrants. As in the United Kingdom, fears over the 'integration' of young people with immigrant backgrounds are particularly evident in the treatment of certain groups framed as 'challenging' based on demographic profiles and statistical information. The targets and the responses to them vary from state to state, depending on, for instance, the states' immigration histories – Australia's multiculturalist policy for dealing with the young people of immigrant origin goes back 40 years, but in Italy and, especially, Finland, the second-generation issue is only starting to emerge and controversies have tended to focus on the '1.5 generation'[5] (those who immigrated as children and have been partly raised and educated in their new home countries). Though there are significant differences, often fears are particularly evident regarding family migration, which has, in the wake of its association with integration challenges, become a subject for analysis after long-standing neglect.[6] In all three states, awareness of the inevitable diversity of young people's trajectories and the challenges they create for national identity, assumed cultural unity and belonging, as well as economic incorporation, is raising questions about successful youth transitions.

The chapter then links these attempts at steering young people's trajectories, which seek to govern both challenges created by global and local economic transformations and anxieties regarding immigrant-origin families and populations, with ideas and expectations regarding young people as potential (rather than actual) citizens. An instrumentalist concern over young people as a future resource whose skills, attitudes and productivity need to be optimised for the good of the nation's economic and social future is a prominent theme in the efforts to manage young people's trajectories to guide them towards proper paths as

---

[5] The term '1.5 generation' has become popular after it was used by Rumbaut and Ima, 'The adaptation' to refer to refugee youth who were born outside the United States but spent the key formative periods of adolescence and early adulthood there.
[6] Kofman, 'Family-related migration'.

citizens. Insofar as young people are framed as the citizen-workers – as well as the reproducers – of the future, they are treated as needing to be equipped to respond to global economic insecurities and to be encouraged to be responsible for ensuring their own successes (and deal with their failures).[7] At the same time, some young people – often, but not exclusively, of immigrant background – emerge as potentially misguided in their transitions, unwilling or unable to move successfully into adult, self-reliant and responsible citizenship, typically because of their backgrounds, which are seen as having negative impacts on their transitions. Such young people are treated as potentially alienated subgroups of troublemakers or, often in the case of girls, as victims of their culture, who require oversight to guide them towards proper paths to successful adulthood. Especially when immigration law is involved (that is, whenever transnational links with their parents' countries of origin are at stake), firmer management of young people on the cusp of adulthood is facilitated by and aligns with perceived demographic interests in immigration policy.

THE UNITED KINGDOM: SHAPING THE CHOICES OF THE YOUNG

Troubled Youth? De-standardised Transitions to Adulthood

There is a widespread perception that young people in Britain are troubled and are struggling to make the transition to adulthood. Demographers have long been interested in the 'youth question', and it has increasingly been of interest to social scientists as well.[8] The young-adult years are 'demographically dense'[9] and involve multiple transitions to adulthood: leaving education, starting a full-time job, leaving the parental home, getting married and becoming a parent for the first time.[10] In the United Kingdom, as elsewhere, youth has come to be seen as an important developmental period that sets in place trajectories impacting on the whole life course, and major shifts have been identified in young people's transitions to adulthood since the 1970s, linked in complex ways to the processes of the 'second demographic transition'.[11] In a nutshell, these changes suggest that the early

---

[7] This belief in the integrative power of employment is discussed further in Chapter 4.
[8] Furstenberg, 'The intersections of social class', 2.
[9] Rindfuss, 'The young adult years', 494.   [10] Shanahan, 'Pathways to adulthood'.
[11] Berrington, 'Transition to adulthood in Britain'; Billari and Liefbroer, 'Towards a new pattern'; Billari and Wilson, 'Convergence towards diversity'.

life course of young adults is becoming de-standardised: where previous generations (such as the 'baby boomers') moved through life transitions more rapidly, the new demographic patterns generally appear to postpone firm commitments and create new complexities. Individuals follow a greater number of sequences of life-course events and take longer to complete them, if they complete them at all.[12] There is concern – often gendered – that for many, the expansion in higher education postpones other transition events, like childbearing and marriage, with some remaining unpartnered, unmarried or childless (as discussed in Chapter 2). At the other end of the spectrum, early school-leaving, teen pregnancy and early lone parenthood can also compromise future prospects for both women and their children.[13] The changing ethnic and religious make-up of Britain's population adds to the complexity of young people's trajectories.[14] Though worries over young people are often expressed at a general level, some groups stimulate more alarm than others. Since the turn of the century, anxiety over the identities and transitions of young British Muslims has become heightened.[15] In short, a host of demographically informed concerns are expressed over young people's willingness and ability to make the right choices to shape their future life trajectories for the better.

When one becomes an adult has, of course, always been a socially and legally defined matter, but arguably the dividing line between adolescence and adulthood has become more complex. As Schaffner notes, 'the legal status of majority, like sanity, is a grant of capacity conferred by the state.'[16] In the United Kingdom, as elsewhere, the age of 18 has emerged as the legal watershed at which parental/state authority over young people ends and individuals are considered to be (chronologically and legally) mature enough to be entrusted with most tasks associated with adult citizenship, including voting, serving in a jury and getting married without parental permission.[17] Yet drawing lines

---

[12] Furlong and Cartmel, *Young People and Social Change*.
[13] Moffitt, 'Teen-aged mothers'. See also Rowlingson and McKay, 'Lone motherhood'.
[14] According to Vertovec, 'Super-diversity', Britain's immigrant and ethnic-minority population can now be characterised as 'super-diverse' (going beyond the established Asian and Afro-Caribbean communities of post-colonial origin): new, small and scattered, multiple-origin, transnationally connected, socioeconomically differentiated and legally stratified groups of immigrants.
[15] Thomas and Sanderson, 'Unwilling citizens?'.   [16] Schaffner, 'An age of reason', 201.
[17] Globally, this trend is now driven by the Convention on the Rights of the Child (Art. 1), which takes 18 as a universal point at which external controls – but also special protection of young people – cease. The Convention on the Rights of the Child was ratified by the United Kingdom in 1991.

between childhood and adolescence,[18] as well as between adolescence and adulthood,[19] is to an extent an arbitrary exercise.[20] Indeed, in the United Kingdom, the age of consent is 16, and 16-year-olds can get married with parental consent, but young people cannot adopt a child until they are 21.[21] Moreover, in the last 20 years, many have argued that social and economic changes in the Global North have postponed the end of adolescence beyond the age of 18.[22] Arnett has even introduced a 'new' developmental phase, 'emerging adulthood', arguing that the period between 18 and 25 is one 'characterized by a high degree of demographic diversity and instability', involving explorations in love, work and worldviews.[23] The causes of these changes are multiple, but they include, most obviously, global economic changes and the changing structural situation regarding labour-market entry, as well as the significance of and opportunities for continued education, including higher education, which have increased for both young men and, especially, young women.[24] Many young people thus enter into permanent employment later and form stable families (with or without marriage) later than previous generations.[25] The social experience is also diverse and commonly includes extended periods of cohabitation, childlessness, single living and unmarried parenthood.[26] Many young people

---

[18] Traditionally, adolescence is conceived as a stage that starts with the onset of puberty. Better nutrition and greater control of infection have lowered the average age for physical maturity, blurring the line between childhood and adolescence (as physical maturity no longer corresponds well to social and emotional maturity).

[19] The physical end of adolescence (especially in terms of physical growth) can also extend into the early twenties.

[20] As Khan, 'Temporality of law', 91, puts it, 'there is no empirical evidence to support the proposition that the eighteenth birthday magically transforms a person from immaturity to maturity, from having an underdeveloped sense of responsibility to a fully developed sense of responsibility, and from having a transitory personality to a fixed personality'.

[21] Or, as Gangoli and Chantler, 'Protecting victims', 277, note, 'child benefit is paid until the age of 16 if the young person has left school or until 19 if they are in full-time education. Therefore, a 16 year old who has left school and is (presumably) in employment is not deemed to be a child, while a 16 year old in education is. Other indicators of maturity in law are marriage and parenthood: under-25 year olds do not have the same rights to housing benefits as over-25 year olds, unless they are married or have dependent children.'

[22] Chisholm and Hurrelman, 'Adolescence in modern Europe'.

[23] Arnett, 'Emerging adulthood', 471. See also Furstenberg et al., 'Growing up'. For debates about the concept, see Arnett, 'Emerging adulthood in Europe'; Bynner, 'Rethinking the youth phase'; Côté and Bynner, 'Changes in the transition'.

[24] Berrington, 'Transition to adulthood in Britain'; France, *Understanding Youth*; Furlong and Cartmel, *Young People and Social Change*; Roberts, 'Education to work transitions'. For a comparative discussion, see Fagan et al., 'Young adults'.

[25] Aassve et al. 'Strings of adulthood'; Buchmann and Kriesi, 'Transition to adulthood'; Francesconi and Golsch, 'The process of globalization'.

[26] Chisholm and Hurrelman, 'Adolescence in modern Europe'; Settersten, 'Passages to adulthood'. For comparative discussions, see Buchmann and Kriesi, 'Transition to adulthood';

leave the parental home later than they did in the past, or return there at some point (for instance, after finishing higher education) in order to plan the next stage of their trajectory.[27]

The new normative 'wisdom' is then that for young adults, in particular middle-class children from the most advantaged sections of society, youth as a period is extended, with states of economic semi-autonomy that can last nearly a decade. However, this trend towards later independence, led by the growing number of young people in higher education, goes hand in hand with increasing diversity of trajectories and divisions between groups. Even for many graduates, the changing educational and employment environment is characterised by insecurity.[28] The British social context also includes relatively high levels of entrenched class inequality and low levels of social mobility.[29] Young people from lower socioeconomic backgrounds spend less time in education and enter the labour market earlier.[30] At the same time, stable work opportunities for unqualified and unskilled young workers are scarce.[31] The role of structural factors – social class, family structure and family economic status – in determining young people's future trajectories has been particularly prominent in discussions around young people who leave education at the minimum age (now being gradually raised from 16 to 18) and then spend a substantial period in the following years outside education and employment.[32] 'Outsider' circumstances are also gendered as well as classed: for many young women, they also mean early motherhood, framed as problematic because of both the norm of postponed childbearing and the subsequent social disadvantage.[33] Though 'the extent to which teenage pregnancy is the cause or consequence of poverty remains

---

Elzinga and Liefbroer, 'De-standardization'; Knijn, *Work, Family Policies*; Settersten et al., 'On the frontier of adulthood'.

[27] On the increased heterogeneity in the living arrangements of young adults in the United Kingdom, see Stone et al., 'The changing determinants'. See also Stone et al. 'Gender, turning points'.

[28] See especially Furlong and Cartmel, *Young People and Social Change*, who argue, following Beck and Giddens, that the past few decades have brought tremendous change in industrialised societies, involving increased individualisation and risk. See also France, *Understanding Youth*, ch. 4.

[29] Bynner, 'British youth transitions'; McKnight and Tsang, 'Divided we fall?'.

[30] On comparative trends, see Buchmann and Kriesi, 'Transition to adulthood', 486.

[31] Bynner, 'Rethinking the youth phase'. See also Schmelzer, 'Increasing employment instability'.

[32] The term now used is 'NEET': a young person who is 'Not in Education, Employment, or Training'. See Furlong and Cartmel, *Young People and Social Change*, 42–3. On heterogeneity, see Furlong, 'Not a very NEET solution'.

[33] Bynner, 'Rethinking the youth phase'. See also Côté and Bynner, 'Changes in the transition'.

unclear',[34] early childbearing (especially teen pregnancy) and lone motherhood can entail long-lasting and often generational disadvantage, especially for women from lower socioeconomic backgrounds.[35] Such patterns of generational disadvantage are a concern as 'the most vulnerable of young people will not only have fewer choices, but they will also have fewer capacities and resources on which to draw as they make those choices, exacerbating still further their existing vulnerabilities.'[36]

Racial and ethnic background is also increasingly examined in terms of its consequences for transitions to full adult citizenship. Being 'second-generation' can be associated with negative effects as well as resiliency and psychological growth.[37] Young people of immigrant background – first-, second- or third-generation – form a rapidly growing and increasingly diverse demographic segment in low-fertility countries. In the US setting, pioneering research into 'segmented assimilation' has identified how socioeconomic inclusion varies across immigrant nationalities.[38] In the British context, as well as elsewhere in Europe, much attention has focused on scrutinising the economic prospects and patterns of the adaptation of various second-generation groups that are identified as ethnic or racial minorities.[39] Research into educational and labour-market statistics confirms a picture of diversity. While certain groups are performing as 'model minorities',[40] others, such as descendants of post-colonial immigrants from Pakistan, are 'worst-performing'[41] in terms of economic incorporation, facing barriers including discrimination in the labour market (which suggest a gap between their formal citizenship and their actual incorporation).[42] British Muslim citizens of South Asian (Pakistani and Bangladeshi)

---

[34] Daguerre and Nativel, *When Children Become Parents*, 5.
[35] See Daguerre, 'Teenage pregnancy'. Despite some progress made in the 2000s, the United Kingdom has relatively high child poverty rates. On lone motherhood and class, see Rowlingson and McKay, 'Lone motherhood'.
[36] Settersten, 'Passages to adulthood', 255.
[37] For an analysis of the multiple factors informing second-generation identity formation, see Rumbaut, 'Sites of belonging'.
[38] Portes, *The New Second Generation*; Portes and Zhou, 'The new second generation'.
[39] For a comparative European overview, see Heath et al., 'The second generation'.
[40] Children of Indian background are often mentioned as a South Asian group that performs well. See e.g. Rothon, 'Can achievement differentials'.
[41] Joppke, *Immigration and the Nation-State*, 246.
[42] See e.g. Berthoud, 'Ethnic employment penalties'; Cheung and Heath, 'Nice work'; Heath and Cheung, 'Ethnic penalties'; Li and Heath, 'Minority ethnic men'; Modood, 'The educational attainment'; Peach, 'Muslims in the 2001 census'; Rothon, 'Can achievement differentials'.

origin who are descendants of low-skilled immigrants have been further scrutinised in the wake of the 2001 disturbances in Oldham, Burnley and Bradford.[43] Though the reasons for the disturbances are complex, official reports have focused on disengagement of young people and community self-segregation, which should be tackled through emphasising social cohesion and making citizenship more meaningful.[44] The terrorist attacks on London's public transportation system in 2005 further focused attention on measuring the cultural tensions between Muslims and mainstream British society, such as the role religion plays in the lives of the second generation,[45] attitudes to extremism[46] and the role of anti-Muslim prejudice.[47]

Awareness of economic 'outcomes' that suggest a failure to 'integrate' is linked with oft-raised questions about the viability of multiculturalism, seen as preventing already poorly performing demographic groups from embracing 'British' family norms and youth behaviours.[48] Further scrutiny has been targeted at Muslim families and young women from these backgrounds. The economic activity levels of British Muslim women of South Asian origin are low, with studies also showing low qualifications and partnerships with strong traditional gender roles.[49] In addition to educational and occupational attainment, demographic information on the marriage patterns of migrants and their descendants has become available in the last few decades, showing a continuation of trans-jurisdictional marriage by the South Asian second and third generation.[50] As 'intermarriage is regarded by many analysts as the ultimate litmus test of integration',[51] the propensity to intermarry, as well as the marriage age, the effect marriage has on employment patterns and the marital instability of South Asian young people, especially Muslims, have all been scrutinised, with particular attention being paid to the high rates of endogamous, often arranged marriage (marriage to

---

[43] On the riots and their aftermath, see Alexander, 'Imagining the Asian gang'. See also Young, 'To these wet and windy'.
[44] Community Cohesion Review Team, 'Community cohesion'; Ministerial Group on Public Order and Community Cohesion, 'Building cohesive communities'. For commentary, see Alexander, 'Imagining the Asian gang'; McGhee, 'The paths to citizenship'.
[45] Voas and Fleischmann, 'Islam moves west'.
[46] Saggar, 'The one per cent world', 'Boomerangs and slingshots'.
[47] Field, 'Islamophobia', 'Revisiting islamophobia'.   [48] Yuval-Davis et al., 'Secure borders'.
[49] Dale et al., 'The labour market prospects', 'A life-course perspective'.
[50] Lucassen and Laarman, 'Immigration, intermarriage'.
[51] Song, 'What happens', 1197. See also Beck-Gernsheim, 'Transnational lives'; Kogan, 'Introduction'.

relatives, especially first cousins).[52] The negative image of cousin marriage, often taking place at young ages and involving relatively early childbearing and stay-at-home motherhood, has become a key symbol of cultural difference, seen as problematic insularity, an 'economically and socially isolated model'.[53] As spouses form the largest single category of migrant settlement in the United Kingdom[54] and the Muslim population has a large proportion of young people,[55] these marriage preferences have attracted considerable attention. Moreover, high-profile instances of immigrant families as violators of women's and children's rights, such as in cases of forced marriage (in which one or both of the parties is married without his or her consent)[56] and so-called 'honour crimes',[57] have added to concerns that Islamic beliefs and family practices impede young Muslim women from aligning quickly enough with contemporary British values.

Governing Misguided Young Citizens

Youth as a period is, as Mizen notes, 'a product of state and government'.[58] The recent attempts to govern the diversifying youth population of the United Kingdom show the state's renewed interest in young people's transitions into adult citizenship. New Labour's approach to the youth question emphasised the concepts of citizenship, community and responsibility, as well as seeking to facilitate transitions to work. Citizenship education was introduced into school curricula in the wake of the Crick report, explicitly placing emphasis on the idea that citizenship (and what it means to be a good citizen) can be promoted and learned.[59] Transitions to work were flagged as a priority for the Labour government as part of its youth policy focused on

---

[52] Carol, 'Like will to like?'; Dale and Ahmed, 'Marriage and employment'; Muttarak, 'Explaining trends'; Qureshi et al., 'Marital instability'; Shaw, 'Kinship, cultural preference', 'The arranged transnational'.

[53] Muttarak, 'Explaining trends', 58.   [54] Charsley et al., 'Marriage-related migration'.

[55] Peach, 'Muslims in the 2001 census', 641.

[56] Reliable figures on forced marriage are obviously hard to obtain, as the problem is often hidden. The latest statistics from the Forced Marriage Unit of the Home Office (set up in 2005) show that the unit gave 1302 cases of advice or support related to a possible forced marriage in 2013. On community perceptions of forced marriage in the Pakistani and Bangladeshi communities, see Samad and Eade, 'Community perceptions'.

[57] Forced marriage can also be considered an 'honour crime', as well as a precursor to violence justified with reference to family honour. Reddy, 'Gender, culture and the law', 306.

[58] Mizen, *The Changing State*, xiii.

[59] Advisory Group on Citizenship, 'Education for citizenship'. Crick also later chaired the Life in the UK advisory group, which formulated the content for the citizenship test (introduced by the Nationality, Immigration and Asylum Act 2002).

education and training, which framed these as a solution for many social ills.[60] The Leitch report, stating that 'our natural resource is our people', emphasised the centrality of a skilled workforce to the United Kingdom's global competitiveness.[61] The emphasis of youth programmes and social-exclusion policies has been on prioritising individual employability and trying to steer young people to prevent their own social exclusion (rather than tackling structural inequalities as such).[62] This is in line with the United Kingdom's general response to economic globalisation, which has involved decreasing state regulation of labour markets and embracing the prospect of a knowledge-driven economy.[63] Though the overall desire has been for less direct state involvement, and instead to encourage young people to take individual responsibility for their future paths, some groups have experienced intensified control amid anxieties around youth, crime and antisocial behaviour.[64] Concerns about and efforts to manage minority youth were given new momentum by the 2001 disturbances, as well as reports of forced marriage and other honour crimes among British South Asians. Multiculturalism, always hesitantly accepted in the British context,[65] has thus given way to 'managing diversity'; that is, management of those groups of immigrant background identified as particularly difficult.[66]

Insofar as recently 'the state's gaze has been on Muslim communities',[67] this can be seen to be part of a pan-European civic integrationist turn amid 'a widespread sense of integration failure'.[68] Since the turn of the millennium, Britain has moved from a relatively liberal approach to the second generation towards a more hands-on approach to managing young adults of migrant origin, involving both 'community cohesion' and citizenship initiatives and criminalisation.[69] One (the most obvious) aspect of the latter relates to the increased criminalisation of young Asian masculinity, especially in the context of counter-terrorism; legislation and policy measures have ranged from

---

[60] Mizen, 'The best days'.   [61] Leitch Review of Skills, 'Prosperity for all'.
[62] France, *Understanding Youth*, ch. 4, 'From being to becoming'; Furlong and Cartmel, *Young People and Social Change*, ch. 3.
[63] Schierup et al., *Migration, Citizenship*, ch. 5.   [64] France, *Understanding Youth*, ch. 6.
[65] For a critical perspective, see Shain, 'Race, nation and education'.
[66] Alexander, 'Imagining the Asian gang', 540. On responses to 'Muslim violence', see Bleich, 'State responses'; Klausen, 'British counter-terrorism'; Mandaville, 'Muslim transnational identity'; Saggar, 'Boomerangs and slingshots'; Young, 'To these wet and windy'.
[67] Gangoli and Chantler, 'Protecting victims', 271.
[68] Thapar-Björkert and Borevi, 'Gender and the "integrationist turn"', 152. See also Wray, 'Moulding the migrant family'.
[69] Alexander, 'Imagining the Asian gang'.

a proliferation of terrorism-related offences to the widespread use of stop and searches in the streets to pre-charge detention for terrorist suspects.[70] Policies aimed at preventing radicalisation and distracting young men from being lured into terrorism, which first appeared in 2005, have sought to employ a range of strategies, often community-based; their impact has been strongly felt by Muslim communities.[71] Such measures have been accompanied by a trend towards stricter use of immigration law in anti-terrorism, for instance through deportation of putative terrorists.[72] Suspected terrorists with dual citizenship can now even be deprived of their British citizenship.[73] Though the government also tried to respond to Muslim claims of Islamophobia,[74] the policies have been accused of constructing a 'suspect community',[75] which some argue has even resulted in a 'wholesale stigmatisation of young Muslims in Britain'.[76] This concern is ongoing – in the wake of young British men and women travelling to Syria and Iraq, new proposals were put forward by the coalition government in 2014. The changes mean, for instance, that suspected foreign fighters will be subject to exclusion orders; that is, blocked from returning to the United Kingdom unless they agree to be monitored. Counter-terror duties have also been imposed on schools, prisons and councils, which much put in place policies or programmes to stop radicalisation.[77]

Fears over the risks posed by antisocial youth and 'home-grown terrorists', disloyal despite being formally citizens, are generally linked to and mixed with anxieties over second-generation *at risk*, especially girls

---

[70] See Terrorism Act 2000; Anti-terrorism, Crime and Security Act 2001; Prevention of Terrorism Act 2005 (now repealed by the Terrorism Prevention and Investigation Measures Act 2011); Terrorism Act 2006.

[71] For criticism of these projects, especially PREVENT (a strand of the counter-terrorist strategy CONTEST), see Birt, 'Promoting virulent envy?'; Choudhury and Fenwick, 'The impact of counter-terrorism'; House of Commons, 'Preventing violent extremism'; Kundnani, 'Spooked!'.

[72] See e.g. Anderson et al., 'Citizenship, deportation'; Bosworth, 'Deportation'; Walker, 'The treatment'. Correspondingly, the governance of migration has become criminalised; see Bosworth and Guild, 'Governing through migration control'. For an overview of Labour's immigration policy, including a discussion of security concerns, see Somerville, *Immigration under New Labour*.

[73] Under the British Nationality Act, the Secretary of State has to be satisfied that the 'deprivation is conducive to the public good'. See further Macklin, 'The securitization'.

[74] For instance, through the criminalisation of religious hatred (see Racial and Religious Hatred Act 2006). While the 2001 amendment of the Crime and Disorder Act had outlawed direct acts of offending or harassing Muslims, the new law added to this the incitement of others to do so.

[75] Pantazis and Pemberton, 'From the "old"'; cf. Greer, 'Anti-terrorist laws'. See also Pantazis and Pemberton, 'Restating the case'.

[76] McDonald, 'Securing identities', 177.   [77] Counter-Terrorism and Security Act 2015.

and young women facing forced marriage, domestic violence and other violations of their human rights by their families.[78] In the wake of highly publicised reports of forced marriage of girls and young women of South Asian descent, particularly Bangladeshi and Pakistani Muslims, the marriage transitions of young people of immigrant origin have attracted the gaze of authorities. Arranged and endogamous marriage, even when consensual, contrasts with the emerging life patterns of middle-class young women, characterised by decreasing gender differentiation, especially when it involves early childbearing and withdrawal from paid work, and thus resonates with arguments about minority community insularity and, especially when occurring at a relatively young age, about young women in particular as lacking the maturity to resist coercion and manipulation by their families.[79] Forced marriage is a genuinely complex form of violence, responses to which in many parts of Europe have been accused of generally treating immigrant families as sites perpetuating inherently patriarchal and oppressive cultural attitudes.[80] In the UK context, a Forced Marriage Unit (FMU) was set up in 2005 to provide support for government policy. The legislative approach has mixed civil law, criminal law and immigration law. Criminalisation of forced marriage was considered but rejected in 2005 as potentially counter-productive.[81] In its place, civil remedies were introduced in 2007.[82] In 2014, despite the initial rejection of the idea, forced marriage was made a criminal offence by the coalition government.[83] Most interestingly, successive governments have also used immigration law to govern transnational arranged marriages in general in the name of eradicating forced marriage.[84]

The changes to family migration were proposed in the context of a changing overall immigration setting. The United Kingdom's immigration policy regarding non-EU citizens has, since the 1990s, been directed away from the previous focus of stemming immigration flows

---

[78] Phillips and Dustin, 'UK initiatives'; Thapar-Björkert and Borevi, 'Gender and the "integrationist turn"'; Wray, 'Moulding the migrant family'.
[79] On similar arguments in other European jurisdictions, see Kofman et al., 'Gendered perspectives', 7.
[80] Razack, 'Imperilled Muslim women', 129.
[81] The respondents to the consultation argued it might make victims less likely to come forward and seek help, as most would not want their family to be prosecuted. See Gangoli and Chantler, 'Protecting victims', 272–3.
[82] Forced Marriage (Civil Protection) Act 2007. For an overview, see Gangoli and Chantler, 'Protecting victims', 273–5. See also Anitha and Gill, 'Coercion, consent'.
[83] See Anti-social Behaviour, Crime and Policing Act 2014. The maximum penalty for the new offence of forced marriage is seven years' imprisonment.
[84] Gangoli and Chantler, 'Protecting victims'.

and towards a selective approach that welcomed skilled migration as part of 'managed migration'.[85] The emphasis on economically useful migration has been accompanied by closer supervision of categories in which selectiveness based on skills and qualifications is not possible but which cannot be completely closed off because of legal entitlements; that is, family migrants and humanitarian entrants.[86] Family migration is based on ideas about the sanctity of the family unit and human rights,[87] and is thus in some ways more open as a migration channel than labour migration, and states' approaches to it are often ambivalent.[88] As Block puts it,

> when family migration is viewed as furthering integration and producing productive inflows, family migration rights might be readily granted. However, when subscribing to the negative arguments of family migration as leading to unproductive, burdensome inflows that also have a negative impact on integration, the admission of family migrants is deemed to be potentially detrimental to the overall interests of society.[89]

The latter view has often been dominant in the United Kingdom, which has a long history of seeking to restrict South Asians citizens from bringing in members of kin groups via marriage (most notoriously, through the 'primary purpose' rule) since postcolonial immigration was largely ended in the 1960s.[90] This legacy has been revived by the recent concerns over the continued growth and reproduction of minority communities that are seen to be out of step with mainstream youth trajectories, gender norms and governmental aspirations for young

---

[85] For a discussion of the UK policies on labour migration, including skilled migration, see Chapter 4.
[86] Regarding family migration and asylum, see Yuval-Davis et al., 'Secure borders'. On the UK concerns over the immigration of EU citizens, see Chapter 4.
[87] The right to a family life is a universally recognised fundamental human right – see e.g. Universal Declaration of Human Rights 1948, Article 16(3); International Covenant on Civil and Political Rights 1966, Article 23(1); European Convention on Human Rights 1950, Article 8. There is, however, no absolute right to be joined by family members. The European Court of Human Rights has acknowledged that a family has no right to choose its common country of residence and that therefore states have the right to exclude family members when joint residence in the country of origin would be sufficiently suitable.
[88] As Wray, 'Moulding the migrant family', 601, puts it, 'family migration undermines state power to select the "best" migrants'.
[89] Block, 'Regulating membership', 6.
[90] The rule required that a person wishing to follow his or her spouse into Britain prove that 'the marriage was not entered into primarily to obtain admission to the UK', effectively asking the applicant to prove a negative. The rule, which was largely seen as targeting men from South Asian, was abolished by Labour in 1997. See Wray, *Regulating Marriage Migration*, for a full account of the history of the efforts to govern family migration. See also Wray, 'Any time, any place'.

THE UNITED KINGDOM: SHAPING THE CHOICES OF THE YOUNG

citizens.[91] As long as the UK remains in the European Union, it cannot unilaterally change family-migration rules that are covered by EU free-movement law,[92] which partly explains the emphasis on seeking to improve the quality of family migration flows in areas where the United Kingdom is not constrained by EU law obligations. The measures on family migration have attempted to balance the right of a family to live together with the state's determination that immigration policy must 'support national interest',[93] defined in terms of economic interests, social cohesion and a desire to crack down on 'sham marriages'.[94]

A host of amendments have been introduced over the years, the most notable of which was the attempt to increase the age limit for sponsoring a spouse from outside the European Union. The discussion around lifting the age limit in 2007 occurred against a background where the age at which a person may act as sponsor for a marriage visa (and the age at which a person may enter the United Kingdom as a spouse) had already been raised from 16 to 18.[95] The government proposal was to further raise the minimum age for a person either to be granted a visa for the purposes of settling in the United Kingdom as a spouse or to sponsor another for the purposes of obtaining such a visa from 18 to 21.[96] In taking this restrictive approach, the United Kingdom followed the example of some other European countries, most notably the Netherlands[97] and Denmark.[98] The change, which took effect in 2008, was

---

[91] However, on the diversity of marriage migration in the UK context, see Charsley et al., 'Marriage-related migration'.

[92] These are in the so-called Citizenship Directive 2004/38/EC and provide EU nationals (including UK citizens) who have exercised their free-movement rights family union with a spouse/partner, children aged under 21 and dependent relatives in the ascending line. The family-migration rights of non-EU citizens (third-country nationals, including persons receiving international protection) are set out in EU Council Directive 2003/86/EC, but the United Kingdom is not bound by this document, though it has adopted many of the measures set out in it.

[93] Border and Immigration Agency (UK), 'Marriage to partners from overseas', 5.

[94] Home Office, 'Secure borders, safe haven'.

[95] Though, as already noted, a 16-year old may generally marry with the permission of their parents.

[96] Border and Immigration Agency (UK), 'Marriage to partners from overseas'.

[97] Dutch law required the Dutch spouse to be at least 21 years old, and to earn a salary of at least 120 per cent the minimum wage (the latter requirement was later challenged, but the former is within EU Council Directive 2003/86/EC, Art. 4.5). In addition, the non-Dutch spouse is required to pass integration exams at the Dutch embassy in their home country, showing a basic mastery of Dutch. On the Dutch reforms, see de Vries, *Integration at the Border*.

[98] Denmark introduced a law in 2003 preventing anyone (except EU citizens exercising free movement rights) from bringing in a spouse from abroad if either party is under 24 years old. Since the year 2000, Danish immigration law has also required that the partners must be at

justified through a direct and sweeping correlation between younger age and likelihood of forced marriages.[99] It was argued that raising the age limit would allow individuals to develop maturity and life skills, enabling them to resist the pressure of being forced into a marriage; it would give them the opportunity to complete education and training; it would delay sponsorship and therefore time spent with the (sometimes abusive) spouse; and it would allow them an opportunity to seek help/advice before sponsorship and extra time to make a decision about whether to sponsor.[100] The demographic assumptions and normative expectations are clear. Young people, especially young women of immigrant origin (clearly the main targets of the provision), should stay in education and – like the average British young person – marry and found a family later, after completing their education and training.[101] Arguments about expected overall transitions to adulthood were supported, moreover, by limited statistics (cases where the FMU had been involved in providing assistance) that did not support the contention that the introduction of a new age limit would prevent forced marriages.[102]

The provision was challenged at court in the Aguilar Quila case.[103] The Supreme Court dismissed the blanket ban on under-21 sponsorship as a breach of Article 8 of the European Convention of Human Rights (and the age limit was consequently dropped back to 18 in 2011). Though the court agreed that state intervention was legitimate to prevent violations of rights such as forced marriages, it considered the efficacy of the measure to be highly debatable as the age-increase requirement was not specific enough to target forced marriages:

<blockquote>
least as strongly affiliated with Denmark as with any other country, measured by their combined number of years of residence in different countries. Denmark, like the United Kingdom, is not bound by the EU's family reunification directive. On Denmark, see Schmidt, 'Law and identity'.

[99] Border and Immigration Agency (UK), 'Marriage to partners from overseas', 'Marriage visas. The way', para 3.1.

[100] Border and Immigration Agency (UK), 'Marriage visas. The way', para 3.4.

[101] Border and Immigration Agency (UK), 'Marriage to partners from overseas', at 2.9 notes that 'The average age at first marriage is going up in the UK and is now around 29 for women and 32 for men ... Our proposal has to be judged against that in terms of whether it is reasonable or not'. For commentary, see Wray, 'Moulding the migrant family', 607.

[102] Border and Immigration Agency (UK), 'Marriage visas. The way'. Indeed, a study by Hester et al., 'Forced marriage', specifically concluded that raising the age was not the way to combat forced marriages. For criticism of the age-related assumptions of the proposal, see also Gangoli and Chantler, 'Protecting victims'.

[103] R (on the application of Quila and another) v Secretary of State for the Home Department; R (on the application of Bibi and another) v Secretary of State for the Home Department [2011] UKSC 45.
</blockquote>

it simply assumed *young* marriages were more likely to be *forced*.[104] Instead, the rule affected the right to family life of many bona fide couples, who would be kept apart (or, alternatively, would be forced to live outside the United Kingdom), in numbers vastly exceeding the number of forced marriages that would be deterred. Perhaps not surprisingly, some commentators have suggested that reducing family-formation migration may have been an underlying motivation of the change, and even that the government was, at best, partially committed to supporting young women of immigrant background, and was using women's oppression to 'legitimise immigration control, policing and surveillance'.[105] What is perhaps less obvious, but is equally worthy of note, is that whether or not the government was consciously using the forced-marriage initiative to pursue an immigration agenda, it was surely using immigration control to address the problem of forced marriage (seeking to prevent at least some forced marriages)[106] and, indeed, in order to regulate transnational marriages overall. Though the endorsement of later marriage may seem neutral in that it sends a message that all young people intending to marry transnationally should wait before getting married, seeing as the actual targets are usually ethnic minorities forming early arranged unions, it rather echoes the Danish message, as Phillips and Dustin phrase it, that 'it would be better all round if people dropped their connections with their countries of origin and abandoned the misguided preference for earlier marriage'.[107]

The age change should also be considered in light of other changes made to family-formation migration rules (as well as the introduction of citizenship and integration tests), which suggest a desire to 'ration' family migration[108] and change the 'socioeconomic characteristics of family migrants' in order to ensure the quality of new entrants.[109] A pre-entry English test was introduced for marriage visa applicants

---

[104] This was, arguably, because it would often be very difficult to test the validity of individual marriages, particularly where spouses might be labouring under family coercion, much of which can take subtle forms. For commentary, see also Yeo, 'Forced marriages II'.
[105] Wilson, 'The forced marriage debate', 26. See also Yeo, 'Forced marriages I', 'Forced marriages II'.
[106] Phillips and Dustin, 'UK initiatives'.
[107] Phillips and Dustin, 'UK initiatives', 544. A 2002 White Paper indicated that the government's expectation was that the number of arranged marriages would decline, as parents would 'seek to choose a suitable partner for their children from among their own communities in this country'. Home Office, 'Secure borders, safe haven', 99.
[108] Legomsky, 'Rationing family values'.   [109] Kofman et al., 'Gendered perspectives', 8.

in 2010.[110] It was justified through claims that it would assist the spouse's integration, improve their employment chances and prepare them for the tests they would need to pass for permanent residence and citizenship.[111] The probationary period during which the marriage must remain intact before a spouse can apply for indefinite leave to remain was raised from one year to two years by the Labour government, and to five years by the coalition government in 2012.[112] As probationary periods leave the immigrant spouse dependent (and vulnerable if there is violence in the marriage), the rule appears to be mostly about removing those family-formation immigrants whose grip on residency is weakened; insofar as it is arguably about helping the vulnerable, it is concerned only with *British*-sponsor victims of violence, rather than the vulnerability of the immigrant spouse.[113] Finally, in 2012, the Home Office introduced an income threshold at £18 600 gross annual income to sponsor a spouse – at about 140 per cent of the minimum wage, roughly half of employed British citizens (especially those from lower sections of society) could not meet this threshold.[114] Though some of these conditions can be argued to target immigrants in order to increase the likelihood of their successful settlement (though probably not the probationary period), they also emphasise economic usefulness, in line with the UK government's 'managed-migration' approach, and are harder to fulfil for 'the young, the low-educated, the ethnic minorities, and the women'.[115] In the context of the Bangladeshi and Pakistani Muslim population, they can thus be argued to be in part an effort to shape communities seen as under-performing, steering them to

---

[110] Previously, language knowledge had to be demonstrated two years after entering the United Kingdom. Border and Immigration Agency (UK), 'Marriage visas: pre-entry' proposed the change in 2007, but resistance meant the change wasn't adopted until November 2010.

[111] But, as admitted by the Immigration Minister, it would also reduce immigration. Migrant Rights Network, 'Damian Green tells Newsnight'. The provision was challenged, but the Court of Appeal rejected the challenge in *Bibi and Ali v Secretary of State for the Home Department* [2013] EWCA Civ 322.

[112] Persons applying for leave to enter/remain will initially be given temporary permission to stay for two-and-a-half years, without recourse to public funds. At the end of the second period, if the relationship is still 'genuine and subsisting' and conforms to other eligibility criterion, they will become eligible to apply for permanent settlement.

[113] Wilson, 'The forced marriage debate'. See also Thapar-Björkert and Borevi, 'Gender and the "integrationist turn"'.

[114] Block, 'Regulating membership', 10, claims that some population segments are particularly disadvantaged; most notably, '58% of jobholders between 20 and 30 years and 61% of female employees... do not earn enough to bring a foreign family member into the country'.

[115] Block, 'Regulating membership', 11. For an assessment, see Children's Commissioner, 'Family friendly?'.

overcome their historical socioeconomic disadvantage, alleged insularity and cultural baggage.

VARIATIONS ON A THEME? AUSTRALIAN, ITALIAN AND FINNISH TRAJECTORIES

Many of the trends visible in the United Kingdom around youth pathways are shared by other contemporary low-fertility states in the Global North: greater individualisation means young people follow a greater number of sequences of life-course events (education, independent living, partnering/marriage, employment, childbearing), taking longer and more complex routes to complete these sequences.[116] This section outlines how immigrant youth transitions have been framed as targets of government in Australia, Italy and Finland, arguing that while there are significant differences between the jurisdictions, in all three, demographic knowledge plays a part in problematising youth transitions and rendering some young people, especially some groups of young people of immigrant origin, subject to special scrutiny and management. In Australia, as in Britain, transitions to adulthood are increasingly prolonged and heterogeneous.[117] Levels of educational involvement have increased, but Australians from lower socioeconomic backgrounds are much less likely to participate in higher education (and young Indigenous Australians continue to be the most disadvantaged group across all areas of life).[118] Italy, as discussed in Chapter 1, is characterised by a strong trend of postponement of transition events; as Billari puts it, 'lowest-low fertility has been associated with latest late transition to adulthood'.[119] With cohabitation rare and a welfare system that favours not autonomy but strong familistic bonds, many Italian young adults stay long in the parental home.[120] In Finland, marriage and childbirth are also postponed (with early cohabitation common); unlike in Australia and Italy, however, most young people leave home early (students are entitled to social-security support if they move away

---

[116] For comparative discussions of transitions to adulthood, see Corijn and Klijzing, *Transitions to Adulthood*; Knijn, *Work, Family Policies*; Settersten et al., 'On the frontier of adulthood'.
[117] On Australian young people's transitions in a comparative context, see Fussell et al., 'Heterogeneity'.
[118] See Wyn, 'Becoming adult', 'Educating for late modernity'; Wyn and Woodman, 'Generation, youth and social change'.
[119] Billari, 'Lowest-low fertility', 5. For an overview of the changes in Italy, see Ongaro, 'Transition to adulthood'.
[120] Billari and Rosina, 'Italian "latest-late" transition'.

from their parents' home when they begin university). Increasing economic instability and insecurity are evident in the rise in youth unemployment.[121]

Out of these three countries, Australia (unsurprisingly) shares most with the United Kingdom in terms of young people's trajectories. Though many young people are spending more time in education, education has increasingly been positioned as a private investment; at the same time, the youth labour market involves 'flexible' practices (non-standard, 'casual' work), and some groups, such as early school leavers, experience youth unemployment and persistent outsider status in terms of access to stable work.[122] As in the United Kingdom, the presence of minorities is longstanding in Australia, but in contrast with the British heritage of Empire, which has attracted (often unwanted) immigrants from former colonies, selective immigration has been central to Australia's nation-building project.[123] At the same time, Australia has always been concerned about the composition of its migrants, initially seeking to maintain a homogeneous society (in terms of race and culture) through the White Australia policy. As a result of immigration (and the erosion of the racially based approach to it), Australia has emerged as a society characterised by a great degree of cultural, religious, linguistic and ethnic diversity (particularly in the largest cities).[124] With the rise of minorities, Australia moved away from assimilationist expectations towards a policy of multiculturalism. Multiculturalism arose as a response to the social inequality experienced by immigrants of non-English-speaking background and their children,[125] and multicultural policies have generally been credited with reducing differences between various ethnic and minority groups.[126] Nonetheless, some groups have been identified as being characterised by socioeconomic disadvantage, for instance second- and third-generation Lebanese, who are more likely to experience unemployment (furthermore, the

---

[121] Salmela-Aro et al., 'Mapping pathways'.
[122] Whiteford, 'Australia'; Wyn, 'Becoming adult'; Wyn and Woodman, 'Generation, youth and social change'. On casual work, see further Chapter 4.
[123] As a result, 'Australia is an immigration nation where immigrants comprise a greater proportion of the population than most other western nations'. Collins, 'Rethinking Australian immigration', 162.
[124] Australia has no predominant minority groups – the Anglo-Australian majority is complemented by a large number of relatively small ethnic groups. While the United Kingdom and New Zealand are still the top two immigrant source countries, Asian countries generally fill most of the rest of the top ten.
[125] For an overview, see Jupp, 'Public policy'.
[126] Inglis, 'The incorporation of Australian youth'.

experiences of the Indigenous minorities, among whom multicultural policies have not been pursued, are far less favourable).[127] While these can be framed as failures of multiculturalism, from a more critical perspective they also highlight fundamental questions about multiculturalism as a tool of measuring and assessing minorities in line with the expectations of the white majority.[128]

Multiculturalism was, in other words, never a straightforward notion. In the last 20 years, it has additionally come under attack from government, following a shift that started with the entry into power of the conservative Howard government in 1996.[129] Sceptical of multiculturalism and Asian immigration, the government (re)asserted the centrality of Anglo-Australianness and questioned the commitment and loyalty of some Australians of immigrant background.[130] Though some immigrants have been judged to be 'problem immigrants' for some time, since the turn of the millennium these anxieties have centred around Muslims, who are seen as a security risk and as posing economic and integration challenges.[131] Whereas in Britain scrutiny has focused around South Asians, in Australia reactions have coalesced around immigrants of mainly Arab background. Especially after the so-called 'Sydney gang rapes'[132] and the 2005 Cronulla riots,[133] young men of Lebanese background and Muslim Lebanese communities were associated with lack of respect for women, a hatred of Western culture and violent sexual aggression towards women.[134] Some have argued that the impact of September 11 and the 2002 Bali bombings was to transform Muslims

---

[127] Inglis, 'The incorporation of Australian youth'. On the Lebanese communities, see also Betts and Healy, 'Lebanese Muslims'. On Indigenous disadvantage, see Campbell et al., 'The problem of Aboriginal marginalisation'.

[128] Hage, White Nation.

[129] Reservations about multiculturalism and Asian immigration were first expressed in the 1980s – see e.g. Blainey, All for Australia – but they were embraced by the Howard government, which found in them a recipe for political success. See e.g. Jupp, From White Australia, especially ch. 6.

[130] Jupp, From White Australia, 'Public policy'.

[131] Humphrey, 'Migration, security and insecurity'. The Muslim population of Australia is even more culturally and geographically diverse than that in the United Kingdom, with communities from the Middle East, South Asia, South East Asia, East Asia and Africa.

[132] The Sydney gang rapes were two series of group sexual assaults in Sydney in 2000 and 2001, involving the use of racist language to degrade the white Australian teenage female victims. These rapes and the subsequent trials created debate about women's rights and intense questioning of the merits of multiculturalism. For discussion, see e.g. Grewal, 'Australia, the feminist nation?'; Warner, 'Gang rape'.

[133] The Cronulla riots involved groups of white 'surfer' youths attacking young people of Middle Eastern appearance. For discussions, see Poynting, 'What caused the Cronulla riot?'; Lattas, 'Cruising'; Stratton, 'Non-citizens'.

[134] Poynting, 'The "lost" girls'.

'from an ethnic/religious minority in a multicultural society to a transnational risk category, potential sources of religiously inspired extremist violence.'[135] This has been reinforced by a series of moral panics about 'Middle Eastern boat people', largely asylum-seekers from Iraq and Afghanistan.[136] In 2006, Prime Minister John Howard explicitly targeted Muslims for their unwillingness to integrate, accusing them of being unwilling to learn English and of not adopting Australian values, especially regarding treating women equally.[137] Australian nationalism has thus been increasingly 'framed against a dangerous Muslim "other"',[138] with young men especially seen as a continuing threat to women (both Muslim and white), as well as society at large.

The recent attempts to govern youth of immigrant background have accordingly emphasised social cohesion, dubbed by some as the 'new integrationism'.[139] Australia's traditionally accessible citizenship and settlement policies have given some way to policies that borrow from European countries, most notably the United Kingdom.[140] Measures aimed at 'extremist' forms of Islam have encouraged internal community surveillance and sponsored 'moderate Islam'.[141] As in Europe, young Muslim women have been at the centre of recent discussions (with an emphasis on the veil, regarded as an oppressive symbol from which young women should be liberated).[142] While the recent public immigration discourse has overwhelmingly focused on stopping asylum-seekers, rather than family migration, family migration had already come to be seen as potentially problematic in the wake of stories of immigration 'marriage rorts' in the 1980s,[143] and changes were made

---

[135] Humphrey, 'Migration, security and insecurity', 182. See also Humphrey, 'Australian Islam'; Mansouri, 'Citizenship, identity and belonging'.
[136] Mansouri, 'Citizenship, identity and belonging'; Poynting et al., *Bin Laden in the Suburbs*. See further Chapter 4.
[137] Department of Prime Minister and Cabinet, 'John Howard transcript'.
[138] Ho, 'Muslim women's new defenders'; Poynting et al., *Bin Laden in the Suburbs*.
[139] A part in this was played by Pauline Hanson and her 'One Nation' party; parts of her platform were subsequently taken into the 'mainstream' by the major parties. Poynting and Mason, 'The new integrationism', 237.
[140] For instance, the Australian citizenship test is directly modelled on that of the United Kingdom. On the test and its legislative history, see Fozdar and Spittles, 'The Australian citizenship test'. Anti-terrorism laws have also been borrowed mainly from the United Kingdom. See Lynch, 'Control orders in Australia'. The same applies to the recent 2015 legislation on stripping dual nationals of citizenship if they have been found guilty of terrorism.
[141] Akbarzadeh, 'Investing in mentoring'; Spalek and Imtoual, 'Muslim communities'. As restrictions on travel to Syria in 2014 show, these efforts are still continuing (new laws designed to stop Australians fighting in overseas conflicts were introduced in 2014, making it illegal for people to travel to areas declared terrorist zones).
[142] On Muslim women in Australia, see Akbarzadeh, *Challenging Identities*.
[143] Birrell, 'Spouse migration'. See also Birrell, 'The chains that bind'.

in the 1990s to limit the right to family migration[144] and to deal with concerns over Australians engaged in 'serial sponsorship'.[145] The diversity of migrant backgrounds and trajectories and the relatively high levels of intermarriage notwithstanding, there remains concern over some second- and third-generation citizens seeking marriage partners from their parents' homeland, echoing developments in the United Kingdom.[146] As in the United Kingdom, spouse visas are already limited in many ways – for instance, the non-Australian spouse will not be granted permanent residency until the marriage relationship has lasted two years.[147] The current context is one in which the old Australian model of immigration and settlement has been transformed to prioritise skilled immigration (with a tighter emphasis on not just skills, but youth and English language fluency).[148] This has entailed reductions in the family components, the largest part of which is the spouse/fiancé category (mainly women).[149] Most recently, public discussion around forced marriage has centred on concerns about 'Australian girls' being coerced to marry, again echoing developments in the United Kingdom; forced marriage was criminalised in 2013.[150]

Italy is in many ways different from longer-established countries of immigration in that with larger immigration flows starting in the 1970s, the second generation has until recently been concentrated in the younger age groups (though some groups of migrant origin are already at the second-generation adult stage). The Italian social context has in some ways been favourable to the inclusion of young people of immigrant background, with relatively easy incorporation of immigrants into (often informal) economic structures, an active charity sector and a public school system open even to irregular migrants.[151] At the same time, it has been difficult even for many groups of Italian young people

---

[144] Family migration had been extended to siblings and parents in the 1970s, but was limited to only partners and dependent children in the late 1980s and the 1990s. Birrell, 'Immigration reform'.
[145] Iredale, 'Patterns of spouse'; Khoo, 'The context of spouse'.
[146] Khoo, 'The context of spouse'; Khoo et al., 'Intermarriage'.
[147] The government recognises an exception to this rule in cases of domestic violence, when it can be documented.
[148] Immigration intake has been at times very high (though fluctuating). Australia has been moving increasingly towards a guest-worker immigration model (see further Chapter 4).
[149] Though over half of those who enter in the skill category are actually accompanying family members. See further Chapter 4.
[150] The Criminal Code Act 1995, as amended in 2013. The offences carry a maximum penalty of four years' imprisonment, or seven years' imprisonment for an aggravated offence.
[151] Alzetta et al., 'Italy: unreceptive climate'.

to transition into the labour market, and precarious non-standard employment has grown in the wake of the flexibilisation of the Italian labour market, especially targeting young workers.[152] Italy's recent economic woes have made the situation worse for many young people.[153] As discussed in Chapter 2, Italians rely on families rather than the state for support, and as a result young people stay in the parental home longer than in other countries. This is the background against which a very diverse group of immigrant-born are growing up and constituting the fastest-growing segment of the Italian population, putting pressure on the Italian school system.[154] Research is now starting to map the educational performance[155] and identity and identifications of the second generation.[156] Poorer outcomes are associated with recent arrival, poor economic situation/parental social capital and certain countries of origin (China, the Philippines, the former Yugoslavia and Peru).[157] In addition to socioeconomic differentiations between young migrant groups, Italian citizenship law keeps many second-generation young people as 'immigrants' on turning 18 (and they then have to obtain a separate legal permit to study or work).[158] Young people of immigrant origin thus face being treated as outsiders despite being raised, and sometimes even born, in Italy. For these young adults, lacking formal citizenship increases the barriers to participation in normal economic and social life even more than for their peers.[159]

---

[152] For analyses of the flexibilisation of the Italian labour market and the emergence of an insider/outsider division and its effects on new entrants, see Barbieri and Scherer, 'Flexibilizing', 'Labour market flexibilization'. See also Bernardi and Nazio, 'Globalization'.

[153] With very high levels of youth unemployment, emigration in search of employment prospects has grown. See Fondazione ISMU, 'Diciannovesimo rapporto'.

[154] Italy has over five million residents of foreign nationality, and almost 800 000 young people of foreign origin in the school system. For demographic overviews, see Caritas/Migrantes, 'Dossier statistico'; Fondazione ISMU, 'Ventesimo rapporto'; Istat, 'Indicatori demografici'.

[155] See e.g. Azzolini, 'A new form'; Azzolini and Barone, 'Do they progress'; Barban and White, 'Immigrants' children's transition'; Mussino and Strozza, 'The delayed school progress'; Queirolo Palmas, *Prove di Seconde Generazioni*.

[156] Colombo et al., 'Different but not stranger', 'Citizenship and multiple belonging'.

[157] Gabrielli et al., 'Just a matter of time?'; Paterno and Gabrielli, 'Two years later'.

[158] As discussed in Chapter 2, children of two foreign parents cannot become Italian nationals until their 18th birthday, when they have one year to request citizenship; this requires that applicants demonstrate uninterrupted residence in the country since birth and that their parents have retained legal residence for all that time. This is very difficult for 'second-generation' adults, who often lack the required documents (e.g. because their parents were irregular at some point – common considering the high rate of informality and subsequent legalisation in Italy – or because their residence was interrupted by visits to the parental homeland). Marchetti, 'Trees without roots'. The levels of naturalisation have been, unsurprisingly, low. Colombo et al., 'Citizenship and multiple belonging', 337.

[159] Bianchi, 'Italiani nuovi', 322. See also Alzetta et al. 'Italy: unreceptive climate'; Ambrosini, 'Il futuro in mezzo a noi'.

Though Italy, as a state unprepared for the demographic changes caused by immigration, can be said to be in a state of constant panic about immigrants from outside the European Union (the so-called *extracomunitari*), the shape of these anxieties is only lately starting to bear resemblance to that in established countries of destination, in that concerns have not traditionally centred around family migration (which has started to grow relatively recently), but around irregular (and often later legalised) work-related immigration and asylum-seeking. New (irregular) arrivals and the security and cultural threats that they allegedly pose have been a focus of aggressive campaigns from the right.[160] This has meant that until recently (legally sanctioned) family immigration has been seen as a 'smooth, regulated, legal and accepted immigration flow', and as a consequence, has been less politicised.[161] However, the politicisation of migration issues and pressure for migration control are now coinciding with large cohorts of children of immigrants (born in Italy or migrated at young ages) moving through the Italian school system, with some of them at least growing up as citizens (and even those not formally citizens being recognised in some ways as 'Italian', even if excluded from 'Italianness' in racial and ethnic terms).[162] Media coverage of the *seconde generazioni* is stigmatising and concentrated on topics related to crime and urban safety, reflecting general trends within the Italian media, with young men of immigrant origin frequently dealt with as members of 'gangs'.[163] The current cohort of young people of immigrant origin is thus 'reaching adulthood at a time when Italian society is characterized by a serious "multiculturalism backlash"'[164] over the reluctance to face the changing character of that society. It is thus unsurprising that immigrant integration has become 'a constant theme in Italian public discourse'.[165]

The dichotomy of being raised in a country and yet being excluded from economic opportunities – along with the hostile atmosphere – presents many challenges for the 1.5 and second generation, who (unlike their parents, who often work on the bottom rungs of the stratified Italian labour market) feel they deserve the same opportunities as

---

[160] Triandafyllidou and Ambrosini, 'Irregular immigration control'.
[161] Ambrosini et al., 'Family migration', 368. See also Bonizzoni and Cibea, 'Family migration policies', 38.
[162] Andall, 'Second-generation attitude', has argued that the terms 'black' and 'Italian' are still seen as mutually exclusive, even when young black individuals have Italian citizenship.
[163] Alzetta et al. 'Italy: unreceptive climate'; Clough Marinaro and Walston, 'Italy's second generations'.
[164] Riccio and Russo, 'Everyday practised citizenship', 360.   [165] Bianchi, 'Italiani nuovi', 322.

native-born Italians.[166] However, much of the official policy response has focused on trying to block immigrant entry and stop the multi-ethnic transformation.[167] Immigration has been treated as a security and law-and-order issue, with recent laws defining unauthorised presence in the country as a crime (the laws also involve the prohibition of all administrative acts, including marriage, for undocumented immigrants).[168] The policing of individuals of immigrant background also occurs at the local level, with some local governments developing policies of exclusion.[169] The recent law-reform proposals regarding citizenship law and young adults have been much debated, but change has been delayed for some time.[170] Though this sluggishness also has to do with the political instability of Italy, it suggests that mainstream opinion rejects the inclusion of immigrants – and their children – as citizens.[171] However, with an emerging 'second generation' and increasing family migration, enduring shifts in national reproduction have been set in motion. There is an increase in family reunifications, including by women performing domestic and care work, who often take a long time to reach a position where they are able to reunite with their children (as they first need to regularise, and then show 'adequate' income and housing, which can be a problem in the Italian labour and housing market).[172] The long separations create new challenges for the integration of young people and their family relationships.[173] Family migration is also becoming increasingly diversified, with inflows of female migrant workers being complemented by more 'traditional' patterns of female migration (as in the case of South Asian women).[174]

Finland, even more so than Italy, is different from longer-established countries of immigration in that immigration flows to this geographically isolated country only started to (re)increase in the 1990s (but, at

---

[166] Ambrosini, 'Il futuro in mezzo a noi'.   [167] Alzetta et al. 'Italy: unreceptive climate'.
[168] See Law 125 of 24 July 2008 and Law 94 of 15 July 2009. For background, see Merlino, 'The Italian (in)security package'. See also Ambrosini, 'Immigration in Italy'. These measures build on the earlier Bossi-Fini law (Law 189/2002), which had already introduced various sanctions in an effort to exclude irregular migrants.
[169] Ambrosini, 'We are against a multi-ethnic society'.
[170] On the approval by the Lower House of the citizenship law changes in October 2015, see Chapter 2. For a discussion of some of the many preceding draft bills, see Marchetti, 'Trees without roots'.
[171] Ambrosini, 'Immigration in Italy'.   [172] Ambrosini, 'Parenting from a distance'.
[173] Ambrosini, 'Migration and transnational commitment'; Bonizzoni, 'Immigrant working mothers'. Regarding adolescents' shifts in family ties, see Bonizzoni and Leonini, 'Shifting geographical configurations'.
[174] Ambrosini et al., 'Family migration'. See De Luca and Arrazola Carballo, 'To work or not to work?', on immigrant women's attitudes to labour-market participation.

little over 200 000, foreigners even now make up only four per cent of the population).[175] Finland is not a multicultural country and is only gradually coming to terms with its new inhabitants of immigrant origin, with much of the early attention focusing on the so-called 1.5 generation who migrated as children. The Finnish education and labour markets have faced many challenges in incorporating newcomers (and also some groups of citizens, such as the Romani minority). The largest groups of immigrants are from neighbouring Estonia and Russia, but much of the attention in terms of youth integration has focused on the smaller non-white Somali minority, who have largely arrived as refugees (the Somali community is by far the largest Muslim group in Finland).[176] The increase in immigration, including the arrival of Somali refugees, coincided with a deep recession in the early 1990s (the same recession also generated high levels of youth unemployment).[177] As elsewhere, youth trajectories in Finland are increasingly individualised, and even young people with high education have at times found it difficult to enter the labour market.[178] Participation in paid work defines membership of Finnish society for both genders, and the unemployed, whether immigrants or not, are to some extent marginalised from society (and unlike in familistic Italy, they are the responsibility of the Finnish welfare state, which struggled to fulfil its universalistic expectations after the recession).[179] Studies have found, not unsurprisingly, that young people with low education and those of immigrant background have a greatly increased risk of being outside the labour market.[180]

Assimilationist concerns have focused largely on those minorities most different from mainstream society in terms of social and cultural practices and civic skills. In this respect, the Somali minority's difficulty in entering the Finnish labour market, along with significant cultural/religious differences, have made it – and lately some other groups

---

[175] Tilastokeskus, 'Väestö'. Note that Finland had experienced some immigration in the past, but received very little between the Second World War and 1990.
[176] Tilastokeskus, 'Väestö'.   [177] Pehkonen, 'Immigrants' paths'.
[178] Salmela-Aro et al., 'Mapping pathways'.
[179] Pehkonen, 'Immigrants' paths'. The increase of youth unemployment in the 1990s led Finland to substantially retrench its welfare state; on this, see Timonen, *Restructuring the Welfare State*. On the low quality of life of unemployed young people (aged 18–24), see Vaarama et al., 'Suomalaisten kokema elämänlaatu', 138–9.
[180] Myrskylä, 'Nuoret työmarkkinoiden', 'Hukassa'. See also Malmberg-Heimonen and Julkunen, 'Out of unemployment?'; Työ-ja elinkeinoministeriö, 'Kotoutumisen kokonaiskatsaus'; Väänänen et al., 'Maahanmuuttajien integroituminen'; Valtonen, 'Cracking monopoly'.

of refugees (and visible outsiders), such as Afghanis and Iraqis – an obvious target of attention. The reality of racism is undeniable and has a significant impact on young people, especially visible minorities like Somalis.[181] How children and adolescents of Somalian origin negotiate two very distinct cultures has been increasingly studied, as have parents' challenges associated with changing generational, gender and family relations.[182] Issues around refugees have become increasingly politicised after the 'cartoon row' in nearby Denmark (2006) and some much-publicised incidents of criminal activity (a series of street robberies in the early 2000s) by groups of Somali youth.[183] While the latter concerns in particular are associated with young men, Somali girls have instead been seen through the lens of victimisation: practices such as female genital mutilation have been much analysed, along with allegations that Somali girls are being brought into the country as (alleged) foster children, only to become maids and 'second wives' in polygamous marriages.[184] The allegations about girls have particularly evoked the role of the Finnish state as a protector of gender equality.[185] Furthermore, as increasing refugee numbers have contributed to higher levels of family reunification, there has been much discussion about this being used as a channel for chain migration. Somali boys, in particular, have been suspected of being 'anchor children'; that is, unaccompanied minors (or young adults claiming to be under 18) who arrive to seek humanitarian protection[186] – often granted to vulnerable unaccompanied young people – who then bring over their parents and sometimes other relatives through family reunion.[187]

---

[181] On racism, see Jasinskaja-Lahti et al., *Rasismi ja syrjintä Suomessa*; Pohjanpää et al., 'Maahanmuuttajien elinolot'. Regarding young people's experiences of discrimination, see Liebkind and Jasinskaja-Lahti, 'Acculturation'; Rastas, 'Racializing categorization', 'Rasismi lasten ja nuorten arjessa'.

[182] Alitolppa-Niitamo, 'Liminalities', 'The generation in-between'; Degni et al., 'Somali parents'; Open Society, 'Somalis in Helsinki'.

[183] For a discussion of the crime and of young men from ethnic minorities, see Honkatukia and Suurpää, 'Panssaroitua kovuutta?'.

[184] Female genital mutilation has been researched by Mölsä, 'Tyttöjen ympärileikkauksen hoito', 'Ajat ovat muuttuneet'. Regarding reports about foster children, see *Uusi Suomi*, 'HS: 5000 somalia jonossa – rahapula pakottaa Suomen vääriin päätöksiin', 29 August 2010.

[185] On violence against young women of immigrant background, see Ala-Lipasti, 'Kunniaväkivalta'; Korhonen and Ellonen, 'Maahanmuuttajanaiset'.

[186] In 2014, there were fewer than 200 unaccompanied children who sought asylum, most from Somalia and Afghanistan. Maahanmuuttovirasto, 'Turvapaikanhakijat. Yksintulleet alaikäiset'.

[187] Despite lack of evidence, successive ministers of home affairs have expressed the view that such children are sent to seek asylum in order to set in motion chain migration. On the debates, see Nykänen, 'Hyöty vai haitta', 44–7.

Finland's naturalisation law is still relatively generous, with legal residence being the biggest hurdle, which also explains the importance of family migration as a legal avenue of migration.[188] Finland has been seeking to readjust its overall immigration policy towards labour migration, which is considered economically necessary and is seen as posing fewer integration challenges. These moves are rooted in the perception, partly based on Finland's own experiences, partly those of other countries, that family-reunification migrants are economically unproductive.[189] This has created pressure to change the law, especially regarding refugees, resulting in tightened rules.[190] As the majority of unaccompanied minors arriving in Finland are boys, often around 16 or 17 years of age (allegedly escaping forced recruitment into the military), suspicions about whether they are over 18 (and thus 'adults') have led to the expansion of forensic age assessment.[191] Stricter rules on who qualifies as a foster child have been introduced to clamp down on false claims and to deal with fears that children, especially girls, are being exploited by manipulative adult relatives seeking entry. Regarding refugees contracting marriages with persons outside Finland, it is now required that the applicant prove they have means of support − a condition which was enacted to prevent insolvent refugees from 'importing wives' from Somalia (this is not required for existing marriages in cases of family reunification).[192] Integration policy, after a hesitant start, is focusing on encouraging young immigrants to find an active role in Finnish society and the Finnish economy.[193] Integration programmes designed by the Finnish state are actively targeting young people with the aim of encouraging their economic participation.[194] While much discussion of the 1.5 generation has focused on employment and labour-market

---

[188] The relative geographical isolation of Finland and its highly formal economy, which is not open to informal work, have kept pressure off formal admission to citizenship (citizenship legislation has been changed twice in the recent past, in 2003 and again in 2011). On Finnish citizenship law, see Fagerlund and Brander, 'Country report: Finland'.
[189] Lippert and Pyykkönen, 'Contesting family'.
[190] See Hallitus, 'HE 240/2009', for background.
[191] Sections 6a–6b of the Aliens Act now provide for clarification of age through forensic examination. Section 38 provides that the underage minor seeking family reunion with parents must still be underage when the claim is decided (often years after application). DNA testing is used to detect fraud concerning family relationships. See Helén and Tapaninen, 'DNA testing'.
[192] Sections 39 and 114 of the Aliens Act.
[193] See Alitolppa-Niitamo and Leinonen, 'Perheet, nuoret'.
[194] The Act on Promotion of Integration (1386/2010 Laki kotoutumisen edistämisestä) entails an obligation for refugees and others admitted on humanitarian grounds to participate in various activities, including education and language tuition, and includes sanctions if they do not (limiting of benefits).

policies, research is now also starting to map the educational attainment of the 1.5 and emerging second generations, showing, for instance, negative impacts of maternal non-employment on some girls' prospects.[195] Such results suggest concerns will continue over the economic and social impact of immigration on existing patterns of youth behaviour, gender and labour participation.

CITIZENSHIP AND THE QUALITY OF THE FUTURE CITIZENRY

> The period of transition from one's family of origin to independent adult life is a crucial one. This is the stage at which young adults make decisions about schooling, housing, careers, conjugal partnerships and childbearing – decisions that will have a long-term effect on their wellbeing and through demographic change the fiscal sustainability of national economies. If they fail to thrive at this critical phase of their life cycle, their ability to develop to their fullest potential in later adult life could be reduced.[196]

This last section discusses the emerging patterns of governing young people, especially of migrant origin, in terms of what they imply about young people as citizens. There are significant differences between states in how they deal with young people, and especially in their approach to those of immigrant background, depending on how long they have dealt with immigration, their approach to immigrant incorporation and citizenship, and their labour market and regulations welfare systems. What they all have in common is a future-orientated concern over young people as a resource of strategic importance as tomorrow's workers (and, implicitly, reproducers). The smaller youth cohorts must not waste their potential, and specific attention thus falls on groups who can be identified as 'failing to thrive' – lacking the ability to perform as reliable citizens – including groups of young people of immigrant origin. How to deal with mixed populations and manage the diversity of the next generations are increasingly crucial questions for migrant-receiving states. Many states have scrambled to gather information on young people of immigrant background and how they perform compared to normative expectations of how and when young people should come to behave as adult citizens, in both economic and

---

[195] Kilpi-Jakonen, 'Does Finnish educational equality', 'Citizenship and educational attainment'.
[196] Sanderson et al., 'Young adult failure', 169.

cultural terms.[197] This section elaborates on two aspects of these processes. First, it discusses the ways in which young people are understood as citizens who should transition to adulthood in a responsible way, negotiating economic insecurities and building a trajectory towards successful, self-sufficient citizenship, with some public support, but ideally without direct intervention. Second, it analyses how some groups who are perceived as misguided in their transitions are singled out for extra management of the risks they are seen to pose or face.

Transitions to adulthood have become much more complex than in the recent past, and in some analyses the implication is that young people's transitions have become 'faulty'[198] as they are not following previously normative sets of behaviours and attitudes. There is, however, also continuity and, moreover, acceptance that at least some of the changed circumstances – in particular, the pressures imposed by the globalised economy – require young people's transitions to change as well, especially as regards the expansion of higher education as an avenue towards more security. Thus, a new normative 'good transition to adulthood' is emerging: a 'successful' young person is one on the route through university and into graduate-type employment.[199] At the same time, marriage as a transitional event has lost much of its power (replaced in many places by cohabitation, though not in places like southern Italy) and independent living is not always a sign of a successful transition (sometimes, it is the reverse). In the context of low fertility, the ideal is becoming more gender-neutral in that both young men and, especially, women should leave family transitions – partnering and children – for later, once they have completed education, found employment and established themselves as self-sufficient individuals (but, of course, they should not be left too late or forgotten (see Chapter 2), and it is at that stage that the de-gendered model breaks down).[200] This aspiration is also open to citizens of migrant background, as the accomplishments of groups of Chinese and Indian background in the United Kingdom show.[201] However, where formal citizenship is exclusively framed, some groups of immigrant origin can find themselves excluded from

---

[197] This can be seen as part of states' general efforts at generating knowledge and expertise about all aspects of youth in order to better regulate it, as Kelly, 'Youth as an artefact', has outlined.
[198] Wyn and Woodman, 'Generation, youth and social change', 498.
[199] They could be argued to be on the way to becoming member of the new 'core population': individuals successful in the competitive labour market. Bommes, 'The shrinking inclusive capacity', 58–9.
[200] See further Chapter 4.   [201] See Bommes, 'The shrinking inclusive capacity', 58.

paths taken for granted by other young people (as in Italy, where turning 18 also turns many second-generation youths into immigrants), but as the UK example shows, citizenship in terms of formal status alone is not enough for all young people – especially those socioeconomically marginalised or racially excluded – to be admitted into the sphere of successful citizenship.[202]

This change towards framing education as the solution for all young people's problems is part of a larger picture that involves the shifting role of the state as the guardian of youth and the general 'transformation of compacts of citizenship'.[203] Economic globalisation has profoundly altered the circumstances of national economies; exposed to new risks, states, in varying degrees, have sought to manage them through encouraging flexible but less secure employment and cuts in the welfare state (including social security for the young) and generally downsizing the social rights of citizenship, often affecting young people most severely.[204] All four governments have progressively reduced support for young people and increasingly reframed their role as supporting young people to transition via study and work, responsibly and flexibly, to learn to self-govern so that they relieve the state of the responsibility.[205] Out of the four states discussed here, the changes in the role of government have arguably been taken furthest in the liberal welfare-state context of the United Kingdom, where the shift from manufacturing to a 'post-industrial' service economy has been accompanied by governments of all stripes dismantling the social guarantees for young people and seeking to encourage individuals to be self-sufficient and accountable for their own fates.[206] The underlying assumption has been that all future employment is in the 'skills economy' and that enhancing skills can address everything from antisocial behaviour to regional economic performance.[207] Even where the government role is stronger and public investments are still substantial, as in Finland, universities are increasingly framed as 'knowledge factories' geared towards economic growth and encouraging young individuals to compete and become useful citizens.[208] Thus, the education system is increasingly seen as being there not so much to educate young people

---

[202] Back and Sinha, 'The UK', 73.   [203] Schierup et al., *Migration, Citizenship*, 249.
[204] Fagan et al., 'Young adults'.
[205] As Rose, 'Government and control', 327, argues, 'the dream of the social state gives way to the metaphor of the facilitating state'.
[206] Furlong and Cartmel, *Young People and Social Change*; Mizen, 'The best days'.
[207] Keep and Mayhew, 'Moving beyond skills'.
[208] For a comparison of British and Finnish education policies, see Lindberg, 'Koulutuspolitiikan'.

as a social right, but to provide educational services to consumers who see education as a private investment that is intended to assist them in dealing with the uncertainties they face as young citizens.[209]

The global economic changes which have transformed young people's labour-market opportunities in the last few decades have been underlined by the global economic crisis, which has, since 2008, hit young people very hard, with severe effects in places like Italy (where youth unemployment rates skyrocketed as a result of the crisis). However, in some ways the recent events are merely exacerbating a number of existing issues, at a time when it is becoming much more important that young people get it right, not just for their own well-being, but arguably for 'the fiscal sustainability of national economies'.[210] Under pressures from demographic ageing, young people's ability and willingness to support the intergenerational arrangements are thus at stake, and their 'failure' to do so is increasingly blamed on them. Though many young adults manage to negotiate successful transitions to work in accordance with established norms on routes to adulthood, the crisis has shown that even those who have followed all the 'right' pathways – the 'successful' young people – are not insured against precariousness.[211] Achieving stable employment and financial independence, while emphasised as a hallmark of adult citizenship, has thus become much harder than before, and remains most difficult for young people who lack qualifications, work experience or personal connections (often, but not exclusively, young people from working-class and ethnic-minority backgrounds, who also face discrimination).[212] Policies seek to deal with these problem groups predominantly by pushing them to upgrade their skills, but questions can be asked about whether extended education is in fact the answer to social advancement in the arguable absence of good 'post-industrial' jobs for everyone and of more substantial policies against inequality and economic marginalisation.[213] It is no longer just 'problem groups', such as young men who lack education, income and employment or young women who, faced with a similar situation, experience early motherhood and lone parenthood,

---

[209] The marketisation of higher education in England culminated in the introduction of the new tuition-fee regime in 2012, after the initial introduction of student fees in 1998.
[210] Sanderson et al., 'Young adult failure', 169.   [211] Fagan et al., 'Young adults'.
[212] On the gender dimensions of labour-market disconnect, see Escott, 'Young women on the margins'.
[213] Keep and Mayhew, 'Moving beyond skills'; MacDonald, 'Youth, transitions and un(der) employment'. For a critique of the idea of a 'post-industrial' society, see Vogt, 'The post-industrial society'.

who may face the prospect of a life of insecure and temporary employment.

In the context where for many people youth is characterised by fragile inclusion as partial citizens, governments increasingly make use of statistical information to target subgroups seen to be 'troublesome' to the state and wider society. With continuing and diversifying immigration, children of immigrants have become an object of knowledge production and speculation. Problem groups – those who cannot or will not successfully manage transitions – can be identified and targeted based on demographic profiles (early school-leavers, teenage mothers, poorly performing groups of second generation, refugees, etc.). States seek to manage problem groups on the one hand by including them, where possible (for instance, by pushing them towards training opportunities), and, on the other, by managing the exclusion of those who are seen to pose dangers that cannot be managed through active inclusion.[214] From this perspective, it can be argued that, for instance, British Muslims of South Asian origin have been targeted for measures that seek to reintegrate Muslim young people into the mainstream (for instance, by steering them away from extremism), while also seeking to contain and control those elements that are considered to be beyond reattachment through tougher measures. It is often young men who are seen as risky and teetering on the brink of permanent marginalisation – apart from fears of extremism, in all four countries a concern over young men of immigrant background centres on their potential for antisociality and criminality – British Muslims of South Asian origin, Australian Lebanese Muslim men, Italy's 'second-generation gangs' and Somali refugee youth in Finland are all straddling the boundary between inclusion and exclusion, treated as subgroups of malcontents in need of careful monitoring.[215]

Concerns over young people of immigrant background take a slightly different form in the case of young women. The role of women as biological, cultural and social reproducers of the ethnic community raises the prospect that 'poorly educated spouses become mothers who raise the next generation but do not have the skills to educate their children to succeed in society'.[216] Instances of forced marriage and female genital mutilation thus raise difficult questions about the best way to address

---

[214] See Rose, 'Government and control'.
[215] For a discussion of a similar comparative trend, see Fangen et al., *Inclusion and Exclusion*, 243–4.
[216] Kofman et al., 'Gendered perspectives', 4.

such practices, and effective responses require investment in resources (such as shelters), long-term engagement and inter-community dialogue about women's changing roles and family authority.[217] It is perhaps not surprising that in seeking faster or cheaper solutions, governments single out (some groups of) young women as too economically marginal, too vulnerable to family pressure and too young to act like adult citizens, especially when they are taking different demographic trajectories than their non-immigrant-background peers. At their most sweeping, such efforts seek to prevent young women from making 'unwise' and misguided choices, such as entering into early marriage with an overseas partner, with the state pre-empting the decisions of young citizens in the name of ensuring their future, as well as the future of the state. In terms of marriage migration, rules such as the raised age requirement for marriage-formation migration in the United Kingdom seek to send a message about the kinds of transition young people should be undergoing: they should not be pressured or encouraged to marry or have children early, but should be busy completing their education first in order to ensure their socioeconomic advancement (and contribute to the progress of their community). This sort of steering may be consistent with the normative extension of youth (or even the infantilisation of young adults), but it does not in itself deal with factors that might impede young women of migrant background from undertaking education and training (be they family pressures, discrimination or lack of opportunity), nor is it interested in the reasons why young people of immigrant origin might want to marry earlier[218] or to strengthen, rather than weaken, their transnational ties.[219]

Immigration law and citizenship rules give the state powerful tools for managing the second generation, whose transnational connections cause anxiety, creating an opening to regulate at least some of the great heterogeneity of individual situations in matters normally beyond their direct reach regarding other citizens, such as their choices over when to marry and settle down to have children.[220] As a result, transnational families are 'confronted with state interference in their family life to

---

[217] Phillips and Dustin, 'UK initiatives'.
[218] For instance, because some communities do not look favourably on unmarried sexual activity or because young individuals wish to establish an independent household.
[219] For a useful exploration of the motivations for transnational marriage in the UK Pakistani context, see Charsley, *Transnational Pakistani Connections*. See also Grillo, 'Marriages, arranged and forced'.
[220] Teitelbaum and Winter, *A Question of Numbers*.

a degree which most non-migrant families will never experience'.[221] Owing to the powers of the state regarding immigrant entry and citizenship attribution, it can manage youth on the cusp of adulthood, for instance preventing young citizens of immigrant origin from marrying what it considers 'unsuitable people' overseas and starting a family too early (in the United Kingdom and Australia), keeping the second generation in a permanent state of precariousness through strict rules of citizenship allocation that force those who cannot fulfil the required conditions to submit to immigration control, sometimes making them perpetual immigrants (Italy), or limiting young refugees' reunion with their 'unproductive' parents (Finland). This nexus with immigration rules allows states to link the management of some young citizens to the perceived demographic national interest in immigration policy (most obviously, the desire for self-sufficient, linguistically skilled people who are assumed to make good new citizens – see also Chapter 4). However, as such policies reflect highly normative notions of 'good members' of society,[222] they also create hierarchies of membership and belonging. These pecking orders are increasingly determined not just in socioeconomic terms but in terms of values – for instance, the UK rules on family-formation migration are arguably part of a broader trend that seeks to use 'culture', as well as economic usefulness, to choose the best newcomers.[223]

The denial of full membership and equal citizenship to young people with transnational backgrounds often stays invisible until it touches on the life of a 'successful' young person. The previously mentioned Aguilar Quila case, in which the 21-year age limit was successfully challenged, is a good example. The case stems from two cases, one involving Mr Diego Aguilar Quila, a Chilean national, who married a (white) British citizen, Amber (Jeffrey) Aguilar,[224] and the other involving Ms Shakira Bibi, a Pakistani national hoping to join her British husband, Suhyal Mohammed, in the United Kingdom (this was an arranged

---

[221] Strasser et al., 'Doing family', 175. See also Friedman, 'Determining "truth"'.
[222] Block, 'Regulating membership', 15.
[223] Distinguishable both from such generally accepted justifications as public order, safety and health, and from such generally unacceptable justifications as race, ethnicity and religion. See Orgad, 'Illiberal liberalism'.
[224] When he applied for a spouse visa at the age of 18, the age restriction to 21 had not been enforced so the rule was still 18 for both sponsor and their spouse, and Mr Quila's wife (the sponsor) was only 17 at the time. By the time his wife had turned 18, the age restriction had been increased to 21 and the Home Office rejected the application for the spouse visa.

marriage). The young 'Western' love-match couple – unusual in marrying early, but otherwise unremarkable – became the incidental victims of the rule, which was not targeted at them, and received public sympathy for their plight. Even the *Daily Mail* lamented that the couple, 'in a genuine marriage', had to choose between living together abroad and Amber Jeffrey's career (she had been offered a place at Royal Holloway to study languages the following year). The irony that the rule, allegedly intended to protect young women and ensure their mature transitions to adult citizenship, was undermining the very values that it sought to support – the young woman's education, subsequent financial independence, etc. – was also noted.[225] The case, framed in the media as involving an emancipated and not at all vulnerable young woman, highlights the assumptions behind the change. Its main targets, young people from certain immigrant communities, were targeted on the basis of generalisations and anxieties about these groups, rather than actual knowledge about the risk involved in such marriages and the various attitudes with which young people and their families approach their marriage choices.[226] Any attempt at case-by-case assessment to establish actual forced marriages was foregone in favour of a blunt instrument to prevent all 'inadvisable' (that is, young) marriages.[227]

It is easy to see why sweeping approaches to dealing with the transnational ties of young citizens would prompt suspicions about barely hidden motivations that have less to do with protecting young people than with preventing the growth of immigrant communities. The broader point is, however, that current policies seek not just to limit family migration, but to screen entrants and facilitate the trajectories of those migrants who are effectively already adapted to living in contemporary societies, both in terms of skills and qualifications and in terms of having suitably 'Western' attitudes to family and gender relations (most notably, marriage based on love and intimacy, as opposed to 'instrumental' and 'patriarchal' motives).[228] As the UK example shows, matters of gender and sexuality are where the cultural fault lines between Islam

---

[225] *Daily Mail*, '"Heartbroken" British wife denied right to live with Chilean husband under Government's forced marriage rules', 8 December 2009.
[226] See Charsley, 'Risk and ritual', 'Risk, trust, gender', on how Pakistani families seek to reduce risks to their daughters. See also Beck-Gernsheim, 'Transnational lives', on why some women marry overseas in the hope of shifting the power balance in gender relations, as well as out of family loyalty and obligation.
[227] Wray, 'Moulding the migrant family', 607.
[228] Beck and Beck-Gernsheim, 'Passage to hope', 409.

and liberal societies can become sticking points.[229] Many commentators have noted that current approaches to family immigration treat family roles and attitudes as fixed and so create inconsistencies – for instance, immigration law, in an age of diversification and individualisation of family life inside contemporary societies, seems to promote an increasingly outmoded ideal of the nuclear family (whereas family law is more quickly reflective of changing family patterns, such as unmarried couples, 'reconstituted families' and same-sex partners). At the same time, while increasing acceptance of the diversity of family life in the contemporary Global North is undeniable, many governments are, in fact, also anxious about the complexities brought on by that diversity, worrying about the rise of individualism, family breakdown and the erosion of 'traditional family values' in secularised societies (not least because of their implications for national reproduction – see Chapter 2). Governmental aims to promote gender equality in the migration context should be viewed against this complex background, where family norms are in flux and women's independence is seen as an essential cultural value of liberal societies, yet something that is causing deep anxiety about the families of the future.[230]

Groenendijk, pointing out the lack of long-term research investigating outcomes of family migrants, has argued that family migration is framed as problematic migration 'mainly because policymakers and the public tend to take a short-term view and expect full integration within one generation, when all evidence points to a process that takes far longer.'[231] Moreover, focusing on the alleged 'deficiencies' of minority groups – whether defined in terms of cultural traditions, values, skills or language – can sideline questions about existing structures of inequality that affect new citizens' substantive inclusion.[232] The recent focus on culture has perhaps obscured that governments neglect socioeconomic inclusion at their peril.[233] In addition, making policy on the basis of group differences in trajectories along ethnic and religious lines can backfire. It treats individuals as members of homogenised groups and lumps together generalisations – like being Muslim and being disadvantaged or overly 'traditional' – which likely hinder rather than help efforts at inclusion.[234] Introducing greater scrutiny without addressing

---

[229] Joppke, 'Europe and Islam'.   [230] Phillips, 'Provocative women'.
[231] Groenendijk, 'Pre-departure integration', 30.
[232] Kostakopoulou, 'Matters of control', 839.   [233] Joppke, 'Europe and Islam', 1332.
[234] Kostakopoulou, 'Matters of control', accordingly suggests a new approach of 'letting be'.

the background conditions behind social practices such as endogenous marriage will further alienate those targeted. Processes of inclusion and exclusion are of course far too complex to be reduced to simplistic terms, but the inconsistencies in the way young people are treated underscore the potential for counter-productiveness. Wray has noted that many of the changes introduced by the United Kingdom regarding marriage-formation migration may not, as intended, reduce the desire to marry someone through arranged transnational marriage, but in fact foster a 'transnational mindset', because being constantly reminded of their problematic identity can encourage young people who take their cultural identity seriously to protect this part of themselves.[235] Similarly, the continuing Italian exclusion of second-generation immigrants who do not fulfil the rigid criteria for citizenship may actually undermine their sense of belonging to the society which treats them with constant suspicion and manages them through legal exclusion.[236]

FINAL REMARKS

Contemporary states in the Global North are increasingly multi-ethnic and diverse. With pressures to incorporate diverse interests, many of them have struggled to redefine themselves as immigration societies and to modify their ideas of national identity. Amid some genuine concern about social disintegration, states often try to manage what they can in circumstances in which there are increasingly many things they either cannot control or choose not to pursue. Young people of immigrant background are caught up in these processes and both treated as a future resource for ageing societies and suspected of being too unreliable to perform what is required of them. Some of the policies discussed in this chapter treat formal citizens as alien citizens (who need to be monitored and whose behaviour needs to be adjusted) in ways that actually treat them as less than full citizens, with lesser rights to family unity. Some of them keep young people outside the sphere of belonging altogether, in an effort to carefully maintain an ethnically defined boundary of citizenship. Attempts to guide young people of immigrant background towards appropriate educational, employment and family behaviours seek to steer them away from the influence of their families based on generalisations and demographic assumptions. Such

---

[235] Wray, 'Any time, any place', 57.   [236] Elliot, 'Legal, social and intimate'.

policies can have unintended consequences (for instance, prompting even earlier, arranged, fake marriages, keeping spouses overseas or encouraging younger and younger unaccompanied children to be sent abroad so that they get protected status). The way they frame adult citizenship may also be contrasted with how adults are actually treated as workers, citizens and immigrants (see further Chapter 4).

CHAPTER FOUR

CASUAL CITIZENS? THE DESIRABLE LABOUR MIGRANT AND CONDITIONAL CITIZENSHIP

This chapter discusses one of the major dimensions of the demographic transformation which has been unfolding in late-modern societies, the decline in the proportion of the working-age population as a result of longstanding lower birth rates, and the way governments in the Global North are using immigration to deal with the challenges posed by this decline.[1] While population ageing is inevitable, governments, armed with demographic projections, are developing strategies to mitigate or postpone its economic impacts (most notably rising dependency ratios) through a combination of policies – such as those aiming at increased labour-force participation (e.g. by groups such as women and older people) and higher productivity, as well as increased levels of immigration. As the demographic ageing process advances over the next few decades, questions concerning labour migration and the issues raised by selecting and admitting immigrants with desirable profiles and turning (some of) them into citizens to counter population decline will become even more important than they are today. Unlike family migration, which is considered culturally problematic or assumed to be economically unproductive (as seen in Chapter 3), states consider some labour (im)migration to be essential for dealing with demographic challenges, though with the assumption that (potentially) large flows of low-skilled immigrants

---

[1] Fertility decline initially reduces dependency ratios by causing labour-force expansion (and low numbers of dependants) – sometimes referred to as the 'demographic dividend' – but once ageing progresses, this demographic window begins to close and the proportion of older people who have left the workforce grows.

from the Global South have to be (and can be) kept at bay. Immigrants are thus seen as both a risk to the nation and vital for its survival, with states seeking to extract the maximum benefits from the resource migrants represent, while limiting the social and economic costs of permanent settlement. States' efforts at population engineering are thus increasingly geared towards identifying, admitting and retaining those immigrants who are most suited to their purposes – currently, skilled migrants in prime working age – and making sure only those most compatible with current priorities are steered towards permanent membership.

As a case study of how states seek to govern the resource (and risks) that labour migrants represent in changing labour markets, this chapter discusses Australia, a traditional country of settlement which has engaged in a partial deregulation of its immigration policy since the 1990s. Australia's immigration framework is 'among the most planned and managed of any OECD country'[2] and has often been held up as model of planned openness to immigration – at the same time, it is an example of 'bad practice' regarding the treatment of less desirable immigrants ('boat people'; that is, refugees arriving by sea). Australia's migration programme, traditionally based on permanent recruitment of immigrants of workforce age, has radically shifted direction in the past 20 years towards a more flexible guest-worker model. It is now attracting increasing numbers of migrants from all over the world, with a significant component from Asia. The prime vehicle for this is the 457 temporary visa programme (introduced in 1996), which bring tens of thousands of migrant workers to Australia every year, but amid claims that temporary migration – via the 457 visas, as well as working holidaymakers and students – creates an insecure underclass of cheap, flexible and compliant workers who can be exploited with impunity and discarded when no longer required. Directing even many of those migrants that have been actively recruited towards increasingly conditional trajectories, as opposed to permanent residence and citizenship, underlines the desire to maximise the benefits of adult migrants in prime working age, while avoiding costs associated with their education and retirement. Important questions are raised about how this is related to broader economic restructuring and the deregulatory trends of the Australian labour market, including an increase in 'casual' work, erosion of social rights and gendered employment patterns.

[2] Hugo, 'Migration and development in Asia', 151.

After the case study, the chapter discusses the efforts at managing labour migration in the other three jurisdictions, which face additional constraints, such as even more unfavourable demographic trends, less familiarity with managing labour immigration and legal limitations imposed by EU law. It examines how the growing desire to find solutions to demographic ageing and eventual decline – especially the prospect of a contracting labour market – has prompted policies that feature immigration as a partial solution to demographic problems, but a solution that creates new challenges in the face of growing hostility towards immigrants and the ongoing economic transformations that are changing the nature of paid work as a foundation of citizenship. In the United Kingdom, the last 20 years have seen moves towards enhancing skilled-labour migration, but migration has more recently become politically contentious (especially since the influx of EU citizens from Central and Eastern Europe has further politicised labour migration); Italy has undergone a huge transformation into a country of immigration; and Finland is struggling to attract the kinds of skilled-labour migration deemed most desirable. Increasingly diverse migrant trajectories are emerging whereby characteristics such as usefulness, self-sufficiency and loyalty are framed as conditions for admission, permanent residence and citizenship, while those deemed to have too little human capital or attitudes that are problematic are either excluded altogether or delegated to precarious trajectories. Similar attributes are increasingly held as valuable in citizens, raising questions not only about the rights and wrongs of entry policy but also about what exactly citizenship entails for those who constitute problem or even 'failed' citizens in economic terms.[3]

The last section analyses the implications of these trends in the governance of labour migration from the point of view of citizenship. The changes in immigration policy are driven by the concurrence of demographic pressures – smaller generations of working age, with increasing cohorts of older people – and economic transformations, such as the move towards knowledge and service economies. Together, these changes, which increase the demand for certain kinds of workers while discounting others, are changing the nature of the link between citizenship and paid work, as well as the gendered pact that has underpinned the breadwinner/carer model of citizenship. They are raising as yet unanswered questions about the citizenship of those who fail to

---

[3] Anderson, *Us and Them?*, 4.

secure good employment in the new precarious labour market or who have to rely on downgraded social entitlements. Immigration fits in this picture as a useful strategy for dealing with demographic challenges, but one that states are now seeking to govern closely, with an eye to the future. Contemporary states are increasingly making a distinction between what they consider desirable migration (often by the highly skilled) and undesirable migration, which needs to be limited to temporary channels or even deterred altogether (for instance, migration by those categorised as low-skilled workers). Though there is increasing competition for the best and the brightest, increased global mobility and reservations about turning newcomers into citizens have implications for conventional assumptions about citizenship as the end of a migration trajectory. The prioritisation of a particular kind of globally competitive worker as an 'ideal future citizen' also raises questions about work and self-sufficiency as conditions for integration and citizenship and the gendered nature of current policies.

AUSTRALIA: WELCOME AND WANTED (CONDITIONS APPLY)

From Nation-Building to Misgivings about Immigration

As is the case in many other developed countries, in Australia demographic challenges have become more acute in the last couple of decades. However, unlike some countries in Europe, which have only recently begun experiencing significant immigration, the demographics of the nation are of longstanding interest in Australia, where immigration has been used for nation-building ever since the white settlers first arrived. The state in Australia has traditionally maintained strong control over immigration entry and selection, using immigration as a way of ordering and modifying the national population.[4] In post-war Australia, it was generally believed that a substantially increased population was needed to keep the country more secure and prosperous (as is evident in the 'populate or perish' sentiment).[5] The longstanding desire to 'keep Australia white and British'[6] was executed through the racially-based immigration-control policy (known as 'White Australia'); this began to be weakened in the 1960s, and a non-discriminatory entry

---

[4] See Jupp, *From White Australia*, ch. 1. [5] Calwell, *How Many Australians*.
[6] Castles et al., 'Rethinking migration', 115.

policy was ushered in by the 1970s.[7] Since then, Australia has rapidly become a multi-ethnic country, whose population reached 23 million in 2013 (compared to 10 million in 1959 and 3.8 million in 1901).[8] Even though the population is growing, new demographic challenges and anxieties have emerged. The enduring decline in the birth rate, together with the end of the baby boomers' working life, means the working-age population faces the prospect of shrinking and demographic ageing is inevitable;[9] at the same time, immigrant diversity has become much more apparent in the last few decades, and popular as well as political attitudes to immigration have become much more critical since the 1990s. Australia has thus gone from having a generally felt desire to fill an 'empty continent'[10] to seeking to find a balance between powerful economic interests embracing immigrants and popular reservations about continuing high levels of immigration and consequent changes in the make-up of the population.

The consensus on the benefits of immigration was unchallenged until the 1970s. Having sought to increase (only) its British and British-descended population since settlement, Australian governments recognised from the mid-twentieth century onwards that birth rates – higher then than they are now[11] – would never be enough to populate the continent.[12] Accordingly, the state's gaze moved away from the birth rate as the only population solution and shifted further towards importing individuals and families to populate the country and meet labour shortages. After the Second World War, subsidised settlement and transportation costs were offered to permanent immigrants, or 'new Australians', of European stock (from Southern Europe, once British and Northern European flows dried up), and as the White Australia policy was phased out, immigrants came from further afield. The traditional

---

[7] On this shift and the various normative, economic, social and political factors behind it, see Tavan, 'Creating multicultural Australia'. For more detail, see also Tavan, *The Long, Slow Death*.

[8] Australian Bureau of Statistics, 'Australian historical population statistics'. For a statistical overview of the changes in immigration that took place over the last century, see Department of Immigration and Multicultural Affairs (Australia), 'Immigration'.

[9] For instance, Commonwealth of Australia, 'Australia to 2050' (the intergenerational report of 2010) flags the consequences of ageing, such as declines in workforce participation, as a major concern for government policy.

[10] Indigenous Australians had inhabited the continent for tens of thousands of years, but despite this, the land was considered uninhabited by the white settlers, who regarded Indigenous Australians as a dying race. On the history of terra nullius, see Banner, 'Why terra nullius?'.

[11] Calwell, *How Many Australians*, 3, highlights the birth rate of 1939 at 2.2 births per woman.

[12] E.g. Markus et al., *Australia's Immigration Revolution*, 54. See also Chapter 2.

narrative has centred on post-war male immigrants in the manufacturing sector (while the immigration of women and family settlement has been little explored).[13] Though many immigrants were incorporated as 'factory fodder',[14] the 'status of the domestic working class' was protected by treating newcomers as permanent settlers and new citizens, rather than guest-workers (unlike in Europe).[15] While immigrants have always been chosen on the basis of their suitability (as well as availability), it was not until the 1970s when, alongside the easing of ethnic restrictiveness, the first attempts were made to sort migrants more systematically, based on social, educational and economic attributes.[16] A more quantitative 'points system' (NUMAS or the Numerical Multifactor Assessment System) was adopted in 1979, borrowed from Canada,[17] and it still forms the basic framework for immigrant selection, giving weight to factors such as occupational and language skills. However, it continued to coexist with and be balanced by the family programme (which was further relaxed amid renewed concerns over the birth rate to include siblings and parents[18]) and the humanitarian intake (including refugees from Vietnam).[19]

The moves towards a points system and its subsequent refinements were connected political decisions that have transformed the Australian economy. The context for emerging discussions over whether immigrant selection would be best based on settlement criteria (family ties) or economic criteria (human capital) is one of economic challenges, periodic recessions (boom–bust cycles) and unemployment. By the early 1970s, increased competitive pressures and rising unemployment focused government attention on the need to ensure the economic viability of immigration.[20] With the decline of manufacturing and agriculture, new economic growth strategies were sought in greater economic openness (the desire to trade with the growing Asian markets and the fading of wartime memories also lessened the fears about Australia's geographic vulnerability).[21] Economic policies seeking the

[13] On family migration, see McDonald, 'The role of family migration', 3–4.
[14] Collins, 'The changing political economy', 9.
[15] Walsh, 'Navigating globalization', 795. See also Collins, 'The changing political economy'; O'Donnell and Mitchell, 'Immigrant labour'.
[16] The first indication of this was the Structured Selection Assessment System, which was introduced in 1973.
[17] Walsh, 'Navigating globalization', 797; Wright, 'Policy legacies', 55–6.
[18] Freeman and Birrell, 'Divergent paths', 532. On changes to family migration involving parents, see further Chapter 5.
[19] Jupp, *From White Australia*, ch. 3.   [20] Jupp, *From White Australia*, 150.
[21] Walsh, 'Navigating globalization'; Wright, 'Policy legacies'.

integration of Australia's economy into the global system were increasingly influenced by a set of ideas influenced by neoliberal rationality, seeking efficiency gains in all areas of public policy.[22] Extensive economic liberalisation since the 1980s was supported by bipartisan consensus and advanced strategies such as the corporatisation and privatisation of state enterprises and functions, deregulation of capital and financial markets, reduction of tariffs and other trade barriers and reduction of business taxation.[23] This has been accompanied by labour-market deregulation and a move away from centralised wage determination and employment protection since the 1990s and a growth in 'casual' (non-standard jobs).[24] As the Australian economy has moved from agriculture and manufacturing towards services (including financial and professional services) and economic activity has become more globalised, the desire has grown for already educated and work-ready (and thus 'cost-free') migrants in sectors of the knowledge economy (and, later, mining).[25]

Post-war population growth in Australia was helped not only by immigration but also by the short-lived 'baby boom', which contributed to the labour-force expansion for some decades.[26] Since then, demand for further immigration has been underpinned by low birth rates, which fell below replacement level in the 1970s and have stayed low ever since.[27] As discussed in Chapter 2, the transition to below-replacement rates is causally complex and is linked to economic, social and cultural dynamics, including women's increasing education and participation in the formal economy.[28] Though the male breadwinner model with the 'family wage' was finally abandoned in the 1970s and women's involvement in paid work has steadily increased, the continuing legacy of women's caregiving duties has disproportionately channelled women into part-time work.[29] Women have also been overrepresented in thinly

---

[22] Beeson and Firth, 'Neoliberalism'.
[23] Collins, 'The changing political economy'; Whiteford, 'Australia'. See also Bell, 'Globalisation, neoliberalism', who argues these policy choices were driven by not only economic internationalisation but also domestic policy choices.
[24] Campbell and Brosnan, 'Labour market deregulation'; Whiteford, 'Australia'.
[25] Walsh, 'Quantifying citizens'. [26] Temple and McDonald, 'Is demography destiny?'.
[27] In 2014, Australia's TFR was 1.80 (see Chapter 2).
[28] For statistics on women's labour force participation, which has increased to about 65 per cent (compared to the male rate, which has declined to 78 per cent), see Australian Bureau of Statistics, 'Gender indicators'. See also Campbell et al., 'Australia'.
[29] Over 40 per cent of women work part-time (compared to little over 1 in 10 men). Australian Bureau of Statistics, 'Gender indicators'. Vosko, *Managing the Margins*, ch. 3, notes that part-time permanent work is a particularly undeveloped sector in Australia, reflecting the slow adjustment to women being in the labour market.

regulated 'casual' jobs, with little employment security.[30] Together with growing life expectancy, decades of low birth rates have gradually resulted in smaller generations entering the workforce, which, as many government reports have pointed out, raises the prospect of a shrinking labour force and tax base at a time when increases in social expenditure are required, with the baby boomers reaching retirement age (and women's workforce participation making them less available for unpaid care).[31] As Temple and McDonald noted in 2008, the Australian labour force grew from 6.5 million in 1980 to 10.3 million in 2005 largely because of a combination of baby-boomer participation, women's increased workforce participation and immigration, and the first two of those growth reasons will disappear in the future.[32] Women's higher work participation will, without serious investment in care services, further exacerbate the care deficit, regarding both children and old people.[33] These demographic processes, which have been gradually unfolding over decades, have made immigration loom even larger as a vital component of policy seeking to address proportionate declines of people in paid employment.[34]

However, awareness of the importance of immigration has been accompanied by increasing demographic anxieties, evident in the rise of nativist and ethno-nationalist sentiments in the last few decades. Though 'immigration has always been a political issue' in Australia,[35] this resurgence of unease has been linked not only to the increase in global mobility (including Asian immigration) and related cultural anxieties since the 1970s (see Chapter 3), but arguably also the economic outcomes of unskilled immigrants following significant expansion of family-migration channels in the 1970s and 1980s (these changes became controversial amid concerns over unemployment and welfare dependency).[36] McNevin has also argued that anxiety about immigration was linked to the strategy of economic liberalisation, which created increased economic uncertainty, especially among precariously placed citizens, such as those with fewer skills, who were displaced with the transition to a globalised skills-driven economy.[37]

[30] Campbell et al., 'Australia'.
[31] Commonwealth of Australia, 'Intergenerational report 2002–03'.
[32] Temple and McDonald, 'Is demography destiny?'.
[33] This is both because it means fewer women will be available to do unpaid care and because more care will be needed for the large elderly age groups (see further Chapter 5).
[34] Markus et al., *Australia's Immigration Revolution*, ch. 2.   [35] Castles et al., 'Australia', 144.
[36] Birrell, 'The chains that bind'; Evans, 'Welfare dependency'.
[37] McNevin, 'The liberal paradox', *Contesting Citizenship*, ch. 3.

As discussed in Chapter 3, in this climate of economic insecurity, multicultural initiatives thus came under attack from the 1980s onwards, and the insecurities about some immigrant-citizens, especially those coming in as family members, continued to fuel debates about the consequences of diversifying immigration.[38] The arrival of small numbers (at least in relative terms) of refugees and migrants by boat from Asia in the early 1990s further raised suspicions about Australia's ability to control immigration flows in a new era of global mobility, and also reminded Australia of its fears of invasion from the north and prompted the introduction of mandatory detention of asylum-seekers arriving by boat.[39] Finally, in addition to social and cultural effects of immigration, increasing concerns over environmental issues and the fragility of Australia's ecosystem have prompted debate about population growth and its impact on the environment.[40] Together, these factors have challenged previous political agreements about the benefits of population growth and immigration.

Australian immigration policy has always been based on 'rational calculations of what the migrant might bring to the Australian state, rather than what the Australian state might offer to the migrant'.[41] These calculations have become more complex and contested in the last few decades. As Hugo wrote in the mid-1990s, public debates on immigration started to become 'increasingly polarised': 'no longer is there a widespread belief that immigration is in Australia's national interest'.[42] In a sense, this is part of a wider well-established tendency among contemporary states towards greater transnational openness in the economic arena, alongside growing pressure for domestic political closure.[43] Australia, though a country built on subsequent waves of immigration, has never been immune from the urge to exclude undesirable immigrants, whether it be on grounds related to race, health or social desirability.[44] These tendencies have resurfaced: immigration

---

[38] See e.g. Jupp, *From White Australia*, ch. 6. See also Chapter 3.
[39] Jupp, *From White Australia*, ch. 10.
[40] Commonwealth Scientific and Industrial Research Organisation (CSIRO), 'Future dilemmas'; Lowe, *Bigger or Better?*. See Jupp, *From White Australia*, ch. 9.
[41] Mares, 'Fear and instrumentalism', 410.   [42] Hugo, 'Introduction', 3.
[43] Hollifield, 'The emerging migration state'.
[44] See e.g. Jupp, *From White Australia*, 138, who points out that in 1901 anyone likely to 'become a charge upon the public or upon any public or charitable institution' was denied entry. Today, most applicants for a temporary or permanent visa to enter Australia are required to fulfil the migration Health Requirements (Migration Regulations 1994) and, where their disease or condition would result in significant cost, their application can be denied. After a 2012 review, the government decided to maintain this exemption from the Disability Discrimination Act

policy, increasingly contested, has started to lack a coherent vision and ambivalence has set in just as the demographic decline and continuing below-replacement birth rates (which became a focus of attention again in the 1990s; see Chapter 2), consequent ageing and fiscal pressures, economic demand for skilled workers, self-perpetuating nature of migration and significant levels of emigration (a challenge for a country of immigration[45]) have all pointed firmly towards the prospect of further immigration. With a population of over 23 million, bringing in new citizens to contribute to nation-building no longer provides a rationale for immigration, and while (im)migration is seen as the answer to both workforce shortages and the prospect of population decline, many more factors have entered the equation: in addition to assessing increasingly complex economic needs and risks, this involves questions about integration, security, national reproduction, cultural belonging, urbanisation and effects on the environment.

Quality or Quantity, Immigrants or Migrants?

In the last 20 years, a paradigm shift has taken place in Australia's immigration governance and, more broadly, in the role non-citizens play in the Australian economy and society. The conservative Howard coalition government (1996–2007) was in charge for much of this period, coming into power at the height of resurging scepticism about immigration (Chapter 3). In this period, economic criteria were conclusively established as primary conditions for entry. The approach adopted was based on the refining and maximising of an 'economically rationalist' approach to immigration in the service of the economy. On the one hand, this has involved the management of public anxiety over a changing population, but on the other, the government has maintained significant immigration flows, both in the shape of the permanent intake and, more importantly, by expanding more temporary forms of migration.[46] The permanent intake has fluctuated in the last 20 years, according to economic circumstances, from a low

---

1992, which means, for instance, that families with children who have Down syndrome can be barred from permanent residence, as Down syndrome can be considered a drain on the nation's resources.

[45] On the concerns that Australia is losing skilled workers to other nations because of increasing emigration since the 1990s, see Birrell et al., 'Skilled labour'; Hugo et al., 'Emigration from Australia'.

[46] On economic rationalism in Australia's immigration policy, see Jupp, *From White Australia*, ch. 8.

of 62 800 in 1993–94 to a high of 190 000 in 2013–14.[47] Following moves towards the prioritisation of skilled and business migration in the 1980s,[48] the emphasis on the skills component of the migration programme has intensified since the 1990s, with limitations on both family and humanitarian entrants, who are (seen as) less likely to possess desirable human capital.[49] Family-migration channels were narrowed in the 1990s.[50] The point-based system has been sharpened amid concerns about labour-market integration, with a further emphasis on language proficiency and qualifications.[51] Human-capital criteria and successful labour-market outcomes have become primary considerations in a pragmatic move that makes it easier to justify immigration to a skeptical public. About two-thirds of the permanent intake is now under the skilled stream.[52] Just as women dominated the family stream in the past, men tend to dominate as primary skilled migrants (and though significant numbers of women do enter as skilled migrants, men are more likely to come with families). Skilled immigrants also have a younger age profile than the Australian population, with emphasis on those in their 20s and 30s.[53]

The newly elected Howard government also presided over a fundamental shift from permanent to more temporary migration. This change is underpinned by changing ideas of national economic interest, reflecting broader trends in economic structures, especially the decline of manufacturing, the growth of the knowledge and service industries and economic openness. Based on a government inquiry (under the previous Labor government), the influential Roach report in 1995 recommended simplifying immigration procedures to allow key business

---

[47] For a historical overview of immigration numbers since federation, see Phillips et al., 'Migration to Australia'. For the 2013–14 figures, see Department of Immigration and Border Protection, '2014–15 migration programme report'.

[48] Mares, 'Fear and instrumentalism', 416.

[49] Though note that many of those who enter under the skilled category are actually family members (not screened in terms of skill, though some extra points are given for spouses' qualifications). On family migration, see Khoo et al., 'Contribution of family migration'; McDonald, 'The role of family migration'.

[50] Freeman and Birrell, 'Divergent paths'. Migration rights of siblings were removed and those of parents much restricted; an attempt to put a cap on spouse visas failed, however. See further Betts, 'Immigration policy'; Birrell, 'Immigration reform'.

[51] See e.g. Freeman and Birrell, 'Divergent paths'; Hawthorne, 'Picking winners'.

[52] In 2014–15, the size of the family stream was 61 085 and the skill stream 127 774. Department of Immigration and Border Protection, '2014–15 migration programme report'.

[53] Australian Bureau of Statistics, 'Perspectives on migrants'. The skilled programme has an age limit of 45. Note that youth is now also a characteristic of much family migration, which is largely limited to spouses and children (Khoo et al., 'Contribution of family migration'). On the migration of parents, see further Chapter 5.

personnel to be more easily brought in for temporary stays.[54] The Howard government implemented this recommendation in 1996 in the form of so-called '457 visas',[55] introduced to allow businesses to react quickly to skill shortages at times of economic growth. Though the 'reforms raised barely a ripple in the popular press' at the time,[56] they have turned out to signify an important break with Australia's past, delegating immigrant selection to employers. Demand-driven, 457 visas largely deregulated immigration control, allowing employers to sponsor skilled workers to fill a vacancy which could not be filled locally.[57] Workers with 457 visas can stay in Australia for up to four years (and enter and leave the country as often as they wish); they can also be joined by their spouses and children.[58] 457 visa holders are eligible to apply for permanent residence, though they are not guaranteed to obtain that status.[59] Contrary to the Roach report's intention that 457 visas would be a temporary stopgap until local training to meet skills shortages could catch up, they have become an enduring and popular migration route. Hundreds of thousands of workers have been sponsored; there was a slight dip during the onset of the financial crisis, but a new record was reached in 2011–12, when there were 125 070 grants (nearly half of whom were dependants).[60]

Even if the 457 visa system is not a pure guest-worker scheme, similar concerns have been expressed regarding it to those often voiced about other temporary-migration schemes.[61] Though surveys have found relatively high levels of satisfaction among migrants on

---

[54] Committee of Inquiry into the Temporary Entry of Business People and Highly Skilled Specialists, 'Business temporary entry'.
[55] The 457 visa program (Temporary Business (Long Stay) (Subclass 457)), now the Temporary Work (Skilled) (Subclass 457) visa program.
[56] Crock, 'Contract or compact', 57.
[57] The occupation has to be on the Australian government's Consolidated Shortage Occupation List (CSOL).
[58] Under the secondary sponsored subclass 457 visa, family members also have work rights. 457 visa holders are excluded from unemployment benefits and public health insurance.
[59] The permanent intake is capped and revised yearly (for 2014–15, it was set at 190 000 places). A significant number of permanent visas are given to individuals who have previously held a temporary visa. For instance, in 2011–12, 79 287 permanent skilled and family visas were granted to migrants in Australia, of which 40 485 went to people who had previously held a 457 visa.
[60] See Department of Immigration and Citizenship, 'Annual report 2011–12'.
[61] Most prominently, that they are discriminatory and deny migrant workers' rights, but also that they are difficult to implement and often have unintended effects. See Castles, 'Guestworkers in Europe'; Dauvergne and Marsden, 'The ideology of temporary labour'; Ruhs, 'The potential of temporary migration'; Ruhs and Martin, 'Numbers vs. rights'.

AUSTRALIA: WELCOME AND WANTED (CONDITIONS APPLY)

457 visas,[62] claims have been made from the beginning (and are still frequently made) that the system, which creates much space for employers to determine whether there is a skill shortage and how important migrant workers are for their business, is being abused by employers who are paying migrants low wages to undercut local workers and fraudulently using 457 visas to fill positions that are in fact unskilled. Indeed, studies have found that some workers on 457 visas are unaware of their entitlements, experiencing exploitation (e.g. being underpaid or unable to access labour protections).[63] Situations of vulnerability are linked to the requirement that migrant workers on 457 visas work for the designated employer; though in theory migrants can change employers to avoid exploitation by someone unscrupulous, they only have a short time (28 days, until 2013) to find a new employer before risking removal. Exploitative practices particularly affect workers in non-unionised sectors (often with few non-migrants), with limited English and with little familiarity with workplace regulations.[64] Workers wishing to become permanent residents (and thus often dependent on their employer as a sponsor for permanent migration[65]) also face precariousness because the system empowers employers to decide their future fate.[66] In light of many concerns expressed about the 457 programme and its huge growth, the Labor government (2007–13) reviewed the programme and enacted some reforms – for instance, a 'no-less-favourable requirement' was introduced regarding terms and conditions; the enforcement regime was tightened; and the period during which a migrant can change employers was lifted to 90 days.[67]

---

[62] Migration Council Australia, 'More than temporary'.
[63] Toh and Quinlan, 'Safeguarding the global'. See also the cases discussed in Howe, 'The Migration Legislation Amendment'.
[64] For an illustrative discussion of Indian 457 visa holders' experiences, which differ markedly by such factors as employment sector, see Velayutham, 'Precarious experiences'.
[65] In order to become a permanent resident, a 457 visa holder must enter one of the streams of the permanent migration programme – and the most accessible of these is the Employer Nomination Scheme.
[66] See Boese et al., 'Temporary migrant nurses', for a discussion regarding nurses' experiences of precariousness.
[67] On the recent reforms, see Howe, 'Is the net cast'. See also Campbell and Tham, 'Labour market deregulation'. Concerns over the exploitation of skilled workers on 457 visas are also addressed by the new offence of forced labour (the Crimes Legislation Amendment (Slavery, Slavery-like Conditions and People Trafficking) Act). Even with these steps towards re-regulation, arguably the vulnerability of temporary migrants cannot be comprehensively addressed without changing the nature of the scheme, as ultimately the right to exclude temporary migrants undermines their position, and the fundamental inequity of the system is thus inbuilt and purposeful. See Dauvergne and Marsden, 'The ideology of temporary labour'.

The other aspect of the 457 visa which has been controversial is its effect on citizens and permanent residents. The Roach report emphasised that the new visa was not to be used for 'overcoming long-term labour market deficiencies which should be resolved by domestic training arrangements'.[68] Nor were the new arrangements meant 'to apply to the traditional skilled trades or to professions like nursing and teaching', and they should not 'provide an avenue for the recruitment of unskilled and semi-skilled workers, or the channelling of overseas workers into low paid and low skilled work'.[69] However, concerns have been expressed for some time about the 457 visa's adverse impacts in trade occupations.[70] Though employers are required to demonstrate their contribution to the training of Australian workers (by providing evidence of meeting training benchmarks), for much of the time there has been no need for employers to show they have actually looked for domestic workers.[71] This is in a context where the vulnerability of the temporary migrant is mirrored by the situation of the most vulnerable Australians, especially those with fewer skills: to increase labour-market flexibility, successive governments have eroded workplace rights since the early 1990s.[72] The vast majority of new jobs created in Australia during the 1990s were for 'casual' (non-standard) workers, disproportionately involving less advantaged workers, such as young people under the age of 25 or women caring for their children or parents.[73] The Labor government (2007–13) made some reforms to 457 visas, just as it slightly wound back some of the previous government's labour-market deregulation.[74] For instance, approval of nominations was tied to a labour market-testing requirement, requiring evidence of a lack

---

[68] Committee of Inquiry into the Temporary Entry of Business People and Highly Skilled Specialists, 'Business temporary entry', 4.
[69] Committee of Inquiry into the Temporary Entry of Business People and Highly Skilled Specialists, 'Business temporary entry', 4.
[70] Kinnaird, 'Current issues'; Toner and Woolley, 'Temporary migration'.
[71] When the programme was enacted in 1996, the scheme did impose a (rather weak) labour market-testing condition, but this requirement was abolished in 2001. For a discussion of the evolution of the programme, see Campbell and Tham, 'Labour market deregulation'; Howe, 'The Migration Legislation Amendment'.
[72] This trend started under the Labor government – see Campbell and Brosnan, 'Labour market deregulation' – but the greatest changes to the industrial relations were made by the Howard government. On the unpopular 2005 Work Choices legislation, see Hall, 'Australian industrial relations', 'First year'. See also Woodward, 'WorkChoices and Howard's defeat'.
[73] See e.g. Burgess and Campbell, 'Casual employment'; Campbell, 'The rise in precarious employment'; Watson, 'Re-assessing'; Watson et al., *Fragmented Futures*. On the persistence of casualisation, see Watson, 'Bridges or traps?'.
[74] On the Fair Work Act 2009 (the successor to Work Choices), see Barnes and Lafferty, 'The Fair Work Act'.

of local workers (many skilled occupations are still exempt, however). Campbell and Tham have argued that these changes amount to a 'partial re-regulation'.[75] In 2015, the conservative coalition government announced a minor changes scheme, which aimed to 'reduce regulation at the same time as it strengthens the integrity'.[76]

While public debate on temporary migration has focused on the 457 visa system, it is part of a far larger trend of temporary migration in Australia. The total number of 457 visa holders currently in Australia is now roughly equal to the annual intake under the permanent migration programme, but this is only a fraction of the over 1 million temporary migrants residing in Australia at any one time.[77] The majority of these other temporary migrants are, apart from New Zealanders,[78] people on working holidaymaker visas and student visas, though there is also now a small proper temporary migration scheme for seasonal agricultural work from the Pacific, which provides no avenues for permanent residence.[79] Because working-holidaymaker visas and student visas are usually associated with tourism and international education, respectively, their significance as forms of labour migration has largely been hidden from public view and is often underplayed (unlike 457 visas, they do not require employer sponsorship or specific skills). Working holidaymakers participate in the labour market in a range of low-skilled jobs, from hospitality to seasonal agricultural work, meeting the demand for flexible workers; a significant number are paid under the national minimum wage.[80] A significant number of international students (embraced by Australian universities to make up for gaps in government funding) also work in unskilled part-time jobs.[81] From

---

[75] Campbell and Tham, 'Labour market deregulation'.
[76] ABC, 'Federal Government announces changes to 457 skilled visa program after review into rorts and abuse', 18 March 2015.
[77] Mares, 'Temporary migration'.
[78] New Zealanders have the right to enter Australia on the basis of a longstanding reciprocal agreement (the 1973 Trans-Tasman Travel Arrangement), but they are no longer automatically treated as de facto permanent residents. On this and its consequences, see Mares, 'Temporary migration'.
[79] On the pilot scheme that trialled temporary visas for seasonal agricultural work, see Reilly, 'The ethics'. On the current arrangement, which is not very popular, thanks to the use of working holidaymakers, unauthorised residents and travellers working without authorisation, see Doyle and Howes, 'Australia's seasonal worker program'; Hay and Howes, 'Australia's Pacific seasonal'.
[80] Tan and Lester, 'Labour market and economic impacts'. See also Mares, 'Temporary migration', 28–9.
[81] There were 339 454 student visa holders in Australia as of 30 June 2014. Department of Immigration and Border Protection, 'Student visa'. Students are allowed to work 40 hours per fortnight during semesters and unlimited hours during scheduled course breaks.

early 2013, international students who have completed at minimum a bachelor's-level qualification are also eligible for a two- to four-year post-study work visa, depending on their level of qualification (485 post-study work visa). As post-study work rights have become an important factor in international students' choice of study destination, this allows Australia to maintain its education export market, as well as to use international students as a reserve semi-permanent labour force.[82] At the same time, international students constitute an in many ways vulnerable workforce, often working in low-status occupations on a casual basis.[83]

Taken together, these forms of temporary migration constitute a major shift away from a permanent skilled migration programme that was built on newcomers entering as future citizens.[84] The temporary workforce is in many cases 'long-term temporary', as migrants can remain on a series of temporary visas for years.[85] This shift signals that Australia welcomes quality entrants on a temporary basis, requiring economic fit as a precondition for permanence.[86] While about half of all 457 holders become permanent residents (transferring into the permanent-residence channel, which is already clogged because of the yearly limits[87]), the other half provide labour-market flexibility and are expected to leave when they are no longer desired. As temporary visas have become a stepping stone to permanent residence, Australia is effectively moving towards a 'two-step' migration programme, where even skilled migrants have to earn their place and to be tried and tested by private employers before inclusion.[88] Indeed, the final step, citizenship, is now also more difficult: the residency requirement has been extended to four years (one of which needs to be as a permanent resident), and a citizenship test was introduced in 2007.[89] These

---

[82] On international students' employment prospects, see Hawthorne and To, 'Australian employer response'.
[83] On the vulnerability of international students as workers, see Nyland et al., 'International student-workers'.
[84] Castles et al., 'Rethinking migration'; Collins, 'Rethinking Australian immigration'; Mares, 'Temporary migration'; Markus et al., *Australia's Immigration Revolution*.
[85] Mares, 'Temporary migration'.
[86] On the role of discrimination in hindering migrants' labour-market integration, see e.g. Hawthorne, 'The question of discrimination'.
[87] Permanent residence is much sought after by migrants from developing countries seeking security. See Khoo et al., 'Which skilled temporary migrants'.
[88] Mares, 'The permanent shift', 69. On the problems skilled migrants face in being incorporated into the Australian labour market, see Birrell and Healy, 'How are skilled migrants'.
[89] See the Australian Citizenship Amendment (Citizenship Testing) Act 2007. The test, introduced to ensure applicants possess an adequate knowledge of Australia, comprises 20 randomly selected multiple-choice questions.

changes – though lenient compared to the citizenship policies of some European states – are part of a restrictive turn, as discussed in Chapter 3.[90] While seeking to respond to public concerns about the extent to which immigrants are developing a feeling of belonging, such efforts could be counter-productive, as with increased temporariness, the issues around belonging may well be exacerbated.[91] Moreover, the assumption that all entrants move towards permanent residence and ultimately citizenship no longer holds. At one end, many vulnerable migrants on temporary visas never make it to permanent residence, and at the other, retention has emerged as an issue, especially among the highly skilled, who have many migration opportunities and do not necessarily want to make Australia home[92] (as Shachar and Hirschl have argued, many of these are the 'super talent' that all states want to attract and retain, but who may not be looking to become citizens).[93]

All of these trends in managing migrant selection are also underpinned by complex gendered dynamics. The shift towards skilled migration (as opposed to family migration) – and temporary migration, at that – is ostensibly neutral, but in fact skills requirements often benefit men (who are, due to global inequalities, more likely to have (better) education or sought-after attributes and skills, such as IT and science qualifications).[94] What counts as a skill, of course, is socially constructed (for instance, caregiving does not count, and the Australian selection system pays little attention to part-time work, which is female-dominated).[95] Family migrants are more often women (wives), and even skilled female migrants are constructed as dependent by immigration law, which categorises one spouse as a primary migrant, the other as a trailing spouse.[96] It could thus be argued that the 'skills turn' and temporariness reinforce existing gender imbalances and encourage men to migrate, with 'trailing spouses' focused more on childrearing than work. The picture is more complex than this, however, in that in feminised professions like nursing, women are often primary migrants, and thanks to women's globally rising education levels and associations

---

[90] See e.g. Joppke, 'Through the European looking glass'; Levey, 'Liberal nationalism'.
[91] Castles et al., 'The internal dynamic', 34–5, 'Australia', 146.
[92] Khoo et al., 'Which skilled temporary migrants'.
[93] Shachar and Hirschl, 'Recruiting "super talent"'. See also Shachar and Hirschl, 'On citizenship'.
[94] Boucher, 'Skill, migration and gender'.
[95] On gendered paths in skilled migration and why women's skills get wasted in migrant selection, see Iredale, 'Patterns of spouse'. See also Kofman, 'Towards a gendered evaluation'.
[96] Boucher, 'Skill, migration and gender'; Dauvergne, 'Gendering permanent residency'.

with the female caring professions, women's roles as primary migrants are increasing.[97] The employment of migrant women is in turn connected to their reproductive roles (Chapter 2). Overall, and especially in the context of the shift from permanent towards temporary migration, the focus on skill often means men enter as primary migrants even when they have skilled spouses.[98] Furthermore, evidence shows migrant wives, even where skilled, often make labour-market sacrifices in order to help the family settle. Even when female migrants come from a strong tradition of paid work, immigration may widen the gender gap, as women subordinate their careers to facilitate family resettlement, assimilating to gendered practices in Australia, where despite the growth in women's employment participation,[99] women's enduring responsibility for the domestic sphere means they leave work or only work part-time (often on a casual basis) when they have young children.[100] The conservative Howard government's work/family reconciliation policies were criticised in particular for actively seeking to discourage the labour-force participation of mothers (with the important exception of sole parents), reflecting the government's ideological ambivalence about whether to support women as home-based childbearer–carers, wage earners or both.[101]

Finally, this turn towards justifying immigrant selection on the basis of economic criteria (while masking low-skilled migration) also explains, in part, Australia's draconian asylum policy, which stands in marked contrast to the country's openness to other forms of migration. Rules that create legal avenues for certain forms of migration are, of course, simultaneously also constraining migration. The focus on raising the skill base of the 'post-industrial' knowledge economy has made it virtually impossible for unskilled or semi-skilled individuals to gain legal entry to Australia for the purposes of work, leaving entry as refugees or family members as the only alternatives.[102] Thanks

[97] For elaboration, see Kofman and Raghuram, 'Gender and global labour'.
[98] Over 70 per cent of primary migrants on 457 visas were male in March 2015. See Department of Immigration and Border Protection, 'Subclass 457 visa holders'.
[99] Borland, 'Labour market and industrial relations'.
[100] On Chinese women, see Ho, 'Migration as feminisation?'. On Malaysian women, see Joseph, '(Re)negotiating cultural and work'. See also Lee and Kim, 'The dynamics of migration', for further analysis of the differences between women according to their country of origin. See McDonald, 'The role of family migration', for a broad discussion of gendered outcomes.
[101] Brennan, 'Babies, budgets, and birthrates'. As discussed in Chapter 2, this is the dilemma of the second demographic transition all advanced societies are grappling with in terms of persistently low birth rates.
[102] These are, of course, the people that sending countries are often most keen to export, while wishing to hold on to their more highly skilled population.

to Australia's geographically isolated location, it has been less affected by irregular migration than European states or the United States, but asylum-seekers arriving by boat have nonetheless been demonised as undesirable migrants. McNevin has argued that Australia's policies on asylum-seekers – inspired by the One Nation party,[103] but subsequently embraced by both major parties – are designed to placate less-skilled and less-wealthy citizens, who were made vulnerable by Australia's trajectory of economic liberalisation, which involved, as already mentioned, casualisation, income inequality and a thinner safety net of social rights.[104] Governments familiar with popular anxieties over immigration know they must be seen to be in control of selecting those who are best for Australia (the highly skilled) and keeping out those who are not (supposedly economically draining and culturally problematic asylum-seekers, or indeed anyone not carefully selected based on economic criteria). Wright has recently argued that the Howard government's carefully cultivated image of being in control gave it political capital that helped it justify taking huge numbers of migrants even in the face of a public backlash against the changing nature of the Australian population.[105] The increasing prominence of immigration (including in the 2010 federal election campaign) shows, however, that this strategy has limits.[106]

VARIATIONS ON A THEME? BRITISH, ITALIAN AND FINNISH TRAJECTORIES

This section outlines the other three jurisdictions' efforts at dealing with declines in the number of working-age people by accepting labour migration, often using countries such as Australia as models for managing migration to their advantage. The other three states face similar demographic realities, owing to demographic processes which have been in motion for some time. As the baby-boom generations move towards retirement, the pressures of population ageing are becoming evident. The fall in fertility rates over the last 40 years and significant rises in life expectancy mean the median ages of the populations in all three jurisdictions are rising, and dependency ratios with them.

[103] On the legacy of One Nation, see Jupp, *From White Australia*, ch. 7.
[104] McNevin, 'The liberal paradox', *Contesting Citizenship*.
[105] Wright, 'How do states'. See also Betts, 'Cosmopolitans and patriots', who argued a decade ago that the tough response to boat people may also have contributed to more favourable attitudes towards immigration.
[106] Mares, 'Fear and instrumentalism', 410.

Unlike Australia, none of the other three countries considers itself as built on immigration, and their relationship with letting in – let alone attracting (and retaining) – immigrants is thus more complex. The United Kingdom's colonial legacy means it approaches immigration with ambivalence, while Italy and Finland have only recently had to face larger-scale immigration, and both are struggling to attract the kinds of migrant they would most like to welcome as new citizens. All three countries are, moreover, Member States of the European Union, meaning their obligations under EU free-movement law further complicate their attempts at emulating countries free of these limitations.[107] This section examines how the growing need to find solutions to demographic ageing (especially the contracting labour market) in these jurisdictions reflects on their attempts to use immigration to ease the issues created by demographic change. All of them have experienced a significant loss of jobs in manufacturing in favour of the services sector, and the ongoing economic and social transformations involved in technological change mean they are seeking to manage the challenge of continuing immigration in the face of growing hostility towards (some) immigrants by actively soliciting some migrants while actively discouraging others.

The United Kingdom, like many other European states, has often been classed as being sceptical of immigration: after clamping down on post-war colonial labour immigration in the 1960s,[108] UK governments from the 1970s to the 1990s sought, with great success, to stem labour immigration flows from former non-white colonies, to the extent that in the late 1990s the United Kingdom could be characterised as a 'zero-immigration country' (though family migration continued, as discussed in Chapter 3).[109] However, in what has been called 'an unprecedented policy reversal',[110] the United Kingdom

---

[107] Freedom of movement for workers (and other economic actors) is a fundamental principle of EU law, guaranteed by the Treaty on the Functioning of the European Union. On the one hand, it allows member states to attract needed workers from other member states; on the other, it makes it difficult for member states to prevent unwanted migrants from entering or to force them to leave when desired.

[108] This migration, largely low-skilled, stemmed from the Empire's colonial legacy and was economically driven by post-war rebuilding, but it was essentially unwanted. See e.g. Hampshire, *Citizenship and Belonging*. On the limitations adopted in immigration and citizenship law since the 1960s, see Cerna and Wietholtz, 'The case of the United Kingdom'; Joppke, *Immigration and the Nation-State*, ch. 4; Sawyer and Wray, 'Country report: United Kingdom'. On family migration in the UK context, see Chapter 3.

[109] Joppke, *Immigration and the Nation-State*, 100.   [110] Hansen, 'Great Britain', 199.

then significantly relaxed its labour immigration controls.[111] The election of the New Labour government in 1997 began an era of significant immigration, which has continued, albeit with renewed efforts to turn the clock back, under the coalition government (2010–15) and now under the culminating in the Brexit referendum.[112] The Labour government, committed to economic openness, saw selective immigration as a way to meet skill demand (not yet met by domestic training) and enhance the country's human capital and global competitiveness.[113] Underpinning these, as Betts points out, was also the demographic reality of an ageing population.[114] In order to make the United Kingdom able to compete for 'the brightest and the best',[115] immigration policy changes were made with the strong backing of the Treasury.[116] As part of the 'managed migration',[117] the government initially significantly relaxed the rules of the work-permit system, dropping the requirement to recruit locally; allowed international students to work (and subsequently also to get work permits on graduation);[118] and made changes to the seasonal-worker scheme and the working-holidaymaker scheme.[119] For skilled migrants from outside the European Union, a points-based system (modelled in large part on Australia's) was eventually developed to restore public trust in immigration management.[120] This system had five tiers, with Tiers 1 and 2 aiming to attract and keep those considered skilled and highly skilled.[121] As in Australia, skilled migration to the United Kingdom shows

---

[111] For a historical overview of UK immigration policy, including this change, see Wright, 'Policy legacies'. Though Labour's explicit embracing of immigration represents a break, Spencer, 'Immigration', notes that the previous Conservative government had already (with little fanfare) increased labour migration, e.g. into the health sector and parts of the private sector.
[112] For a discussion of the immigration policies of Labour governments since 1997, see Somerville, *Immigration under New Labour*.
[113] Hansen, 'Great Britain'; Layton-Henry, 'Britain'; Somerville, *Immigration under New Labour*; Wright, 'Policy legacies'.
[114] Betts, 'Commentary', 222. See also Layton-Henry, 'Britain', 299.
[115] As put by Minister for Immigration Barbara Roche. BBC, 'Call for immigration rethink', 12 September 2000.
[116] Hansen, 'Great Britain'. On other causal factors, see Consterdine and Hampshire, 'Immigration policy'. See also Somerville, *Immigration under New Labour*.
[117] For an example of rhetoric on how immigration needs to be 'managed', see e.g. Home Office, 'Secure borders, safe haven'.
[118] Significant numbers of foreign students have come to study at British universities since 1999.
[119] Hansen, 'Great Britain', 202.
[120] On the points system, see Somerville, 'The politics and policy'. For context, see Anderson, *Us and Them?*, ch. 3.
[121] Tier 1 was aimed at the highly skilled, Tier 2 at skilled workers with a job offer, Tier 3 at low-skill workers (never opened because of EU enlargement), Tier 4 at students and Tier 5 at youth mobility and temporary workers.

gendered patterns, evident especially in the medical sector, which is highly dependent on skilled migrants.[122]

While the points-based system was very much focused on skilled immigration, considered justifiable in terms of its economic benefits, unskilled channels were also significantly expanded, most importantly through the decision to immediately open the UK labour market when the European Union expanded in 2004.[123] This openness to workers from the accession countries resulted in over 200 000 Central and Eastern Europeans registering each year to work over the subsequent two years, meeting demand for lower-skilled migrants in low-paid jobs in sectors such as food processing, agriculture and construction.[124] Much greater levels of EU migration than were expected have continued, and though the numbers dipped during the economic crisis, net migration of EU citizens more than doubled from 72 000 in the year ending June 2010 to 162 000 in the year ending September 2014.[125] Moves towards openness were justified in terms of avoiding migrants resorting to irregular migration alternatives.[126] At the same time, as in Australia, the government sought to maintain a distinction between wanted and unwanted migration. Asylum-seekers were readily identified as a major category of 'unwanted',[127] and many high-profile restrictions were introduced to deal with public pressure to clamp down on those seeking asylum.[128] Failed asylum-seekers, like others with irregular migration status (such as visa over-stayers), are a feature of the UK labour immigration picture: though officially denounced, they fill positions at the bottom of the labour-market hierarchy that are unattractive to others.[129] While they are particularly vulnerable to exploitation, they are merely the end of the spectrum of various categories of migrants and ethnic minorities working in the low-paid and often deregulated

---

[122] Kofman, 'Towards a gendered evaluation'; Raghuram, 'The difference that skills make'.
[123] The United Kingdom had been bound by the European rules on the free movement of labour since it joined the EEC in 1973. In the run-up to Eastern European states joining, member states were given discretion (for up to seven years) as to whether to restrict or postpone the free-movement rights of workers from the so-called 'A8' states, the largest and most significant of which was Poland. The United Kingdom, unlike most member states, allowed free movement (the only requirement was that the workers had to register with the Worker Registration Scheme).
[124] Spencer, *The Migration Debate*, 91.
[125] Migration Observatory, 'Net migration'. [126] Spencer, 'Immigration'.
[127] Asylum applications rose to a historic high of 84 130 in 2002. For more figures, see Mulvey, 'Immigration under New Labour', 1478.
[128] See e.g. Hansen, 'Great Britain'; Mulvey, 'Immigration under New Labour'; Spencer, 'Immigration'.
[129] Jordan and Düvell, *Irregular Migration*; Schierup et al., *Migration, Citizenship*, ch. 5. On polarisation, see Goos and Manning, 'Lousy and lovely jobs'.

sectors of the flexible and increasingly polarised UK labour market.[130] A good example of how work categorised as demanding lower skills is gendered is migrant work in the care services sectors: these sectors rely on migrant women to make up for the gap created by British women's increasing participation in the labour market,[131] which makes them less available to provide care for an ageing population.[132]

While immigration was not initially politically important, by 2005 it had become relevant, despite (Australian-style) attempts to demonstrate control over selection via draconian treatment of the unwanted, largely because of the influx of EU citizens from Central and Eastern Europe.[133] The recession has accentuated concerns about economic immigration and whether it is 'needed' or simply desired by some employers keen on low pay and flexibility.[134] After the 2010 election, the coalition government was under pressure to limit overall immigration, in line with the Conservative pledge to reduce net migration[135] from a level of over 250 000 per year to 'tens of thousands' by 2015.[136] Various restrictive measures were adopted: for instance, a cap was imposed on the number of skilled migrants (under Tier 2),[137] students' ability to switch into skilled work after graduation was limited and in family migration, the earnings threshold for the UK spouse was set at £18 600 (see Chapter 3). The government has also been keen to sharpen the rules for the eligibility of skilled migrants and to make settlement in the United Kingdom (and, by implication, acquisition of citizenship) more difficult.[138] However, the tens-of-thousands

---

[130] On Central and East European migrants in low-wage occupations, see e.g. Anderson et al., 'Fair enough?'. On the role of migration in the UK labour market, see Anderson, *Us and Them?*, ch. 4.

[131] On government policies to facilitate (largely women's) reconciliation of paid work and family, see Lewis and Campbell, 'UK work/family balance'.

[132] Cangiano et al. 'Migrant care workers'.

[133] Hansen, 'Great Britain'; Mulvey, 'Immigration under New Labour'; Somerville, 'The politics and policy'.

[134] The argument is that much of labour demand is constructed by the poor wages, conditions and social statuses of some occupations, such as construction and hospitality. See Ruhs and Anderson, *Who Needs Migrant Workers?*.

[135] Net migration is a crude measure, calculated by subtracting the number of people leaving the country from the number coming in. For a discussion, see Anderson, *Us and Them?*, ch. 3.

[136] Prime Minister David Cameron made the promise to return net migration to the levels of the 1990s, when it was 'tens of thousands per year', in 2010, and restated it in 2011. BBC, 'In full: David Cameron immigration speech', 14 November 2011.

[137] However, intra-company transfers (skilled workers moving to the United Kingdom within a multinational company) were not included in the cap. For a full discussion of the changes, see Gower, 'Immigration and asylum'.

[138] The coalition government introduced a new minimum salary requirement for most Tier 2 migrants applying for permanent settlement after April 2016 (£35 000 per annum).

pledge, which experts generally regarded as unachievable when it was announced (considering the government could not limit the movement of UK or EU citizens),[139] was abandoned in 2014 (figures show net migration to the United Kingdom rose to 260 000 in the year to June 2014). As the rise of the UK Independence Party (UKIP) and the surprise 2016 Brexit vote indicate, immigration and free movement are now firmly politicised, but as long as the United Kingdom remains in the European Union, the latter is difficult to curb.[140] The dilemma between the perceived political need to clamp down on migration and the economic desire for more migrants will not go away (and the demographic need in sectors like care work will continue – see Chapter 5). This means successive UK governments – including the current Conservative government – will continue to seek strategies to maintain an uneasy balance between the powerful forces driving for more migration and the public anxiety over its continuation.

In Italy, demographic needs due to population ageing and decline are particularly acute,[141] and labour immigrants are essential in that 'to keep the working age population (those ages 20–59) constant in Italy for the twenty-year period between 2007 and 2026 ... around 300 000 per year will be required'.[142] Indeed, because of these challenges, Italy has opened itself to an unprecedented degree to labour immigration over the last couple of decades and has become one of the main labour migrant-importing countries in Europe (this continues to the case despite the economic crisis, especially in the social care sector).[143] Migrant workers have helped to substantially reduce existing labour shortages, particularly in low- and medium-skilled occupations (sectors relying heavily on immigrant workers are domestic and caring services, agriculture, construction and small industries).[144] These are sectors of the stratified Italian labour market – divided into labour-market insiders with secure employment and outsiders with precarious employment – which are increasingly deserted by Italian workers, which explains why

---

[139] Migration Observatory, 'Commentary'.
[140] Geddes, 'The EU, UKIP'. The Cameron government's desire (and limited capacity) to rewrite EU free movement rules was, of course, one of the crucial factors in the referendum on the United Kingdom's EU membership.
[141] Italy's very low birth rates mean the population is now growing because of immigration. See Chapter 2.
[142] Perlmutter, 'Italy', 342.
[143] In 2013, Italy was estimated to have over 5.4 million migrants (about eight per cent of the total population); irregular migrants were estimated to constitute six per cent. Blangiardo and Cesareo, 'Foreign population in Italy', 12.
[144] OECD, 'Jobs for immigrants'; Sciortino, 'Fortunes and miseries'.

migrant workers have largely been seen as not being in competition with Italians.[145] The crucial role played by migrants in an ageing society is emphasised in the care and domestic work sectors: in the large and growing feminised family work sector, immigrant women fill the gap between the Italian state's failure to modernise welfare systems based on male breadwinner/female carer roles and women's rising participation in paid employment (as discussed in Chapter 2).[146] Migrant care work partly remedies the gender care gap, as many groups of migrant women are involved in domestic and care work (for instance, eighty per cent of Ukrainians in Italy are women),[147] which is also a more secure sector in terms of labour demand than, for instance, construction or manufacturing.[148]

In terms of governance, the most striking feature of this expansive trend is the extent to which most labour migrants have accessed Italy through the back door,[149] despite a system which has, since the 1990s, actually foreseen labour-migration inflows and tried to regulate the entry of migrant workers through a national planning programme.[150] In other words, Italian policies have acknowledged the existence of a large structural demand for foreign labour and, in theory, actively plan for immigration via yearly quotas.[151] In practice, the rigidities of the planning system and its 'conservative forecasts',[152] combined with easy access to Italy's shadow economy by irregular migrants,[153] have meant that most migrant workers enter, work or stay irregularly and subsequently legalise their status, often via misuse of the quota system or an ad hoc regularisation campaign.[154] Migrants integrate easily into the flexible and exploitable workforce of Italy's informal economy.[155]

[145] Massetti, 'Mainstream parties', 2. See also Campani et al., 'Labour market, migration'; Zanfrini, 'Immigration and labour market'.
[146] Sciortino, 'Immigration in a Mediterranean welfare state'.
[147] Zanfrini, 'Immigration and labour market'.
[148] Hence, it appears male migrants were harder hit by the economic crisis. OECD, 'Jobs for immigrants'. For discussion of this, see Farris, 'Migrants' regular army'.
[149] Note, however, that the scale and significance of irregularity, as well as arguments about continuing Italian exceptionalism in terms of inability to control immigration, can be exaggerated – for a recent discussion, see Colombo, *Fuori controllo?*; Sciortino, 'Commentary'.
[150] The current legislative framework is a consolidated text of legislative decree 286/1998 (as amended subsequently). Often referred to as the Turco-Napolitano law, the 1998 Act provided the first comprehensive framework for the management of immigration in Italy.
[151] These quotas represent annual ceilings and can be further divided into sub-quotas – often there is a very large sub-quota for domestic and care work. For further details, see Salis, 'Labour migration governance', pt 3.
[152] Ambrosini, 'Immigration in Italy', 177.   [153] Reyneri, 'Underground economy'.
[154] See e.g. Perlmutter, 'Italy'; Salis, 'Labour migration governance'; Sciortino, 'Fortunes and miseries'.
[155] Reyneri, 'Immigrants'.

Policy has oscillated between practical acceptance of immigrants, as long as they are useful for the national economy (and most foreigners in Italy do indeed have very high activity rates in the labour market), and harsh attempts to disrupt (or at least to be seen to disrupt) the existing irregular migration system.[156] Recurrent regularisations are a means of post-entry management, which accepts that immigrant workers already in the country may stay and continue to work (though with the condition that their road to permanent residence, never mind citizenship, will be long and arduous).[157] At the same time, the increased visibility of immigrants has generated strong anxieties about the changing nature of Italian society, and immigration policy has become strongly politicised (especially by the anti-immigrant Lega Nord). Centre-right governments have attempted to stop irregular immigration via the use of criminal law, but this has proved largely unsuccessful.[158] Italy's reaction to EU eastward enlargements in this context is illustrative of its equivocality – despite ostensibly setting limitations on workers from Central and Eastern Europe, the governing centre-right coalition was in fact very generous in terms of entry.[159]

One of the consequences of a (de facto) reactive policy that focuses on absorbing already present irregulars without being able to manage new entries (in terms of either quantity or quality) is the lack of a systemic capacity to actually choose and value immigrants on the basis of skills. In theory, Italian immigration policy allows for extra-quota entries for some highly skilled workers (e.g. intra-company transferees and academics), but the main quota system does not take into account educational or professional qualifications.[160] At the same time, the segregation of immigrant workers to the low-skilled sectors is due not to poor education but to a lack of access to the insider labour market.[161] Moreover, like Australia, Italy is experiencing a loss of local

---

[156] For a summary of immigration policy since 1990, see Perlmutter, 'Italy'.
[157] Regularisations have taken place in 1986, 1990, 1995, 1998, 2002 and 2009. The 2002 regularisation, passed by a centre-right government, was the largest, with more than 600 000 people regularised. See Zincone, 'The case of Italy'. On regularisations, see also Barbagli et al., *I sommersi e i sanati*.
[158] The Bossi-Fini law of 2002 and the 2008–09 security package (125/2008, 94/2009) are examples of measures particularly aimed at irregular migrants. For a discussion of Bossi-Fini, see Totah, 'Fortress Italy'.
[159] Sciortino, 'Fortunes and miseries'. In 2010, Romanians, who became EU citizens in 2007 (and had been exempt from visas since 2000), amounted to 1 million people, constituting almost 20 per cent of the immigrant population. See Pegna, 'Italy'.
[160] Salis, 'Labour migration governance'.
[161] Fullin and Reyneri, 'Low unemployment and bad jobs'.

workers through emigration (and not for the first time),[162] but in contrast with Australia, which actively seeks to attract skilled migrants to make up for this loss, it has been unable to devise ways to attract foreign skilled workers to replace those who have left (especially in the scientific and technological fields). There are many reasons for this, including recent economic woes and lack of investment, the closed nature of the Italian labour market, doubts about meritocratic career progression and corruption,[163] but the fact that immigration policies do not place emphasis on the education levels of incoming foreigners is also relevant.[164] Remedying this would require not just grudging acceptance of low-skilled immigration as necessary (though socially regrettable) from the point of view of the Italian economy,[165] but public commitment to valuing immigrants and even solicitation of highly skilled immigrants through incentives.[166] This is a difficult bullet for any Italian government to bite.[167] As with the delayed reform of the restrictive 1992 citizenship law (discussed in Chapter 2),[168] the issue of comprehensive immigration reform towards a more proactive policy has been postponed because it involves facing an uncomfortable reality, and not just because of Italy's notorious political instability, which has not improved in recent years.[169] As a response to this skill waste, self-employment is emerging as a way out of migrant subordination.[170]

Finland, like Italy, has been alert to the issues around future labour-force contraction for some time. Finland has one of the most rapidly ageing populations in Europe, and the population of working age is

---

[162] Highly regulated systems of movement control were instituted to regulate exit from Italy in the past. Caporali and Golini, 'Births and fertility'.
[163] Morano Foadi, 'Key issues'.
[164] Breda, 'How to reverse'. Note that Italy has also transposed Council Directive 2009/50/EC (the Blue Card) into its domestic legislation (in 2012). The Blue Card aims to facilitate the movement of high-skilled non-EU citizens to work in the European Union by harmonising entry and residence conditions throughout the European Union and by providing for a legal status and a set of rights. However, little use of this has been made in Italy to date. See European Commission, 'Communication from the Commission'.
[165] Campani et al., 'Labour market, migration'.
[166] Ambrosini, 'Immigration in Italy', 183, has argued that 'immigrants are relatively well accepted in the labor market and, gradually in society too, as long as they remain at the lowest levels of the social and professional scale, ready to perform the least pleasant tasks'.
[167] Sciortino, 'Fortunes and miseries'.
[168] In 1992, when immigration was already a fact, the law governing citizenship was made more restrictive (for those with no Italian heritage). See e.g. Zincone, 'The case of Italy'. See also Chapter 2.
[169] For overviews of the political landscape of immigration management, see Massetti, 'Mainstream parties'; Perlmutter, 'Italy'; Zincone, 'The case of Italy'.
[170] Ambrosini, 'Immigration in Italy'.

decreasing as the large post-war generations reach retirement age.[171] Smaller generations of working-age adults will need to provide the fiscal resources necessary to finance public services, including care for the ageing population.[172] Awareness of these demographic pressures is widespread, and labour migration is discussed in terms of its ability assist with (if not to solve) the problems associated with a rapidly ageing population.[173] Indeed, Finland has already been transformed into an immigration destination, though to a much more modest degree than most other countries. The change started with the collapse of the Soviet Union (which particularly increased immigration by ethnic Finns from the former Soviet Union[174]) and with increasing refugee numbers. Since 1990, the proportion of foreign citizens legally residing in Finland has increased sixfold, but it is still under five per cent.[175] Unlike in Italy, where immigration is perceived to be out of the government's control, Finland's labour market is still comparatively highly regulated and closed to outsiders, and even highly educated immigrants can find it difficult to find employment.[176] The approach to labour migration, despite concerns over the dependency ratio, has been tightly managed (indeed, a long-term preference for raising fertility over immigration has also been expressed, though this is difficult[177]). Labour migration rules still require labour-market testing – that is, for prospective employers to prove the necessity of recruiting foreign workers[178] – and the numbers have consequently been low. However, limited moves towards greater openness have been made. At the more skilled end, international students are now subject to a lighter immigration process, recognising their desirability as future skilled workers.[179] Estonians (and

---

[171] Valtioneuvoston kanslia, 'Väestön ikärakenteen muutos'.
[172] On the growth of the over-65s and the challenge it is posing, see Chapter 5.
[173] Asa and Bärlund, 'Satisfying labour demand'; Honkatukia et al., 'Työvoiman tarve'; Tuomaala and Torvi, 'Kohti työperusteista maahanmuuttoa'. Myrskylä and Pyykkönen, 'Tulevaisuuden Tekijät', estimate Finland would need to double its immigrant intake to avoid labour-force contraction.
[174] 'Ethnic Finns', or Ingrians, living in the Soviet Union were granted, somewhat controversially, 'return migrant' rights in 1990. This resulted in some tens of thousands of ethnic Finns immigrating, many of whom experienced significant language and cultural barriers and ended up in less skilled employment. Saarinen, 'Non-work migration'.
[175] Tilastokeskus, 'Väestö'.   [176] Kyhä, 'Koulutetut maahamuuttajat'.   [177] See Chapter 2.
[178] Employers or job applicants must apply for authorisation from the Public Employment Service. The post, unless it is on the regional shortage list, must be listed for 2–4 weeks, while local labour-market authorities check the skill level and the compliance with collective agreements.
[179] Non-EU graduates of Finnish educational establishments can, following amendments to the Aliens Act in 2006, obtain a work permit to search for a job for up to six months and a residence permit to allow a job search for up to 10 months.

other citizens of accession states) were given free-movement rights two years after the European Union's eastward enlargement.[180]

Despite small moves towards openness, the flow of economic migrants to Finland has consistently been lower than that experienced by other advanced economies, and Finland can still be described as a reluctant country of immigration.[181] As in other Nordic countries, where a highly regulated labour market and concerns over the sustainability of the welfare system have created a tension between immigration and the desire to maintain welfare standards,[182] Finland's strong labour unions and general concerns about the welfare state have prevented the importation of large numbers of immigrant workers into low-skill jobs (as has occurred in Italy), apart from small numbers of seasonal agricultural workers exempted from normal labour law.[183] Many immigrants have instead arrived as family members or humanitarian entrants, and the unwillingness to embrace labour immigration more fully is also rooted in these experiences. High rates of unemployment and high concentrations of immigrants in low-skilled work suggest many immigrants have found it difficult to become full participants in the Finnish labour market, which requires Finnish language skills and occupational expertise (and the lack of experience in designing integration policies has not improved matters).[184] Immigration per se is not seen as a solution. Finland is yet to develop policies to support the economic incorporation of its immigrants, including female immigrants, many of whom are neglected by policies that automatically assume rather than seek to facilitate women's labour-market participation (as Finnish women generally work full-time).[185] Thus, how to ensure labour immigration of suitably high-skilled workers has remained a thorny issue: as discussed already in relation to Australia

---

[180] For those two years, Act 309/2004 (Laki Tšekin, Viron, Latvian, Liettuan, Unkarin, Puolan, Slovenian ja Slovakian kansalaisten ansiotyön edellytyksistä) required citizens from the accession countries to apply for a work permit before working in Finland. During that time, many came not as employees but as temporary transferees.

[181] Asa and Bärlund, 'Satisfying labour demand'.   [182] Brochmann, 'Scandinavia'.

[183] Seasonal agricultural workers are entitled to work in Finland without a residence permit if the working period is less than three months. Largely berry pickers, most seasonal agricultural workers come from Thailand. See Rantanen and Valkonen, 'Ulkomaalaiset metsämarjapoimijat'.

[184] It is well documented that immigrant–native employment gaps are larger in Finland than in many other states. Työ- ja elinkeinoministeriö, 'Kotoutumisen kokonaiskatsaus'; Väänänen et al., 'Maahanmuuttajien integroituminen'. See Chapter 3. Note that eventual naturalisation requires fluency in Finnish or Swedish, making it difficult for many to obtain.

[185] On the experiences of migrant women, see Saarinen, 'Non-work migration'.

and the United Kingdom, global competition – especially for those with skills – is intense, and many skilled migrants regard Finland as a remote, cold destination with a difficult language and deep reservations about immigrants.[186] It is not a coincidence that one of the largest and most successful groups of labour migrants and immigrants is Estonians, who come from a nearby country with a similar language (but with much lower wage and welfare levels).[187]

The pressure to enhance work-based immigration has been growing, but the adoption of firm steps to facilitate it has proved difficult and the financial crisis and rising unemployment since 2008 put a stop to tentative moves towards enticing immigrants. The decision to increase labour migration was included in the government's official programme in 2007.[188] The second Vanhanen government started phasing in measures intended to foster labour migration and, in 2009, proposed to remove the requirement to assess whether there was a labour-market need for recruiting a foreign worker over Finnish residents in the work-permit application process.[189] In the wake of a slowing economy and surging anti-immigration sentiments,[190] this proposal ran into trouble, splitting the government, and eventually failed.[191] The more cautious government programme in 2011[192] stresses the need to support immigration 'based on genuine demand for workers' and suggests that Finland ought to carefully examine what unfolds in neighbouring Sweden, which has partly removed the 'necessity' requirement.[193] The government strategy for the future of immigration for 2013–20 aims to pave

[186] Though Finland has transposed Council Directive 2009/50/EC (the Blue Card) into its domestic legislation, only five Blue Cards were issued in 2013. See European Commission, 'Communication from the Commission'.
[187] Estonians numbered 44 000 in 2014, nearly twice as many as in 2008. Immigration from Estonia, a small country with low fertility levels, will not provide a long-term solution to Finland's population concerns. Moreover, many Estonians do not stay permanently in Finland. See Kangasniemi and Kauhanen, 'Who leaves and who stays?'.
[188] Valtioneuvoston kanslia, 'Matti Vanhasen II hallituksen ohjelma', 11.
[189] Hallitus, 'HE 269/2009'. The requirement is in Aliens Act (301/2004), s.72. The government also proposed to shorten the period of residence required for Finnish citizenship, with an eye towards encouraging immigration of workers – this change took effect in 2011. See Law 579/2011 (Laki kansalaisuuslain muuttamisesta). See also Fagerlund and Brander, 'Country report: Finland'.
[190] Politically, immigration has become a difficult issue since 2008, when the True Finns party (Perussuomalaiset) emerged as an anti-immigration force that has politicised migration policy.
[191] Nykänen, 'Hyöty vai haitta'.
[192] This programme was adopted after the 2011 elections, where the True Finns party surged in the polls, though ultimately opted to stay out of government. The True Finns party joined government in 2015.
[193] Valtioneuvoston kanslia, Pääministeri Jyrki Kataisen, 7, 29. In 2011, two-thirds of work-permit decisions involved establishing labour-market necessity. See Sisäasiainministeriö, 'Työvoiman maahanmuuton', 7.

the way for a more active and predictable immigration policy, recognising the need for young and skilled labour immigrants.[194] Its implementation plan aims for better international recruitment of necessary immigrants (already piloted in the social and medical fields), improved strategies for retaining international students[195] and simplified immigration administration.[196] These steps, cautious as they are, suggest a similar desire as elsewhere to attract, in a focused way, those immigrants seen as most useful – in the Finnish context, highly skilled and with a special focus on the health and welfare sectors, which are most in need of workers to provide services to an ageing population. At the same time, it can be said that even though the window for labour immigration opened later in Finland than elsewhere, it has already partially closed again, before dramatic changes could be made.

CITIZENSHIP AND THE GOVERNANCE OF LABOUR MIGRATION

This last section discusses what the trends and policies of labour migration discussed in this chapter imply not only about the inclusion of migrants in contemporary states, but also about the gendered expectations of and the meaning of work as a foundation for citizenship. The situations of the states discussed differ in terms of their immigration histories, their systems of labour regulation and their ability to attract immigrants. Nevertheless, a strong shared theme is a view of the necessity of immigration either at the top end of the labour market (highly skilled work) or at the bottom end (low-skilled work), or both. Immigration is considered, if not the only viable means through which contemporary states can alleviate the inevitable strains of population ageing (the prospect of labour shortages and shrinking economies) and the prospect of population decline, then an essential component of efforts to this end.[197] This is the case not just in Australia, but in states with less experience of immigration. At the same time, this acceptance of immigration is grudging, in the sense that it comes with a marked reluctance to fully admit all or even most newcomers into permanent membership, even in Australia (which, out of all the states discussed, is still

---

[194] Sisäministeriö, 'Valtioneuvoston periaatepäätös'.
[195] The proposal that graduates from Finnish educational establishments be allowed to obtain permits to search for a job for up to 12 months (see HE 219/2014) was adopted in 2014 (Aliens Act (301/2004), ss. 54–5).
[196] Sisäministeriö, 'Maahanmuuton tulevaisuus'.
[197] On the costs of looking after ageing citizens, see Chapter 5.

most welcoming to a large number of entrants every year). All of the states in question are seeking to govern migration in order to maximise its economic benefits, while shedding as many of the (real and imagined) costs as possible, and as a result seek to engage in various strategies to attract and retain migrants deemed desirable, while stemming, redirecting or temporarily utilising other flows. This section discusses two aspects of these strategies. First, it discusses what the framing of skilled immigration as the acceptable face of (im)migration reveals about the qualities desirable in citizens and the consequences of policies seeking to identify migrants in terms of their desirability and to test them before fully incorporating them. Second, it turns to the flipside of the endless search for the best and the brightest: the contested issue of temporary and low-skilled migration, its demographic drivers and its relationship with economic transformations.

Concerns over current and future labour supply at the advanced stages of the demographic transition are rooted in low birth rates, which have gradually produced smaller generations since the 1970s and have raised the prospect of smaller populations and labour-force contraction as larger generations gradually leave the workforce.[198] As discussed in Chapter 2, the historic shift to low birth rates that has stagnated natural population growth was and is coupled with women's increasing education and labour-force participation. As women have joined men in the paid labour force, women's citizenship has started to resemble that of men.[199] In fits and starts, the Global North is moving from the ideological male worker breadwinner citizen towards a dual-citizen (or 1.5 citizen) model (with women still carrying more of the care burden and thus only working part-time). Some have argued the extension of gender-equality policies, such as those discussed in Chapter 2, is aimed at enabling the utilisation of women's economic potential at a time when improved productivity is essential because of global ageing (though they have not fully resolved the conflict in women's paid work being both a contributing factor to low birth rates and a necessity in dealing with its consequences).[200] There is undoubtedly much truth to this – at the same time, these policies are also debated in the shadow of the only other obvious demographic lever by which to counter the economic

---

[198] For a summary of these prospects in the EU context, see Fargues, 'International migration and Europe's demographic challenge'.
[199] Esping-Andersen, *The Incomplete Revolution*; Fraser, 'After the family wage'.
[200] Repo, 'The governance of fertility'.

effects of ageing in market economies: 'replacement migration'.[201] The 'replacement' of missing citizens of workforce age by migrants highlights the concern that ongoing immigration is gradually more literally 'replacing' the native populations of contemporary states with 'immigrant' populations.[202] Thus, while immigration is firmly in the frame as something states in the advanced stage of the demographic transition cannot avoid, at the same time states in the Global North have become increasingly concerned about the increased diversity of their societies and the permanent settlement of immigrants (Chapter 3).

As this demographic shift has unfolded, producing smaller generations, advanced market economies have undergone economic transformation from Fordist mass production to a 'post-industrial' service and knowledge economy.[203] In the place of manufacturing jobs, contemporary states in the Global North have seen a growth of skilled jobs in the growing internationalised service economy (including finance and IT sectors). The role of governments has also changed: they now aim to gain and maintain a competitive advantage in emerging knowledge-based industries, supporting innovation and directing resources to enhance the global competitiveness of growth sectors.[204] Even with women's increasing involvement in the paid labour market (still limited by their caregiving roles – see Chapter 2) and the growing education levels of the general population (Chapter 3), the change to a knowledge-based economy and the rise of new technologies have also entailed demand for not just workers but skilled workers. Against this background, the emergence of the new good migrant subject is entirely logical. The desirable migrant that states wish to add to their population is one who enhances their productiveness and competitiveness. This migrant is ideally already highly skilled, self-sufficient, responsible and productive, requires little direction from government to navigate the risks of the knowledge economy and poses few risks themselves in terms of economic and social integration in societies on high alert about their changing populations.[205] Australia has fine-tuned this strategy. With the help of the points system, the best would-be citizens, who continuously and successfully self-regulate, invest in and enhance their

---

[201] Apart from these two key demographic components, states can also raise retirement age. Fargues, 'International migration and Europe's demographic challenge'. On retirement age, see Chapter 5.
[202] Coleman, 'Immigration and ethnic change'.
[203] Jessop, 'Towards a Schumpeterian workfare state?'.
[204] Jessop, 'Towards a Schumpeterian workfare state?'. [205] Walsh, 'Quantifying citizens'.

'human capital', can be identified and rewarded.[206] Because of the supposed objectivity of this selection based on economic criteria, the government can sell these immigrants to a sceptical public, as 'the focus on productive, highly-skilled migrants allows them to convey a message of control, while internationally signaling to those with high-demand skills and extraordinary talent that they are "wanted and welcome"'.[207]

As Sassen has put it, despite all the talk about closed borders, borders increasingly serve as 'transmitting membranes', letting in those deemed useful based on their desirability.[208] In this entirely utilitarian calculus, migrants are reduced to their labour-market attributes, and those with the highest points values are the targets of increasing competition (especially highly skilled and specialised migrant workers, such as doctors and IT specialists).[209] Australia has refined its system furthest in this regard, in order to identify the most likely 'winners', but even Finland, faced with many constraints not applicable to Australia, aspires to similar strategies to compete for highly skilled students and get them to contribute to the knowledge economy, counter workforce shortages and counter population decline. It is assumed such individuals make the best new citizens, avoiding integration concerns and the need for further education and resource spending (however, when permanent, immigrants do eventually contribute to ageing).[210] They are also assumed to be less problematic in terms of their childbearing and childrearing than migrants entering on the basis of family relations. Though skilled female migrants are still something of an afterthought in immigration policy, women are increasingly admitted as skilled migrants in their own right, thanks to women's globally increasing education.[211] As educated and working women have fewer children, they contribute less to improving birth rates, but they do not raise the same integration concerns and anxieties as low-skilled ethnic-minority women (for instance in Finland; see Chapter 3). However, even this type of migrant is not automatically admitted to full membership. Skilled-migration policies allow migrants to be chosen on the basis of assumed self-sufficiency, which can be monitored post-entry via the expectations set by permanent-residency and citizenship rules. Citizenship is 'earned' on the basis of successful self-management over time.

[206] Walsh, 'Quantifying citizens'. For an analysis of the broader change in governance in which this approach represents a new politics of citizenship, see Rose, 'Governing liberty'.
[207] Shachar and Hirsch, 'On citizenship', 236   [208] Sassen, *Guests and Aliens*, 150.
[209] Abella, 'Global competition'; Shachar, 'The race for talent'.
[210] Fargues, 'International migration and Europe's demographic challenge'.
[211] Kofman, 'Towards a gendered evaluation'.

The good future citizen navigates a successful route in an employment landscape of relaxed labour-market regulations and survives periods of hardship without resorting to government assistance.

The downsides and risks of this approach are rarely explicitly stated. One question is whether mobile and cosmopolitan knowledge workers want to become citizens, and if they do, whether they make the best new citizens. The systems states have devised to identify those most desirable prioritise easily measurable attributes such as qualifications and language skills, not soft skills such as communication and team work.[212] The neoliberal worker-citizen these systems prioritise is one who has few affective ties (or none beyond immediate family), who is not rooted in one location (they could get on with their working life anywhere) and who is autonomous and self-interested (they are not obviously invested in contributing to the well-being of their community, or not without expectation of remuneration or reward). Their obvious ideal subjectivity as worker-citizens notwithstanding, leaving social cohesion on the shoulders of atomised individuals as active citizens, as Soysal has argued, may not be enough to sustain social cohesion.[213] The related but more frequently raised question is whether the issue of increasing conditionality might be corrosive to citizenship. Being kept temporary for years affects not only family relationships but also the ability to feel settled. In Australia, 457 visa holders can bring spouses and dependants, but they have limited access to public education and social security. Is the eventual transformation of temporariness into permanence sufficient to turn migrants into members of a society that has kept them at arm's length?[214] Finally, the relentless quest for economically useful and skilled migrants raises obvious issues of demographic sustainability. On the one hand, much discussed global justice issues, most notably brain drain, are ignored when richer countries target poorer ones as a source of useful citizens, such as when the United Kingdom's National Health Service (NHS) recruits medical workers[215] or when Australia seeks highly skilled migrants and students with an eye on keeping them for permanent settlement.[216] Current policies fall far short of the ideals of moral cosmopolitanism advocated by many immigration theorists.[217] On the other hand, it is unclear how long

---

[212] Kofman, 'Towards a gendered evaluation', 118. [213] Soysal, 'Citizenship, immigration'.
[214] Mares, 'Temporary migration'. [215] Raghuram, 'The difference that skills make'.
[216] Hugo, 'Migration and development in low-income countries'.
[217] Bader, 'The ethics of immigration'; Brock, 'Immigration and global justice'; Seglow, 'The ethics of immigration'; Ypi, 'Justice in migration'.

the skill focus can continue when competition is likely to stiffen from other countries facing demographic decline (China) and from emerging economies seeking to retain skilled workers (or even attract return migration).[218]

The issues of justice and temporariness also raise the question of what this picture of desirable migration so explicitly favoured by states obscures. The growth of knowledge and financial service sectors in advanced economies has not meant that routine low-end jobs have disappeared.[219] In fact, contrary to some expectations, lower-paid, lower-skilled service jobs have proliferated in sectors such as hospitality, care and retail, while technology has substituted many middle jobs and employment flexibility and 'casualness' have increased, especially in liberal welfare states such as Australia.[220] Many critiques of these trends are based on Beck's famous argument about the 'Brazilianisation of the West': labour markets in the developed world are taking on some of the characteristics that have been associated with less developed labour markets, such as employment insecurity, informality and precariousness.[221] Though claims about insecurity and the temporariness of employment can easily be overstated,[222] forms of precarious work have characterised young people's and women's employment. Such precarious work can be considered either as a way for these workers to enter the paid labour market or as a type of employment that those with little experience and gendered caregiving obligations are often powerless to avoid. Insofar as such divisions are regarded as a 'syndrome of the post-industrial, globalized economies', they have particular consequences in the context of migration.[223] The skills agenda dedicated to the nation's desire to 'up-skill' does not officially acknowledge the demand for low-skilled workers, and labour-immigration policies regarding low-skilled migrants are much more restrictive than those that apply to skilled and highly skilled migrants. Low-skilled immigration, while useful for many employers, is also difficult to sell to a population that is facing unemployment itself, as the UK case shows. Yet sectors like hospitality, construction, cleaning, agriculture and food processing have structural demand for low-skilled workers.

---

[218] Münz, 'Demography and migration'.
[219] See Vogt, 'The post-industrial society', for an analysis of how practical work is rendered invisible in discussion of the 'post-industrial' society.
[220] Campbell at al., 'Australia'; Vosko, *Managing the Margins*.
[221] Beck, *The Brave New World*.   [222] Doogan, *New Capitalism?*.
[223] Soysal, 'Citizenship, immigration', 7.

Because of the limited channels for migration for this kind of work, employers in contemporary states have relied heavily on various forms of temporary migration, both legal and informal. States have, in varying degrees, encouraged or tolerated this, not only because it meets demand by employers but also because it provides labour while avoiding the need to manage anxieties around permanent integration, migrant reproduction and the costs of ageing migrants.[224] In Australia, low-skilled temporary-migrant workers are typically working holidaymakers and international students, but even the allegedly skilled 457 visas have sometimes been used to meet employer demand for flexible less-skilled workers, thanks to lax oversight. In the United Kingdom, Finland and Italy, EU citizens from Central and Eastern Europe have entered using their free-movement rights, and both the United Kingdom and, in particular, Italy make use of irregular migrants (Finland, on the other hand, remains largely closed to irregular low-skilled migrants, showing that a domestically well-regulated labour market does make a difference in this regard). Both legal but temporary workers and, in particular, irregular workers are vulnerable. There has been some debate over whether immigration for low-skilled work is really needed or whether it is just preferred by employers for this reason. Ruhs and Anderson have argued that economic need in some sectors in the United Kingdom is constructed via poor wages, conditions and status – as long as immigrants are available, they will continue to be preferred over improving pay and conditions.[225] Rather than talk about a need for migrant labour, Ruhs and Anderson advocate analysing a demand promoted by powerful economic and political interests. In other words, though some states face greater pressures than others, they are not merely helpless bystanders in the face of demographic changes – they choose to accommodate employers demanding cheap and flexible temporary workers (though as the UK case again shows, public resistance is growing). Finland's reticence emphasises the role of the state in facilitating the expansion of informal work and the growth of low-paid migrant sectors.

The expansion of the migrant care-work sector in both the United Kingdom and Italy can be seen as an example of the dynamic whereby states govern immigration via temporariness and informality, but it is also a good example of where demographic factors will continue to play a part in maintaining the demand for migration in the Global

---

[224] Fargues, 'International migration and Europe's demographic challenge'.
[225] Ruhs and Anderson, *Who Needs Migrant Workers?*.

North. A comparison with the Finnish and Australian care sectors shows that economic and social circumstances and state choices matter in the development and expansion of a low-skilled migrant-worker segment.[226] However, as discussed in Chapter 5, the care sector is also one which, even in Finland and Australia, will be characterised by growing labour shortages in the future, because of strong demographic drivers.[227] Women's increased labour-market participation (which makes them unavailable for informal caregiving) and the need for caregiving among an ageing population (and, possibly, the increase in highly educated young people who aspire to better jobs[228]) together mean that states face a 'care deficit' which requires more (paid) carers. The redistribution of care work that has already taken place between different groups of women also draws attention to both the new inequalities between women and the global demographic imbalance which allows the Global North to attract more immigrants than it wants to admit.[229] However, the strategy of recruiting women from the Global South to do care work may, again, prove difficult in the long run. Despite global population growth, the rest of the world is following the Global North in terms of the demographic transition, which means the supply of migrants – certainly the kind that is readily justified to a sceptical public – may eventually dry up.[230] Assuming that the rest of the world will 'provide unlimited reserves of labour with the necessary skills and attributes'[231] is likely to prove questionable as a general proposition in the future. The race to find suitable labour will not be over any time soon.

Mares has argued that the Australian response to immigration has been based on fear and instrumentalism.[232] This is a charge that can increasingly be applied to other states that seek to use immigration for economic purposes, yet fear the individuals who will come and seek to manage the anxiety over their presence. This view, that 'migrants are nothing but economic input, a useful addition to the machinery of production that can be discarded when no longer needed',[233] reflects a self-interest approach, whereby migrants, especially in low-paid sectors, are wanted to make up for shortfalls in the labour market, but not as future members of society. Temporary migration brings workers who

---

[226] On Finland, see Chapter 5. On Australia, see Howe, 'Migrant care workers'.
[227] On Australia, see Hugo, 'Care worker'. See also Hugo, 'Migration and development in Asia'.
[228] Castles, 'Guestworkers in Europe', 745.   [229] See Chapter 5.
[230] Castles, 'The forces driving'.   [231] Castles, 'Migration, crisis', 318.
[232] Mares, 'Fear and instrumentalism', 407.   [233] Mares, 'Fear and instrumentalism', 418.

will leave before they contribute to ageing, which makes it attractive as a strategy to counter the effects of ageing on the economy (if not population decline). Increased temporariness among migrants may, however, further undermine the social cohesion towards which it is intended to contribute.[234] As with guest-worker regimes, inviting labour but not treating those who come as people accentuates social divides and is corrosive for the long-term legitimacy of contemporary states. Long-term permanent temporariness creates seeds for the kinds of marginalisation that states are now seeking to avoid because of integration concerns triggered by past immigration (Chapter 3). In addition, the idolisation of the neoliberal worker who is focused on maximising their own economic benefit is inimical to a society of citizens in a more insidious way. Even in Australia, the majority of immigrants are actually not taken in on a purely economic selective basis – what are the consequences of the 'dominant political rhetoric'?[235] It leaves behind not just some immigrants, but anyone 'unable to exercise and live up to the highest form of life of being productive; those who are stuck in secondary or temporary jobs, and not able to climb the social ladder; and those who face ethnic and religious discrimination'.[236] At worst, it suggests they brought their misfortune on themselves by failing to make the most of their opportunities.

FINAL REMARKS

The demographic shrinkage of the workforce in the Global North has no easy solutions – women's participation, improved productivity and later retirement are all part of the mix, but are not enough to make states entertain the possibility that they can sustain economic growth without any migration. At the same time, states are not merely helpless bystanders in the face of these changes, and they have a significant role in terms of resisting, adapting to and encouraging economic and demographic change. International migration has become an essential component in assisting the Global North to keep up workforce growth. It takes time to create new citizens via reproduction (if you can convince women to make them) and taking in immigrants involves no immediate cost when they are predominantly of workforce age. However, permanent immigrants also grow old, contributing to population ageing

---

[234] Castles et al., 'The internal dynamic', 34–5, 'Australia', 146. On how temporary migration can transform citizenship, see also Bauböck, 'Temporary migrants'.
[235] Castles et al., 'Rethinking migration', 117.   [236] Soysal, 'Citizenship, immigration', 15.

(see Chapter 5). Immigration can only ever postpone the issues around ageing and, where birth rates are very low, mitigate the prospect of population decline. At the same time, some states in the Global North still treat migrants as an endless resource, meaning they are not thinking very hard about how to adjust their economies to the possibility of population stagnation, if not decline. Because of the concern over integration and the assumption that more educated immigrants assimilate more easily, contemporary states are more willing to accept them. This trend will likely continue, alongside more temporary migration, in an attempt to alleviate public concerns. The long-term success of this approach remains to be seen.

CHAPTER FIVE

DEPLETING CITIZENS? AGEING POPULATIONS, CARE AND MIGRATION

This chapter explores a much-lamented success story: that of increasing longevity and growth in the proportion of older people in contemporary societies. The cause of this demographic ageing of states in the Global North is the transition from high to low levels of fertility and mortality (and many less wealthy states will be, or are already on their way to experiencing the same phenomenon).[1] The 'maturing' of contemporary states, where people live far longer and healthier lives than previous generations, is in many ways a great and unprecedented achievement. However, and importantly, increasing longevity is hardly ever framed in this way in public debates – instead, it is typically discussed in negative and fearful, even apocalyptic[2] terms, focusing on the problems associated with ageing, from concerns over economic growth and the sustainability of pension and social security systems to pressures on health and social services related to the increased care needs of the growing elderly population. Demographic ageing thus has many implications for debates on the future of citizenship, especially in the context of funding and providing care for ageing populations. These are not only manifested in changes in the way the citizenship of older persons is conceived, but also linked to increased mobility, regarding both people migrating to provide care for older people and older people wishing to migrate with their future care needs in mind. Though much has been written about the women, including migrant care workers, who provide

---

[1] Kalache et al., 'Global ageing'.   [2] Robertson, 'The politics of Alzheimer's'.

formal and informal care for the older people, and about the international division of caretaking labour these care patterns implicate, some of the other links between the ageing of populations and international migration, including the migration of older people to join their adult children abroad, have been relatively under-explored.[3]

As a case study, this chapter examines Finland, which is noteworthy because of its particularly advanced state of demographic ageing, which is putting increasing pressures on the Finnish welfare state.[4] The proportion aged 65 years old and older is growing more rapidly than in any other EU Member State, and Finland's old age-dependency ratio will be among the highest of all EU countries by around 2020–25.[5] As a frontrunner in dealing with ageing, Finland faces significant challenges in terms of addressing declining support ratios, with smaller young age cohorts, already high female labour-market participation and, as discussed in Chapter 4, limited public appetite for large-scale labour migration. In light of the growing numbers of older people, questions regarding the funding and practical organisation of care have prompted much discussion about the rights of citizens in their old age, the future of the welfare state and the role of immigration in ameliorating and exacerbating the pressures caused by demographic ageing. As older citizens are increasingly steered to work longer and to look after themselves for as long as possible (with the help of markets and their families), the outer boundaries of the Finnish state have also been reinforced against older people considered to be a future economic burden that might deplete the nation's economic resources and competitiveness. Attempts by adult immigrant-citizens to bring their older dependent relatives, usually their mothers, to join them (whether so that they can care for them in their old age or so that the older relatives can themselves provide help, for instance by providing childcare) have resulted in controversial legal challenges. Demographically driven anxieties about public spending emerge starkly in a cross-border context, trumping immigrant-citizens' caring obligations to their parents.

After the case study, the chapter examines the other three jurisdictions in terms of their patterns of ageing, demographic anxieties and changes in citizenship and migration policy. While ageing is particularly advanced in Finland, owing to its special demographic profile

---

[3] van der Geest et al., 'Linkages between migration', 436. See also Blakemore, 'International migration'.
[4] Piekkola, 'Active ageing'.   [5] Valtioneuvoston kanslia, 'Väestön ikärakenteen muutos'.

(including an early and very short post-war baby boom), the other three states face a similar situation in terms of the increase in the elderly population, including growing numbers of the very old, many of whom will have intensive needs for care and assistance in the coming decades. Italy, like Finland, is also ageing very rapidly, and though it is currently still behind Finland in this regard, it faces a steeper adjustment curve at a time when its familistic welfare model is already deeply stretched. The United Kingdom and Australia face less extreme prospects but are not far behind the ageing curve, and their liberal welfare models have already privatised responsibility for elder care to a great degree. All states face the prospect of making adjustments to their existing models of providing support to old people due to the growth of the ageing population, and they are using demographic arguments to justify restructuring of pension and care policies, largely with the aim and effect of making citizens more responsible for their own old age. In all three states, albeit in slightly different ways than in Finland, the relevance of immigration is rising in various ways. All are using migration rules both to facilitate the management of pressures on care systems – for instance by utilising their ability to attract immigrants as a new segment of the care workforce – and to minimise the entry of new immigrants who are, because of their age, deemed to be potentially expensive in the future.

Finally, the last section discusses, more broadly, the impact that states' approaches to managing demographic ageing are having on the content and boundaries of citizenship. It explores changing ideas about who should (and who should not) be cared for at the end of their life in a world of increasing longevity and international mobility, and by whom (in terms of obligations of self, family, state and the market). Unlike children and young people, who are framed as a demographic resource (if also a risk – see Chapter 3), the growing numbers of older people are seen not as individuals whose expertise and experience is valuable but more systematically in negative terms as a mass of unproductive people who, at best, contribute little in later life, and then primarily by minimising the burden they impose on others for as long as possible. As such, older people, especially those who are oldest and frailest, are framed as a numerical threat to the sustainability of social security and welfare arrangements which were put in place at a different demographic stage and with a different set of demographic assumptions. The responses to the risks posed by the demographic shift seek to mitigate the costs via postponing retirement and emphasising self-sufficiency but have uneven effects on citizens along gender, class and racial lines.

Moreover, they seek to escape from and, when that is not possible, contain the risks of (rather than accept and adjust to the inevitability of) human dependency at the very end of life. Furthermore, increased geographical mobility and the 'non-citizen' are shaping the approaches to ageing in destination countries. Migrants add a further contradiction: they are needed as providers of essential care, but as those in need of care they are conceived of as undeserving of the diminishing substantive benefits of citizenship.

FINLAND: WALLED OR WEAKENED WELFARE?

Ageing Pains of a Welfare State?

Finland is in the middle of an unprecedented demographic transformation of its age structure, owing to a combination of low birth-rate patterns (see Chapter 2), increasing longevity (as life expectancy has risen steadily since the Second World War[6]) and low levels of working-age immigration. The transition from high birth and death rates to low ones initially increased the population (including the working-age population – this is sometimes called a 'demographic gift or bonus' phase[7]), but later decreased birth cohorts while earlier and larger cohorts (especially the post-war baby-boom cohort) moved forward through retirement. Individuals over the age of 65 constituted seven per cent of the population in the 1960s, but their proportion has steadily risen and is expected to rise from 20 per cent in 2015 to 26 per cent by 2030 (and to 29 per cent by 2060).[8] In contrast, those under the age of 15 will only constitute 16 per cent of the population in 2030 and 14 per cent in 2060.[9] As the proportions of young and older persons have reversed, the meaning of ageing has also changed. Just as transitions to adulthood have been transformed because of demographic changes (Chapter 3), so has the nature and meaning of old age. Thanks to the post-war rise in living standards, many older people are living healthier and longer lives, meaning retirement age can no longer be treated as synonymous

---

[6] The life expectancy for children born in 2013 was 77.8 for boys and 83.8 for girls. Tilastokeskus, 'Elinajanodote'.
[7] Lee, 'The demographic transition', 182. In Finland, this lasted until the 1970s, corresponding to the expansive stage of the Finnish welfare state.
[8] Tilastokeskus, 'Väestöennuste 2015'. In Finland, the largest baby-boom cohorts occurred in the immediate post-war period, but the boom was comparatively short. See Piekkola, 'Demographic aspects'.
[9] Tilastokeskus, 'Väestöennuste 2015'.

with decrepitude and dependency. However, the increasing older population is also ageing, and the over-85 demographic, which needs high-intensity support and care, is expected to grow to seven per cent by 2060.[10] While longevity is officially affirmed as a good development, increasing numbers of these 'oldest-old' citizens help explain why in policy terms ageing is framed as Finland's crucial 'ageing problem'.[11]

As this demographic shift is taking place in Finland slightly earlier than in other European countries, it has been clear for some time that the changing age profile will require some structural adjustments.[12] At the heart of the debate have been the economic consequences of demographic ageing, framed as the main threat to Finland's economic growth and the sustainability of its welfare state arrangements.[13] Population ageing does have many consequences – it has 'an impact on economic growth, savings, investment and consumption, labour markets, pensions, taxation and intergenerational transfers'.[14] In Finland, these started to be considered seriously in the 1990s, at a time when a deep recession reinforced fears over the economic sustainability of the welfare state.[15] In workforce terms, demographic ageing means smaller numbers of workers are entering productive age, while larger cohorts enter retirement age (and live longer lives after retirement).[16] This means the dependency ratio will rise (despite smaller younger generations), arguably with an adverse effect on Finnish competitiveness and economic growth.[17] Due to its comparatively large post-war cohorts (baby boomers), some have argued the projected stark rise of Finnish dependency ratios will only be rivalled by that of Japan.[18] The economic consequences are exacerbated by labour-market patterns such as those related to relatively early retirement, despite the official public retirement age of 65 (since 1961).[19] How to plan for the sustainability

[10] Tilastokeskus, 'Väestöennuste 2009–2060'.
[11] Valtioneuvoston kanslia, 'Hyvä yhteiskunta kaikenikäisille', 115.
[12] See e.g. Antolín et al., 'How will ageing'. For a comparative view, see Piekkola, 'Demographic aspects'.
[13] Valtioneuvoston kanslia, 'Hyvä yhteiskunta kaikenikäisille', 'Ikääntymisraportti'.
[14] United Nations, 'World population ageing: 1950–2050', xxviii.
[15] On the recession, see Kiander, 'Laman opetukset'.
[16] Parjanne, 'Väestön ikärakenteen muutoksen vaikutukset'; Parkkinen, 'Suomen väestömuutokset'; Valtioneuvoston kanslia, 'Hyvä yhteiskunta kaikenikäisille'.
[17] Antolín et al., 'How will ageing'; Kilponen and Romppanen, 'Julkinen talous'; Luoma et al., 'Seniori-Suomi'; Valtioneuvoston kanslia, 'Hyvä yhteiskunta kaikenikäisille', 'Ikääntymisraportti'.
[18] Parkkinen, 'Suomen väestömuutokset', 320.
[19] On retirement patterns, see Haataja, 'Ikääntyvät työmarkkinoilla'; Hytti, 'Early exit'; Rantala, 'Varhainen eläkkeelle siirtyminen'. The early retirement pattern matches the preferences of

of the economy has thus emerged as a big question with no easy demographic solutions.[20] Finnish women are not an untapped labour resource, as women's labour-market participation is already comparatively high,[21] and, as discussed in Chapter 4, immigration does not provide immediate answers.

In light of the future care needs of the growing cohorts of older people, in particular members of the over-85 demographic who are intensive users of health care and other services, population ageing particularly affects the Finnish welfare state.[22] Finland's welfare system was built largely after the Second World War and, in the model of the Nordic countries, the citizen was constructed as a member of a state providing services on the basis of universalism and decommodification.[23] The Finnish Constitution promises that the state will be responsible for meeting the needs of citizens in terms of basic welfare.[24] The welfare-state system, based on public service provision, was built during the demographic dividend period, when the post-war baby-boomer generation was in working age.[25] It was expanded up until the 1980s, following the assumption of universal guarantees.[26] Care for older people accordingly become largely publicly financed and provided. Though care provided for older citizens can be divided into institutional care (care in residential homes for the elderly and long-term inpatient care in health centres) and home care (care both at home and in service housing), the ability of older citizens to continue to remain in their home for as long as possible has been supported with arguments about the right of citizens to live in their own home.[27] Home-living has been supported via home help (for instance, support in personal tasks, necessary daily housekeeping), support services (meals on wheels, cleaning) and home nursing care.[28] In terms of support for more informal care, often

some employees but has often been promoted by employers and policies. The 1990s recession had a particularly strong impact on the employment of older workers.
[20] For an overview, see Schleutker, 'Väestön ikääntyminen'.
[21] Parkkinen, 'Suomen väestömuutokset', 321.
[22] Luoma et al., 'Seniori-Suomi'; Parkkinen, 'Hoivapalvelut ja eläkemenot'; Sonkin et al., 'Seniori 2000'.
[23] Esping-Andersen, *The Three Worlds*.
[24] The Finnish Constitution (731/1999), s. 19 provides that basic maintenance in old age must be guaranteed by the state. On fundamental rights as the starting point for establishing quality care, see Räty, 'Perus- ja ihmisoikeudet'. For an overview, see Anttonen, 'Hoivan yhteiskunnallistuminen'.
[25] Parkkinen, 'Suomen väestömuutokset', 320.
[26] Häikiö et al., 'Vastuullinen ja valitseva', 240. On the contested meanings and reinterpretations of universalism, see Anttonen et al., *Welfare State*.
[27] Anttonen, 'Hoivan yhteiskunnallistuminen'.
[28] Anttonen, 'Hoivan yhteiskunnallistuminen'.

provided by family members, a so-called 'home care allowance' was introduced in the 1970s to provide support for those looking after disabled or older adults, offering a cash payment for direct provision of care.[29] These systems have come under pressure as aged cohorts have grown, and cuts were made in the recession in the early 1990s.

As already mentioned, the post-war baby-boomer generation that is now approaching later life is, though large, undeniably healthier and wealthier than previous age cohorts.[30] In that sense, it is, as a cohort, easily identifiable with Laslett's 'third-agers' who challenge stereotypes of ageing as a time of decline and idleness.[31] Many older Finnish people, including women, have, compared to their parents, higher education levels, more assets and different consuming habits and attitudes, and many of them stay active longer and live independently in their own homes.[32] Many are providing care for grandchildren or their own old parents.[33] The retiring and the recently retired also form an increasingly diverse group, and there are large divisions between older people in terms of health: many are able to take care of themselves, with the support of family and networks and eventually by moving to service housing or residential homes, while others, typically those with poor health and few resources, are in need of more sustained support.[34] Thus, though older citizens put less pressure on the system than the pure numbers of retirees might suggest, new solutions will be needed for a diverse group of older citizens or 'seniors' whose lives after retirement stretch for much longer than before.[35] Moreover, despite better health and wealth, these baby-boom cohorts will eventually age further. The health of older persons typically deteriorates with increasing age (especially after 75), with ill health increasingly concentrated at the end of life, creating greater demand for long-term care as the numbers of the oldest-old, or frail elderly (or those in the 'fourth age'), increase. The fastest-growing age group in Finland (as well as the rest of the world) is

---

[29] The allowance ('*omaishoidon tuki*') was initially introduced in an ad hoc manner by some municipalities; a formal legal framework was put in place in the 1980s – see Anttonen, 'Hoivan yhteiskunnallistuminen'.
[30] Parjanne, 'Väestön ikärakenteen muutoksen vaikutukset'; Sainio et al., 'Iäkkään väestön'.
[31] Laslett, *A Fresh Map of Life*, has described the various historical influences which have made possible a period of active life after formal work (the Third Age).
[32] Helldán and Helakorpi, 'Eläkeikäisen väestön terveyskäyttäytyminen'; Karisto, 'Finnish baby boomers'. See also Valtioneuvoston kanslia, 'Ikääntyminen voimavarana'.
[33] Hämäläinen and Tanskanen, 'Autetaanko lapsia'.
[34] Helldán and Helakorpi, 'Eläkeikäisen väestön terveyskäyttäytyminen'; Karisto, 'Finnish baby boomers'; Valtioneuvoston kanslia, 'Ikääntyminen voimavarana'.
[35] Sonkin et al., 'Seniori 2000'.

the oldest-old, those aged 80 years or older.[36] The greatest pressures on the health and welfare sector are thus expected in the 2030s and 2040s, when the baby boomers reach this stage.[37]

In line with the social-democratic welfare-state model, where the state has, over the decades, taken on many of the health and social care functions traditionally provided by families, it is not surprising that much attention has focused on the challenges to universalist commitments that increasing numbers will cause, especially regarding formal care services.[38] Attention has particularly focused on municipalities (the local level of administration), which bear the frontline responsibility for the practical provision of services to residents (funded directly from the state and municipal tax).[39] Municipalities have some autonomy over how they organise home help, housing services and institutional care and how they choose to support informal care for the elderly. Various scandals related to stretched municipal services providing substandard residential care because of a lack of resources have focused attention on the variable standards of municipal services.[40] However, demographic ageing has also entailed increased pressure on families and resurfacing questions about the division of care between publicly provided services and private care.[41] Indeed, discussions over the welfare state sometimes obscure the fact that even in Finland's service-state model, care provided by relatives has remained a significant source of support for older people, involving substantial economic savings for the welfare state.[42] This is despite the fact that in Finland, adult children are no longer legally responsible for their ageing parents.[43] It is estimated that there are about 300 000 people who provide informal family care,[44] and the majority of these carers do not fall under the semi-formal support offered via municipal care allowances (that is, financial support

---

[36] Tilastokeskus, 'Väestöennuste 2009–2060'.
[37] Valtioneuvoston kanslia, 'Ikääntyminen voimavarana'.
[38] Antolín et al., 'How will ageing'; Luoma et al., 'Seniori-Suomi'.
[39] Parkkinen, 'Väestön ikääntymisen vaikutukset'. See also Kröger, 'Hoivapolitiikan rajanvetoja'.
[40] For the report of the parliamentary ombudsman who looked into these claims, see Paunio and Linnakangas, 'Ympärivuorokautisessa hoidossa'.
[41] Kehusmaa, 'Hoidon menoja'.
[42] Kehusmaa, 'Hoidon menoja', 85, puts the figure at 2.8 billion euros.
[43] The requirement of the Poor Act (Köyhäinhoitolaki, 125/1922) that people look after their parents was repealed in 1970 as incompatible with the welfare state. This is in line with the Finnish Constitution and its stance that the state is responsible for providing for the basic needs of citizens.
[44] Anttonen, 'Hoivan yhteiskunnallistuminen', 79.

for home carers who have made an official contract with the municipality regarding the provision of care to a family member).[45]

Many of these informal carers are over 65 themselves, and the patterns of informal care are, unsurprisingly, also gendered (so are, of course, the patterns of formal care, thanks to a predominantly female workforce in the public sector).[46] Many of the people who provide unpaid care to family members are women (a significant proportion often also work in the paid labour force) – typically, female caregivers provide care for an infirm and older husband.[47] Often, informal carers' long-term wealth and capacity to provide for their own care in old age are adversely affected by the expectation that they will provide unpaid care for others. In particular, long-term caring commitments can hamper the ability to work in the paid labour market, and even when carers do engage in paid work, women typically earn less than men and caring obligations (not just for older people, but also for children) often make their working careers more fragmented. Patchy employment histories and the provision of informal care to others thus explain why women over the age of 75 are one of the poorest groups in society, with more limited savings and pension entitlements.[48] Older women's relative marginalisation and poverty also have to do with increasing changes in family compositions and living arrangements (most notably divorce, which disadvantages women disproportionally, and is especially difficult for women who have not been engaged in paid work) and the fact that women's higher life expectancy means they often survive their husbands.[49] Despite improving male lifespans, many women will have no spouse to care for them in old age, unlike men, who can usually rely on their wife for assistance.[50] Eventually, there will also be fewer children (daughters) available to give care, because of both lower birth rates and increasing mobility. All these factors mean ageing is 'appropriately defined as a gender issue'.[51]

---

[45] About 40 000 people received the care allowance in 2012. Sosiaali- ja terveysministeriö, 'Kansallinen omaishoidon kehittämisohjelma'.
[46] Sosiaali- ja terveysministeriö, 'Kansallinen omaishoidon kehittämisohjelma'. See also Vilkko et al., 'Läheisapu iäkkään ihmisen arjessa'.
[47] Sosiaali- ja terveysministeriö, 'Kansallinen omaishoidon kehittämisohjelma'; Zechner, 'Informaali hoiva'.
[48] van Aerschot, 'Vanhusten hoiva ja eriarvoisuus', 69.
[49] van Aerschot, 'Vanhusten hoiva ja eriarvoisuus', 69–70.
[50] For a comparative study of poverty in old age and living alone, see Ahonen and Bach-Othman, 'Vanhuusköyhyyden jäljillä'.
[51] Estes, 'Women, ageing and inequality', 552.

The future need for workers in the health and social welfare sectors also implicates the role of immigrants as part of the future care workforce. The rising demand for health care and nursing services in the public sector coincides with the retirement of large numbers of (mostly female) workers in the public health and welfare sectors, and employers have started to experience difficulties in filling vacant posts.[52] Traditionally, Finland has exported rather than imported health and social welfare workers, and the proportion of immigrants in the health care and social welfare sectors has been low, suggesting both difficulties in immigrant insertion and growth potential as an immigrant-employment sector.[53] Labour shortages in the field of social and health care have already created a need for immigrant labour, and it has become clear that, considering the extent of future needs, immigrants could compensate for at least some of the future labour shortage.[54] As discussed in Chapter 4, the Finnish policy landscape has been characterised by disagreements over whether there will be a consistent need for skilled or unskilled migration in the first place and whether sufficient numbers of skilled migrant workers could be recruited given the high proportion of asylum-seekers and family migrants in Finnish migration flows (and growing global competition for skilled workers). The issue of foreign care workers is accordingly frequently discussed.[55] The desire to avoid the prospect of bringing in immigrants as a low-paid workforce has been a principled sticking point (considering the generally high education levels of the Finnish care workforce); in terms of practical hurdles, language difficulties and recognition of qualifications, as well as the lack of multicultural accommodation in the workplace, are frequently raised.[56]

Immigration is linked to ageing in many other ways – most obviously because immigrants grow old and old people may immigrate.[57] Not only are many Finnish pensioners moving to Spain,[58] wishing to take their

---

[52] Koivuniemi, 'Maahanmuuttajataustainen koulutettu hoitohenkilöstö'; Markkanen and Tammisto, 'Maahanmuuttajat hoitoalan työyhteisöissä'. Koponen et al., 'Mistä tekijät', note that in 2011 social and health care sectors employed 400 000 workers (16 per cent of the workforce): 73 per cent worked in the public sector and 37 per cent were over 50.

[53] Of all immigrants who entered Finland between 1989 and 2001, only 0.9 per cent worked in health and 1.4 per cent in social welfare. Markkanen and Tammisto, 'Maahanmuuttajat hoitoalan työyhteisöissä', 13.

[54] Koivuniemi, 'Maahanmuuttajataustainen koulutettu hoitohenkilöstö'.

[55] Laurén and Wrede, 'Immigrants in care work'.

[56] Koivuniemi, 'Maahanmuuttajataustainen koulutettu hoitohenkilöstö'; Markkanen and Tammisto, 'Maahanmuuttajat hoitoalan työyhteisöissä'.

[57] Kröger and Zechner, 'Migration and care'. [58] Karisto, *Suomalaiselämää Espanjassa*.

pension and health care entitlements with them, but immigrants to Finland are also growing old, further challenging the assumed homogeneity of old age. As immigration numbers have grown, the increasingly diverse composition of the older population has started to raise questions about multicultural ageing and Finland's preparedness to deal with socially excluded older people from minorities.[59] The need for specialised services and language support for older people is only gradually being recognised in integration programmes (which are generally focused on working-age immigrants and supporting them to find employment).[60] This issue is still emerging, unlike that of older people wishing to immigrate to Finland to join their adult children there. The issue raises questions both about the lack of support for transnational care of ageing parents overseas[61] and, most crucially, about the extension of stretched welfare-state services to 'latecomers' who want to migrate in order to overcome the transnational care problem. The Finnish welfare state's universalism was arguably built on assumptions of mutual trust and a homogenous population, based on the maintenance of effective closure.[62] Social heterogeneity and demands for entry by older relatives of immigrant-citizens have challenged these conditions and are testing the official commitment to providing universal services to all residents. These controversies around the migration of dependent adult parents recently came to a head in so-called 'granny cases' (*Antonova* and *Fadayel*) in which two older women, both of whom had adult children who had become Finnish citizens, wanted to join their children as family members.

The Turn Towards Familialism – But 'Why Can't Granny Stay?'[63]
Ageing has been studied intensively since the 1980s, with calculations of tax burdens and costs, and from the 1990s onwards, Finnish debates about cuts in public spending and the future of the welfare state have been dominated by the 'challenges and threats' of population ageing.[64]

---

[59] Most current older immigrants came as Ingrian 'return' migrants – see Heikkinen, 'Exclusion of older immigrants'. See also Linderborg, 'De ryskspråkiga anhörigvårdarnas upplevelser'.
[60] Laki kotoutumisen edistämisestä 2011. Heikkinen and Lumme-Sandt, 'Ikääntyvä maahanmuuttaja.
[61] Baldassar and Baldock, 'Linking migration'; Zechner, 'Care of older persons'.
[62] For a discussion of this assumption and challenges to it, see Häikiö and Hvinden, 'Finding the way'.
[63] 'Miksi mummo ei saa jäädä?' – title of http://uusi.voima.fi/blog/arkisto-voima/miksi-mummo-ei-saa-jaada-2/.
[64] Luoma et al., 'Seniori-Suomi', 6.

The 1990s recession also put pressure on universalist principles.[65] The economic burden of an ageing population has become the dominant narrative in the discussion of demographic change, and it is to be addressed via various 'active ageing' policies aimed at keeping older people economically and socially active for longer.[66] The attention given to how to successfully manage all aspects of ageing culminated with the governmental report on the future in 2004.[67] Since then, and especially after the financial crisis, the realities of demographic ageing have been used to warn about the constant need to prioritise economic sustainability. Most notably, arguments about social security-financing problems arising from people living longer and retiring 'too early' were prominent in justifying changes to the pension system (pensions being one of the largest items of public expenditure).[68] Delaying retirement is an attractive strategy for governments, because it both postpones the time at which pensions will have to be paid out and raises individuals' contributions.[69] Pension reforms were introduced in 2005 to discourage early retirement and encourage further labour-force participation among older workers up until the age of 68, for instance via higher occupational pensions as a reward for later retirement (a further pension reform will take place from 2017).[70] This has gone hand in hand with the slow recognition of age discrimination as barrier for older people's employment.[71] The general trend towards postponed retirement, especially strong among women, shows that the strategies have indeed encouraged people to retire later.[72] In terms of care, ongoing questions remain, because of the tension between the push to reduce the pressure on public services and the desire to uphold the welfare-state guarantees of the constitution (with a continued high level of public support for the welfare state).

The general way in which this tension has been managed in the last two decades is via further encouraging the shifting of responsibility away from the state, including redefining its role and diversifying

---

[65] Anttonen and Häikiö, 'Care "going market"'; Julkunen, *Suunnanmuutos*.
[66] For a summary, see Piekkola, 'Active ageing'. See also Parjanne, 'Väestön ikärakenteen muutoksen vaikutukset'.
[67] Valtioneuvoston kanslia, 'Hyvä yhteiskunta kaikenikäisille'.
[68] Moisio, 'Sosiaali- ja terveysmenojen rakenne'.
[69] Esping-Andersen, *The Incomplete Revolution*, 157–8.
[70] On the 2005 reforms, see Börsch-Supan, 'The 2005 pension reform'. On the 2014 changes, which further shift retirement ages for those born after 1954, see Lassila et al., 'Työeläkeuudistus 2017'.
[71] Jyrkämä and Nikander, 'Ikäsyrjintä'. [72] Myrskylä and Pyykkönen, 'Tulevaisuuden tekijät'.

the system through which old people are supported.[73] As a result, the earlier universalist foundation is arguably being replaced with new practices and principles.[74] The state is moving away from service production, making space for services provided by non-profit (including non-governmental organisations and foundations) or market actors (changes include introducing vouchers to promote choice and encouraging the formation of care markets and tax rebates as incentives to buy services).[75] In residential care, the earlier shift away from institutional care towards home care and community-based services has been pushed further, in the hope that this will introduce savings.[76] The emphasis has further moved away from residential homes and towards home-based living (including user-paid serviced housing that provides 24-hour care).[77] In contrast to many other states that have expanded their home care provisions, public-coverage levels in Finland have dropped dramatically – while those with the highest needs do receive increased amounts of support, others, assessed to be less needy, have become excluded from publicly funded provisions and often need to rely on family members.[78] Indeed, increasing public responsibility has correspondingly resulted in an increasing reliance on family carers.[79] The home care-allowance scheme supporting informal family carers, which was regulated in 1993 and 2005,[80] has been one of the very few forms of social support that has actually been expanded.[81] The growing emphasis on home-care allowance presupposes the availability of a family member to provide basic care.[82] In contrast, formal services are

---

[73] Anttonen, 'Hoivan yhteiskunnallistuminen'; van Aerschot, 'Vanhusten hoiva ja eriarvoisuus'.
[74] Häikiö et al., 'Vastuullinen ja valitseva'.
[75] Anttonen and Häikiö, 'Care "going market"'; Kröger and Leinonen, 'Transformation by stealth'.
[76] The aim of supporting people's living at home is not new, and some have questioned whether it will in fact create economic savings, considering the increased need to provide support for those who choose to do so. Rintala, 'Vanhustenhuoltoa ikääntyville', 645.
[77] Noro et al., 'Ikäihmisten palvelujen kehityslinjoja'.
[78] Valtioneuvoston kanslia, 'Ikääntymisraportti'.
[79] Kröger and Leinonen, 'Transformation by stealth'; see also Kröger, 'Hoivapolitiikan rajanvetoja'. On developments in home care neighbouring Sweden and Norway, see Vabø and Szebehely, 'A caring state'.
[80] Law on Care Allowance (Omaishoidon tuesta annettu laki), 937/2005.
[81] Kröger and Leinonen, 'Transformation by stealth'. Home-care allowance is still discretionary for municipalities, in that they allocate the budget for it, meaning often there is not enough money to support all those who apply. Ellilä, 'Kunnan omaishoidon tuki'.
[82] Compared to support for caring for children (see Chapter 2), care-leave guarantees for those caring for other relatives, introduced in 2011, are more limited. The Act on Employment Contracts (Työsopimuslaki), 55/2001, s. 7a obliges the employer to seek to accommodate such absences – meaning it can be refused – and this type of care leave does not come with earnings compensation.

now very strictly targeted, to the extent that some commentators argue that 'familialism by default' has become the model for those old people who do not yet need intensive help – for those who need more help, home care allowance means 'supported familialism', while 'defamilisation' (that is, public provision) is only for those with the highest needs.[83] Thus, there is movement from universalism towards more targeted services.

In practice, this transformation has created a two-fold construction, where older citizens are assumed to be either able to get by largely without the full involvement of the state or comprehensively helpless. The first group consists of those who are, with some support from the municipalities (care allowance, tax credit for domestic help), still able to be responsible for themselves and live relatively independently. Such citizens are 'incentivised' and expected to use family members, the care market and network solutions – and their own savings and resources – to take responsibility for their own care and to manage their own risks as active, participating, choosing and responsible citizens.[84] Public responsibility for such citizens is conceived in terms of strengthening individuals' choices, and the state shares responsibility for such citizens with their family members, companies and others.[85] This emphasis on the citizen-consumer's choice does recognise self-determination and the differences between old people, and allows independence and customised support. However, it also assumes a citizen who can look after him- or herself – a quintessential third-ager – and may risk blaming older and more frail citizens (and their family members) who make the wrong choices or otherwise fail to manage themselves appropriately.[86] Moreover, it has gone hand in hand with limitations to substantive entitlements, as shown by the recent Act on supporting the capacity of older people and social and health services for older people. The Act offers no new substantive rights (nor guarantees as to how much personnel must be allocated to care – that depends on the municipality's available funds and workers).[87] Instead, it offers a 'right to have needs assessed': what Kotkas identifies as a procedural right supporting active

---

[83] Kröger and Leinonen, 'Transformation by stealth', 323.
[84] Häikiö et al., 'Vastuullinen ja valitseva'.
[85] Anttonen, 'Hoivan yhteiskunnallistuminen'; Häikiö et al., 'Vastuullinen ja valitseva'.
[86] Häikiö et al., 'Vastuullinen ja valitseva'.
[87] Laki ikääntyneen väestön toimintakyvyn tukemisesta sekä iäkkäiden sosiaali- ja terveyspalveluista ('vanhuspalvelulaki') or Act on Supporting the Capacity of Older People and Social and Health Services for Older People, 980/2012. See Hoppania, 'Elder care policy'.

citizenship.[88] With procedural rights, citizens are encouraged to self-determine and be active in terms of their social rights, the focus being not on guaranteeing social rights as universal guarantees but on providing universal access to whatever services the municipality can afford to make available.

The second kind of citizen is the one who requires the state to step in more fully, despite tightened eligibility criteria. Behind active and independent citizens, who use their resources to purchase services and ensure a comfortable later life, are those who cannot self-manage an independent life as an active old person.[89] Typically, these are individuals over the age of 75 or, increasingly, 80 (thus, approaching 'fourth-agers') who are physically frail and/or have multiple illnesses, few resources and few informal supporters and who are unable to make effective choices about their care for themselves.[90] The shift from collective responsibility to individual risk-management for those who can be active and cope by themselves or who can cope with the support of their family has enabled states to focus limited resources regarding home care, other services and institutional care (where it cannot be avoided) on those who are most clearly in need.[91] Though the 'frail old' are treated as residual in discourse about active and successful ageing, there is, of course, a continuum between dependence and independence, and indeed more significant numbers of old people are in need of intensive care and support (and in need of help in receiving care and support), and more will be so in the future.[92] Studies show that these citizens are among the most vulnerable. Women over 80, usually widows, have the lowest quality of life.[93] The home is now a central place for many old and frail people, even those who need more support than they receive.[94] Others have to rely on already stretched institutional care, with fewer carers per person than other Nordic countries.[95] The rights of oldest-old people have caused fraught debate amid reports of mistreatment and lack of assistance in the public sector.[96] While the dreaded fate of the

---

[88] Kotkas, 'Terveyden ja sosiaalisen turvallisuuden hallinnointi'.
[89] Häikiö et al., 'Vastuullinen ja valitseva'.
[90] On the differences between groups, see Valtioneuvoston kanslia, 'Ikääntymisraportti'.
[91] Kröger and Leinonen, 'Transformation by stealth'; Rintala, 'Vanhustenhuoltoa ikääntyville'.
[92] Häikiö et al., 'Vastuullinen ja valitseva'; Valtioneuvoston kanslia, 'Ikääntymisraportti'.
[93] Vaarama et al., '80 vuotta täyttäneiden', 'Suomalaisten kokema elämänlaatu'. See also van Aerschot, 'Vanhusten hoiva ja eriarvoisuus'.
[94] Kröger and Leinonen, 'Transformation by stealth'; van Aerschot, 'Vanhusten hoiva ja eriarvoisuus', 86.
[95] Kröger and Vuorensyrjä, 'Suomalainen hoivatyö'.
[96] Paunio and Linnakangas, 'Ympärivuorokautisessa hoidossa'.

small minority who do not get enough assistance from the public sector is prompting citizens to seek private assistance, not all can. As municipalities have more support to provide, without increased income from the state, they are tempted to respond by minimising what they can, such as staff-to-client ratios in institutional care.[97] Further retrenchment of state standards for care institutions was flagged in 2015.[98]

Who will provide the formal and informal care for the redefined 'problem group' of fourth-age citizens has prompted much anxiety (obscuring from view the increasing amounts of care provided by older people, both to their grandchildren and their peers). Hoping for an expansion in family carers – largely women – is problematic for both demographic and economic reasons.[99] Care-worker shortages, which are already visible in some areas, are projected to become significant by 2025.[100] Despite the Finnish reticence about immigration, there have been moves to utilise immigrants to make up for declining numbers of workers in health care and social welfare. Indeed, despite the imposition of a transition period in 2004,[101] the number of Estonians working in health care has increased.[102] Though the number of immigrant care workers is still small, pressures to find care workers are growing; importantly, while the state has been slow to act, private employers and staff-recruitment agencies have already recruited immigrant care workers – sometimes from further afield than Estonia, such as from the Philippines.[103] Targeting nearby countries (such as Russia and Poland) is seen as the most promising avenue for educated workers (such as nurses), but recruitment from overseas is not the only solution: given Finland has high proportions of family migrants, it is possible to train already-resident immigrants (and the young and unemployed) to be the new care workforce.[104] Occupations such as practical nursing (*lähihoitaja*), which require shorter formal training, are increasingly viewed as ones into which it is not only possible, but

---

[97] Virkki et al., 'Talouden ja hoivan ristipaineissa'.
[98] *Helsingin Sanomat*, 'Hallitus aikoo pienentää mitoitusta', 16 October 2015.
[99] Despite low fertility, family carers (daughters) are still available in theory. Murphy et al., 'Demographic change'. However, the fact that women work and are encouraged to do so, and are now also encouraged to work much later, makes many of them unavailable.
[100] Koponen et al., 'Mistä tekijät'.
[101] Act 309/2004 (Laki Tšekin, Viron, Latvian, Liettuan, Unkarin, Puolan, Slovenian ja Slovakian kansalaisten ansiotyön edellytyksistä).
[102] Markkanen and Tammisto, 'Maahanmuuttajat hoitoalan työyhteisöissä'.
[103] Koivuniemi, 'Maahanmuuttajataustainen koulutettu hoitohenkilöstö'. Opteam recruits from the Philippines.
[104] Koivuniemi, 'Maahanmuuttajataustainen koulutettu hoitohenkilöstö'. See later.

desirable to recruit recently arrived immigrants and second-generation citizens. Both immigrant women and second-generation young people are thus increasingly encouraged to work in the care sectors, with mixed success.[105] Though Finland is still at the early stages of diversifying the workforce in care, some research has suggested that such incipient trends may give rise to the emergence of ethnic hierarchies and increase the segmentation of the care-work labour market according to ethnicity, as has already happened in other countries.[106]

The division of old people into those expected to manage by themselves or with the support of networks and those who need the state's care has also come to frame discussions and policy choices regarding the entry of older migrants and explains the recent controversies around older family members (mothers) wishing to join their adult children in Finland. With increased migration to Finland, the receipt of care has emerged as a transnational issue.[107] The so-called 'granny cases' (*Antonova*[108] and *Fadayel*[109]) tested the provision originally added into the Aliens Act in 1999, but maintained in 2004.[110] The Aliens Act 2004 defines a family member for the purposes of the Aliens Act and family reunion in terms of the nuclear family (described as the 'Finnish concept'[111]): the spouse and any unmarried children under 18 years of age.[112] As per s. 50(2) of the Act, a relative other than a member of the nuclear family ('muu omainen') may join a Finnish citizen living in Finland (the provision does not apply to non-citizens,[113] and EU citizens have their own set of rights[114]) only under two circumstances: if refusing a residence permit would be unreasonable either because the persons concerned intend to resume their close family life in Finland or because the relative is fully dependent on the Finnish citizen living in

---

[105] Koponen et al., 'Mistä tekijät'.
[106] Laurén and Wrede, 'Immigrants in care work'; Näre, 'Ideal workers'; Olakivi, 'In case you can'.
[107] Linderborg, 'De ryskspråkiga anhörigvårdarnas upplevelser'; Zechner, 'Care of older persons'.
[108] Korkein hallinto-oikeus (Supreme Administrative Court, KHO 8.3.2010/436, 8 March 2010). The Court denied leave to appeal, meaning the Helsinki District Court decision was upheld (21.9.2009: 09/1269/3).
[109] Korkein hallinto-oikeus (Supreme Administrative Court, KHO 8.3.2010/444, 8 March 2010). The Court gave leave to appeal and examined the substance of the applicant's arguments.
[110] The original section in the Aliens Act (Ulkomaalaislaki) was s. 18c(3).
[111] Hallitus, 'HE 50/1998', 21.   [112] Aliens Act 301/2004 (Ulkomaalaislaki), s. 37(1).
[113] However, s. 115 of the Aliens Act contains a similar provision that applies to refugees and others receiving international protection.
[114] See so-called Citizenship Directive (2004/38/EC): EU citizens falling under the scope of the directive are entitled to family reunion with dependent direct relatives in the ascending line, and those of their spouse or partner, as long as the relative is 'dependent'. *Complete* dependence is not required. See Aliens Act s. 154.

Finland. The aim of the provision is 'humane': to protect actual family unity, regardless of the formal characterisation of the relationship between family members. The usual requirement of the Aliens Act that the applicant must be shown to be financially supported does not apply to such cases, but according to the travaux préparatoires, the provision should be interpreted strictly.[115]

Irina Antonova (Russian, born 1928) and Eveline Fadayel (Egyptian, born 1945), both of whom were widowed and had children who had moved to Finland and become Finnish citizens, sought, while visiting their children in Finland, to challenge the prevailing interpretation of s. 50(2), which made it very difficult permanently to join their children as family members. In deciding these granny cases (Fadayel being the significant one in terms of elaborating on the reasoning applied), the Supreme Administrative Court maintained a strict interpretation of s. 50. In terms of resumption of close family life, it is required that the parent and child lived together immediately before emigration of the adult child – otherwise, for instance if adult children formed families of their own before emigrating, they are seen as voluntarily separated (even if they stay in touch or provide financial support).[116] The rule does not apply if the adult children have voluntarily emigrated and/or seek permission to bring their parent only after a long period has passed. Complete dependence on a Finnish citizen does mean just that: full dependence on the adult child, demonstrated with medical and other evidence.[117] In assessing dependency, the parent's health and mental state are relevant considerations, as is age, but normal ageing and deteriorating health are not enough to create dependency.[118] What is crucial is the parent's (in)ability to cope with everyday life and the lack of support for them in their country of origin (in terms of other children, a spouse, relatives, etc.). If there is anyone in the country of origin who can look after the parent, no permit will be granted. Similarly, the Court stated that a customary expectation in some countries that children (e.g. the eldest son) look after parents is not enough to create full dependency; nor is there full dependency if the parent can get medical treatment in their home country (with financial support

---

[115] See Hallitus, 'HE 50/1998', 24–5. See also Nykänen et al. *Migration Law in Finland*, 66.
[116] KHO 8.3.2010/444. In Fadayel's case, all three of her sons had emigrated and settled in Finland.
[117] KHO 8.3.2010/444.
[118] KHO 8.3.2010/444. In Fadayel's case, she provided evidence of her various illnesses, but this was not enough to establish complete dependence.

from the children).[119] Individuals, like Antonova and Fadayel, who have children who have voluntarily emigrated and who are not completely dependent under the strict definition (as a result of illnesses for which they cannot get treatment in the country of origin) do not qualify (Fadayel also provided care for her grandchildren, countering claims of complete dependency).[120] The interpretation, consistent with the Court's strict approach in past cases,[121] was confirmed in *Senchishak*, which also withstood a challenge to the European Court of Human Rights.[122]

The interpretation treats older immigrants from outside the European Union in a similar fashion to citizens, in that those who can look after themselves in old age, or who can rely on anything except formal assistance from the Finnish state (including their children in their country of origin), are expected to do so. However, in contrast to old Finnish citizens, the parents of immigrant-citizens to Finland are expected to accept that their emigrated children have assimilated to the 'Finnish family model', which, for them (if not for other Finnish citizens), means *not* looking after their aged parents – at least, not providing day-to-day assistance. The undifferentiated approach obviously allows for little consideration of transnational caring relationships or the ability of parents to contribute to their adult children's families in mutual reciprocity (e.g. by providing unpaid childcare). Instead, it is assumed that any older people will, if not now, eventually drain the nation's dwindling resources as non-productive non-workers, and they are excluded on that basis. At the same time, Finland has no policies to support transnational caring – there is, for instance, no right to flexible working even for those who might have parents in a different country, and no right to the care allowance to help an old parent who is not living in Finland.[123] Interestingly, however, entry is still allowed – in theory, at least – for those who are *completely* unable to cope on their own, when there is no one else that can be made to look after them. Such biologically and functionally completely declined individuals – a

---

[119] KHO 8.3.2010/444. The Court rejected as unproven the allegation that Fadayel could not get assistance and medical treatment in Egypt.
[120] It would also be possible to grant permits for compassionate reasons, if they were manifestly unreasonable to deny, on the basis of s. 52 of the Aliens Act, but this is hardly ever accepted (for an exception, see KHO: 24.10.2007/2719).
[121] The Supreme Administrative Court has consistently rejected appeals arguing that this interpretation is too strict. Nieminen, 'Selvitys edellytyksistä myöntää'.
[122] *Senchishak v. Finland*, application no. 5049/12 judgment 18 November 2014.
[123] On this, see e.g. Zechner, 'Care of older persons'.

tiny minority – *are* grudgingly let in on the basis of the sanctity of family unity, effectively to die in the arms of their child. Once in, they officially have the right to the pared-down benefits of the stretched welfare state, though in line with increasing familialism, the assumption in 'dependency' on the adult child is that the family (daughters and daughters-in-law) will look after the dependent relative. Mirroring dependent fourth-ager citizens, such migrants are ultimately at the mercy of whatever public services are made available.

The granny cases prompted enormous public debate and some civic activism to save the women from threatened removals (churches, for instance, volunteered to protect them).[124] The President of the Republic, the Prime Minister and the President of the Supreme Administrative Court (in the minority) all criticised the law for its lack of compassion.[125] Despite this, promises that the law would be changed never bore fruit.[126] Immigration became a hot potato in the aftermath of the 2008 elections and the economic crisis, and political appetite for the change disappeared. A large factor in this reaffirmation of the status quo was anxiety over the potential numerical threat of mass immigration by older people from poorer countries seeking to join their children as a risk to the already stretched social welfare system, which allegedly could barely provide services to Finnish people.[127] It was thus for the protection of the already at-risk welfare state that border closure had to be kept tight, where possible (within international obligations[128]). Alternatively, there was some suggestion that the right of access to the welfare system for the parents of naturalised citizens be limited to absolutely necessary treatment or that the children be required to make a commitment to repay certain of their parents' welfare entitlements (as is done in Australia; see later). This option was rejected, however, as 'un-Finnish' and contrary to universal access. Indeed, a similar high-profile proposal by a professor of family law that all adult Finnish citizens be made responsible for their parents' care in the aged welfare system,

---

[124] Antonova's departure from Finland was eventually organised by her family, and she died later in Russia. Fadayel was diagnosed with pancreatic cancer and died while in Finland on a temporary permit (pending a challenge to the European Court of Human Rights).
[125] For discussion of this aspect, see Nykänen, 'Hyöty vai haitta', 49–53.
[126] Nykänen, 'Hyöty vai haitta', 53.
[127] *Iltalehti*, 'Mummojen hinta', 1 June 2010, estimated, on the basis of the crude assumption that 10 per cent of immigrants would seek to have an elderly relative join them, that the change would involve 5000 elderly parents, costing 1.5 million euros.
[128] The most important of which relates to EU citizens who are exercising their free-movement rights on the basis the Treaty on the Functioning of the European Union.

if the parents cannot cover the costs themselves, was also rejected.[129] Despite the clear trend towards re-familialising responsibility for elder care, where possible, both of these proposals were seen as going too far towards formally abandoning the logic of universality. Given that many adult children now informally support their parents, the argument that it would be fairer to create a general expectation has some force – however, such a move is, at least for now, still too explicit a departure from universalist principles.

VARIATIONS ON A THEME? ITALIAN, BRITISH AND AUSTRALIAN TRAJECTORIES

Population ageing has been unfolding for many decades now, and it has risen in political importance as the magnitude of its consequences, which will unfold over the next several decades (until the proportion of those over 65 stabilises and the age pyramid is no longer a pyramid but a rectangle[130]), has dawned on contemporary societies in the Global North. This section discusses how the other three jurisdictions are reacting to the growing proportion of greying citizens, especially in the context of care and migration. Though ageing is very advanced in Finland, the upward trajectories faced by the other three states are broadly similar: because of a combination of low birth rates and increasing life expectancy, a growing proportion of their citizens are over 65, and their populations will age further in the next few decades. Italy faces the deepest change: the proportion of the population aged over 65 years, already at 20.3 per cent in 2011, is projected to rise to 32 per cent by 2043.[131] The projections for the United Kingdom show that by 2035, those aged 65 and over will account for 23 per cent of the population, up from 17 per cent in 2010.[132] In Australia, the over-65 age group is projected to increase from 14 per cent in 2012 to 22 per cent by 2061.[133] As in Finland, the percentage of the population aged 85 and over, which is also the heaviest user of health care and care services, will grow particularly fast, making the care needs of the very old a

---

[129] Yle, 'Professori: suomalaiset pitäisi velvoittaa elättämään omat vanhempansa', 26 February 2014.
[130] Putney and Bengtson, 'Intergenerational relations', 152.
[131] Istat, 'Il future demografico', 1.
[132] Office of National Statistics, 'Population ageing'. Wales is the most aged constituent country, while Northern Ireland is the least aged.
[133] In the same period, the number of people aged 85 years and over is projected to grow to five per cent by 2061. Australian Bureau of Statistics, 'Population projections'.

topic of concern. To a greater degree than Finland, where the state has developed a strong universalist approach to guaranteeing the security of old-age citizens, the other states have more strongly built on the family and the private sector as sources of old-age support. This section also examines both the shifting nature of care provision, including provision of care by migrants, and states' responses to older people's migration.

Like Finland, Italy is already feeling the pressures of ageing. Moreover, though Italy is behind Finland in terms of the timing of demographic ageing, its curve will be much steeper than Finland's. Based on current trends, it is projected that the old age-dependency ratio will grow dramatically by 2050 (the youth-dependency ratio will be stable; of course, the accuracy of this depends largely on the level of immigration).[134] The sharpness of the demographic shift is thanks largely to a combination of very high life expectancy and lowest-low fertility (as discussed in Chapter 2) – the latter, together with ageing, has been characterised as one of 'the main changes in Italian society'.[135] Growing concern about the sustainability of public pension systems, owing to high public pension spending and relatively early retirement, have prompted policy initiatives in the active ageing domain aimed at extending working life. Indeed, pension reforms have been a political priority since the 1990s, with changes both raising retirement ages and decreasing levels of coverage.[136] The 2008 economic crisis prompted even more attention to be paid to pensions, and further changes were introduced to limit public spending.[137] Along with pension reforms and efforts to encourage later-life participation in the labour market, care of the growing ageing population has become a crucial issue in terms of who will perform the necessary work and how it will be organised. With the state withdrawing further, the role of non-state sectors in care provision is on the rise.[138] In contrast to Finland, with its more

---

[134] Istat, 'Il future demografico', 7–8.
[135] Naldini and Saraceno, 'Social and family policies', 734. On the current patters of Italian retirement transitions, see Barbieri and Scherer, 'Retirement in Italy'.
[136] Agudo and García, 'Pension reform'. Retirement ages were increased from 60 to 65 years for men and from 55 to 60 years for women, the minimum number of years of contributions necessary for early retirement was increased, pension calculations were changed and a mixed system with pension funds was introduced. On gendered effects, see Naldini and Saraceno, 'Social and family policies', 739–40.
[137] The changes have been controversial, and in 2015 the Constitutional Court held that the temporary removal of inflation adjustment for pensions, brought in by the Monti government in 2012, was unconstitutional (Judgment 70/2015).
[138] For a fascinating account of how the state's withdrawal from its always limited role in care provision is accompanied by the mobilisation of the volunteer sector, involving increasing numbers of retired but 'active' citizens, see Muehlebach, *The Moral Neoliberal*.

social-democratic model, public long-term care for old people has always been much more limited in Italy (though it is similar in that it is characterised by great regional and local variations).[139] The social care system in Italy has always been largely familistic, based on intra-familial loyalty and the unpaid care work of women.[140] This is even more true for the old than for children.[141] Women's increasing employment is therefore putting great pressures on the family obligation – which, in Italy, is also a legal obligation – to provide care for older family members.[142]

The solution to the care dilemma has been for care to 'go private', in more ways than one.[143] Families (often their female members) are still mainly responsible for care, but with financial support from the state, they now increasingly buy care services from the private sector. The main mechanism for this is the generous so-called 'care or attendance allowance' (*indennità di accompagnamento*), which was established in 1980, initially in order to cope with the demand for care by disabled and/or poor citizens, but soon to care for older people, too.[144] The allowance is based on a needs assessment and can be used in whatever way the recipients see fit. With its support, the decline of informal family care has been met by the new category of paid carers (*badanti*), especially in the north, where increasingly educated women are more likely to be engaged in paid work, making them unavailable and unwilling to perform informal care work.[145] This phenomenon is driven by need and a lack of public care provision, but a host of other factors also contribute to it, such as the availability of a cheap immigrant workforce, a large informal sector and sustained tolerance of employment irregularity.[146] Since the mid-1990s, Italian families have increasingly hired immigrants – often immigrants without regular immigration status, who are particularly flexible and can be induced to work long hours (or even round-the-clock as live-in carers) – to substitute the diminishing

---

[139] Gori, 'Solidarity'. For a comparison of the different institutional contexts in Finland and Italy and their effects on caring, see Zechner, 'Family commitments'; Zechner and Valokivi, 'Negotiating care'.
[140] Da Roit, 'Changing intergenerational solidarities'; Naldini, *The Family*; Saraceno, *Mutamenti della famiglia*.
[141] Naldini and Saraceno, 'Social and family policies', 743. Chapter 2.
[142] Naldini, *The Family*, 122–3.   [143] Da Roit and Sabatinelli, 'Nothing on the move'.
[144] On the allowance, see e.g. Bettio et al., 'Change in care regimes'; Da Roit, 'Changing intergenerational solidarities'; Da Roit and Sabatinelli, 'Nothing on the move'.
[145] Da Roit, 'Changing intergenerational solidarities'.
[146] Ambrosini, 'The role of immigrants'; Reyneri, 'Underground economy', 'Immigrants'; Sciortino, 'Immigration in a Mediterranean welfare state'.

supply of other carers.[147] This development from a 'family' care model to a 'migrant-in-the-family' care model[148] has become *the* solution, so crucial that the state will single out irregular workers in the caregiving sector to benefit from regularisation campaigns.[149] Public services, in contrast, are increasingly provided by the 'third sector' and are targeted at those whose condition is seriously deteriorated and who have no family.[150] The care policy regarding old people has thus followed a different logic from that emerging with regard to small children (Chapter 2) – rather than contesting familialism, it has further entrenched the care of the old as a family matter.[151]

Immigrants obviously play a crucial role in the functioning of this system – as discussed in Chapter 4, the care sector is particularly characterised by the presence of immigrants who are poorly paid and willing to work long hours, and who often initially have irregular migration status and are hoping to be legalised. At the same time, Italian immigration law has made it very difficult for such migrant workers to be reunited with their children (Chapter 3), and a similar difficulty applies to older migrants wishing to join their children who have migrated to Italy for work. After the Bossi-Fini law, adopted in 2002 in the middle of a general backlash against immigration, parents' migration rights were also restricted from the more generous stance of the earlier Turco-Napolitano law.[152] After the change, parents under the age of 65 could be reunited with their adult children in Italy only if they had no other children living in their own country; parents over the age of 65 could be reunited only if any other children in the country of origin could not take care of them due to serious health conditions (for instance, inability to work). These requirements were temporarily relaxed in 2007 by the Prodi government, but quickly restored after a change of government in 2008, and a further requirement regarding private health insurance (or privately funded registration with the National Health System) was added for relatives aged 65 and above.[153] As Bonizzoni and Cibea point out, 'the largest percentage of Italian immigrants originate

---

[147] Da Roit, 'Changing intergenerational solidarities'.
[148] Bettio et al., 'Change in care regimes'.
[149] Da Roit and Sabatinelli, 'Nothing on the move'; van Hooren, 'When families need immigrants'.
[150] Muehlebach, *The Moral Neoliberal*.
[151] Naldini and Saraceno, 'Social and family policies', 743.
[152] Bossi-Fini law (Law No. 189 of 30 July 2002).
[153] This was done as part of the overall 'security package' passed by the Berlusconi government. On the requirements, see Bonizzoni, 'Uneven paths'; Favilli, *Migration Law in Italy*.

from countries where the life expectancy hardly reaches 65 years and fertility rates are such that it is difficult for their parents not to have other offspring',[154] so these conditions severely limit parental migration. Indeed, they argue this was precisely the intent: to limit the migration of older people amid concerns about welfare costs (these provisions obviously also pay no attention to any simultaneous care responsibilities that migrant workers, including carers of Italian citizens, might have towards their own parents).

In the United Kingdom, a similar if less extreme demographic profile also suggests increases in pension costs and a growing demand for social and health care services. These demographic trends have provided an additional rationale for justifying changes in pension systems and reductions in state welfare spending.[155] As in Finland, discussions over deterring early retirement and the cost of public pension spending have emerged as predominant preoccupations for successive governments.[156] In line with the active ageing discourse, government measures focus on encouraging people to look after themselves, on encouraging people to stay in the labour market into later life and on making older people more attractive to employers.[157] In terms of pension reform, changes brought in by the Pensions Acts of 2007 and 2008 have sought not only to postpone retirement (the state pension age is now 65 for men and will increase to 65 for women; it will then rise to 66 by 2020 and then increase further) but generally to make people save more and take personal responsibility for their security in old age. The 2012 reforms passed by the coalition government include 'automatic enrolment' into private pensions (and a new 'single-tier' state pension).[158] The emphasis on encouraging older people to rely on occupational pensions and accumulated resources rather than the small basic pension has continued to raise significant issues of inequality, including over those older citizens (often women) who are less likely to have access to significant pension entitlements and savings.[159] On the whole, the active

---

[154] Bonizzoni and Cibea, 'Family migration policies', 22.
[155] Lloyd et al., 'Look after yourself'.
[156] The UK government's Foresight Programme has, since 1993, been examining future challenges, including ageing (especially in the Ageing Population Panel). For a recent overview, see House of Lords, 'Ready for ageing'.
[157] See e.g. Department for Work and Pensions (UK), 'Opportunity age', 'Employing older workers'.
[158] For an overview, see Berry, 'Austerity, ageing'. See also Macnicol, *Neoliberalising Old Age*, ch. 3.
[159] See Gilleard and Higgs, *Cultures of Ageing*, ch. 3, for a discussion of part-time work, caregiving roles and gendered retirement experiences. On inequalities at the retirement stage, see

ageing agenda has become inextricably linked with the broader desire to reduce older people's use of public resources since the 1980s. This ongoing aim can particularly be linked to a projected increase in the number of people aged 85 and over (who are heavy users of services) to 3.5 million, or five per cent of the total population, by 2035.[160] Who should be eligible for publicly funded care and under what conditions has been much discussed.[161]

The United Kingdom's social care system has been extensively modified in the last few decades as successive governments have looked for ways of adjusting the United Kingdom's liberal public service model via management theories from the private sector and the use of market options to save costs and enhance choice for citizens (qua clients).[162] A longstanding favouring of care in the community has also meant that families have retained an important role in providing care, sometimes combined with support from formal and paid services (as in Italy, this is affected by women's participation in the labour market and their ability to provide informal care).[163] The Labour government strategy after 1997 continued in line with earlier trends and involved attempts to personalise services (e.g. via 'direct payments', and then 'personal budgets' from local authorities to enable old people to purchase their own care).[164] The personalisation agenda is intended to increase 'user choice' and older citizens' control over the care they receive, but, crucially, it is also seen as a way of limiting the expansion of public spending in response to demographic trends.[165] The desire to maintain controls over expenditure has increasingly meant that publicly funded or subsidised social services are limited to those who are deemed to be have 'substantial' or 'critical' needs.[166] In line with the premise of active ageing, there is now a strong emphasis on individual responsibility and ability to manage one's own care, which can be difficult for the most

---

Schmelzer, 'Income development'. On accumulation of inequality over the life course, see Vincent, *Inequality and Old Age*.

[160] Office of National Statistics, 'Population ageing'.
[161] On the debates around the long-term care of older people, see Royal Commission on Long Term Care, 'With respect to old age'; Wanless et al., 'Securing good care'.
[162] For discussion, see Gilleard and Higgs, *Cultures of Ageing*, ch. 5. For a discussion of the changes since 1990, see Lewis and West, 'Re-shaping social care'. Note that this trend varies as a result of devolution and is strongest in England. Moffatt et al., 'Choice, consumerism and devolution'.
[163] Cangiano and Shutes, 'Ageing, demand for care'; Hoff, 'Current and future challenges'.
[164] Lewis and West, 'Re-shaping social care'. For an analysis of the personalisation agenda, see Lloyd, 'The individual in social care'.
[165] Lloyd et al., 'Look after yourself'. [166] Lloyd et al., 'Look after yourself'.

vulnerable.[167] The personalisation agenda has continued to be pursued, with the Coalition government (2010–15) working under the assumption that more choice would provide improvements and savings under conditions of austerity.[168] As in Italy, though to a lesser degree, there have been changes in who provides care within the formal system: migrants, predominantly female, have come to make up a significant proportion of the paid care workforce, especially in the private sector.[169] As discussed in Chapter 4, low pay and unsocial working hours (as well as immigration policies) frame the context in which foreign-born workers fill the gap in demand.[170]

The United Kingdom has recently dramatically curtailed the entry of immigrants aged over 65 as family members. This is in line with increasingly restrictive regulations on family migration (see Chapter 3). Up until 2012, settlement for parents of British citizens or permanent residents aged over 65 was possible, if not easy (requirements included having financial dependence on the UK relative, having a lack of other family abroad and being excluded from recourse to public funds for five years).[171] In 2012, the coalition government announced that 'in view of the significant NHS and social care costs to which these cases can give rise', the expectation of settlement in the United Kingdom for dependent parents and grandparents aged 65 or over (from outside the European Economic Area) would be terminated.[172] The new Adult Dependent Relative rule came into force in July 2012.[173] Relatives must now demonstrate that, as a result of 'age, illness or disability, [they] require long-term personal care to perform everyday tasks' and are 'unable even with the practical and financial help of a sponsor to obtain a required level of care in the country where they are living'.[174] As before, sponsors are also required to show that they can care for the dependent relative for five years without recourse to public funds. These changes mean that, as in Finland, relatively fit and healthy older people, who are not completely dependent on their adult children (never mind those who might still be relatively active and, for instance, able to provide help

[167] Moran et al., 'Older people's experiences'.
[168] Moran et al., 'Older people's experiences'; Lewis and West, 'Re-shaping social care'.
[169] Lewis and West, 'Re-shaping social care'.
[170] Cangiano and Shutes, 'Ageing, demand for care'; Cangiano et al., 'Migrant care workers'; Shutes and Chiatti, 'Migrant labour'.
[171] For an overview of previous family-reunion rules, see Kofman et al., 'Family migration'.
[172] Home Office, 'Statement of intent: family migration', 28.
[173] Immigration Directorate Instructions, Appendix FM, Adult Dependent Relatives (in effect from 13 December 2012).
[174] Immigration Directorate Instructions, Appendix FM, Adult Dependent Relatives.

in caring for grandchildren), will not be able to migrate to join their children. The only people who might be able to do so are, as under the Finnish system, those frail old people who are totally dependent and have no medical assistance or care available in their own country (but, unlike in Finland, such people will have no access to the public welfare system). It has been argued that the changes have, in effect, closed this visa category.[175] In the UK context, the change also affects much large numbers of families than in Finland – often from backgrounds where family is assumed to be a source of support for older people.

Finally, as in the other states, in Australia, demographic trends, and what they mean for likely increases in public pensions and health care expenditure, have been discussed for some time in light of projections that show an increase in the proportion of older people.[176] In fact, despite Australia's ageing trends, which are the least dramatic among the states discussed, population ageing has been identified by successive governments as one of Australia's most significant social challenges and has been used as a major rationale for changes in public policy. Reports including the Treasury's regular Intergenerational Reports have highlighted, with increasing emphasis, the government's desire to address the productivity issues of ageing, by improving the workforce-participation rates of older adults, lengthening labour market-participation periods in later life and removing incentives for early retirement.[177] In terms of pensions, Australia is less affected than the other states in that the government only provides the first pillar of retirement income, the age pension (and means tests this), and, encouraged by successive governments since the 1990s, superannuation (private pension fund) benefits have been growing (further reducing entitlement to the age pension).[178] Despite this, raising of the pension eligibility age to 70 (it is already scheduled to increase from 65 to 67 in 2023) was floated recently as a further response to population ageing.[179]

---

[175] The All Party Parliamentary Group on Migration, 'Report of the inquiry', 6–7, notes that even if the sponsor earns a reasonable salary, being thus able to prove no recourse to public funds, they fail under the new rules as this means they can afford to pay for care in their parent's country of residence.

[176] Productivity Commission, 'An ageing Australia'. For a demographic overview, see Biddle et al., 'Indigenous Australia'.

[177] Commonwealth of Australia, 'Intergenerational report 2002–03', 'Australia's demographic challenges', 'Intergenerational report 2007', 'Australia to 2050'.

[178] On Australia's retirement income system and the risks of its superannuation (private), see Borowski, 'Risky by design'.

[179] Productivity Commission, 'An ageing Australia'. For discussion, see Biggs et al., 'Work, aging, and risks'.

As elsewhere, Australian governments (at federal, state and local levels) have adopted the language of healthy, productive and successful ageing, where ageing is discussed in terms of a deficit that must be managed, primarily by individuals who must be responsible for the outcomes of their choices regarding health, work and family (albeit with some community support and state provision of infrastructure to help in making appropriate choices).[180]

Considerations of costs and shifting demographics have shaped the Australian approach to aged care since the 1980s – even earlier than in the United Kingdom – and though many of the changes have embraced market solutions, Australia has retained a greater emphasis on national planning than has the United Kingdom.[181] Several series of reforms aimed at containing the costs of providing care for older citizens have reduced the earlier emphasis (prevalent from the 1960s to the 1980s) on nursing home care, have introduced payment requirements, have targeted services towards those most in need and have heavily increased the emphasis on community-based services (which rely significantly on the unpaid work of informal family carers, principally women).[182] Recent proposals by the Productivity Commission suggested further measures to make individuals contribute more to the cost of their care (for instance, using older adults' housing equity to fund aged care services).[183] In terms of compensating family members for informal care, there are two types of payment available specifically for carers, but they offer very limited support for informal carers.[184] Nor do Australian workplaces adequately accommodate the flexibility needs of unpaid carers.[185] In terms of paid carers, the care workforce

---

[180] Asquith, 'Positive ageing'. See also Aberdeen and Bye, 'Challenges for Australian sociology'; Biggs et al., 'Work, aging, and risks'.
[181] For a comparison between Australia and the United Kingdom, see Healy, 'The care of older people'.
[182] Angus and Nay, 'The paradox'; Clare et al., 'Planning aged care'; Courtney et al., 'Aged care'; Gibson et al., 'The changing availability'. For a critical overview of the gender implications, see Dodds, 'Gender, ageing and injustice'.
[183] Productivity Commission, 'An ageing Australia'.
[184] The Carer Allowance, for the extra medical and health service costs associated with caring in the home (not subject to an income or asset test, but with strict eligibility requirements; accessed by less than 15 per cent of the total carer population), and the Carer Payment (even stricter eligibility criteria; it also includes an income and asset test and a health professional's report). Carers relying solely on the Carer Payment plus the Carer Allowance are paid $200 per week below the minimum wage. Hughes, 'Caring for carers'. On the savings informal carers bring, see Deloitte, 'The economic value'.
[185] A recent amendment to the Australian Fair Work Act 2009 entitles older workers with caring responsibilities to request flexible working arrangements, where previously this was available only to workers with children of school age Biggs et al., 'Work, aging, and risks'.

is overwhelmingly female, part-time and casual. Unlike in Italy, and to some extent in the United Kingdom, in Australia there is no clearly identifiable recent immigrant carer flow; Australia's migration programme limits the entry of low-skilled care workers (not included on the skilled list) and the state offers few cash benefits that could be used to pay workers.[186] At the same time, migrant workers are, as a result of sustained migration over many decades, strongly represented in the aged care workforce, which is largely female, part-time and casual,[187] but care workers are drawn from diverse migration backgrounds (with, however, some birthplace groups concentrated in lower-pay, low-status entry positions).[188] Studies suggest a pending shortfall as the number of older people requiring care grows and the availability of carers, informal and formal, diminishes.[189]

As to the entry of older relatives, as discussed in Chapter 4, Australia's focus since the 1990s has shifted towards a skills-based, economically driven model, and the family-migration stream has been curtailed. In fact, parents of naturalised citizens or permanent residents were first flagged as a likely economic burden in the late 1980s, and a 'balance of family' rule and an 'assurance of support' were introduced to limit such migration and its economic costs.[190] The Howard government restricted this migration further, allowing for the capping of all sections of the family programme (except spouses and dependent children).[191] This significantly limited the ability of aged parents to gain visas.[192] In response to the increasingly long queue for parent visas and the perceived cost of these migrants, the government succeeded in introducing contributory-parent visas – involving higher costs and a bond – in 2003.[193] Further changes were put forward in 2014, when, rather quietly, four visa subclasses were scrapped, including those for

---

[186] Howe, 'Migrant care workers'. [187] Fine, 'Economic restructuring', 5.
[188] Fine and Mitchell, 'Immigration and the aged'.
[189] Fine and Mitchell, 'Immigration and the aged'; Hugo, 'Contextualising the "crisis in aged care"'.
[190] Birrell, 'The chains that bind'; Evans, 'Welfare dependency'. The 'balance of family' rule requires that the parents have at least half of their children permanently resident in Australia or have more children living permanently in Australia than in any other country. The 'assurance of support' is a legal commitment by a person (not necessarily the sponsor) to repay to the Australian government certain welfare payments paid to migrants during a specific residency period.
[191] Betts, 'Immigration policy'; Birrell, 'Immigration reform'.
[192] Betts, 'Immigration policy', 178, states that in 2002–03, just 500 visas were set aside for parents.
[193] Since then, the contributory subclasses have come to dominate, being allocated about three-quarters of parent-visa places.

relative-carers and non-contributory parents.[194] Carer visas enabled needy permanent residents or citizens to sponsor a family member to care for them.[195] The parent-visa changes removed the parent-or-aged-parent visas (already capped and with very long waiting periods[196]), meaning the contributory-parent visa (at a cost of nearly AU$50 000, plus a bond of AU$10 000 to cover any welfare payments made over a 10-year period) was left as the only optionfor permanent entry.[197] The change was blocked by the Senate and the visas were reinstated some months later – but now with even longer queues. The move on parents highlights the dominance of a purely economic reasoning over any other perspective; the one on carer visas is more baffling (carers generally bring savings, taking pressure off the welfare and health care systems) but may be driven by a perception that carer migration does not fit with the precedence given to 'skilled' migration.[198]

CITIZENSHIP AND THE MANAGEMENT OF AGEING POPULATIONS

This last section discusses the emerging patterns of states' management of ageing populations and what they mean for both older citizens and the inclusion of migrants, as both providers and recipients of care. Despite differences in terms of the steepness of their ageing curves, all of the states examined face real demographic changes that necessitate adjustments to policies designed at different stages of their demographic cycles; at the same time, considering the inherent uncertainty of demographic projections, the overriding narrative of demographic pressures has also used an excuse for pursuing policy choices that may not be demographically justified, following alarmist logics rather than

---

[194] The other visas removed were the aged dependent-relative visa (for relatives of retirement age who were wholly or substantially dependent on the Australian sponsor for financial support to meet their basic needs) and the remaining-relative visa (for relatives left alone in their country of origin, with no family or support outside of the family in Australia).

[195] The sponsor had to have a medical condition requiring direct assistance with the practical aspects of everyday life that could not reasonably be obtained from a relative or services in Australia.

[196] The planning levels for 2014–15 reserved 1500 places for non-contributory parents and 7175 for contributory parents, giving existing non-contributory visa applicants a queue time of about 13 years.

[197] Contributory-parent visas, involving higher application fees and the lodgement of a substantial bond, have much shorter processing times (around 12 months).

[198] The official reason was that the (still unfolding) rollout of the National Disability Insurance Scheme will render these visas redundant. Minister for Immigration and Border Protection, 'Explanatory statement'.

empirical evidence.[199] All four states are engaged in similar problematisations of ageing and increasing longevity, founded on statistical knowledge and crude demographic projections of dependency ratios, which frame them as a burden and a threat, posing various risks to both individuals and society that have to be managed. Strategies that encourage greater personal responsibility are clearly dominant, but the concern over those who, for various reasons, fail to 'age responsibly' shows the limits of this approach, requiring more direct involvement and ongoing attention. This section elaborates on two aspects of these processes. First, it discusses the effects on older people of the imperative that pushes them to be active, self-reliant and productive. While strategies that emphasise self-sufficiency have helped redefine and postpone the 'problem of old age', they have uneven effects along gender, class and racial lines and cannot eliminate the inevitability of human dependency, especially at the very end of life. The exclusion of older migrants also starkly shows how states maintain their outer boundary to manage the risks that such dependency poses. Second, it discusses contemporary states' approaches to the inevitability of care provision that hopes to utilise both families and migrants to minimise the costs of care – such approaches do not remove the costs, but simply redistribute them, and in the case of migrants, they do so across state boundaries, while failing to grasp the centrality of care for human relations.

It is well established that the last few decades have seen significant changes in terms of how older people are imagined as citizens. As part of broader de-standardisation of the life course, 'old age' as a distinct phase has been eclipsed by the rise of the 'third age' and dependency has been pushed to the later 'fourth age'. In part, this is a response to demographic change, which has gradually weakened the hold of age-specific categories over age cohorts. Citizens over 65 are no longer treated as a homogenous, separate, dependent population but are now commonly framed as independent individuals who resist generalisations and choose their own paths.[200] There has thus been a move away from the old-person dependency discourse (used to build the welfare state) towards a discourse focused on getting older people to stay active, and especially to stay in employment longer.[201] The new ideal is expressed by the European Union's Active Ageing Index as 'the situation where people continue to participate in the formal

---

[199] For a recent example in the Australian context, see Birrell and Betts, 'The 2015 intergenerational report'.
[200] Gilleard and Higgs, *Cultures of Ageing*.   [201] Walker and Maltby, 'Active ageing'.

labour market, as well as engage in other unpaid productive activities (such as care provision to family members and volunteering), and live healthy, independent and secure lives as they age.'[202] Active-ageing discourses, initially from the World Health Organization (WHO) and United Nations (UN), have come to have widespread purchase and are accepted, for instance, as a Europe-wide strategy to counter the effects of demographic ageing.[203] At the same time, this move away from the dependency discourse towards a focus on the individual is underpinned by a more traditional collective framing – suggested by demographic projections and projected dependency ratios – such that 'older people are *en masse* a financial problem'[204] from the point of view of future economic growth and competitiveness.[205] Active and successful ageing and policies against age discrimination are the positive face of the shift in which citizens' pension ages are lifted and entitlements limited in order to minimise the risk of older citizens depleting the nation's vitality. The ideal role of old citizens is thus transformed from a passive 'pensioner population' to individuals encouraged to engage in work or work-like activities, which Biggs has argued is a form of new 'age imperialism' or more sophisticated ageism, where work and the provision of care to others (in the voluntary sector or in terms of caring for grandchildren or older parents) are never over.[206] This simply widens, rather than counters, the dominant discourse on the value of work for citizenship.

In terms of care as well, older citizens are asked to shoulder the risks of their old age as active individuals – organise savings, plan their care options, look after their health, etc. – and citizenship is thus redefined from a relationship with the state to a relationship mediated by the state but including private, corporate and semi-public actors. Even in the Finnish context, which has long emphasised universalism, the welfare state is shedding some of its universal aspirations and citizens are expected to make independent solutions to help themselves and their families.[207] These changes position older citizens as consumers and frame them as active decision-makers and participants in their own

---

[202] European Commission and United Nations Economic Commission for Europe, 'Introducing the Active Ageing Index'. The Active Ageing Index was developed during 2012, the Year on Active Ageing and Solidarity between the Generations.
[203] On the UN and WHO frameworks, see Kalache et al., 'Global ageing'.
[204] Lloyd, 'A caring profession?', 1173.
[205] As Katz, 'Alarmist demography', has outlined, there is a long history of constructing the elderly as a danger to intergenerational harmony and social prosperity.
[206] Biggs, 'New ageism'. [207] Yeandle et al., 'Voice and choice'.

care, asserting their rights to choose their preferred options. Market solutions for older people are so far under-developed in Finland, but as the other jurisdictions show, the economic possibilities connected to population ageing can be rapidly discovered if mechanisms are put in place to facilitate this and as existing welfare supports are limited. In all four states, care options are increasingly a mix of private and public, paid and unpaid – with direct payments recognising, in part, the care provided and with states giving up their role as provider and instead acting as regulators and facilitators.[208] There has been some discussion about whether the restructuring of welfare systems for older citizens, which combines different solutions and aims for more individual treatment, necessarily equates to reduction.[209] In some ways, it is also about the reluctant recognition of both the ongoing state role in care (even if this is different from its function in the past) and the value of care work (especially private and informal care provided by women; see later). This recognition of the gendered labour of care is forced upon states by the demographic shift, not just in terms demand for care but also in terms of women's changing roles in the economy.[210] While contexts and developments vary regarding these mixed arrangements of formal and informal care as complementary aspects of a whole (as is clear with cash benefits), they all represent experiments with similar multiple aims.[211]

While there is merit in recognising the increasingly diverse needs of older people and developing options to support them that suit their personal situations, this individualisation also entails the possibility that the focus on minimising the neediness of older people and encouraging them to stay at home as long as possible gets subsumed under the overwhelming aim of reducing government expenditure, which may be particularly dangerous for those citizens who are most vulnerable.[212] These vulnerable people are the redefined problem of old age that the moves to create an optimal older population – healthy, active, with morbidity compressed at the very end of life – are trying to minimise:

> the number of people reaching retirement age – 60 or 65 – has become of less import compared with the numbers of older people who will continue to age, ending up as denizens of a 'fourth age' – people worn down

---

[208] Fine, 'The social division of care'.
[209] Pavolini and Ranci, 'Restructuring the welfare state'. See also Fine, 'Individualising care'.
[210] Daly and Lewis, 'The concept of social care', 288.
[211] Daly and Lewis, 'The concept of social care'; Timonen et al., 'Care revolutions'; Ungerson, 'Commodified care work'.
[212] On how vulnerability is obscured by liberal assumptions of competency, self-sufficiency and personal responsibility, see Fineman, 'The vulnerable subject'.

by the weight of their own ageing, and no longer able to manage as 'senior citizens' without the aid and assistance of others.[213]

This focus on minimising the real problem of old age – dependency – cannot change the actual life chances of vulnerable older people whose trajectories have already progressed. For one thing, the ideas behind active ageing that encourage people to provide for themselves are gendered in many ways and have different implications for women, who live longer than men, often end up widowed, frequently have histories of working part-time or taking career breaks to provide care, or who indeed may have been full-time home-makers.[214] Similarly, raised retirement ages disadvantage manual workers, who are often less healthy and wealthy – and indeed die earlier – than other workers.[215] Growing inequalities mean that wealthy people buy services while the poor rely on their families[216] – but what about those who have neither money nor loved ones? Moreover, while the recent shifts in policy have not made it easy for those nearing retirement, in particular, to plan for their active ageing, they also risk blaming those who fail to conform to the new norm. As Asquith puts it, 'if you are incapable of meeting the benchmarks of a positive ageing experience, then you have negatively (or unhealthily, unsuccessfully, or unproductively) aged, and with it, you must bear the weight of failure'.[217]

Most importantly, however, 'real old age', or the fourth age of illness, frailty and dependence, while postponed, cannot be eliminated altogether. This prospect is imagined as an ever-present threat to economic growth and is a constant source of anxiety because of the idea of 'deep old age – the fourth age – as a demographic black hole depleting society's resources as it grows ever larger'.[218] With the intensifying need for care over the next few decades and already stretched public services, enormous unresolved questions are raised about the citizenship of the frailest and the oldest, the poorest and the loneliest. What constitutes good care at the end of life, and how can such care be provided for growing numbers of old and dependent people when states have taken the back seat and are unwilling to commit more resources for even the most vulnerable segment of citizens? While, alongside treating older citizens

---

[213] Gilleard and Higgs, *Rethinking Old Age*, 43.
[214] Foster and Walker, 'Gender and active ageing'. See also Arber and Ginn, 'Gender dimensions'.
[215] Esping-Andersen, *The Incomplete Revolution*, 158.
[216] Kröger and Leinonen, 'Transformation by stealth'.
[217] Asquith, 'Positive ageing', 266. See also Fineman, 'The vulnerable subject'.
[218] Gilleard and Higgs, *Rethinking Old Age*, 56.

as active and participating, there is also a discourse around maintaining a core of services and protecting the vulnerable citizen who can no longer be 'active', such a 'divided discourse' does not easily lend itself to coherent policy towards the very old and vulnerable.[219] Indeed, current discourse around ageing policy does not really seem to be able to envisage the dependent old citizen in any other way except in terms of risk management. At a time of scarce funding, limited staff and growing time pressures, the frail old are increasingly framed as at risk (of falling out of bed or of forgetting where they are and wandering off), creating scope for seeking to manage this risk by monitoring and controlling old people more extensively and isolating them from sources of potential danger. Such warehousing of old people is more typically a female experience. Even though the proportion of men in older age groups is increasing, there is, as Gilleard and Higgs point out, something 'inherently gendered in current thinking about unsuccessful ageing such that men succeed or die, while women linger on in their ever deepening fragility'.[220] At a deeper level, the inability to envisage better ways of looking after the frail elderly is rooted in their vulnerability and dependency, which make them far removed from the 'competent social actor' who underpins ideas about the facilitating state.[221]

Ideas about risk also underpin changes to rules limiting the migration of older people, and specifically that of immigrant-citizens' parents. The increasing role of the economic perspective in family migration was discussed in Chapter 3, but the remarkably uniform trend of shutting down family-migration routes for older people whose children have migrated and settled in the Global North showcases the explicit use of immigration law to prioritise the avoidance of the financial risk to host countries from immigrant-citizens' dependent family members. Such individuals are excluded on the basis of a blanket assumption that people over 65 are at the end of their formal economic productivity and thus particularly at risk of excessive dependence on 'societal resources', which leaves no space for their 'active ageing' in the company of their children. Australia takes the 'assumed economic burden' approach furthest with the straightforward requirement that significant amounts of money be provided in order to guarantee the entry of dependent relatives. As stressed by Baldassar, the assumption is clear: that 'the flows

---

[219] Biggs and Powell, 'A Foucauldian analysis'.
[220] Gilleard and Higgs, *Rethinking Old Age*, 77. [221] Fineman, 'The vulnerable subject', 10.

of caring resources are unilateral: either from child to ageing parent and/or from the State to the elderly.'[222] In reality, the lengthening lives of parents and grandparents allow them to provide various forms of support to their families, including caregiving (allowing the next generation – in particular, women – to engage in paid work). However, the primacy of the avoidance of economic risk posed by older migrants trumps the social and, arguably, economic benefits of family-reunion migration. It also highlights the degree to which immigrants are expected to leave their family loyalties behind once and for all when they emigrate. In effect, this creates a two-tier citizenship: it deprives families with migrant background of grandparental links and imposes heavy burdens on migrant-citizens, who have to organise care for their parents in a transnational setting (in the European context, EU law adds further layers of complexity by privileging the relatives of mobile EU citizens). Even where, in theory, the completely dependent 'fourth-ager' is welcome as a token nod towards family ties and filial duties (for instance, in Finland), the practical reality is that the possibility of family reunion is remote.

The 'crisis in care' is not just a crisis for those who need it, but for those who provide it, and both groups disproportionately involve women.[223] The care issue is really about a structural change in society that not only involves an increasing need for care, but has seen a reduction in the availability – until now taken for granted – of women of all ages to fill the gendered pact of citizenship via unpaid family caregiving. This change can no longer be ignored, and it is for this reason that care has been gradually moving into the public sphere (even if only in part, and still with an element of gendered invisibility).[224] Insofar as it is still the case that '"community" should read "family" and, in turn, "family" should read "women"',[225] it is evident that the 'community' alone cannot provide the caregiving that will be needed in the future. Yet the increasing turn towards family as support in old age is still wedded to the idea that women can carry 'a double, if not triple load, as mothers, workers and carers'.[226] There is also a telling difference between childcare and care for older people, in that directing resources towards childcare is supported by arguments about encouraging women to produce more

---

[222] Baldassar, 'Transnational families', 278.
[223] Chappell and Penning, 'Family caregivers', 459.
[224] Fine, 'The social division of care', 'Employment and informal care'.
[225] Courtney et al., 'Aged care', 238.   [226] Coole, 'Reconstructing the elderly', 59.

children, who are a future resource (Chapter 2), while care for older people is seen as, if not a waste of resources, at least less of an investment in the future. While there is growing support for reconciling paid work and childcare duties, there is little such support in the case of the care of older people.[227] As already mentioned, the issues around family caregiving are further exacerbated by geographical borders, which now define where family sentiment is meant to end; but many migrants are separated from their parents by borders and yet continue to maintain mutual caregiving relationships in a transnational setting.[228] As many countries of origin do not have such an extensive welfare state as, for example, Finland, the practical reality is quite different from the expectation set by immigration law.[229] Indeed, transnational caring is also consistent with ideas about the 'beanpoling' of generations – the idea that, with few people in each *generation*, family intergenerational ties are strengthened, contrary to popular assumptions.[230]

States' maintenance of firm outside boundaries in the context of those (potentially) needing care stands in stark contrast with their openness to (or, in the case of Finland, at least willingness to accept) migrants providing care. Migrant labour has served as a means of containing the crisis in care in many contemporary states, with many governments in the Global North benefiting from the economic inequalities of globalisation that allow them to use immigrants as an 'asymmetrical geopolitical solution' to the care deficit.[231] The continuing and, indeed, growing need for carers at a time of rising anti-immigration pressure raises questions about the future of this approach. This need means the pattern of migrant carers, particularly evident in Italy (and the family-orientated care regimes of Southern Europe in general), will probably be a permanent feature. The increasing demand for paid care and domestic work (which persists in recessions) is a result of structural drivers, involving not only an ageing population that is still largely spatially fixed[232] and women's participation in the labour

---

[227] In Finland, for instance, there is no automatic right to carer's leave when caring for parents, unlike when caring for children; nor does care leave in the case of parents come with earnings compensation.
[228] Baldassar, 'Transnational families'.   [229] Zechner, 'Care of older persons'.
[230] Putney and Bengtson, 'Intergenerational relations'.
[231] Williams, 'Migration and care', 385. See also Anderson, *Doing the Dirty Work?*; Anderson and Shutes, *Migration and Care Labour*; Calavita, *Immigrants at the Margins*; Hochschild, 'Global care chains'; Lutz and Palenga-Möllenbeck, 'Care workers'.
[232] However, see the *Guardian*, 'Germany "exporting" old and sick to foreign care homes', 27 December 2012.

market, but also the commodification of care and the states' migration regimes (Chapter 4).[233] As part of the global restructuring of care regimes, even Finland is now seeking to contain cost in order to get caregiving done as cheaply as possible by those who are not members (or are only partial members). The differences between the four states discussed show the importance of state action – where a state has supported arrangements that encourage migrants as a care force amid a difficulty in getting trained carers (as in the United Kingdom, with its chronic difficulties in the recruitment and retention of care workers over the past decade, due to low wages and unfavourable working conditions), immigrants easily fill the niche. However, it is clear that the construction of immigrants as an exploitable workforce is just that: a construction. As Shutes has argued, the differential rights accorded to migrants on the basis of citizenship and immigration status, as well as gender, race, ethnicity and class, all shape who works in particular sectors, if and how they are incorporated as workers and whether they are constructed as future citizens or temporary migrants.[234]

Finally, there are broader questions about care and its meaning for citizenship. The historical division between public and private and the associated devaluation of women's caregiving have involved a failure to acknowledge the reality of human dependency. The sidelining of care as secondary in debates about citizenship has been widely critiqued by feminist scholars.[235] While it is now to some degree being addressed, at the same time the utopia of a post-industrial economy obscures the continuing reality of practical work,[236] and arguably the focus on active ageing is reifying work as key to citizenship for everyone, including older people. The focus on the economics of the future 'care burden' conceives of care as an unfortunate inevitability, a series of tasks to be completed as quickly and cheaply as possible. This is rather a far cry from the argument made by Tronto and others that care is central to human life and a crucial political issue, requiring a 'shift in our values'.[237] The implications of ignoring dependency and vulnerability as core concepts in the provision of care are huge.[238] When care is understood merely as a set of physical tasks to be performed under

---

[233] Farris, 'Migrants' regular army'.   [234] Shutes, 'The employment'.
[235] Held, *The Ethics of Care*; Kittay, *Love's Labor*; Tronto, *Moral Boundaries*.
[236] Vogt, 'The post-industrial society'.   [237] Tronto, *Moral Boundaries*, 157.
[238] See Fineman, 'The vulnerable subject', for a discussion of the links and differences between dependency and vulnerability, and what these concepts mean for the role of the state.

time pressure, it can be conceived of as low-skilled and manual, requiring little training and involving low pay, and something that can be measured and rationed. When care is understood as a human need that everyone has and something that involves a relationship between carer and cared-for, it is difficult work, requiring a set of skills and a disposition based on compassion, empathy and listening.[239] The contradictory actions that have both moved care into the public domain and simultaneously re-privatised it can be seen as part of an incomplete transition riddled with tensions. Focusing on informal care, Fine has argued for changes that would be needed to sustain the recognition of care as a human experience, involving the need to accommodate carers via care leave and flexible working.[240] A similar reimagining of caregiving as a skilled profession would be required to counter the public perception that it is simple work that can be done by anyone or that it is low-paid 'migrant work'. Finally, most importantly, the gendered nature of care and the issue of men's participation are still largely overlooked.[241]

FINAL REMARKS

'Old age' has lost its distinct status as a stage of life that everyone goes through in the same way. Contemporary states have moved from mass society, where the population can be divided into easily manageable blocks, to having diverse populations whose interests cannot be defined in homogenous terms. These changes have led to reassessments of what being old means – older people are now largely framed as independent and able to choose their own paths, and also their own services. This heterogeneity also comes with a price tag: never-ending activity and individual responsibility. The recent transformations have postponed but not eliminated questions regarding dependency and inequality in old age and states' responsibility for those who are most vulnerable in later life. Similarly, the changing configuration of care provision, where states encourage the market and the family to take on the day-to-day responsibilities of care, does not remove the economic and social costs of care; it simply spreads them differently. When this redistribution of care involves of migrant caregivers, as well as older people receiving

---

[239] Daly and Lewis, 'The concept of social care'; Fine, 'The social division of care'; Tronto, *Moral Boundaries*.
[240] Fine, 'Employment and informal care'. [241] Tronto, *Creating Caring Institutions*, ch. 3.

care in transnational settings, it distributes the consequences of care-giving across international borders. Finally, the current governance of care reframes it as nothing but a drain on resources, which is a deeply impoverished way to treat something that is fundamental to human dignity and relationships.

CHAPTER SIX

CONCLUSION

The previous four chapters have sought to elaborate on the multitude of demographic challenges facing contemporary migrant-receiving states in the Global North, examining the implications of international mobility against the broader demographic picture of low birth rates, increasing diversity and population ageing. States in the Global North have entered a new demographic phase in which all three of the basic components of population change (births, deaths and migration) are constant sources of demographic anxiety and are, together and separately, resulting in policy responses that are at times full of contradictions. The intention of this book, in bringing together analyses of low birth rates and demographic ageing with investigations into immigration, was to add new and much broader perspectives to the debates about the meaning and regulation of citizenship in an age of increasing international mobility. The aim was to discuss the implications of increasing international migration and its relevance to citizenship, and to place this discussion within a larger demographic context. This focus has allowed for an approach where immigration has been treated as part of the overall picture of demographic governance, in which citizenship could be explored in terms of both its boundary-crossing aspect and its inward-looking dimensions. This conclusion does not intend to summarise the book; instead, it takes a brief look at the issues explored and arguments made regarding the three components of demographic change – births, deaths and migration – and outlines how states' attempts to govern them will continue to change citizenship, as well as fleshing out some of the many interconnections between them.

Births are, in many ways, at the heart of the anxieties around population change, owing to the essential role national reproduction plays in nation-making. Chapter 2 discussed the demographic challenge posed by low birth rates, arguing that anxieties over population decline are crucially implicated in debates about both women's citizenship duties and the changing demographic make-up resulting from immigrant births. Population growth via above-replacement birth rates has been, until recently, the norm for most states. It has been so much the norm that most systems in contemporary states – their economic structures, most obviously – are based on the assumption of population growth: the age pyramid has been pyramid-shaped for a reason. Below-replacement-level birth rates have made population stagnation and population decline real prospects – prospects that states have no experience dealing with and no desire to face. Smaller populations may be good for the planet, but they raise enduring anxieties about shrinking economies and relative loss of power in the international system of states. At the heart of these challenges stands the issue of women's citizenship. Women's lives in contemporary societies have been radically transformed, and as much as states have sought to stop these changes, or indeed adjust to them in the name of 'family-friendliness', birth rates remain below replacement, casting doubt on the hope that a new reproductive equilibrium can easily be reached. It may well be that higher birth rates, if achievable, will require a more comprehensive revolution in gender roles – and, indeed, economic structures – than states are willing to contemplate at present, despite women's entry into economic and political realms. Hence the anxiety around immigration: amid worries about 'too few' births and the decline of the national population, the understandable solution is to bring in people from other places (Chapter 4), but that entails a change in the meaning of 'national'. Multi-ethnicity and 'super-diversity' bring new demographic risks, such as inter-ethnic rivalry, socioeconomic marginalisation and cultural challenges, which require new strategies (Chapter 3).

Deaths are also a source of anxiety – or, rather, the fact that deaths are now postponed to very late in life, with many citizens living longer, 'unproductive' lives, sometimes for decades, poses further economic challenges to states. Chapter 5 investigated the increasing proportion of people in older age groups, which is complicating states' desire to maximise 'productive' gains and achieve a global competitive edge via a growing, not shrinking, workforce. Anxiety over having 'too many' old people for the working-age population to support obviously complicates the pursuit of economic growth in a globally competitive economy. Having large age cohorts go through possibly long periods of dependency prior to death will test the social commitments of states to their citizens. The gendered nature of support and care provided in old age is evident in both the increasing practice of importing care workers and the outsourcing of care to private actors and families (especially women whose employment and retirement are affected as a result). The ageing of the Global North will unfold over the next few decades, after which the age pyramid will be more of a rectangle. Until then, states are again hoping to use both the unpaid and paid work of women, including migrant women, to deal with caregiving demands. They are also using immigration to mitigate the challenge of a shrinking workforce – and yet, permanent migrants also eventually add to ageing, which explains the attractiveness of temporary migration (Chapter 4). In the current unequal world system, states in the Global North are well placed to extract labour from the Global South. At the same time, states accept, in the name of countering population decline (and not just ageing), that they also want migrants as new citizens, even if these newcomers contribute to ageing at some point. Again, however, they are seeking to do so on their own terms, preferring skilled and 'Western-valued' migrants – but such migrants also have low fertility rates. To truly counter population decline, states would have to encourage immigrants from high-fertility countries – but this would not only involve migrants who do not have the 'skills', but also tap into the already high anxiety around migrant reproduction (Chapter 2).

Migration, as the demographic component that pierces the boundaries of populations carefully kept separate by the modern state system, is therefore likely to remain a source of demographic anxiety in the decades to come. Chapter 3 analysed the changes in transitions to adulthood and discussed the interconnections between economic and cultural anxieties over young people's transitions and the efforts made to ensure appropriate work and reproductive patterns among young people of immigrant background. Increasing international mobility and the diversity that results from this have already made states anxious about the consequences of demographic change (social cohesion and trust, fragmented identities, role of religion in public life, etc.). At the same time, the retreating welfare state leaves young people to their own devices and, at times, excludes migrants from measures helpful for their integration, risking further fragmentation (as treating young people of immigrant background as permanent outsiders will backfire). These 'integration challenges' are ongoing: not only is migration to the Global North further diversifying – in terms of both types of migration and source countries – but the source countries of most of the current wave of refugees into Europe are largely Muslim, as are many of the likely pools of migrants for the coming decades. With the increase in scepticism about immigrant integration and the rise of right-wing nationalism, states are further tempted to focus only on 'immaculate' migrants and to develop ways of picking and choosing newcomers on the basis of their desirable attributes. Chapter 4 discussed the dynamics of labour migration into low-fertility societies concerned about increasing diversity. It argued that highly skilled labour migration is constructed as the acceptable face of migration; however, the realities of labour migration are more complex, especially as regards low-skilled and temporary migration. The encouragement of temporariness and reservations about turning newcomers into citizens ('testing before buying') are impeding state efforts to achieve integration.

Despite all this, at present the prospect of population decline or even stagnation seems to outweigh these concerns. Torn between the desire to minimise demographic diversity on the one hand and the desire to counter population ageing and population decline (via immigration) on the other, states seem reconciled to accepting immigration – as long as it is at 'manageable' levels. The demographic realities may only be postponed, however, as the supply of skilled labour migrants (so desired by contemporary states) will, if not run out, at least result in a competition between contemporary states that not all of them can win. Indeed, in the long run at least, states in the Global North may finally have to learn to collaborate with states in the Global South, investing in education there and generally taking a more balanced approach to labour migration. At the same time, to continue to counter the effects of declining birth rates, especially in countries where they are at an extreme low, would require a continuous intake of migrants in such large numbers that no government would be politically able to keep admitting them, even as temporary entrants. States with less than perfect records in integrating immigrants from culturally different backgrounds in particular lack the capacity to manage such continuous immigration, but even established countries of immigration show signs of unease about their ability to absorb migrants. Ultimately, then, in the long term it will be necessary to question the unquestionable: the idea of economic growth based on population growth. If population growth in the Global North does peak, it will be considered obviously economically harmful, as it counters the very model on which contemporary capitalist states operate. Even with higher productivity and women's labour-market participation (and, indeed, older people working longer), population decline, however modest, will require a fundamental adjustment in perspective. At the same time, having to manage such a decline may reinforce states' desire to find more sustainable ways of ensuring national reproduction; it may also encourage attempts to build more sustainable economies and systems of global coexistence.

BIBLIOGRAPHY

Books and Articles

Aassve, A., Billari, F. C. and Piccarreta, R., 'Strings of adulthood: a sequence analysis of young British women's work-family trajectories', *European Journal of Population*, 23 (2007), 369–88

Abbasi-Shavazi, M. J. and McDonald, P., 'Fertility and multiculturalism: immigrant fertility in Australia, 1977–1991', *International Migration Review*, 34 (2000), 215–42

Abella, M., 'Global competition for skilled workers and consequences' in C. Kuptsch and E. F. Pang (eds), *Competing for Global Talent* (Geneva: International Labour Office, 2006), 11–32

Aberdeen, L. and Bye, L. 'Challenges for Australian sociology. Critical ageing research – ageing well?', *Journal of Sociology*, 49 (2011), 3–21

Addis, E., 'Gender in the reform of the Italian welfare state', *South European Society and Politics*, 4 (1999), 122–49

Agudo, L. F. and García, M. A., 'Pension reform in Italy: description and evaluation', *Pensions*, 16 (2011), 96–106

Akbarzadeh, S. (ed.), *Challenging Identities: Muslim Women in Australia* (Melbourne University Press, 2010)

'Investing in mentoring and educational initiatives: the limits of deradicalisation programmes in Australia', *Journal of Muslim Minority Affairs*, 33 (2013), 451–63

Albanese, P., *Mothers of the Nation. Women, Families, and Nationalism in Twentieth-Century Europe* (University of Toronto Press, 2006)

Alexander, C., 'Imagining the Asian gang: ethnicity, masculinity and youth after "the riots"', *Critical Social Policy*, 24 (2004), 526–49

Alitolppa-Niitamo, A., 'Liminalities: expanding and constraining the options of Somali youth in the Helsinki metropolitan area', *Finnish Yearbook of Population Research*, 37 (2001), 126–47

'The generation in-between: Somali youth and schooling in metropolitan Helsinki', *Intercultural Education*, 13 (2002), 275–90

Alitolppa-Niitamo, A. and Leinonen, E., 'Perheet, nuoret ja maahanmuutto' in A. Alitolppa-Niitamo, S. Fågel and M. Säävälä (eds), *Olemme muuttaneet – ja kotoudumme. Maahan muuttaneen kohtaaminen ammatillisessa työssä* (Helsinki: Väestöliitto, 2013), 96–113

Alzetta, R., Lagomarsino, F. and Ravecca, A., 'Italy: unreceptive climate and forced adulthood' in K. Fangen, K. Fossan and F. A. Mohn (eds), *Inclusion and Exclusion of Young Adult Migrants in Europe: Barriers and Bridges* (Alderhot: Ashgate, 2010), 109–37

Ambrosini, M., 'The role of immigrants in the Italian labour market', *International Migration*, 39 (2001), 61–83

'Il futuro in mezzo a noi. Le seconde generazioni scaturite dall'immigrazione nella società italiana dei prossimi anni' in M. Ambrosini and S. Molina (eds), *Seconde generazioni. Un'introduzione al futuro dell'immigrazione in Italia* (Torino: Edizioni della Fondazione Giovanni Agnelli, 2004), 1–53

'Immigration in Italy: between economic acceptance and political rejection', *Journal of International Migration and Integration*, 14 (2013), 175–94

'"We are against a multi-ethnic society": policies of exclusion at the urban level in Italy', *Ethnic and Racial Studies*, 36 (2013), 136–55

'Acting for immigrants' rights: civil society and immigration policies in Italy' in C. Sandelind (ed.), *European Populism and Winning the Immigration Debate* (Falun: ScandBook, 2014), 213–46

'Migration and transnational commitment: some evidence from the Italian case', *Journal of Ethnic and Migration Studies*, 40 (2014), 619–37

'Parenting from a distance and processes of family reunification: a research on the Italian case', *Ethnicities*, 15 (2015), 440–59

Ambrosini, M., Bonizzoni, P. and Triandafyllidou, A., 'Family migration in Southern Europe: integration challenges and transnational dynamics: an introduction', *International Review of Sociology*, 24 (2014), 367–37

Andall, J., 'Organizing domestic workers in Italy: the challenge of gender, class and ethnicity', in F. Anthias and G. Lazaridis, *Gender and Migration in Southern Europe* (Oxford: Berg, 2000), 145–71

'Second-generation attitude? African-Italians in Milan', *Journal of Ethnic and Migration Studies*, 28 (2002), 389–407

Anderson, B., *Doing the Dirty Work? The Global Politics of Domestic Labour* (London and New York: Zed Books, 2000)

Us and Them? The Dangerous Politics of Immigration Control (Oxford University Press, 2013)

Anderson, B. and Shutes, I. (eds), *Migration and Care Labour: Theory, Policy and Politics* (London: Palgrave Macmillan, 2014)

Anderson, B., Gibney, M. J. and Paoletti, E., 'Citizenship, deportation and the boundaries of belonging', *Citizenship Studies*, 15 (2011), 547–63

Angus, I. and Butler, S., *Too Many People? Population, Immigration, and the Environmental Crisis* (Chicago, Ill: Haymarket Books, 2011)

Angus, J. and Nay, R., 'The paradox of the Aged Care Act 1997: the marginalisation of nursing discourse', *Nursing Inquiry*, 10 (2003), 130–8

Anitha, S. and Gill, A., 'Coercion, consent and the forced marriage debate in the UK', *Feminist Legal Studies*, 17 (2009), 165–84

Anthias, F. and Lazaridis, G., *Gender and Migration in Southern Europe* (Oxford: Berg, 2000)
Anttonen, A., 'Vocabularies of citizenship and gender: Finland', *Critical Social Policy*, 18 (1998), 355–73
'Hoivan yhteiskunnallistuminen ja politisoituminen' in A. Anttonen, H. Valokivi and M. Zechner (eds), *Hoiva – tutkimus, politiikka ja arki* (Tampere: Vastapaino, 2009), 59–98
Anttonen, A. and Häikiö, L., 'Care "going market": Finnish elderly-care policies in transition', *Nordic Journal of Social Research*, 2 (2011), 70–90
Anttonen, A., Häikiö, L. and Stefánsson, K. (eds), *Welfare State, Universalism and Diversity* (Edward Elgar, 2012)
Arber, S. and Ginn, J., 'Gender dimensions of the age shift' in M. L. Johnson (ed.), *The Cambridge Handbook of Age and Ageing* (Cambridge University Press, 2005), 527–37
Arena, M., Nascimbene, B. and Zincone, G., 'Italy', in R. Bauböck (ed.), *Acquisition and Loss of Nationality*, Vol. 2 (Amsterdam University Press, 2006), 329–66
Arnett, J. J., 'Emerging adulthood. A theory of development from the late teens through the twenties', *American Psychologist*, 55 (2000), 469–80
'Emerging adulthood in Europe: a response to Bynner', *Journal of Youth Studies*, 9 (2006), 111–23
Asquith, N., 'Positive ageing, neoliberalism and Australian sociology', *Journal of Sociology*, 45 (2009), 255–69
Astudillo, O., 'Protests grow against Spain's draft abortion law', *The Lancet*, 383 (2014), 587
Azzolini, D., 'A new form of educational inequality? What we know and what we still do not know about the immigrant-native gap in Italian schools', *Italian Journal of Sociology of Education*, 3 (2011), 197–222
Azzolini, D. and Barone, C., 'Do they progress or do they lag behind? Educational attainment of immigrants' children in Italy: the role played by generational status, country of origin and social class', *Research in Social Stratification and Mobility*, 1 (2013), 82–96
Back, L. and Sinha, S., 'The UK: imperial spectres, new migrations and the state of "permanent emergency"' in K. Fangen, K. Fossan and F. A. Mohn (eds), *Inclusion and Exclusion of Young Adult Migrants in Europe: Barriers and Bridges* (Ashgate: Aldershot, 2010), 51–80
Bader, V., 'The ethics of immigration', *Constellations*, 12 (2005), 331–61
Baird, B., 'Maternity, whiteness and national identity', *Australian Feminist Studies*, 21 (2006), 197–221
Baldassar L., 'Transnational families and aged care: the mobility of care and the migrancy of ageing,' *Journal of Ethnic and Migration Studies*, 33 (2007), 275–97

Baldassar, L. and Baldock, C., 'Linking migration and family studies: transnational migrants and the care of ageing parents' in B. Agozino (ed.), *Theoretical and Methodological Issues in Migration Research* (Ashgate: Aldershot, 2000), 61–89

Balibar, É., *We, the People of Europe. Reflections on transnational citizenship* (Princeton University Press, 2004)

Ballarino, G., Braga, M., Bratti, M., et al., 'Italy' in B. Nolan, W. Salverda, D. Checchi, et al. (eds), *Changing Inequalities and Societal Impacts in Rich Countries: Thirty Countries' Experiences* (Oxford University Press, 2014)

Banner, S., 'Why terra nullius? Anthropology and property law in early Australia', *Law and History Review*, 23 (2005), 95–131

Barbagli, M., Colombo, A. and Sciortino, G. (eds), *I Sommersi e i Sanati. Le Regolarizzazioni degli Immigrati in Italia* (Bologna: Il Mulino, 2004)

Barban, N. and White, M. J., 'Immigrants' children's transition to secondary school in Italy', *International Migration Review*, 45 (2011), 702–26

Barbieri, P. and Scherer, S., 'Flexibilizing the Italian labor market: unanticipated consequences of partial and targeted labor market deregulation' in H. Blossfeld, S. Buchholz, E. Bukodi and K. Kurz (eds), *Young Workers, Globalization and the Labor Market. Comparing Early Working Life in Eleven Countries* (Cheltenham: Edward Elgar, 2008), 155–79

'Labour market flexibilization and its consequences in Italy', *European Sociological Review*, 25 (2009) 677–92

'Retirement in Italy. Rising social inequalities across generations' in H. Blossfeld, S. Buchholz, and K. Kurz (eds), *Aging Populations, Globalization and the Labor Market. Comparing Late Working Life and Retirement in Modern Societies* (Cheltenham: Edward Elgar, 2011), 91–119

Barnes, A. and Lafferty, G., 'The Fair Work Act: as good as it gets?', *The Economic and Labour Relations Review*, 21 (2010), 1–12

Bartram, D., 'Conspicuous by their absence: why are there so few foreign workers in Finland?', *Journal of Ethnic and Migration Studies*, 33 (2007), 767–82

Basa, C., Harcourt, W. and Zarro, A., 'Remittances and transnational families in Italy and the Philippines: breaking the global care chain', *Gender & Development*, 19 (2011), 11–22

Bauböck, R., 'Temporary migrants, partial citizenship and hypermigration', *Critical Review of International Social and Political Philosophy*, 14 (2011), 665–93

Bauböck, R., Perchinig, B. and Sievers, W. (eds), *Citizenship Policies in the New Europe*, 2nd edn (Amsterdam University Press, 2009)

Beck, U., *Risk Society. Towards a New Modernity* (London: Sage, 1992)

World Risk Society (Cambridge: Polity Press, 1998)

The Brave New World of Work (Cambridge: Polity Press, 2000)

Beck, U. and Beck-Gernsheim, E., *Individualization: Institutionalized Individualism and its Social and Political Consequences* (London: Sage, 2002)

'Passage to hope: marriage, migration, and the need for a cosmopolitan turn in family research', *Journal of Family Theory & Review*, 2 (2010), 401–14

Beck-Gernsheim, E., 'Transnational lives, transnational marriages: a review of the evidence from migrant communities in Europe', *Global Networks*, 7 (2007), 271–88

Beeson, M. and Firth, A., 'Neoliberalism as a political rationality: Australian public policy since the 1980s', *Journal of Sociology*, 34 (1998), 215–31

Bell, S., 'Globalisation, neoliberalism and the transformation of the Australian state', *Australian Journal of Political Science*, 32 (1997), 345–68

Benegiano, G. and Gianaroli, L., 'The new Italian IVF legislation', *Reproductive BioMedicine Online*, 9 (2004), 117–25

Benhabib, S., *The Rights of Others: Aliens, Residents and Citizens* (Cambridge University Press, 2004)

Benhabib, S. and Resnik, J. (eds), *Migrations and Mobilities: Citizenship, Borders, and Gender* (New York University Press, 2009)

Bernardi, F. and Nazio, T., 'Globalization and the transition to adulthood in Italy' in H. Blossfeld, E. Klijzing, M. Mills and K. Kurz (eds), *Globalization, Uncertainty and Youth in Society* (London and New York: Routledge, 2005), 349–69

Berrington, A., 'Transition to adulthood in Britain', in M. Corijn and E. Klijzing (eds), *Transitions to Adulthood in Europe* (Dordrecht: Kluwer, 2001), 67–99

Berry, C., 'Austerity, ageing and the financialisation of pensions policy in the UK', *British Politics*, 11 (2016), 2–25

Bertagna, F. and Maccari-Clayton, M., 'Italy: migration 1815 to present' in I. Ness (ed.), *The Encyclopedia of Global Human Migration* (Hoboken, NJ: Wiley-Blackwell, 2013), 1–13

Berthoud, R., 'Ethnic employment penalties in Britain', *Journal of Ethnic and Migration Studies*, 26 (2000), 389–416

Bettio, F., Simonazzi, A. and Villa, P. 'Change in care regimes and female migration: the "care drain" in the Mediterranean', *Journal of European Social Policy*, 16 (2006), 271–85

Betts, A., 'Commentary: contesting Hansen's claim of liberalism and exceptionalism under Labour', in J. F. Hollifield, P. L. Martin and P. M. Orrenius (eds), *Controlling Immigration: A Global Perspective*, 3rd edn (Stanford University Press, 2014), 220–3

Betts, K., 'Immigration policy under the Howard government', *Australian Journal of Social Issues*, 38 (2003), 169–92

'Cosmopolitans and patriots: Australia's cultural divide and attitudes to immigration', *People and Place*, 13 (2005), 29–40

Betts, K. and Healy, E., 'Lebanese Muslims in Australia and social disadvantage', *People and Place*, 14 (2006), 24–42

Bianchi, G. E., 'Italiani nuovi o nuova Italia? Citizenship and attitudes towards the second generation in contemporary Italy', *Journal of Modern Italian Studies*, 16 (2011), 321–33

Biddle, N., Khoo, S. and Taylor, J., 'Indigenous Australia, white Australia, multicultural Australia: the demography of race and ethnicity in Australia', in R. Sáenz, D. G. Embrick and N. P. Rodríguez (eds), *The International Handbook of the Demography of Race and Ethnicity* (Dordrecht: Springer, 2015), 599–622

Biggs, S., 'New ageism: age imperialism, personal experience and ageing policy' in S. O. Daatland and S. Biggs, *Ageing and Diversity* (Bristol: Policy Press, 2004) 95–106

Biggs, S. and Powell, J. L., 'A Foucauldian analysis of old age and the power of social welfare', *Journal of Aging & Social Policy*, 12 (2001), 93–112

Biggs, S., Carr, A. and Haapala, I., 'Work, aging, and risks to family life: the case of Australia', *Canadian Journal on Aging*, 34 (2015), 321–33

Billari, F. C., 'Lowest-low fertility in Europe: exploring the causes and finding some surprises', *Japanese Journal of Population*, 6 (2008), 2–18

Billari, F. C. and Liefbroer, A. C., 'Towards a new pattern of transition to adulthood?', *Advances in Life Course Research*, 15 (2010), 59–75

Billari, F. C. and Rosina, A., 'Italian "latest-late" transition to adulthood: an exploration of its consequences on fertility', *Genus*, 60 (2004), 71–88

Bimbi, F., 'The family paradigm in the Italian welfare state (1947–1996)', *South European Society and Politics*, 4 (1999), 72–88

Birrell, B., 'Spouse migration to Australia', *People and Place*, 3 (1995), 9–16

Birrell, B. and Healy, E. 'How are skilled migrants doing?', *People and Place*, 16 (2008), 1–19

Birt, Y., 'Promoting virulent envy?', *The RUSI Journal*, 154 (2009), 52–8

Blainey, G., *All for Australia* (Sydney: Methuen, 1984)

Blakemore, K., 'International migration in later life: social care and policy implications', *Ageing and Society*, 19 (1999), 761–74

Blangiardo, G. C. and Cesareo, V. (2013) 'Foreign population in Italy: statistical framework and integration', in V. Cesareo (ed.), *Migration: A Picture from Italy* (Milan: Fondazione Ismu, 2013), 11–28

Bleich, E., 'State responses to "Muslim" violence: a comparison of six West European countries', *Journal of Ethnic and Migration Studies*, 35 (2009), 361–79

Block, L., 'Regulating membership: explaining restriction and stratification of family migration in Europe', *Journal of Family Issues*, 36 (2015), 1433–52

Bloemraad, I., Korteweg A. and Yurdakul, G., 'Citizenship and immigration: multiculturalism, assimilation, and challenges to the nation-state', *Annual Review of Sociology*, 34 (2008), 153–79

Blomgren, J., Hiilamo, H., Kangas, O. and Niemelä, M., 'Finland: growing inequality with contested consequences' in B. Nolan, W. Salverda, D. Checchi, et al. (eds), *Changing Inequalities and Societal Impacts in Rich Countries: Thirty Countries' Experiences* (Oxford University Press, 2014)

Bloom, D. E, Canning, D., Fink, G. and Finlay, J. E., 'The cost of low fertility in Europe', *European Journal of Population*, 26 (2010), 141–58

Boccuzzo, G., Caltabiano, M., Dalla Zuanna, G. and Loghi, M., 'The impact of the bonus at birth on reproductive behaviour in a lowest-low fertility context: Friuli-Venezia Giulia (Italy), 1989–2005', *Vienna Yearbook of Population Research*, 6 (2008), 125–47

Boese, M., Campbell, I., Roberts, W. and Tham J., 'Temporary migrant nurses in Australia: sites and sources of precariousness', *Economic and Labour Relations Review*, 24 (2013), 316–39

Bommes, M., 'The shrinking inclusive capacity of the national welfare state: international migration and the deregulation of identity formation' in G. Brochmann (ed.), *Multicultural Challenge* (Oxford: Elsevier, 2003), 43–67

Bonizzoni, P., 'Immigrant working mothers reconciling work and childcare: the experience of Latin American and Eastern European women in Milan', *Social Politics*, 21 (2014), 194–217

'Uneven paths: Latin American women facing Italian family reunification policies', *Journal of Ethnic and Migration Studies*, 41 (2015), 2001–20

Bonizzoni, P. and Leonini, L., 'Shifting geographical configurations in migrant families: narratives of children reunited with their mothers in Italy', *Comparative Population Studies*, 38 (2013), 465–98

Booth, H., 'Demographic forecasting: 1980 to 2005 in review', *International Journal of Forecasting*, 22 (2006), 547–81

Borland J. I., 'Labour market and industrial relations' in I. McAllister, S. Dowrick, R. Hassan (eds), *The Cambridge Handbook of Social Sciences in Australia* (Cambridge University Press, 2003), 94–117

Borowski, A., 'Risky by design: the mandatory private pillar of Australia's retirement income system', *Social Policy & Administration*, 47 (2013), 749–64

Bosniak, L., 'Universal citizenship and the problem of alienage', *Northwestern University Law Review*, 94 (2000), 963–84

The Citizen and the Alien. Dilemmas of Contemporary Membership (Princeton University Press, 2006)

'Making sense of citizenship', *Issues in Legal Scholarship*, 9 (2011), 1–17

Bosworth, M., 'Deportation, detention and foreign-national prisoners in England and Wales', *Citizenship Studies*, 15 (2011), 583–95

Bosworth, M. and Guild, M., 'Governing through migration control. Security and citizenship in Britain', *British Journal of Criminology*, 48 (2008), 703–19

Boucher, A., 'Skill, migration and gender in Australia and Canada: the case of gender-based analysis', *Australian Journal of Political Science*, 42 (2007), 383–401

Breda, V., 'How to reverse the Italian brain drain: a master class from Australia', *International Migration*, 52 (2014), 64–77

Brennan, D., 'Babies, budgets, and birthrates: work/family policy in Australia 1996–2006', *Social Politics*, 14 (2007), 31–57

Brettel, C. 'Gender, family, and migration' in M. R. Rosenblum and D. J. Tichenor (eds), *Oxford Handbook of the Politics of International Migration* (Oxford University Press, 2012), 478–508

Brewer, M., Ratcliffe, A. and Smith, S., 'Does welfare reform affect fertility? Evidence from the UK', *Journal of Population Economics*, 25 (2012), 245–66

Brewster, K. L. and Rindfuss, R. R., 'Fertility and women's employment in industrialized nations', *Annual Review of Sociology*, 26 (2000), 271–96

Broberg, G. and Roll-Hansen, N. (eds), *Eugenics and the Welfare State: Sterilization Policy in Denmark, Sweden, Norway, and Finland* (Michigan State University Press, 2005)

Brochmann, G., 'Scandinavia. Governing immigration in advanced welfare states', in J. F. Hollifield, P. L. Martin, P. M. Orrenius (eds), *Controlling Immigration: A Global Perspective*, 3rd edn (Stanford University Press, 2014), 281–301

Brock, G., 'Immigration and global justice: what kinds of policies should a cosmopolitan support?' *Etica & Politica*, XII (2010), 362–76

Brown, J. A. and Ferree, M. M., 'Close your eyes and think of England: pronatalism in the British print media', *Gender & Society*, 19 (2005), 5–24

Brown, W., *Undoing the Demos: Neoliberalism's Stealth Revolution* (New York: Zone Books, 2015)

Brubaker, R. W., *Citizenship and Nationhood in France and Germany* (Cambridge, MA: Harvard University Press, 1992)

  'Migration, membership, and the modern nation-state: internal and external dimensions of the politics of belonging', *Journal of Interdisciplinary History*, 41 (2010), 61–78

Brysk, A., 'Children across borders: patrimony, property, or persons?' in A. Brysk and G. Shafir (eds), *People Out of Place: Globalization, Human Rights, and the Citizenship Gap* (New York: Routledge, 2004), 153–73

Buchanan, A. and Rotkirch, A. (eds), *Fertility Rates and Population Decline: No Time for Children?* (Basingstoke: Palgrave Macmillan, 2013)

Buchmann, M. C. and Kriesi, I., 'Transition to adulthood in Europe', *Annual Review of Sociology*, 37 (2011), 481–503

Burgess, J. and Campbell, I., 'Casual employment in Australia: growth characteristics, a bridge or a trap?', *Economic and Labour Relations Review*, 9 (1998), 31–54

Bussemaker, J., 'Citizenship and changes in life courses in post-industrial welfare states' in J. Bussemaker (ed.), *Citizenship and Welfare State Reform in Europe* (London: Routledge, 1999), 69–83
Bussemaker, J. and Voet, R., 'Citizenship and gender: theoretical approaches and historical legacies', *Critical Social Policy*, 18 (1998), 277–307
Bynner, J., 'British youth transitions in comparative perspective', *Journal of Youth Studies*, 4 (2001), 5–23
'Rethinking the youth phase of the life-course: the case for emerging adulthood?', *Journal of Youth Studies*, 8 (2005), 367–84
Calavita, K., *Immigrants at the Margins: Law, Race, and Exclusion in Southern Europe* (Cambridge University Press, 2005)
Caldwell, J. C., 'Demographic theory: a long view', *Population and Development Review*, 30 (2004), 297–316
Caldwell, L., 'Women as the family: the foundation of a new Italy' in N. Yuval-Davis and F. Antheas (eds), *Woman-Nation-State* (Basingstoke: MacMillan, 1989), 169–83
Italian Family Matters. Women, Politics and Legal Reform (Basingstoke and London: MacMillan, 1991)
Calwell, A., *How Many Australians Tomorrow?* (Melbourne: Reed & Harris, 1945)
Caltabiano, M., Castiglioni M. and Rosina, A., 'Lowest-low fertility: signs of a recovery in Italy?', *Demographic Research*, 21 (2009), 681–718
Campani, G., Chiappelli, T. and Salimbeni, O., 'Labour market, migration and populism: the subordinated integration of third country migrants' in M. Pajnik and G. Campani (eds), *Precarious Migrant Labour Across Europe* (Ljubljana: Peace institute, 2011), 45–71
Campbell, I., 'The rise in precarious employment and union responses in Australia' in C. Thornley, S. Jefferys and B. Appay (eds), *Globalization and Precarious Forms of Production and Employment. Challenges for Workers and Unions* (Cheltenham: Edward Elgar, 2010), 114–32
Campbell, I. and Brosnan, P., 'Labour market deregulation in Australia: the slow combustion approach to workplace change', *International Review of Applied Economics*, 13 (1999), 353–94
Campbell, I. and Tham, J., 'Labour market deregulation and temporary migrant labour schemes: an analysis of the 457 visa program', *Australian Journal of Labour Law*, 26 (2013), 239–72
Campbell, I., Whitehouse, G. and Baxter, J., 'Australia: casual employment, part-time employment and the resilience of the male-breadwinner model' in L. F. Vosko, M. MacDonald and I. Campbell (eds), *Gender and the Contours of Precarious Employment* (Hoboken, NJ: Taylor & Francis, 2009), 60–75
Cangiano, A. and Shutes, I., 'Ageing, demand for care and the role of migrant care workers in the UK', *Journal of Population Ageing*, 3 (2010), 39–57

Caporali, A. and Golini, A., 'Births and fertility in interwar Italy: trends, images, policies and perception', *Population Review*, 49 (2010), 30–46

Carol, S., 'Like will to like? Partner choice among Muslim migrants and natives in Western Europe', *Journal of Ethnic and Migration Studies*, 42 (2016), 261–76

Castiglioni, M. and Dalla Zuanna, G., 'Innovation and tradition: reproductive and marital behaviour in Italy in the 1970s and 1980s', *European Journal of Population*, 10 (1994), 107–41

'Marital and reproductive behavior in Italy after 1995: bridging the gap with Western Europe?', *European Journal of Population*, 25 (2009), 1–26

Castiglioni, M., Dalla Zuanna, G. and Loghi, M., 'Planned and unplanned births and conceptions in Italy, 1970–1995', *European Journal of Population*, 17 (2001), 207–33

Castles, F. G., 'The world turned upside down: below replacement fertility, changing preferences and family-friendly public policy in 21 OECD countries', *Journal of European Social Policy*, 13 (2003), 209–27

Castles, S., 'Guestworkers in Europe: a resurrection?', *International Migration Review*, 40 (2006), 741–66

'Migration, crisis, and the global labour market', *Globalizations*, 8 (2011), 311–24

'The forces driving global migration', *Journal of Intercultural Studies*, 34 (2013), 122–40

Castles, S. and Davidson A., *Citizenship and Migration: Globalization and the Politics of Belonging* (New York: Routledge, 2000)

Castles, S., Hugo, G. and Vasta, E., 'Rethinking migration and diversity in Australia: introduction', *Journal of Intercultural Studies*, 34 (2013), 115–21

Castles, S., Vasta, E. and Ozkul, D., 'Australia: a classical immigration country in transition' in J. F. Hollifield, P. L. Martin and P. M. Orrenius (eds), *Controlling Immigration: A Global Perspective*, 3rd edn (Stanford University Press, 2014), 128–50

Cerna, L. and Wietholtz, A., 'The case of the United Kingdom' in G. Zincone, R. Penninx and M. Borkert (eds), *Migration Policymaking in Europe* (Amsterdam University Press, 2011), 195–244

Chappell, N. L. and Penning, M. J., 'Family caregivers: increasing demands in the context of 21st-century globalization?' in M. L. Johnson (ed.), *The Cambridge Handbook of Age and Ageing* (Cambridge University Press, 2005), 455–62

Charsley, K., 'Risk and ritual: the protection of British Pakistani women in transnational marriage', *Journal of Ethnic and Migration Studies*, 32 (2006), 1169–87

'Risk, trust, gender and transnational cousin marriage among British Pakistanis', *Ethnic and Racial Studies*, 30 (2007), 1117–31

Transnational Pakistani Connections. Marrying 'Back Home' (London and New York: Routledge, 2013)

Chavez, L. R., *The Latino Threat. Constructing Immigrants, Citizens, and the Nation*, 2nd edn (Stanford University Press, 2013)

Chell-Robinson, V. 'Female migrants in Italy: coping in a country of new migration' in F. Anthias and G. Lazaridis, *Gender and Migration in Southern Europe* (Oxford: Berg, 2000), 103–23

Cherlin, A. J., 'Demographic trends in the United States: a review of research in the 2000s', *Journal of Marriage and Family*, 72 (2010), 403–19

Chesnais, J., *The Demographic Transition. Stages, Patterns, and Economic Implications* (Oxford: Clarendon Press, 1992)

'Fertility, family, and social policy in contemporary Western Europe', *Population and Development Review*, 22 (1996), 729–39

'Below-replacement fertility in the European Union (EU-15): facts and policies, 1960–1997', *Review of Population and Social Policy*, 7 (1998), 83–101

'A march toward population recession', *Population and Development Review*, 27(Supp.) (2001), 255–9

Cheung, S. Y. and Heath, A. F., 'Nice work if you can get it: ethnic penalties in Great Britain' in A. F. Heath and S. Y. Cheung (eds), *Unequal Chances. Ethnic Minorities in Western Labour Markets*, Proceedings of the British Academy 137 (Oxford University Press, 2007), 507–50

Chisholm, L. and Hurrelman, K., 'Adolescence in modern Europe. Pluralized transition patterns and their implications for personal and social risks', *Journal of Adolescence*, 18 (1995), 129–58

Clare, J., De Bellis, A. and Jarrett, D., 'Planning aged care in Australia: a review and critique of the reforms 1975–96', *Collegian*, 4 (1997), 22–9

Clarke, T. and Galligan, B., 'Protecting the citizen body: the commonwealth's role in shaping and defending an "Australian" population', *Australian Journal of Political Science*, 30 (1995), 452–68

Clough Marinaro, I. and Walston, J., 'Italy's second generations: the sons and daughters of migrants', *Bulletin of Italian Politics*, 2 (2010), 5–19

Coleman, D., 'Europe's demographic future: determinants, dimensions, and challenges', *Population and Development Review*, 32 (2006) 52–95

'Immigration and ethnic change in low-fertility countries: a third demographic transition', *Population and Development Review*, 32 (2006), 401–46

'The demographic effects of international migration in Europe', *Oxford Review of Economic Policy*, 24 (2008), 452–76

'Divergent patterns in the ethnic transformation of societies', *Population and Development Review*, 35 (2009), 449–78

Coleman, D. and Dubuc, S., 'The fertility of ethnic minorities in the UK, 1960s–2006', *Population Studies*, 64 (2010), 19–41

Coleman, D. and Rowthorn, R., 'Who's afraid of population decline? A critical examination of its consequences', *Population and Development Review*, 37(Supp.) (2011), 217–48

Collins, J., 'The changing political economy of Australian immigration', *Tijdschrift voor economische en sociale geografie*, 9 (2006), 7–16

'Rethinking Australian immigration and immigrant settlement policy', *Journal of Intercultural Studies*, 34 (2013), 160–77

Colombo, A., *Fuori controllo? Miti e realtà dell'immigrazione in Italia* (Il Mulino: Bologna, 2012)

Colombo, E., Leonini, L. and Rebughini, P., 'Different but not stranger: everyday collective identifications among adolescent children of immigrants in Italy', *Journal of Ethnic and Migration Studies*, 35 (2009), 37–59

Colombo, E., Domaneschi, L. and Marchetti, C., 'Citizenship and multiple belonging. Representations of inclusion, identification and participation among children of immigrants in Italy', *Journal of Modern Italian Studies*, 16 (2011), 334–47

Connelly, M., *Fatal Misconception. The Struggle to Control World Population* (Cambridge, MA and London: The Belknap Press, 2008)

Consterdine, E. and Hampshire, J., 'Immigration policy under New Labour: exploring a critical juncture', *British Politics*, 9 (2014), 275–96

Cooke, L. P., 'Gender equity and fertility in Italy and Spain', *Journal of Social Policy*, 38 (2009), 123–40

Coole, D., 'Reconstructing the elderly: a critical analysis of pensions and population policies in an era of demographic ageing', *Contemporary Political Theory*, 11 (2012), 41–67

Corijn, M., and Klijzing, E. (eds), *Transitions to Adulthood in Europe* (Dordrecht: Kluwer Academic Publishers, 2001)

Côté, J. and Bynner, J. M., 'Changes in the transition to adulthood in the UK and Canada: the role of structure and agency in emerging adulthood', *Journal of Youth Studies*, 11 (2008), 251–68

Courtney, M., Minichiello, V. and Waite, H., 'Aged care in Australia: a critical review of the reforms', *Journal of Aging Studies*, 11 (1997), 229–50

Cover, R., 'Biopolitics and the baby bonus: Australia's national identity, fertility, and global overpopulation', *Continuum: Journal of Media & Cultural Studies*, 25 (2011), 439–51

Crock, M., 'Contract or compact: skilled migration and the dictates of politics and ideology' in M. Crock and K. Lyon (eds), *Nation Skilling: Migration, Labour and the Law in Australia, Canada, New Zealand and the United States* (Sydney: Desert Pea Press, 2002), 49–66

Crompton, R., 'Class and family', *The Sociological Review*, 54 (2006), 658–77

Cruikshank, B., *The Will to Empower: Democratic Citizens and Other Subjects* (Ithaca, NY: Cornell University Press, 1999)

Daguerre, A., 'Teenage pregnancy and parenthood in England' in A. Daguerre and C. Nativel (eds), *When Children Become Parents: Welfare State Responses to Teenage Pregnancy* (Bristol: Policy Press, 2006), 67–88

Daguerre, A. and Nativel, C. (eds), *When Children Become Parents: Welfare State Responses to Teenage Pregnancy* (Bristol: Policy Press, 2006), 67–88

Dale, A. and Ahmed, S., 'Marriage and employment patterns amongst UK-raised Indian, Pakistani, and Bangladeshi women', *Ethnic and Racial Studies*, 34 (2011), 902–24

Dale, A., Fieldhouse, E., Shaheen, N. and Kaira, V., 'The labour market prospects for Pakistani and Bangladeshi women', *Work, Employment and Society*, 16 (2002), 5–25

Dale, A., Lindley, J. and Dex, S., 'A life-course perspective on ethnic differences in women's economic activity in Britain', *European Sociological Review*, 22 (2006), 459–76

Dalla Zuanna, G., 'Population replacement, social mobility and development in Italy in the twentieth century', *Journal of Modern Italian Studies*, 11 (2006), 188–208

Dalla Zuanna, G. and Micheli, Giuseppe A., *Strong Family and Low Fertility: A Paradox? New Perspectives in Interpreting Contemporary Family and Reproductive Behaviour* (New York: Kluwer, 2004)

Daly, M. and Lewis, J., 'The concept of social care and the analysis of contemporary welfare states', *British Journal of Sociology*, 5 (2000), 281–98

Da Roit, B., 'Changing intergenerational solidarities within families in a Mediterranean welfare state. Elderly care in Italy', *Current Sociology*, 55 (2007), 251–69

Da Roit, B. and Sabatinelli, S., 'Nothing on the move or just going private? Understanding the freeze on child- and eldercare policies and the development of care markets in Italy', *Social Politics*, 20 (2013), 430–53

Dauvergne, C., 'Gendering permanent residency statistics', *Melbourne University Law Review*, 24 (2000), 280–309

Making People Illegal: What Globalization Means for Migration and Law (Cambridge University Press, 2008)

Dauvergne, C. and Marsden, S., 'The ideology of temporary labour migration in the post-global era', *Citizenship Studies*, 18 (2014), 224–42

Dean, M., *Governmentality: Power and Rule in Modern Society* (London: Sage, 1999)

Degni, F., Pöntinen, S. and Mölsä, M., 'Somali parents' experiences of bringing up children in Finland: exploring social-cultural change within migrant households', *Forum: Qualitative Social Research*, 7 (2006), Art. 8

de Lepervanche, M., 'Breeders for Australia: a national identity for women', *Australian Journal of Social Issues*, 24 (1989), 163–82

De Luca, D. and Arrazola Carballo, J., 'To work or not to work? Immigrant women and work between constraints and opportunities: a comparison between Lombardy and Cataluña', *International Review of Sociology*, 24 (2014), 422–35

Demeny, P., 'Population policy dilemmas in Europe at the dawn of the twenty-first century', *Population and Development Review*, 29 (2003), 1–28

'Population policy and the demographic transition: performance, prospects, and options', *Population and Development Review*, 37(Supp.) (2011), 249–74

Demeny, P. and McNicoll, G., 'The political demography of the world system, 2000–2050' in P. Demeny and G. McNicoll (eds), *The Political Economy of Global Population Change, 1950–2050* (New York: Population Council, 2006), 254–87

De Rose, A., Racioppi, F. and Zanatta A. L., 'Italy: delayed adaptation of social institutions to changes in family behaviour', *Demographic Research*, 19 (2008), 665–704

de Vries, K., *Integration at the Border. The Dutch Act on Integration Abroad and International Immigration Law* (Oxford: Hart Publishing, 2013)

Docquier, F., and Rapoport, H., 'Globalization, brain drain, and development', *Journal of Economic Literature*, 50 (2012), 681–730

Dodds, S., 'Gender, ageing, and injustice: social and political contexts of bioethics', *Journal of Medical Ethics*, 31 (2005), 295–8

Doogan, K., *New Capitalism? The Transformation of Work* (Cambridge: Polity, 2009)

Dorbritz, J., 'Germany: family diversity with low actual and desired fertility', *Demographic Research*, 19 (2008), 557–98

Douglass, C. B. (ed.), *Barren States: The Population Implosion in Europe* (Oxford and New York: Berg, 2005)

Douglass, C. B., Nash, R., Erikson, S. L. and Lim, A., 'Introduction' in C. B. Douglass (ed.), *Barren States: The Population Implosion in Europe* (Oxford and New York: Berg, 2005), 2–28

Dummett, A., 'United Kingdom' in R. Bauböck (ed.), *Acquisition and Loss of Nationality*, Vol. 2 (Amsterdam University Press, 2006), 551–85

Dyson, T., *Population and Development. The Demographic Transition* (London and New York: Zed Books, 2010)

Eager, P. W., *Global Population Policy: From Population Control to Reproductive Rights* (Aldershot and Burlington, VT: Ashgate, 2004)

Elzinga, C. H. and Liefbroer, A. C., 'De-standardization of family-life trajectories of young adults: a cross-national comparison using sequence analysis', *European Journal of Population*, 23 (2007), 225–50

Escott, K., 'Young women on the margins of the labour market', *Work, Employment and Society*, 26 (2012), 412–28

Esping-Andersen, G., *The Three Worlds of Welfare Capitalism* (Princeton University Press, 1990)

The Incomplete Revolution. Adapting to Women's New Roles (Cambridge: Polity Press, 2009)

Estes, C. L., 'Women, ageing and inequality: a feminist perspective' in M. L. Johnson (ed.), *The Cambridge Handbook of Age and Ageing* (Cambridge University Press, 2005), 552–9

Evans, S., 'Welfare dependency amongst recently arrived aged migrant parents', *People and Place*, 2 (1994), 35–9

Fagan, C., Kanjuo-Mrčela, A. and Norman, H., 'Young adults navigating European labour markets: old and new social risks and employment policies' in T. Knijn (ed.), *Work, Family Policies and Transitions to Adulthood in Europe* (Basingstoke: Palgrave Macmillan, 2012), 130–54

Fagerlund, J., 'Finland' in R. Bauböck (ed.), *Acquisition and Loss of Nationality*, Vol. 2 (Amsterdam University Press, 2006), 149–86

Fallaci, O., *The Rage and the Pride* (New York: Rizzoli, 2002)

Fangen, K., Fossan, K. and Mohn, F. A. (eds), *Inclusion and Exclusion of Young Adult Migrants in Europe. Barriers and Bridges* (Farnham: Ashgate, 2010)

Fargion, V., 'Children, gender and families in the Italian welfare state' in M. Ajzenstadt and J. Gal (eds), *Children, Gender and Families in Mediterranean Welfare States* (Dordrecht: Springer, 2010), 105–28

'Italy: a territorial and generational divide' in A. Evers and A. Guillemard (eds), *Social Citizenship, Social Policy and Citizenship. The Changing Landscape* (Oxford University Press, 2013), 173–92

Fargues, P., 'International migration and the demographic transition: a two-way interaction', *International Migration Review*, 45 (2011), 588–614

Farris, S., 'Migrants' regular army of labour: gender dimensions of the impact of the globaleconomic crisis on migrant labor in Western Europe', *The Sociological Review*, 63 (2015), 121–43

Favilli, C., *Migration Law in Italy* (Alphen aan den Rijn: Kluwer Law International, 2013)

Fenton, R. A., 'Catholic doctrine versus women's rights: the new Italian law on assisted reproduction', *Medical Law Review*, 14 (2006), 73–107

Ferrarini, T., *Families, States and Labour Markets. Institutions, Causes and Consequences of Family Policy in Post-War Welfare States* (Cheltenham: Edward Elgar, 2006)

Ferrera, M., 'The "southern model" of welfare in social Europe', *Journal of European Social Policy*, 6 (1996), 17–37

Field, C. D., 'Islamophobia in contemporary Britain: the evidence of the opinion polls, 1988–2006', *Islam and Christian–Muslim Relations*, 18 (2007), 447–77

Field C. D., 'Revisiting Islamophobia in contemporary Britain: opinion-poll findings for 2007–10' in M. Helbling (ed.), *Islamophobia in the West: Measuring and Explaining Individual Attitudes* (London: Routledge, 2012), 147–61

Fine, M., 'The social division of care', *Australian Journal of Social Issues*, 42 (2007), 137–49

'Employment and informal care: sustaining paid work and caregiving in community and home-based care', *Ageing International*, 37 (2012), 57–68

'Individualising care. The transformation of personal support in old age', *Ageing and Society*, 33 (2013), 421–36

'Economic restructuring and the caring society. Changing the face of age care work' in B. Aulenbacher, B. Riegraf and H. Theobald (eds) *Soziale Welt: Sonderband 20*, Baden-Baden: Nomos, 2014), 269–78

Fine, M. and Mitchell, A., 'Immigration and the aged care workforce in Australia: meeting the deficit', *Australasian Journal on Ageing*, 26 (2007), 157–61

Fineman, M., 'The vulnerable subject: anchoring equality in the human condition', *Yale Journal of Law and Feminism*, 20 (2008), 1–23

Forcucci, L. E., 'Battle for births: the fascist pronatalist campaign in Italy 1925 to 1938', *Journal of the Society for the Anthropology of Europe*, 10 (2010), 4–13

Foster, L. and Walker, A., 'Gender and active ageing in Europe', *European Journal of Ageing*, 10 (2013), 3–10

Foucault, M., *Discipline and Punish: The Birth of the Prison* (London: Penguin Books, 1977)

The History of Sexuality, Vol. 1 (New York: Random House, 1990)

Society Must Be Defended: Lectures at the College de France 1975–76 (New York: Palgrave, 2003)

The Birth of Biopolitics: Lectures at the College de France 1978–1979 (New York: Palgrave, 2008)

Fozdar, F. and Spittles, B., 'The Australian citizenship test: process and rhetoric', *Australian Journal of Politics and History*, 55 (2009), 496–512

France, A., *Understanding Youth in Late Modernity* (Maidenhead: Open University Press, 2007)

'From being to becoming: the importance of tackling youth poverty in transitions to adulthood', *Social Policy and Society*, 7 (2008), 495–505

Francesconi, M. and Golsch, K., 'The process of globalization and transition to adulthood in Britain' in H. Blossfeld, E. Klijzing, M. Mills and K. Kurz (eds), *Globalization, Uncertainty and Youth in Society* (London and New York: Routledge, 2005), 249–76

Fraser, N., 'After the family wage: gender equity and the welfare state', *Political Theory*, 22 (1994), 591–618

Freeman, G., 'Modes of immigration politics in liberal democratic states', *International Migration Review*, 29 (1995), 881–902

Freeman, G. and Birrell, B., 'Divergent paths of immigration politics in the United States and Australia', *Population and Development Review*, 27 (2001), 525–51

Frejka, T. and Calot, G., 'Cohort reproductive patterns in low-fertility countries', *Population and Development Review*, 27 (2001), 103–32

Frejka, T. and Sobotka, T., 'Overview chapter 1: fertility in Europe: diverse, delayed and below replacement', *Demographic Research*, 19 (2008), 15–46

Frejka, T., Sobotka, T., Hoem, J. M. and Toulemon, L., 'Summary and general conclusions: childbearing trends and policies in Europe', *Demographic Research*, 19 (2008), 5–14

Friedman, S. L., 'Determining "truth" at the border: immigration interviews, Chinese marital migrants, and Taiwan's sovereignty dilemmas', *Citizenship Studies*, 14 (2010), 167–83

Fullin, G. and Reyneri, E., 'Low unemployment and bad jobs for new immigrants in Italy', *International Migration*, 49 (2011), 118–47

Furedi, F., *The Culture of Fear* (London: Cassells, 1997)

Furlong, A., 'Not a very NEET solution', *Work, Employment and Society*, 20 (2006), 553–69

Furlong, A. and Cartmel, F., *Young People and Social Change: New Perspectives*, 2nd edn (Buckingham: Open University Press, 2007)

Furstenberg, F., 'Reflections on the future of the life course' in J. T. Mortimer and M. J. Shanahan (eds), *Handbook of the Life Course* (New York: Kluwer, 2004), 661–70

'The intersections of social class and the transition to adulthood', *New Directions for Child and Adolescent Development*, 119 (2008), 1–10

Furstenberg, F. F. Jr, Kennedy, S., McLoyd, V. C., Rumbaut, R. G. and Settersten, R. A. Jr, 'Growing up is harder to do', *Contexts*, 3 (2004), 33–41

Fussell, E., Gauthier, A. H. and Evans, A., 'Heterogeneity in the transition to adulthood: the cases of Australia, Canada, and the United States', *European Journal of Population*, 23 (2007), 389–414

Gabrielli, G., Paterno, A. and Dalla-Zuanna, G., 'Just a matter of time? The ways in which the children of immigrants become similar (or not) to Italians', *Journal of Ethnic and Migration Studies*, 39 (2013), 1403–23

Gangoli, G. and Chantler, K., 'Protecting victims of forced marriage: is age a protective factor?', *Feminist Legal Studies*, 17 (2009), 267–88

Gauthier, A. H., 'The impact of family policies on fertility in industrialized countries: a review of the literature', *Population Research and Policy Review*, 26 (2007), 323–46

'Family policy and fertility: do policies make a difference?' in A. Buchanan and A. Rotkirch (eds), *Fertility Rates and Population Decline: No Time for Children?* (Basingstoke: Palgrave Macmillan, 2013), 269–28

Geddes, A., 'The EU, UKIP and the politics of immigration in Britain', *The Political Quarterly*, 85 (2014) 289–95

Gibson, D., Liu, Z. and Choi, C., 'The changing availability of residential aged care in Australia', *Health Policy*, 32 (1995), 211–24

Giddens, A., *The Consequences of Modernity* (Stanford University Press, 1990)

Runaway World: How Globalization is Reshaping Our Lives (London: Profile, 2002)
Gilleard, C. and Higgs, P., *Cultures of Ageing: Self, Citizen, and the Body* (Harlow: Prentice Hall, 2000)
  Rethinking Old Age. Theorising the Fourth Age (London: Palgrave Macmillan, 2015)
Goerres, A., *The Political Participation of Older People in Europe: The Greying of our Democracies* (Basingstoke: Palgrave Macmillan, 2009)
Golder, B. and Fitzpatrick, P., *Foucault's Law* (Abingdon: Taylor & Francis, 2009)
Goldscheider, F., Oláh L. Sz. and Puur, A., 'Reconciling studies of men's gender attitudes and fertility: response to Westoff and Higgins', *Demographic Research*, 22 (2010), 189–97
Goldstein, J. R., Sobotka, T. and Jasilioniene, A., 'The end of "lowest-low" fertility?', *Population and Development Review*, 35 (2009), 663–99
Goos, M. and Manning, A., 'Lousy and lovely jobs: the rising polarization of work in Britain', *Review of Economics and Statistics*, 89 (2007), 118–33
Gori, C., 'Solidarity in Italy's policies towards the frail elders: a value at stake', *International Journal of Social Welfare*, 9 (2000), 261–9
Greene, M. E. and Biddlecom, A. E., 'Absent and problematic men: demographic accounts of male reproductive roles', *Population Research and Policy Review*, 26 (2000), 81–115
Greenhalgh, S. and Winckler, E. A., *Governing China's Population: From Leninist to Neoliberal Biopolitics* (Stanford University Press, 2005)
Greer, S., 'Anti-terrorist laws and the United Kingdom's "suspect Muslim community": a reply to Pantazis and Pemberton', *British Journal of Criminology*, 50 (2010), 1171–90
Grewal, K., 'Australia, the feminist nation? Discourses of gender, "culture" and nation in the "K Brothers" gang rapes', *Journal of Intercultural Studies*, 33 (2012), 509–28
Grillo, R., 'Marriages, arranged and forced: the UK debate' in A. Kraler, E. Kofman, M. Kohli Martin and C. Schmoll (eds), *Gender, Generations and the Family in International Migration* (Amsterdam University Press, 2011), 77–97
Grimshaw, P., Lake, M., McGrath, A. and Quartly, M., *Creating a Nation* (Ringwood, Vic: Penguin, 1996)
Groenendijk, K., 'Pre-departure integration strategies in the European Union: integration or immigration policy?', *European Journal of Migration and Law*, 13 (2011), 1–30
Guest, R., 'The baby bonus: a dubious policy initiative', *Policy*, 23 (2007), 11–15
Hage, G., *White Nation: Fantasies of White Supremacy in a Multicultural Society* (Annandale, NSW: Pluto Press, 1998)

BIBLIOGRAPHY

Häikiö, L. and Hvinden, B., 'Finding the way between universalism and diversity: a challenge to the Nordic model' in A. Anttonen, L. Häikiö and K. Stefánsson (eds), *Welfare State, Universalism and Diversity* (Edward Elgar, 2012), 69–89

Häikiö, L, Anttonen, A. and van Aerschot, L., 'Vastuullinen ja valitseva kansalainen: vanhushoivapolitiikan uusi suunta', *Yhteiskuntapolitiikka*, 76 (2011), 239–50

Halsaa, B., Roseneil, S. and Sümer, S. (eds), *Remaking Citizenship in Multicultural Europe. Women's Movements, Gender and Diversity* (Basingstoke and New York: Palgrave Macmillan, 2012)

Hall, R., 'Australian industrial relations in 2005 – the WorkChoices revolution', *Journal of Industrial Relations*, 48 (2006), 291–303

'First year of Work Choices: industrial relations in Australia', *Journal of Industrial Relations*, 49 (2007), 307–10

Hämäläinen, H. and Tanskanen, A., 'Autetaanko lapsia enemmän kuin vanhempia? Suurten ikäluokkien lapsilleen ja vanhemmilleen antama käytännön apu ja hoiva', *Yhteiskuntapolitiikka*, 79 (2014), 365–74

Hampshire, J., *Citizenship and Belonging. Immigration and the Politics of Demographic Governance in Postwar Britain* (Basingstoke: Palgrave, 2005)

Hanafin, P., 'Gender, citizenship and human reproduction in contemporary Italy', *Feminist Legal Studies*, 14 (2006), 329–52

Conceiving Life: Reproductive Politics and the Law in Contemporary Italy (Aldershot, Ashgate, 2007)

Hansen, K., Hawkes, D. and Joshi, H., 'The timing of motherhood, mothers' employment and child outcomes' in D. Kneale, E. Coast and J. Stillwell (eds), *Fertility, Living Arrangements, Care and Mobility* (Dordrecht: Springer, 2009), 59–80

Hansen, R., 'Great Britain. Paradigm and policy shifts: British immigration policy, 1997–2011' in J. F. Hollifield, P. L. Martin and P. M. Orrenius (eds), *Controlling Immigration: A Global Perspective*, 3rd edn (Stanford University Press, 2014), 199–219

Hartmann, B., *Reproductive Rights and Wrongs. The Global Politics of Population Control* (Boston, MA: South End Press, 1995)

Hawthorne, L., 'The question of discrimination: skilled migrants' access to Australian employment', *International Migration*, 35 (1997), 395–420

'"Picking winners": the recent transformation of Australia's skilled migration policy', *International Migration Review*, 39 (2005), 663–96

Hawthorne, L. and To, A., 'Australian employer response to the study-migration pathway: the quantitative evidence 2007–2011', *International Migration*, 52 (2014), 99–115

Healy, J., 'The care of older people: Australia and the United Kingdom', *Social Policy and Administration*, 3 (2002), 1–19

Heard, G., 'Pronatalism under Howard', *People and Place*, 14 (2006), 12–25

Heath, A. F., Rothon, C. and Kilpi, E., 'The second generation in Western Europe: education, unemployment, and occupational attainment', *Annual Review of Sociology*, 34 (2008), 211–35

Heikkinen, S. J., 'Exclusion of older immigrants from the former Soviet Union to Finland: the meaning of intergenerational relationships', *Journal of Cross Cultural Gerontology*, 26 (2011), 379–95

Heikkinen, S. J. and Lumme-Sandt, K., 'Ikääntyvä maahanmuuttaja kuntien kotouttamisohjelmissa ja vanhuspoliittisissa ohjelmissa', *Gerontologia*, 28 (2014), 168–83

Heitlinger, A., 'Pronatalism and women's equality policies', *European Journal of Population*, 7 (1991), 343–75

Held, V., *The Ethics of Care* (Oxford University Press, 2005)

Helén, I. and Tapaninen, A., 'Closer to the truth: DNA profiling for family reunification and the rationales of immigration policy in Finland', *Nordic Journal of Migration Research*, 3 (2013), 153–61

Hiilamo, H. and Kangas, O., 'Trap for women or freedom to choose? The struggle over cash for child care schemes in Finland and Sweden', *Journal of Social Policy*, 38 (2009), 457–75

Ho, C., 'Migration as feminisation? Chinese women's experiences of work and family in Australia', *Journal of Ethnic and Migration Studies*, 32 (2006), 497–514

'Muslim women's new defenders: women's rights, nationalism and Islamophobia in contemporary Australia', *Women's Studies International Forum*, 30 (2007), 290–8

Hobson, B. (ed.), *Making Men into Fathers* (Cambridge University Press, 2002)

Hochschild, A. R., 'Global care chains and emotional surplus value' in W. Hutton and A. Giddens (eds), *On The Edge: Living with Global Capitalism* (London: Jonathan Cape, 2000), 130–46

Hochschild, A. R., with Machung, A., *The Second Shift* (New York: Viking, 1989)

Hodgson, D., 'Abortion, family planning, and population policy: prospects for the common-ground approach', *Population and Development Review*, 35 (2009), 479–518

Höhn, C., 'Population policies in advanced societies: pronatalist and migration strategies', *European Journal of Population*, 3 (1987), 459–81

Hollifield, J., 'The emerging migration state', *International Migration Review*, 38 (2004), 885–912

Hollifield, J. F. Martin, P. L. and Orrenius P. M. (eds), *Controlling Immigration: A Global Perspective*, 3rd edn (Stanford University Press)

'The dilemmas of migration control' in J. F. Hollifield, P. L. Martin and P. M. Orrenius (eds), *Controlling Immigration: A Global Perspective*, 3rd edn (Stanford University Press, 2014), 3–34

Holton, S., Fisher, J. and Rowe, H., 'To have or not to have? Australian women's childbearing desires, expectations and outcomes', *Journal of Population Research*, 28 (2011), 353–79

Honkatukia, P. and Suurpää, L., 'Panssaroitua kovuutta? Etnisiin vähemmistöihin luokiteltujen nuortenmiesten ryhmäsuhteet ja rikollisuus', *Oikeus*, 37 (2008), 162–80

Hoppania, H., 'Elder care policy in Finland: remedies for crisis?' in G. Jónsson and K. Stefánsson (eds), *Retrenchment or Renewal? Welfare States in Times of Economic Crisis* (Helsinki: NordWel Studies in Historical Welfare State Research 6, 2013), 252–69

Howe, A., 'Migrant care workers or migrants working in long-term care? A review of Australian experience', *Journal of Aging & Social Policy*, 21 (2009), 374–92

Howe, J., 'The Migration Legislation Amendment (Worker Protection) Act 2008: long overdue reform, but have migration workers been sold short?', *Australian Journal of Labor Law*, 24 (2010)

'Is the net cast too wide? An assessment of whether the regulatory design of the 457 visa meets Australia's skill needs', *Federal Law Review*, 41 (2013), 443

Hughes, J., 'Caring for carers: the financial strain of caring', *Family Matters*, 76 (2007), 32–3

Hughes, R., *The Fatal Shore, The Epic of Australia's Founding* (New York: Alfred A. Knopf, 1987)

Hugo, G., 'Introduction' in M. Wooden, R. Holton, G. Hugo and J. Sloan (eds), *Australian Immigration: A Survey of the Issues* (Canberra: Bureau of Immigration and Population Research, 1994), 1–27

'Contextualising the "crisis in aged care" in Australia: a demographic perspective', *Australian Journal of Social Issues*, 42 (2007), 162–82

'Care worker migration, Australia and development', *Population, Space and Place*, 15 (2009), 189–203

'Migration and development in low-income countries: a role for destination country policy?', *Migration and Development*, 1 (2012), 24–49

'Migration and development in Asia and a role for Australia', *Journal of Intercultural Studies*, 34 (2013), 141–59

Humphrey, M., 'Australian Islam, the new global terrorism and the limits of citizenship' in S. Akbarzadeh and S. Yasmeen (eds), *Islam and the West: Reflections from Australia* (Sydney: University of New South Wales Press, 2005), 132–48

'Migration, security and insecurity', *Journal of Intercultural Studies*, 34 (2013), 178–95

Hvistendahl, M., *Unnatural Selection: Choosing Boys Over Girls, and the Consequences of a World Full of Men* (New York: Public Affairs, 2011)

Hytti, H., 'Early exit from the labour market through the unemployment pathway in Finland', *European Societies*, 6 (2004), 265–97
Inda, J. X., *Targeting Immigrants. Government, Technology, and Ethics* (Malden, MA: Blackwell Publishing, 2006)
Inglis, C., 'The incorporation of Australian youth in a multicultural and transnational world' in M. Clyne and J. Jupp (eds), *Multiculturalism and Incorporation* (Canberra: ANU E Press, 2011), 151–77
Iredale, R., 'Patterns of spouse/fiancé sponsorship to Australia', *Asian and Pacific Migration Journal*, 3 (1994), 547–66
Isola, A., 'Fertility concern in Finland and Russia: economic thinking and ideal family size in the rhetoric of population policies', *Finnish Yearbook of Population Research*, 43 (2008), 63–84
  'Hyviä työntekijöitä ja veronmaksajia: syntyvyysretoriikka 2000-luvun alun Suomessa', *Janus*, 20 (2012), 334–52
Jacobson, D., *Rights across Borders: Immigration and the Decline of Citizenship* (Baltimore, MD: Johns Hopkins University Press, 1996)
Jackson, N., 'When is a baby boom not a baby boom? Nine points of caution when interpreting fertility trends', *People and Place*, 14 (2006), 1–13
Jackson, N. and Casey, A., 'Procreate and cherish: a note on Australia's abrupt shift to pro-natalism', *New Zealand Population Review*, 35 (2009), 129–48
Jamieson, L., Backett Milburn, K., Simpson, R. and Wasoff, F., 'Fertility and social change: the neglected contribution of men's approaches to becoming partners and parents', *The Sociological Review*, 58 (2010) 463–85
Jasinskaja-Lahti, I., Liebkind, K. and Vesala, T., *Rasismi ja syrjintä Suomessa. Maahanmuuttajien kokemuksia* (Helsinki: Gaudeamus, 2002)
Jessop, B., 'Towards a Schumpeterian workfare state? Preliminary remarks on post-Fordist political economy', *Studies in Political Economy*, 40 (1993), 7–39
Jones, B., 'The dangers of muddling through: why Australia needs a clear national population policy' in S. Vizard, H. J. Martin and T. Watts (eds), *Australia's Population Challenges* (Camberwell: Penguin, 2003), 140–50
Joppke, C., 'Why liberal states accept unwanted immigration', *World Politics*, 50 (1998), 266–93
  Challenge to the Nation-State: Immigration in Western Europe and the United States (Oxford University Press 1998)
  'How immigration is changing citizenship: a comparative view', *Ethnic and Racial Studies*, 22 (1999), 629–52
  Immigration and the Nation-State: The United States, Germany, and Great Britain (Oxford University Press, 1999)
  Selecting by Origin: Ethnic Migration in the Liberal State (Cambridge, MA: Harvard University Press, 2005)
  'Comparative citizenship: a restrictive turn in Europe?', *Law & Ethics of Human Rights*, 2 (2008), Art. 6

Citizenship and Immigration (Cambridge: Polity Press, 2010)

'Through the European looking glass: citizenship tests in the USA, Australia, and Canada', *Citizenship Studies*, 17 (2013), 1–15

'Europe and Islam: alarmists, victimists, and integration by law', *West European Politics*, 37 (2014), 1314–35

Jordan, B. and Düvell, F., *Irregular Migration. The Dilemmas of Transnational Mobility* (Edward Elgar, 2002)

Joseph, C., '(Re)negotiating cultural and work identities pre and post-migration: Malaysian migrant women in Australia', *Women's Studies International Forum*, 36 (2013), 27–36

Julkunen, R., *Suunnanmuutos* (Tampere: Vastapaino, 2001)

Jupp, J., *From White Australia to Woomera: The story of Australian immigration*, 2nd edn (Cambridge University Press, 2007)

'Politics, public policy and multiculturalism' in M. Clyne and J. Jupp (eds), *Multiculturalism and Incorporation* (Canberra: ANU E Press, 2011), 151–77

Jyrkämä, J. and Nikander, P., 'Ikäsyrjintä, ageismi' in O. Lepola and S. Villa (eds), *Syrjintä Suomessa 2006* (Helsinki: Ihmisoikeusliitto, 2007), 181–218

Kalache, A., Barreto, S. M. and Keller, I., 'Global ageing: the demographic revolution in all cultures and societies' in M. L. Johnson (ed.), *The Cambridge Handbook of Age and Ageing* (Cambridge University Press, 2005), 30–46

Karisto, A. (ed.), *Suomalaiselämää Espanjassa* (Helsinki: Suomalaisen Kirjallisuuden Seura, 2000)

'Finnish baby boomers and the emergence of the third age', *International Journal of Ageing and Later Life*, 2 (2007), 91–108

Katz, S., 'Alarmist demography: power, knowledge, and the elderly population', *Journal of Aging Studies*, 6 (1992), 203–25

Keep, E. and Mayhew, K., 'Moving beyond skills as a social and economic panacea', *Work, Employment and Society*, 24 (2010), 565–77

Kelly, P., 'Youth as an artefact of expertise: problematizing the practice of youth studies in an age of uncertainty', *Journal of Youth Studies*, 3 (2000), 301–15

Keskinen, S., Rastas, A. and Tuori, S., *En ole rasisti, mutta . . . Maahanmuutosta, monikulttuurisuudesta ja kritiikistä* (Tampere: Vastapaino, 2009)

Khan, L. A., 'Temporality of law', *McGeorge Law Review*, 40 (2009), 55–106

Khoo, S., 'The context of spouse migration to Australia', *International Migration* 39 (2001), 111–32

Khoo, S., Birrell, B. and Heard, G., 'Intermarriage by birthplace and ancestry in Australia', *People and Place*, 17 (2009), 15–28

Khoo, S., Hugo, G. and McDonald, P., 'Which skilled temporary migrants become permanent residents and why?', *International Migration Review*, 42 (2008), 193–226

Kilpi-Jakonen, E., 'Does Finnish educational equality extend to children of immigrants?', *Nordic Journal of Migration Research*, 2 (2012), 167–81
   'Citizenship and educational attainment amongst the second generation: an analysis of children of immigrants in Finland', *Journal of Ethnic and Migration Studies*, 40 (2014), 1079–96
Kilponen, J. and Romppanen, A., 'Julkinen talous ja väestön ikääntyminen pitkällä aikavälillä', *Kansantaloudellinen aikakauskirja*, 98 (2002), 275–90
Kinnaird, B., 'Current issues in the Skilled Temporary Subclass 457 visa', *People and Place*, 14 (2006), 49–65
Kirk, D., 'Demographic transition theory', *Population Studies*, 50 (1996), 361–87
Kittay, E. F., *Love's Labor: Essays on Women, Equality and Dependency* (New York and London: Routledge, 1999)
Klausen, J., 'British counter-terrorism after 7/7: adapting community policing to the fight against domestic terrorism', *Journal of Ethnic and Migration Studies*, 35 (2009), 403–20
Kligman, G., 'A reflection on barren states: the demographic paradoxes of consumer capitalism' in C. B. Douglass (ed.), *Barren States: The Population Implosion in Europe* (Oxford and New York: Berg, 2005), 249–59
Knijn, T. (ed.), *Work, Family Policies and Transitions to Adulthood in Europe* (Basingstoke: Palgrave Macmillan, 2012)
Kofman, E., 'Family-related migration: a critical review of European Studies', *Journal of Ethnic and Migration Studies*, 30 (2004), 243–62
   'Towards a gendered evaluation of (highly) skilled immigration policies in Europe', *International Migration*, 52 (2014), 116–28
Kofman, E., and Raghuram, P., 'Gender and global labour migrations. Incorporating skilled workers', *Antipode*, 38 (2006), 282–303
Kofman, E., Phizacklea, A., Raghuram, P. and Sales, R., *Gender and International Migration in Europe: employment, welfare and politics* (Routledge, 2000)
Kofman, E., Saharso, S. and Vacchelli, E., 'Gendered perspectives on integration discourses and measures', *International Migration*, 53 (2015), 77–89
Kogan, I., 'Introduction to the special issue on minority ethnic groups' marriage patterns in Europe', *Zeitschrift für Familienforschung*, 22 (2010), 3–10
Kohler, H., Billari, F. C. and Ortega, J. A., 'The emergence of lowest-low fertility in Europe during the 1990s', *Population and Development Review*, 28 (2002), 641–80
Koslowski, R., *Migrants and Citizens. Demographic Change in the European State System* (Ithaca, NY and London: Cornell University Press, 2000)
Kostakopoulou, D., 'Matters of control: integration tests, naturalisation reform and probationary citizenship in the United Kingdom', *Journal of Ethnic and Migration Studies*, 36 (2010), 829–46

Kotkas, T., 'Terveyden ja sosiaalisen turvallisuuden hallinnointi 2000-luvun Suomessa – menettelylliset oikeudet ja aktiivinen kansalaisuus', *Lakimies* (2009) 2, 207-25

Kraler, A., Kofman, E., Kohli, M. and Schmoll, C. (eds), *Gender, Generations and the Family in International Migration* (Amsterdam University Press, 2011)

Kramer, S. P., *The Other Population Crisis. What Governments Can DO about Falling Birth Rates* (Washington, DC/Baltimore, MD: Woodrow Wilson Center Press/Johns Hopkins University Press, 2014)

Krause, E. L., '"Empty cradles" and the quiet revolution: demographic discourse and cultural struggles of gender, race, and class in Italy', *Cultural Anthropology*, 16 (2001), 576-611

A Crisis of Births. Population Politics and Family-Making in Italy (Belmont, CA: Wadsworth, 2005)

'"Toys and perfumes": imploding Italy's population paradox and motherly myths' in C. B. Douglass (ed.), *Barren States: The Population Implosion in Europe* (Oxford and New York: Berg, 2005), 159-82

Krause, E. L. and Marchesi, M., 'Fertility politics as "social Viagra": reproducing boundaries, social cohesion, and modernity in Italy', *American Anthropologist*, 109 (2007), 350-62

Kröger, T., 'Hoivapolitiikan rajanvetoja' in A. Anttonen, H. Valokivi and M. Zechner (eds), *Hoiva – tutkimus, politiikka ja arki* (Tampere: Vastapaino, 2009), 99-125

Kröger, T. and Leinonen, A., 'Transformation by stealth: the retargeting of home care services in Finland', *Health and Social Care in the Community*, 20 (2012), 319-27

Kröger, T. and Vuorensyrjä, M., 'Suomalainen hoivatyö pohjoismaisessa vertailussa. Vanhuspalvelujen koti- ja laitoshoitotyön piirteitä ja ongelmia', *Yhteiskuntapolitiikka*, 73 (2008), 250-66

Kröger, T. and Zechner, M., 'Migration and care: giving and needing care across national borders', *Finnish Journal of Ethnicity and Migration*, 4 (2009), 17-26

Kymlicka W., *Multicultural Citizenship: A Liberal Theory of Minority Rights* (Oxford: Clarendon, 1995)

Politics in the Vernacular: Nationalism, Multiculturalism and Citizenship (Oxford University Press, 2001)

Kymlicka, W. and Norman, W., 'Return of the citizen: a survey of recent work on citizenship theory', *Ethics*, 104 (1994), 352-81

Lain, S. J., Ford, J. B., Raynes-Greenow, C. H., et al., 'The impact of the baby bonus payment in New South Wales: who is having "one for the country"?', *Medical Journal of Australia*, 190 (2009), 238-41

Laslett, P., *A Fresh Map of Life* (Cambridge, MA: Harvard University Press, 1991)

Lattas, J., 'Cruising: "moral panic" and the Cronulla riot', *Australian Journal of Anthropology*, 18 (2007), 320–35

Laurén, J. and Wrede, S., 'Immigrants in care work: ethnic hierarchies and work distribution', *Finnish Journal of Ethnicity and Migration*, 3 (2008), 20–31

Layton-Henry, Z., 'Britain: from immigration control to migration management' in W. Cornelius, T. Tsuda, P. Martin and J. Hollifield (eds), *Controlling Immigration: A Global Perspective*, 2nd edn (Stanford University Press, 2004), 297–333

Lee, R., 'The demographic transition: three centuries of fundamental change', *Journal of Economic Perspectives*, 17 (2003), 167–90

Lee, R. and Mason, A., 'Fertility, human capital, and economic growth over the demographic transition', *European Journal of Population*, 26 (2010), 159–82

Legomsky, S. H., 'Rationing family values in Europe and America: an immigration tug of war between states and their supra-national associations', *Georgetown Immigration Law Journal*, 26 (2012), 807–58

Leisering, L., 'Government and the life course' in J. T. Mortimer and M. J. Shanahan (eds), *Handbook of the Life Course* (New York: Kluwer, 2004), 205–25

Lemke, T., '"The birth of bio-politics": Michel Foucault's lecture at the Collège de France on neo-liberal governmentality', *Economy and Society*, 30 (2001), 190–207

Lesthaeghe, R., 'The unfolding story of the second demographic transition', *Population and Development Review*, 36 (2010), 211–51

Lesthaeghe, R. and van de Kaa, D. J., 'Twee demografische transities?' in D. J. van de Kaa and R. Lesthaeghe (eds), *Bevolking: Groei en Krimp* (Deventer, Van Loghum Slaterus, 1986), 9–24

Levey, G. B., 'Liberal nationalism and the Australian citizenship tests', *Citizenship Studies*, 18 (2014), 175–89

Lewis, J. and Campbell, M., 'UK work/family balance policies and gender equality, 1997–2005', *Social Politics*, 14 (2007), 4–30

Lewis, J. and West, A., 'Re-shaping social care services for older people in England: policy development and the problem of achieving "good care"', *Journal of Social Policy*, 43 (2014), 1–18

Li, Y. and Heath, A., 'Minority ethnic men in British labour market (1972–2005)', *International Journal of Sociology and Social Policy*, 28 (2008), 231–44

Liebkind, K. and Jasinskaja-Lahti, I., 'Acculturation and psychological well-being among immigrant adolescents in Finland: a comparative study of adolescents from different cultural backgrounds', *Journal of Adolescent Research*, 15 (2000), 446–69

Lindberg, M., 'Koulutuspolitiikan uusliberalisoitumisen vääjäämättömyys?', *Tieteessä Tapahtuu*, 2 (2013), 8–14
Linderborg, H., 'De ryskspråkiga anhörigvårdarnas upplevelser i vårdandet av sina dementa anhöriga', *Nordisk sosialt arbeid*, 1 (2008), 55–68
Lippert, R. and Pyykkönen, M. 'Contesting family in Finnish and Canadian immigration and refugee policy', *Nordic Journal of Migration research*, 2 (2012), 45–56
Lister R., *Citizenship: Feminist Perspectives* (Basingstoke: Palgrave Macmillan 2003)
Lister, R., Williams, F., Anttonen, A., et al., *Gendering Citizenship in Western Europe* (Bristol: Policy Press, 2007)
Livi-Bacci, M. 'Modernization and tradition in the recent history of Italian fertility', *Demography*, 4 (1967), 657–72
  'Population policy in Western Europe', *Population Studies*, 28 (1974), 191–204
  A History of Italian Fertility during the Last Two Centuries (Princeton University Press, 1977)
  'Too few children and too much family', *Daedalus*, 130 (2001), 139–55
  A Concise History of World Population, 5th edn (Chichester: Wiley Blackwell, 2012)
Lloyd, L., 'A caring profession? The ethics of care and social work with older people', *British Journal of Social Work*, 36 (2006), 1171–85
  'The individual in social care: the ethics of care and the "personalisation" agenda in services for older people in England', *Ethics and Social Welfare*, 4 (2010), 188–200
Lloyd, L., Tanner, D., Milne, A., et al., 'Look after yourself: active ageing, individual responsibility and the decline of social work with older people in the UK', *European Journal of Social Work*, 17 (2014), 322–35
Lowe, I., *Bigger or Better? Australia's Population Debate* (St Lucia, Qld: University of Queensland Press, 2012)
Lucassen, L. and Laarman, C., 'Immigration, intermarriage and the changing face of Europe in the post war period', *History of the Family*, 14 (2009), 52–68
Lutz, H. and Palenga-Möllenbeck, E., 'Care workers, care drain, and care chains: reflections on care, migration, and citizenship', *Social Politics*, 19 (2012), 15–37
Lutz, W., 'Fertility rates and future population trends: will Europe's birth rate recover or continue to decline?', *International Journal of Andrology*, 29 (2006), 25–33
Lutz, W. and Skirbekk, V., 'Low fertility in Europe in a global demographic context' in J. C. Tremmel (ed.), *Demographic Change and Intergenerational Justice* (Berlin: Springer, 2008), 3–19

Lutz, W., Skirbekk, V. and Testa, M. R., 'The low fertility trap hypothesis: forces that may lead to further postponement and fewer births in Europe', *Vienna Yearbook of Population Research*, 4 (2006), 167–92

Lynch, A., 'Control orders in Australia: a further case study in the migration of British counterterrorism law', *Oxford University Commonwealth Law Journal*, 8 (2008), 159–85

MacDonald, R., 'Youth, transitions and un(der)employment: plus ça change, plus ça même chose', *Journal of Sociology*, 47 (2010), 427–44

Mackinnon, A., 'From one fin de siècle to another: the educated woman and the declining birth-rate', *Australian Educational Researcher*, 22 (1995), 71–86

 '"Bringing the unclothed immigrant into the world": population policies and gender in twentieth-century Australia', *Journal of Population Research*, 17 (2000), 109–23

Macleod, C. and Durrheim, K., 'Foucauldian feminism: the implications of governmentality', *Journal for the Theory of Social Behaviour*, 32 (2002), 41–60

Macklin, A., 'The securitization of dual citizenship' in T. Faist and P. Kivisto (eds), *Dual Citizenship in Global Perspective: From Unitary to Multiple Citizenship* (New York: Palgrave Macmillan, 2007), 42–66

Macnicol, J., *Neoliberalising Old Age* (Cambridge University Press, 2015)

Malmberg-Heimonen, I. and Julkunen, I., 'Out of unemployment? A comparative analysis of the risks and opportunities longer-term unemployed immigrant youth face when entering the labour market', *Journal of Youth Studies*, 9 (2006), 575–92

Malthus, R. T., *An Essay on the Principle of Population* (Oxford University Press, 2008)

Mandaville, P., 'Muslim transnational identity and state responses in Europe and the UK after 9/11: political community, ideology and authority', *Journal of Ethnic and Migration Studies*, 35 (2009), 491–506

Mansouri, F., 'Citizenship, identity and belonging in contemporary Australia' in S. Akbarzadeh and S. Yasmeen (eds), *Islam and the West: Reflections from Australia* (Sydney: University of New South Wales, 2005), 149–64

Marchesi, M., 'Reproducing Italians: contested biopolitics in the age of "replacement anxiety"', *Anthropology & Medicine*, 19 (2012), 171–88

Marchetti, C., '"Trees without roots": the reform of citizenship challenged by the children of immigrants in Italy', *Bulletin of Italian Politics*, 2 (2010), 45–67

Mares, P., 'The permanent shift to temporary migration' in S. Perera, G. Seal and S. Summers (eds), *Enter at own risk? Australia's Population Questions for the 21st Century* (Perth, WA: Black Swan Press, 2010), 65–89

'Fear and instrumentalism: Australian policy responses to migration from the Global South', *The Round Table: The Commonwealth Journal of International Affairs*, 100 (2011), 407–22

'Temporary migration and its implications for Australia', *Papers on Parliament*, 57 (2012), 23–58

Markus, A., Jupp, J. and McDonald, P., *Australia's Immigration Revolution* (Sydney: Allen and Unwin, 2009)

Massetti, E., 'Mainstream parties and the politics of immigration in Italy: a structural advantage for the right or a missed opportunity for the left?', *Acta Politica*, 50 (2015), 486–505

May, J., 'Population policy' D. L. Poston and M. Micklin (eds), *Handbook of Population* (New York: Kluwer Academic/Plenum Publishers, 2005), 827–52

May, J. F., *World Population Policies: Their Origin, Evolution, and Impact* (Washington: Springer, 2012)

Mayer, K. U., 'New directions in life course research', *Annual Review of Sociology*, 35 (2009), 413–33

Mayer, K. U. and Schoepflin, U., 'The state and the life course', *Annual Review of Sociology*, 15 (1989), 187–209

Mayton, W. T., 'Birthright citizenship and the civic minimum', *Georgetown Immigration Law Journal*, 22 (2008), 221–58

McDaniel, S. and Zimmer, Z (eds), *Global Ageing in the Twenty-First Century: Challenges, Opportunities and Implications* (Farnham, Surrey: Ashgate, 2013)

McDonald, L. Z., 'Securing identities, resisting terror: Muslim youth work in the UK and its implications for security', *Religion, State and Society*, 39 (2011), 177–89

McDonald, P., 'Gender equity, social institutions and the future of fertility', *Journal of Population Research*, 17 (2000), 1–16

'Gender equity in theories of fertility transition', *Population and Development Review*, 26 (2000), 427–39

'An assessment of policies that support having children from the perspectives of equity, efficiency and efficacy', *Vienna Yearbook of Population Research*, 4 (2006), 213–34

'Low fertility and the state: the efficacy of policy', *Population and Development Review*, 32 (2006), 485–510

McDonald, P. and Moyle, H., 'Why do English-speaking countries have relatively high fertility?', *Journal of Population Research*, 27 (2010), 247–73

McGhee, D., 'The paths to citizenship: a critical examination of immigration policy in Britain since 2001', *Patterns of Prejudice*, 43 (2009), 41–64

McIntosh, C. A., *Population Policy in Western Europe: Responses to Low Fertility in France, Sweden, and West Germany* (Armonk, NY: M. E. Sharpe, 1983)

McKnight, A. and Tsang, T., 'Divided we fall? The wider consequences of high and unrelenting inequality in the UK' in B. Nolan, W. Salverda, D. Checchi, et al. (eds), *Changing Inequalities and Societal Impacts in Rich Countries: Thirty Countries' Experiences* (Oxford University Press, 2014)

McNevin, A., 'The liberal paradox and the politics of asylum in Australia', *Australian Journal of Political Science*, 42 (2007), 611–30

Contesting Citizenship. Irregular Migrants and New Frontiers of the Political (New York: Columbia University Press, 2011)

Mencarini, L. and Tanturri, M. L. 'High fertility or childlessness: micro- level determinants of reproductive behaviour in Italy', *Population*, 61 (2006), 389–415

Messerschmidt, R. '"Garbled demography" or "demographization of the social"? – A Foucaultian discourse analysis of German demographic change at the beginning of the 21st century', *Historical Social Research*, 39 (2014), 299–335

Metzler, I., '"Nationalizing embryos": the politics of human embryonic stem cell research in Italy', *BioSocieties*, 2 (2007), 413–27

Meyers, D. T., 'The rush to motherhood – pronatalist discourse and women's autonomy', *Signs*, 26 (2001), 735–73

Milewski, N., 'First child of immigrant workers and their descendants in West Germany: interrelation of events, disruption, or adaptation?', *Demographic Research*, 17 (2007), 859–96

Mishtal, J., 'Irrational non-reproduction? The "dying nation" and thepostsocialist logics of declining motherhood in Poland', *Anthropology & Medicine*, 19 (2012), 153–69

Mizen, P., 'The best days of your life? Youth, policy and Blair's New Labour', *Critical Social Policy*, 23 (2003), 453–76

The Changing State of Youth (Basingstoke: Palgrave, 2004)

Modood, T., 'The educational attainment of ethnic minorities in Britain' in G. C. Loury, T. Modood and S. M. Teles (eds), *Ethnicity, Social Mobility and Public Policy: Comparing the US and UK* (New York: Cambridge University Press, 2005), 288–308

Moffatt, S., Higgs, P., Rummery, K. and Jones, I. R., 'Choice, consumerism and devolution: growing old in the welfare state(s) of Scotland, Wales and England', *Ageing and Society*, 32 (2012), 725–46

Moffitt, T. E. 'Teen-aged mothers in contemporary Britain', *Journal of Child Psychology and Psychiatry*, 43 (2002), 727–42

Moisio, P., 'Sosiaali- ja terveysmenojen rakenne ja kehitys' in M. Vaarama, S. Karvonen and P. Moisio (eds), *Suomalaisten hyvinvointi 2010* (Helsinki: Terveyden ja hyvinvoinnin laitos, 2010), 20–7

Moran, N., Glendinning, C., Wilberforce, M., et al., 'Older people's experiences of cash-for-care schemes: evidence from the English Individual Budget pilot projects', *Ageing and Society*, 33 (2013), 826–51

Morano Foadi, S., 'Key issues and causes of the Italian brain drain', *Innovation*, 19 (2006), 209–23

Morgan, L. M. and Roberts, E. F. S., 'Reproductive governance in Latin America', *Anthropology & Medicine*, 19 (2012), 241–54

Mouffe, C. (ed.), *Dimensions of Radical Democracy: Pluralism, Citizenship, Community* (New York: Verso, 1992)

Muehlebach, A., *The Moral Neoliberal* (University of Chicago Press, 2012)

Mulvey, G., 'Immigration under New Labour: policy and effects', *Journal of Ethnic and Migration Studies*, 37 (2011), 1477–93

Murphy, M., Martikainen, P. and Pennec, S., 'Demographic change and the supply of potential family supporters in Britain, Finland and France in the period 1911–2050', *European Journal of Population*, 22 (2006), 219–40

Mussino, E. and Strozza, S., 'Does citizenship still matter? Second birth risks of migrants from Albania, Morocco, and Romania in Italy', *European Journal of Population*, 28 (2012), 269–302

'The delayed school progress of the children of immigrants in lower-secondary education in Italy', *Journal of Ethnic and Migration Studies*, 38 (2012), 41–57

'The fertility of immigrants after arrival: the Italian case', *Demographic Research*, 26 (2012), 99–130

Mussino, E. and Van Raalte, A. A., 'Immigrant fertility: a comparative study between Italy and Russia', *International Migration*, 51 (2013), 148–64

Muttarak, R., 'Explaining trends and patterns of immigrants' partner choice in Britain', *Zeitschrift für Familienforschung*, 22 (2010), 37–64

Mythen, G. and Walklate, S. 'Criminology and terrorism', *British Journal of Criminology*, 46 (2006), 379–98

Naldini, M., *The Family in Mediterranean Welfare States* (London and Portland, OR: Frank Cass, 2003)

Naldini, M. and Saraceno, C., 'Social and family policies in Italy: not totally frozen but far from structural reforms', *Social Policy & Administration*, 42 (2008), 733–48

Näre, L., 'Ideal workers and suspects. Employers' politics of recognition and the migrant division of care labour in Finland', *Nordic Journal of Migration Research*, 3 (2013), 72–81

Neyer, G., 'Should governments in Europe be more aggressive in pushing for gender equality to raise fertility? The second "No"', *Demographic Research*, 24 (2011), 225–50

'Welfare states, family policies, and fertility in Europe' in G. Neyer, G. Andersson, H. Kulu, L. Bernardi and C. Bühler, *The Demography of Europe* (Dordrecht: Springer, 2013), 29–53

Neyer, G. and Andersson, G., 'Consequences of family policies on childbearing behavior: effects or artifacts?', *Population and Development Review*, 34 (2008), 699–724

Neyer, G., Lappegård, T. and Vignoli, D., 'Gender equality and fertility: which equality matters?', *European Journal of Population*, 29 (2013), 245–72

Ngai, M. M., *Impossible Subjects: Illegal Aliens and the Making of Modern America* (Princeton University Press, 2004)

Nykänen, E., Pirjatanniemi, E., Sorainen, O. and Staffans, I., *Migration Law in Finland* (Alphen aan den Rijn: Kluwer Law International, 2012)

Nyland, C., Forbes-Mewett, H., Marginson, S., et al., 'International student-workers in Australia: a new vulnerable workforce', *Journal of Education and Work*, 22 (2009), 1–14

O'Donnell, A. and Mitchell, R., 'Immigrant labour in Australia: the regulatory framework', *Australian Journal of Labour Law*, 14 (2001), 269–305

Okin, S. M. (eds Cohen, J., Howard, M. and Nussbaum, M. C.), *Is Multiculturalism Bad for Women?* (Princeton University Press, 1999)

Olakivi, A., '"In case you can speak Finnish, there's no problem." Reconstructing problematic identity-positions in migrant care workers' organizational discourse', *Nordic Journal of Migration Research*, 3 (2013), 91–9

O'Malley, P., *Risk, Uncertainty and Government* (London: Glasshouse, 2004)

O'Neill, B., Balk, D., Brickman, M. and Ezra, M., 'A guide to global population projections', *Demographic Research*, 4 (2001), 203–88

Ong, A. *Neoliberalism as Exception. Mutations in Citizenship and Sovereignty* (Durham, NC and London: Duke University Press, 2006)

Ongaro, F. 'Transition to adulthood in Italy' in M. Corijn and E. Klijzing (eds), *Transitions to Adulthood in Europe* (Dordrecht: Kluwer, 2001), 173–205

Orgad, L., 'Illiberal liberalism: cultural restrictions on migration and access to citizenship in Europe', *American Journal of Comparative Law*, 58 (2010), 53–105

Orloff, A. S., 'Gender and the social rights of citizenship: the comparative analysis of gender relations and welfare states', *American Sociological Review*, 58 (1993), 303–28

Orsini-Jones, M. and Gattullo, F., 'Migrant women in Italy: national trends and local perspectives' in F. Anthias and G. Lazaridis, *Gender and Migration in Southern Europe* (Oxford: Berg, 2000), 125–44

Pantazis, C. and Pemberton, S., 'From the "old" to the "new" suspect community: examining the impacts of recent UK counter-terrorist legislation', *British Journal of Criminology*, 49 (2009), 646–66

'Restating the case for the "suspect community". A reply to Greer', *British Journal of Criminology*, 51 (2011), 1054–62

Parekh, B., *Rethinking Multiculturalism* (Palgrave Macmillan, 2006)

Parkkinen, P., 'Suomen väestömuutokset ja kilpailukyky', *Yhteiskuntapolitiikka*, 65 (2000), 315–22

Parr, N. and Guest, R., 'The contribution of increases in family benefits to Australia's early 21st-century fertility increase: an empirical analysis', *Demographic Research*, 25 (2011), 215–44

Pastore, F., 'A community out of balance: nationality law and migration politics in the history of post-unification Italy', *Journal of Modern Italian Studies*, 9 (2004), 27–48

Paterno, A. and Gabrielli, G., 'Two years later: assimilation process of children of immigrants in Italy', *Journal of Population Research*, 31 (2014), 29–50

Patosalmi, M., *The Politics and Policies of Reproductive Agency* (Helsinki: Unigrafia, 2011)

Pavolini, E. and Ranci C., 'Restructuring the welfare state: reforms in long-term care in Western European countries', *Journal of European Social Policy*, 18 (2008), 246–59

Peach, C., 'Muslims in the 2001 census of England and Wales: gender and economic disadvantage', *Ethnic and Racial Studies*, 29 (2006), 629–55

Pearce, F., *Peoplequake. Mass Migration, Ageing Nations and the Coming Population Crash* (London: Eden Project Book, 2010)

Pegna, S. 'Italy: migration from 1990s to 2010s' in I. Ness (ed.), *The Encyclopedia of Global Human Migration* (Hoboken, NJ: Wiley-Blackwell, 2013), 1–11

Pehkonen, A., 'Immigrants' paths to employment in Finland', *Finnish Yearbook of Population Research*, 42 (2006), 113–28

Perelli-Harris, B. and Isupova, O., 'Crisis and control: Russia's dramatic fertility decline and efforts to increase it' in A. Buchanan and A. Rotkirch (eds), *Fertility Rates and Population Decline: No Time for Children?* (Basingstoke: Palgrave Macmillan, 2013), 141–56

Perlmutter, T., 'Italy. Political parties and Italian policy 1990–2009' in J. F. Hollifield, P. L. Martin and P. M. Orrenius (eds), *Controlling Immigration: A Global Perspective*, 3rd edn (Stanford University Press, 2014), 341–65

Phillips A. and Dustin, M., 'UK initiatives on forced marriage: regulation, dialogue and exit', *Political Studies*, 52 (2004), 531–51

Phillips, K., 'Provocative women in the border zone: articulations of national crisis and the limits of women's political status', *Continuum*, 23 (2009), 597–612

Portes, A., *The New Second Generation* (New York: Russell Sage Foundation, 1996)

Portes, A. and Zhou, M., 'The new second generation: segmented assimilation and its variants among post-1965 immigrant youth', *Annals of the American Academy of Political and Social Science*, 530 (1993), 74–96

Poston, D. L., 'Age and sex' in D. L. Poston and M. Micklin (eds), *Handbook of Population*, (Springer, 2005), 19–58

Poynting, S., 'What caused the Cronulla riot?', *Race & Class*, 48 (2006), 85–92

'The "lost" girls: Muslim young women in Australia', *Journal of Intercultural Studies*, 30 (2009), 373–86

Poynting, S. and Mason, V., 'The new integrationism, the state and islamophobia: retreat from multiculturalism in Australia', *International Journal of Law, Crime and Justice*, 36 (2008), 230–46

Poynting, S., Noble, G., Tabar, P. and Collins, J., *Bin Laden in the Suburbs* (Sydney: Institute of Criminology, 2004)

Presser, H. B., 'Demography, feminism, and the science-policy nexus', *Population and Development Review*, 23 (1997), 295–331

Putney, N. M. and Bengtson, V. L., 'Intergenerational relations in changing times' in J. T. Mortimer and M. J. Shanahan (eds), *Handbook of the Life Course* (New York: Kluwer, 2004), 149–64

Puur, A. Olah, L. Sz., Tazi-Preve, M. I. and Dorbritz, J., 'Men's childbearing desires and views of the male role in Europe at the dawn of the 21st century', *Demographic Research*, 19 (2008), 1883–912

Queirolo Palmas, L., *Prove di Seconde Generazioni: Giovani di origine immigrata tra scuole e spazi urbani* (Milan: FrancoAngeli, 2006)

Qureshi, K., Charsley, K. and Shaw, A., 'Marital instability among British Pakistanis: transnationality, conjugalities and Islam', *Ethnic and Racial Studies*, 37 (2014), 261–79

Rabinow, P. and Rose, N., 'Biopower today', *Biosocieties*, 1 (2006), 195–217

Raghuram, P., 'The difference that skills make: gender, family migration strategies and regulated labour markets', *Journal of Ethnic and Migration Studies*, 30 (2004), 303–21

Raissiguier, C., *Reinventing the Republic. Gender, Migration, and Citizenship in France* (Stanford University Press, 2010)

Rastas, A., 'Racializing categorization among young people in Finland', *Young*, 13 (2005), 147–66

Rasismi lasten ja nuorten arjessa (Tampere University Press, 2007)

Räty, T., 'Perus- ja ihmisoikeudet ovat vanhusten hoidon laadun lähtökohtia', *Sosiaalitieto*, (2012) 12, 26–7

Razack, S. H., 'Imperilled Muslim women, dangerous Muslim men and civilised Europeans: legal and social responses to forced marriages', *Feminist Legal Studies*, 12 (2004), 129–74

Reddy, R., 'Gender, culture and the law: approaches to "honour crimes" in the UK', *Feminist Legal Studies*, 16 (2008), 305–21

Reher, D. S., 'Towards long-term population decline: a discussion of relevant issues', *European Journal Population*, 23 (2007), 189–207

'Economic and social implications of the demographic transition', *Population and Development Review*, 37(Supp.) (2011), 11–33

Reilly, A., 'The ethics of seasonal labour migration', *Griffith Law Review*, 20 (2011), 127–52

Repo, J., 'The governance of fertility through gender equality in the EU and Japan', *Asia Europe Journal*, 10 (2012), 199–214

Repo, K., 'Finnish child home care allowance – users' perspectives and perceptions' in J. Sipilä, K. Repo and T. Rissanen (eds), *Cash-for-Childcare. The Consequences for Caring Mothers* (Cheltenham: Edward Elgar Publishing Limited, 2010), 46–64

Reyneri, E., 'The role of the underground economy in irregular migration to Italy: cause or effect?', *Journal of Ethnic and Migration Studies*, 24 (1998), 313–31

'Immigrants in a segmented and often undeclared labour market', *Journal of Modern Italian Studies*, 9 (2004), 71–93

Riccio, B. and Russo, M., 'Everyday practised citizenship and the challenges of representation: second-generation associations in Bologna', *Journal of Modern Italian Studies*, 16 (2011), 360–72

Rindfuss, R. R., 'The young adult years: diversity, structural change, and fertility', *Demography*, 28 (1991), 493–512

Rintala, T., 'Vanhustenhuoltoa ikääntyville vai ikääntyneille?', *Yhteiskuntapolitiikka*, 69 (2004), 642–7

Risse, L., '"... And one for the country." The effect of the baby bonus on Australian women's childbearing intentions', *Journal of Population Research*, 27 (2010), 213–40

Roberts, K., 'Education to work transitions: how the old middle went missing and why the new middle remains elusive', *Sociological Research Online*, 18 (2013)

Robertson, A., 'The politics of Alzheimer's disease: a case study in apocalyptic demography', *International Journal of Health Services*, 20 (1990), 429–42

Roche, M., *Rethinking Citizenship. Welfare, Ideology and Change in Modern Society*. (Cambridge: Polity Press, 1992)

Rose, N., 'Governing liberty' in R. V. Ericson and N. Stehr (eds), *Governing Modern Societies* (University of Toronto Press, 2000), 141–76

'Government and control', *British Journal of Criminology*, 40 (2000), 321–39

Rose, N. and Miller, P., 'Political power beyond the state: problematics of government', *British Journal of Sociology*, 43 (1992), 173–205

Rose, N. and Novas, C., 'Biological citizenship' in A. Ong and S. Collier (eds), *Global Assemblages* (Malden, MA: Blackwell Publishing, 2005), 439–63

Rose, N. and Valverde, M., 'Governed by law?', *Social & Legal Studies*, 7 (1998), 541–51

Rosenbluth, F. M. (ed.), *The Political Economy of Japan's Low Fertility* (Stanford University Press, 2007)

Rothon, C., 'Can achievement differentials be explained by social class alone? An examination of minority ethnic educational performance in England and Wales at the end of compulsory schooling', *Ethnicities*, 7 (2007), 306–22

Rowlingson, K. and McKay, S., 'Lone motherhood and socio-economic disadvantage: insights from quantitative and qualitative evidence', *Sociological Review*, 53 (2005), 30–49

Rubenstein, K., 'Citizenship and the centenary – inclusion and exclusion in 20th century Australia', *Melbourne University Law Review*, 24 (2000), 576–608

Ruhs, M., 'The potential of temporary migration programmes in future international migration policy', *International Labour Review*, 145 (2006), 7–36

Ruhs, M. and Anderson, B. (eds), *Who Needs Migrant Workers? Labour Shortages, Immigration, and Public Policy* (Oxford University Press, 2010)

Ruhs, M. and Martin, P., 'Numbers vs. rights: trade-offs and guest worker programs', *International Migration Review*, 42 (2008), 249–65

Rumbaut, R., 'Sites of belonging: acculturation, discrimination, and ethnic identity among children of immigrants' in T. S. Weiner (ed.), *Discovering Successful Pathways in Children's Development: Mixed methods in the Study of Childhood and Family Life* (University of Chicago Press, 2005), 111–64

Saarinen, A., 'Non-work migration, employment and welfare in Finland: three third country migrant cases/four phases of immigration policies' in M. Pajnik and G. Campani (eds), *Precarious Migrant Labour Across Europe* (Ljubljana: Peace Institute, 2011), 45–71

Saggar, S., 'The one per cent world: managing the myth of muslim religious extremism', *The Political Quarterly*, 77 (2006), 314–27

'Boomerangs and slingshots: radical islamism and counter-terrorism strategy', *Journal of Ethnic and Migration Studies*, 35 (2009), 381–402

Sainsbury, D., *Gender, Equality and Welfare States* (Cambridge University Press, 1996)

Salmela-Aro, K., Kiuru, N. Nurmi, J. and Eerola, M., 'Mapping pathways to adulthood among Finnish university students: Sequences, patterns, variations in family- and work-related roles', *Advances in Life Course Research*, 16 (2011), 25–41

Salmio, T., 'Kylmän sodan loppuminen ja EU-jäsenyys muuttivat Suomen maahanmuuttopolitiikkaa', *Siirtolaisuus*, 2 (2000), 21–6

Sanderson, W. C., Skirbekk, V. and Stonawski, M., 'Young adult failure to thrive syndrome', *Finnish Yearbook of Population Research*, 48 (2013), 169–87

Santarelli, E. 'Economic resources and the first child in Italy: a focus on income and job stability', *Demographic Research*, 25 (2011), 311–36

Saraceno, C., *Mutamenti della famiglia e politiche sociali in Italia* (Bologna: Il Mulino, 2003)

Sassen, S., *Losing Control? Sovereignty in an Age of Globalization* (New York: Columbia University Press, 1996)

Guests and Aliens (New York: New Press, 1999)

Satterthwaite, D., 'The implications of population growth and urbanization for climate change', *Environment and Urbanization*, 21 (2009), 545–67

Schaffner, L., 'An age of reason: paradoxes in the U.S. legal construction of adulthood', *International Journal of Children's Rights*, 10 (2002), 201–32
Schierup, C., Hansen, P. and Castles, S., *Migration, Citizenship, and the European Welfare State. A European Dilemma* (Oxford University Press, 2006)
Schleutker, E., 'Väestön ikääntyminen ja hyvinvointivaltio: mitä vaihtoehtoja meillä on?', *Yhteiskuntapolitiikka*, 78 (2013), 425–36
'Women's career strategy choices and fertility in Finland', *Finnish Yearbook of Population Research* 48 (2013), 103–26
Schmelzer, P., 'Increasing employment instability among young people? Labor market entries and early careers in Great Britain since the 1980s' in H. Blossfeld, S. Buchholz, E. Bukodi and K. Kurz (eds), *Young Workers, Globalization and the Labor Market. Comparing Early Working Life in Eleven Countries* (Cheltenham: Edward Elgar, 2008), 181–205
'Income development of older people: consequences of pension reforms and unstable careers in the UK' in H. Blossfeld, S. Buchholz, and K. Kurz (eds), *Aging Populations, Globalization and the Labor Market. Comparing Late Working Life and Retirement in Modern Societies* (Cheltenham: Edward Elgar, 2011), 259–82
Schmidt, G., 'Law and identity: transnational arranged marriages and the boundaries of Danishness', *Journal of Ethnic and Migration Studies*, 37 (2011), 257–75
Schneider, J. (ed.), *Italy's 'Southern Question': Orientalism in One Country* (Oxford: Berg, 1998)
Sciortino, G., 'Immigration in a Mediterranean welfare state: the Italian experience in comparative perspective', *Journal of Comparative Policy Analysis*, 6 (2004), 111–29
Sciortino, G., 'Commentary' in J. F. Hollifield, P. L. Martin and P. M. Orrenius (eds), *Controlling Immigration: A Global Perspective*, 3rd edn (Stanford University Press, 2014), 366–70
Seglow, J., 'The ethics of immigration', *Political Studies Review*, 3 (2005), 317–34
Sen, A., 'Missing women: social inequality outweighs women's survival advantage in Asia and north Africa', *British Medical Journal*, 304 (1992), 587
Settersten, R. A., 'Age structuring and the rhythm of the life course' in J. T. Mortimer and M. J. Shanahan (eds), *Handbook of the Life Course* (New York: Kluwer, 2004), 81–98
'Passages to adulthood: linking demographic change and human development', *European Journal of Population*, 23 (2007), 251–72
Settersten, R. A., Furstenberg, F. F. and Rumbaut, R. G., 'On the frontier of adulthood' in R. A. Settersten Jr, F. F. Furstenberg, and R. G. Rumbaut (eds), *On the Frontier of Adulthood: Theory, Research, and Public Policy* (University of Chicago Press, 2005), 3–28

Shachar, A., 'The race for talent: highly skilled migrants and competitive immigration regimes', *York University Law Review*, 81 (2006), 148–206
  The Birthright Lottery: Citizenship and Global Inequality (Cambridge, MA: Harvard University Press, 2009)
Shachar, A. and Hirschl, R., 'On citizenship, states, and markets', *Journal of Political Philosophy*, 22 (2014), 231–57
  'Recruiting "super talent": the new world of selective migration regimes', *Indiana Journal of Global Legal Studies*, 20 (2013), 71–107
Shain, F., 'Race, nation and education. An overview of British attempts to "manage diversity" since the 1950s', *Education Inquiry*, 4 (2013), 63–85
Shanahan, M. J., 'Pathways to adulthood in changing societies: variability and mechanisms in life course perspective', *Annual Review of Sociology*, 26 (2000), 667–92
Shaw, A., 'Kinship, cultural preference and immigration: consanguineous marriage among British Pakistanis', *Journal of the Royal Anthropological Institute*, 7 (2001), 315–34
  'The arranged transnational cousin marriages of British Pakistanis: critique, dissent and cultural continuity', *Contemporary South Asia*, 15 (2006), 315–34
Sheldon, S., *Beyond Control. Medical Power and Abortion Law* (London and Chicago: Pluto Press, 1997)
Shutes, I., 'The employment of migrant workers in long-term care: dynamics of choice and control', *Journal of Social Policy*, 41 (2012), 43–59
Shutes, I. and Chiatti, C., 'Migrant labour and the marketisation of care for older people: the employment of migrant care workers by families and service providers', *Journal of European Social Policy*, 22 (2012), 392–405
Siedlecky, S. and Wyndham, D., *Populate and Perish. Australian Women's Fight for Birth Control* (Sydney: Allen & Unwin, 1990)
Sigle-Rushton, W., 'England and Wales: stable fertility and pronounced social status differences', *Demographic Research*, 19 (2008), 455–502
  'Fertility in England and Wales: a policy puzzle', *Demografie*, 51 (2009), 258–65
Siim, B., *Gender and Citizenship. Politics and Agency in France, Britain and Denmark* (Cambridge University Press, 2000)
Smith, S. and Ratcliffe, A., 'Women's education and childbearing: a growing divide' in D. Kneale, E. Coast and J. Stillwell (eds), *Fertility, Living Arrangements, Care and Mobility* (Dordrecht: Springer, 2009), 41–58
Sobotka, T., 'Overview chapter 7: the rising importance of migrants for childbearing in Europe', *Demographic Research*, 19 (2008), 225–48
Söderling, I., 'Suomen väestökysymys ja maahanmuutto' in A. Alitolppa-Niitamo, I. Söderling and S. Fågel (eds), *Olemme muuttaneet. Näkökulmia maahanmuuttoon, perheiden kotoutumiseen ja ammatillisen työn käytäntöihin* (Helsinki: Väestöliitto, 2005), 13–23

Soloway, R. A., *Demography and Degeneration. Eugenics and the Declining Birthrate in Twentieth-Century Britain* (Chapel Hill, NC: University of North Carolina Press, 1990)

Somerville, W., *Immigration under New Labour* (Bristol: Policy Press, 2007)

'The politics and policy of skilled economic immigration under New Labour, 1997–2010' in T. Triadafilopoulos (ed.), *Wanted and Welcome?* (New York: Springer, 2013), 257–71

Somers, M. R., *Genealogies of Citizenship. Markets, Statelessness, and the Right to Have Rights* (Cambridge University Press, 2008)

Song, M., 'What happens after segmented assimilation? An exploration of intermarriage and "mixed race" young people in Britain', *Ethnic and Racial Studies*, 33 (2010), 1194–213

Soysal, Y. N., 'Citizenship, immigration, and the European social project: rights and obligations of individuality', *The British Journal of Sociology*, 63 (2012), 1–21

Spalek, B. and Imtoual, A., 'Muslim communities and counter-terror responses: "hard" approaches to community engagement in the UK and Australia', *Journal of Muslim Minority Affairs*, 27 (2007), 185–202

Spencer, S., 'Immigration' in A. Seldon (ed.), *Blair's Britain 1997–2007* (Cambridge University Press, 2007), 341–60

The Migration Debate (Bristol: Policy Press, 2011)

Stone, J., Berrington, A. and Falkingham, J., 'The changing determinants of UK young adults' living arrangements', *Demographic Research*, 25 (2011), 629–66

'Gender, turning points, and boomerangs: returning home in young adulthood in Great Britain', *Demography*, 51 (2014), 257–76

Strasser, E., Kraler, A., Bonjour, S. and Bilger, V., 'Doing family', *The History of the Family*, 14 (2009), 165–76

Stratton, J., 'Non-citizens in the exclusionary state: citizenship, mitigated exclusion, and the Cronulla riots', *Continuum*, 25 (2011), 299–316

Summers, A., 'Women and the birth rate' in S. Vizard, H. J. Martin and T. Watts (eds), *Australia's Population Challenges* (Camberwell: Penguin, 2003), 237–41

Tan, Y. and Lester, L. H., 'Labour market and economic impacts of international working holiday temporary migrants to Australia', *Population, Space and Place*, 18 (2012), 359–83

Tanturri, M. L. and Mencarini, L. 'Childless or childfree? Paths to voluntary childlessness in Italy', *Population and Development Review*, 34 (2008), 51–77

Tavan, G., *The Long, Slow Death of White Australia* (Carlton North, Vic: Scribe, 2005)

'Creating multicultural Australia: local, global and trans-national contexts for the creation of a universal admissions scheme, 1945–1983' in

T. Triadafilopoulos (ed.), *Wanted and Welcome?* (New York: Springer, 2013), 39–59

Teitelbaum M. S. and Winter, J. M., *The Fear of Population Decline* (Orlando, FL: Academic Press, 1985)

A Question of Numbers. High Migration, Low Fertility, and the Politics of National Identity (New York: Hill and Wang, 1998)

Temple, J. B. and McDonald, P., 'Is demography destiny? The role of structural and demographic factors in Australia's past and future labour supply', *Journal of Population Research*, 25 (2008), 29–49

Thapar-Björkert, S. and Borevi, K., 'Gender and the "integrationist turn". Comparative perspectives on marriage migration in the UK and Sweden', *Tijdschrift voor Genderstudies*, 17 (2014), 149–65

Thévenon, O. and Gauthier, A. H. 'Family policies in developed countries: a "fertility-booster" with side-effects', *Community, Work & Family*, 14 (2011), 197–216

Thomas, P. and Sanderson, P., 'Unwilling citizens? Muslim young people and national identity', *Sociology*, 45 (2011), 1028–44

Thomassen, B., '"Second generation immigrants" or "Italians with immigrant parents"? Italian and European perspectives on immigrants and their children', *Bulletin of Italian Politics*, 2 (2010), 21–44

Timonen, V., *Restructuring the Welfare State: Globalization and Social Policy Reform in Finland and Sweden* (Cheltenham: Edward Elgar, 2003)

Timonen, V., Convery, J. and Cahill, S., 'Care revolutions in the making? A comparison of cash-for-care programmes in four European countries', *Ageing and Society*, 26 (2006), 455–74

Toh, S. and Quinlan, M., 'Safeguarding the global contingent workforce? Guestworkers in Australia', *International Journal of Manpower*, 30 (2009), 453–71

Toner, P. and Woolley, R., 'Temporary migration and skills formation in the trades: a provisional assessment', *People and Place*, 16 (2008), 47–57

Totah, M., 'Fortress Italy: racial politics and the new immigration amendment in Italy', *Fordham International Law Journal*, 26 (2003), 1438–504

Toulemon, L., 'Should governments in Europe be more aggressive in pushing for gender equality to raise fertility? The first "yes"', *Demographic Research*, 24 (2011), 179–200

Toulemon, L., Pailhé, A. and Rossier, C., 'France: high and stable fertility', *Demographic Research*, 19 (2008), 503–56

Tremmel, J. C. (ed.), *Demographic Change and Intergenerational Justice* (Berlin: Springer, 2008)

Triandafyllidou, A. and Ambrosini, M., 'Irregular immigration control in Italy and Greece: strong fencing and weak gate-keeping serving the labour market', *European Journal of Migration and Law*, 13 (2011), 251–73

Tronto, J. C., *Moral Boundaries. A Political Argument for an Ethic of Care* (New York and London: Routledge, 1993)
Creating Caring Institutions (New York University Press, 2013)
Turner, B. S., 'Ageing, status politics and sociological theory', *British Journal of Sociology*, 40 (1989), 588–606
'Citizenship, reproduction and the state: international marriage and human rights', *Citizenship Studies*, 12 (2008), 45–54
Ungerson, C., 'Commodified care work in European labour markets', *European Societies*, 5 (2003), 377–96
Vaarama, M., Siljander, E., Luoma, M. and Meriläinen, S., '80 vuotta täyttäneiden koettu elämänlaatu' in M. Vaarama, S. Karvonen and P. Moisio (eds), *Suomalaisten hyvinvointi 2010* (Helsinki: Terveyden ja hyvinvoinnin laitos, 2010), 150–66
'Suomalaisten kokema elämänlaatu nuoruudesta vanhuuteen' in M. Vaarama, S. Karvonen and P. Moisio (eds), *Suomalaisten hyvinvointi 2010* (Helsinki: Terveyden ja hyvinvoinnin laitos, 2010), 126–49
Vabø, M. and Szebehely, M., 'A caring state for all older people?' in A. Anttonen, L. Häikiö and K. Stefánsson (eds), *Welfare State, Universalism and Diversity* (Edward Elgar, 2012), 121–43
Vallin, J., 'Is a population policy really necessary?', *Population and Societies*, 489 (2012), 1–4
Valtonen, K., 'Cracking monopoly: immigrants and employment in Finland', *Journal of Ethnic and Migration Studies*, 27 (2001), 421–38
van Bavel, J. and Reher, D. S., 'The baby boom and its causes: what we know and what we need to know', *Population and Development Review*, 39 (2013), 257–88
van der Geest, S., Mul, A. and Vermeulen, H., 'Linkages between migration and the care of frail older people: observations from Greece, Ghana and The Netherlands', *Ageing and Society*, 24 (2004), 431–50
van Hooren, F., 'When families need immigrants: the exceptional position of migrant domestic workers and care assistants in Italian immigration policy', *Bulletin of Italian Politics*, 2 (2010), 21–38
van Klink, B. and Taekema, S., 'On the border. Limits and possibilities of interdisciplinary research' in B. van Klink and S. Taekema (eds), *Law and Method. Interdisciplinary Research into Law* (Tübingen: Mohr Siebeck, 2011)
van Nimwegen, N. and van der Erf, R., 'Europe at the crossroads: demographic challenges and international migration', *Journal of Ethnic and Migration Studies*, 36 (2010), 1359–79
Vincent, J. A. *Inequality and Old Age* (New York: St Martin's Press, 1996)
Velayutham, S., 'Precarious experiences of Indians in Australia on 457 temporary work visas', *Economic and Labour Relations Review*, 24 (2013), 340–61

Vertovec, S., 'Super-diversity and its implications', *Ethnic and Racial Studies*, 30 (2007), 1024–54

Vikat, A., 'Women's labor force attachment and childbearing in Finland', *Demographic Research*, S3 (2004), 177–212

Vilkko, A., Muuri, A. and Finne-Soveri, H., 'Läheisapu iäkkään ihmisen arjessa' in M. Vaarama, S. Karvonen and P. Moisio (eds), *Suomalaisten hyvinvointi 2010* (Helsinki: Terveyden ja hyvinvoinnin laitos, 2010), 60–77

Vink, M. P. and de Groot, G., 'Citizenship attribution in Western Europe: international framework and domestic trends', *Journal of Ethnic and Migration Studies*, 36 (2010), 713–34

Virkki, T., Vartiainen, A. and Hänninen, R., 'Talouden ja hoivan ristipaineissa', *Yhteiskuntapolitiikka*, 77 (2012), 253–64

Voas, D. and Fleischmann, F., 'Islam moves west: religious change in the first and second generations', *Annual Review of Sociology*, 38 (2012), 525–45

Vogt, K. C., 'The post-industrial society: from utopia to ideology', *Work, Employment and Society*, 30 (2016), 366–76

Volpp, L., 'Impossible subjects: illegal aliens and alien citizens', *Michigan Law Review*, 103 (2004), 1595–630

Vosko, L. F., *Managing the Margins: Gender, Citizenship and the International Regulation of Precarious Employment* (Oxford University Press, 2009)

Vuori, J., 'Men's choices and masculine duties: fathers in expert discussions', *Men and Masculinities*, 12 (2009), 45–72

Waite, L. J., 'Marriage and family' in D. L. Poston and M. Micklin (eds), *Handbook of Population* (New York: Kluwer Academic/Plenum Publishers, 2005), 87–108

Walby, S., 'Is citizenship gendered?', *Sociology*, 28 (1994), 379–95

Walker, A. and Maltby, T., 'Active ageing: a strategic policy solution to demographic ageing in the European Union', *International Journal of Social Welfare*, 21(Supp.) (2012), 117–30

Walker, C., 'The treatment of foreign terror suspects', *Modern Law Review*, 70 (2007), 427–57

Walklate, S. and Mythen, G., 'Agency, reflexivity and risk: cosmopolitan, neurotic or prudential citizen?', *British Journal of Sociology*, 61 (2010), 45–62

Walsh, J., 'Navigating globalization: immigration policy in Canada and Australia, 1945–2007', *Sociological Forum*, 23 (2008), 786–813

'Quantifying citizens: neoliberal restructuring and immigrant selection in Canada and Australia', *Citizenship Studies*, 15 (2011), 861–79

Warner, K., 'Gang rape in Sydney: crime, the media, politics, race and sentencing', *Australian and New Zealand Journal of Criminology*, 37 (2004), 344–61

Watson, I., 'Re-assessing casual employment in Australia', *Journal of Industrial Relations*, 47 (2005), 371–92

'Bridges or traps? Casualisation and labour market transitions in Australia', *Journal of Industrial Relations*, 55 (2013), 6–3

Watson, I., Buchanan, J., Campbell, I. and Briggs, C., *Fragmented Futures: New Challenges in Working Life* (Sydney: Federation Press, 2003)

Weiner, M. and Teitelbaum, M. S., *Political Demography, Demographic Engineering* (New York and Oxford: Berghahn Books, 2001)

Westoff, C. F. and Higgins, J., 'Relationships between men's gender attitudes and fertility: response to Puur et al.'s "Men's childbearing desires and views of the male role in Europe at the dawn of the 21st century"', *Demographic Research*, 21 (2009), 65–7

Williams, F., 'Migration and care: themes, concepts and challenges', *Social Policy and Society*, 9 (2010), 390–2

Wilson, A., 'The forced marriage debate and the British state', *Race & Class*, 49 (2007), 25–38

Winter, J. and Teitelbaum, M., *The Global Spread of Fertility Decline. Population, Fear and Uncertainty* (New Haven, CT and London: Yale University Press, 2013)

Whiteford, P., 'Australia. Inequality and prosperity and their impacts in a radical welfare state' in B. Nolan, W. Salverda, D. Checchi, et al. (eds), *Changing Inequalities and Societal Impacts in Rich Countries: Thirty Countries' Experiences* (Oxford University Press, 2014)

Woodward, D., 'WorkChoices and Howard's defeat', *The Australian Journal of Public Administration*, 69 (2010), 274–88

Wray, H., 'Moulding the migrant family', *Legal Studies*, 29 (2009), 592–618

Regulating Marriage Migration into the UK. A Stranger in the Home (Farnham: Ashgate, 2011)

'Any time, any place, anywhere: entry clearance, marriage migration and the border' in K. Charsley, (ed.), *Transnational Marriage: New Perspectives from Europe and Beyond* (Routledge, 2012), 41–59

Wright, C.F. 'How do states implement liberal immigration policies? Control signals and skilled immigration reform in Australia', *Governance*, 27 (2014), 397–421

Wyn, J., 'Becoming adult in the 2000s', *Family Matters*, 68 (2004), 6–12

'Educating for late modernity' in A. Furlong (ed.), *Handbook of Youth and Young Adulthood* (London and New York: Routledge, 2009), 97–104

Wyn, J. and Woodman, D., 'Generation, youth and social change in Australia', *Journal of Youth Studies*, 9 (2006), 495–514

Yeandle, S., Kröger, T. and Cass, B., 'Voice and choice for users and carers? Developments in patterns of care for older people in Australia, England and Finland', *Journal of European Social Policy*, 22 (2012), 432–44

Yeo, C., 'Forced marriages and the spouse visa age: part I', *Journal of Family Law and Practice*, 2 (2011), 44–9

'Forced marriages and the spouse visa age: part II', *Journal of Family Law and Practice*, 2 (2011), 38–42

Young, J., 'To these wet and windy shores', *Punishment & Society*, 5 (2003), 449–46

Ypi, L., 'Justice in migration: a closed borders utopia?' in J. S. Fishkin and R. E. Goodin (eds), *Population and Political Theory* (Chichester: Wiley-Blackwell, 2010), 256–84

Yuval-Davis, N., 'Gender and nation', *Ethnic and Racial Studies*, 16 (1993), 621–32

'Women and the biological reproduction of "the nation"', *Women's Studies International Forum*, 19 (1996), 17–24

Gender and Nation (London: Sage, 1997)

Yuval-Davis, N., Anthias, F. and Kofman, E., 'Secure borders and safe haven: the gendered politics of belonging beyond social cohesion', *Ethnic and Racial Studies*, 28 (2005), 513–35

Zanfrini, L., 'Immigration and labour market' in V. Cesareo (ed.), *Migration: A Picture from Italy* (Milan: Fondazione Ismu, 2013), 39–55

Zappalà, G. and Castles, S., 'Citizenship and immigration in Australia' in T. Aleinikoff and D. Klusmeyer (eds), *From Migrants to Citizens: Membership in a Changing World* (Washington, DC: Carnegie Endowment for International Peace, 2000), 32–81

Zarkovic Bookman, M., *The Demographic Struggle for Power. The Political Economy of Demographic Engineering in the Modern World* (London and Portland, OR: Frank Cass, 1997)

Zechner, M., 'Family commitments under negotiation: dual carers in Finland and in Italy', *Social Policy and Administration*, 38 (2004), 640–53

'Care of older persons in transnational settings', *Journal of Ageing Studies*, 22 (2008), 32–44

'Informaali hoiva sosiaalipoliittisessa kontekstissa', *Janus*, 18 (2010), 403–12

Zechner, M. and Valokivi, H., 'Negotiating care in the context of Finnish and Italian elder care policies', *European Journal of Ageing*, 9 (2012), 131 40

Ziguras, C. and Law, S., 'Recruiting international students as skilled migrants: the global "skills race" as viewed from Australia and Malaysia', *Globalisation, Societies and Education*, 4 (2006), 59–76

Zincone, G., 'The case of Italy' in G. Zincone, R. Penninx and M. Borkert (eds), *Migration Policymaking in Europe* (Amsterdam University Press, 2011), 247–90

Other Sources (Including Research Papers, Reports, Government Documents, Statistics, Dissertations, Online Resources)

Advisory Group on Citizenship, 'Education for citizenship and the teaching of democracy in schools', final report of the Advisory Group on Citizenship ('Crick report') (Qualifications and Curriculum Authority, 1998)

BIBLIOGRAPHY

Ahonen, K. and Bach-Othman, J., 'Vanhuusköyhyyden jäljillä – kotitalouden rakenteen merkitys sukupuolten välisiin köyhyysriskieroihin kahdeksassa EU-maassa', Eläketurvakeskuksen keskustelualoitteita 2009:8 (Helsinki: Eläketurvakeskus)

Ala-Lipasti, R., 'Kunniaväkivalta' (Helsinki: Vihreä sivistysliitto, 2009)

All Party Parliamentary Group on Migration, 'Report of the inquiry into new family migration rules', London, June 2013

Anderson, B., Ruhs, M., Rogaly, B. and Spencer, S., 'Fair enough? Central and East European migrants in low wage employment in the UK', report for the Joseph Rowntree Foundation (2006)

Antolín, P., Oxley, H. and Suyker, W., 'How will ageing affect Finland?', OECD Economics Department Working Papers, No. 295 (OECD Publishing, 2001)

Asa, R. and Bärlund, R., 'Satisfying labour demand through migration', European Migration Network (2010)

Attenborough, D., 'People and planet', RSA President's Lecture 2011, 10 March 2011

Australian Bureau of Statistics, 'Perspectives on migrants' (2009), at: www.abs.gov.au/AUSSTATS/abs@.nsf/Lookup/3416.0Main+Features32009

'Population projections, Australia, 2012' (2012), at: www.abs.gov.au/ausstats/abs@.nsf/mf/3222.0

'Australian historical population statistics' (2014), at: www.abs.gov.au/AUSSTATS/abs@.nsf/DetailsPage/3105.0.65.0012014?OpenDocument

'Births, Australia, 2014' (2014), at: www.abs.gov.au/ausstats/abs@.nsf/Latestproducts/3301.0Main%20Features42014?opendocument&tabname=Summary&prodno=3301.0&issue=2014&num=&view=

'Gender indicators, Australia, Feb 2016' (2016), at: www.abs.gov.au/ausstats/abs@.nsf/mf/4125.0

Billari, F. C. and Wilson, C., 'Convergence towards diversity? Cohort dynamics in the transition to adulthood in contemporary Western Europe', MPIDR Working Paper WP 2001–039

Birrell, B., 'Immigration reform in Australia: Coalition Government proposals and outcomes since March 1996', Centre for Population and Urban Research, Monash University (1997)

'The chains that bind: family reunion migration to Australia in the 1980s', Bureau of Immigration Research (1990)

Birrell, B. and Betts, K., 'The 2015 intergenerational report: misleading findings and hidden agendas', The Australian Population Research Institute, Research Report, July 2015

Birrell, B., Dobson, I. R., Rapson, V. and Smith, T. F., 'Skilled labour: gains and losses', Centre for Population and Urban Research, Monash University (2001)

Bonizzoni, P. and Cibea, A., 'Family migration policies in Italy', NODE Policy Report (Vienna: Austrian Ministry for Science and Research/International Centre for Migration Policy Development, 2009)

Border and Immigration Agency (UK), 'Marriage to partners from overseas. A consultation paper', December 2007
  'Marriage visas: pre-entry English requirements for spouses', December 2007
  'Marriage visas. The way forward', July 2008

Börsch-Supan, A., 'The 2005 pension reform in Finland', Finnish Centre for Pensions Working Papers 2005:1

Campbell, P., Kelly, P. and Harrison, L., 'The problem of Aboriginal marginalisation: education, labour markets and social and emotional well-being', Alfred Deakin Research Institute, Working Papers Series Two, No. 31 (2012)

Cangiano, A., Shutes, I., Spencer, S. and Leeson, G., 'Migrant care workers in ageing societies: research findings in the UK' (Centre on Migration, Policy and Society, University of Oxford, 2009)

Caritas/Migrantes, 'Dossier statistico immigrazione: 22° Rapporto' (Rome: IDOS-Redazione, 2012)

Castles, S., Vasta, E. and Ozkul, D., 'The internal dynamics of migration processes and their consequences for Australian government migration policies', Working Paper for the Department of Immigration and Citizenship (DIAC) (2012)

Charsley, K., Van Hear, N., Benson, M. and Storer-Church, B., 'Marriage-related migration to the UK', Home Office Occasional Paper 96 (2011)

Children's Commissioner, 'Family friendly? The impact on children of the Family Migration Rules: a review of the financial requirements', August 2015

Choudhury, T. and Fenwick, H., 'The impact of counter-terrorism measures on Muslim communities', Equality and Human Rights Commission Research report 72 (Manchester, 2011)

Committee of Inquiry into the Temporary Entry of Business People and Highly Skilled Specialists, 'Business temporary entry: future directions' ('Roach report') (Canberra, 1995)

Commonwealth of Australia, 'Intergenerational report 2002–03' (Canberra, 2002)
  'Australia's demographic challenges' (Canberra, 2004)
  'Intergenerational report 2007' (Canberra, 2004)
  'Australia to 2050: future challenges. Intergenerational report' (Canberra, 2010)
  'Sustainable Australia – sustainable communities. A sustainable population strategy for Australia' (Canberra, 2011)

Commonwealth Scientific and Industrial Research Organisation (CSIRO), 'Future dilemmas. Options to 2050 for Australia's population, technology, resources and environment', CSIRO Working paper series 02/01 (2002)

Community Cohesion Review Team, chaired by Cantle, T., 'Community cohesion' ('Cantle report') (London: Home Office, 2001)

Coole, D., 'Population stories: European narratives of over- and under-population', Paper prepared for the ECPR General Conference, Reykjavik, Iceland, 25–27 August 2011 d'Addio, A. C. and d'Ercole, M. M., 'Trends and determinants of fertility rates in OECD countries: the role of policies', OECD Social, Employment and Migration Working Papers, DELSA/ELSA/WD/SEM(2005)6

Deloitte, 'The economic value of informal care in Australia in 2015' (Deloitte Access Economics/Carers Australia, 2015)

Department of Immigration and Multicultural Affairs (Australia), 'Immigration. Federation to century's end 1901–2000' (2001)

Department of Immigration and Citizenship, 'Annual report 2011–12' (Commonwealth of Australia, 2012)

Department of Immigration and Border Protection, 'Student visa and temporary graduate visa programme trends 2006–07 to 2013–14' (2014)

'Subclass 457 visa holders quarterly pivot table 31 March 2015' (2015), at: www.border.gov.au/about/reports-publications/research-statistics/statistics/work-in-australia

'2014–15 migration programme report. Programme year to 30 June 2015' (2015), at: www.immi.gov.au/media/statistics/statistical-info/temp-entrants/subclass-457.htm#

Department of Prime Minister and Cabinet, 'John Howard transcript of interview with Chris Smith', Radio 2GB, Sydney, 31 August 2006, at: pmtranscripts.dpmc.gov.au/release/transcript-22450

Department for Work and Pensions (UK), 'Opportunity age', Seventh Annual Report 2005

'Employing older workers' (2013)

Doyle, J. and Howes, S., 'Australia's seasonal worker program: demand-side constraints and suggested reforms' (Washington, DC: World Bank Group, 2015)

Dunnell, K., 'Policy responses to population ageing and population decline – United Kingdom' (Office for National Statistics, 2000)

Ellilä, K., 'Kunnan omaishoidon tuki sosiaalipalveluna', Edilex 2011/23

Elliott, A., 'Legal, social and intimate belonging: Moroccan and Albanian second generation migrants in Italy', University College London Anthropology Working Paper No. 05/2009

European Commission, 'Green Paper "Confronting demographic change: a new solidarity between the generations"', COM(2005) 94 final

'The 2012 Ageing Report, Economic and budgetary projections for the 27 EU Member States (2010–2060)', European Economy 2/2012

'Communication from the Commission to the European Parliament and the Council on the Implementation of Directive 2009/50/EC on the conditions of entry and residence of third-country nationals for the purpose of highly qualified employment', COM(2014) 287 final

European Commission and United Nations Economic Commission for Europe, 'Introducing the Active Ageing Index', policy brief, April 2013

EVA, 'Tuomitut vähenemään – suomalaiset ja lisääntymisen vaikea taito' (Helsinki: Elinkeinoelämän valtuuskunta, 2003)

Fagerlund, J. and Brander, S., 'Country report: Finland' (EUDO Citizenship Observatory, EUI: Robert Schuman Centre for Advanced Studies, 2013)

Fargues, P., 'International migration and Europe's demographic challenge', background paper EU-US Immigration Systems 2011/09 (European University Institute, 2011)

Farina, P. and Ortensi, L. E., 'When low fertility affects immigrants. The case of Italy', paper presented at European Population Conference, Stockholm, June 2012

Fondazione ISMU, 'Diciannovesimo rapporto sulle migrazioni 2013' (Milano: FrancoAngeli, 2014)

'Ventesimo rapporto sulle migrazioni: 1994–2014' (Milano: FrancoAngeli, 2015)

General Register Office for Scotland, 'Vital events reference tables' (2014), at: www.nrscotland.gov.uk/statistics-and-data/statistics/statistics-by-theme/vital-events/general-publications/vital-events-reference-tables/2014

Gower, M., 'Immigration and asylum: changes made by the coalition government 2010–2015', House of Commons Library briefing, 2015

Gray, M., Qu, L. and Weston, R., 'Fertility and family policy in Australia', research paper no 41, Australian Institute of Family Studies (2008)

Haataja, A., 'Ikääntyvät työmarkkinoilla 1989–2005', Sosiaali- ja terveysministeriön selvityksiä 2006:42

Hallitus, 'HE 50/1998 vp, Hallituksen esitys Eduskunnalle laiksi ulkomaalaislain muuttamisesta'

'HE 240/2009 vp, Hallituksen esitys Eduskunnalle laiksi ulkomaalaislain muuttamisesta'

'HE 269/2009 vp, Hallituksen esitys Eduskunnalle laeiksi ulkomaalaislain ja ulkomaalaisrekisteristä annetun lain 3 §:n muuttamisesta'

Hay, D. and Howes, S., 'Australia's Pacific Seasonal Worker pilot scheme: why has take-up been so low?', Discussion Paper 17, Development Policy Centre (Canberra, 2012)

Heath, A. H. and Cheung, S. Y., 'Ethnic penalties in the labour market: employers and discrimination', Department for Work and Pensions Research Report No. 341 (London: HMSO, 2006)

Helldán, A. and Helakorpi, S., 'Eläkeikäisen väestön terveyskäyttäytyminen ja terveys keväällä 2013 ja niiden muutokset 1993–2013', Terveyden ja hyvinvoinnin laitos, Raportti 15/2014

Hester, M., Chantler, K., Gangoli, G., et al., 'Forced marriage: the risk factors and the effect of raising the minimum age for a sponsor, and of leave to enter the UK as a spouse or fiance(e)' (Home Office, 2006)

Hoff, A., 'Current and future challenges of family care in the UK, Future of an ageing population: evidence review' (Government Office for Science, 2015)

Home Office, 'Secure borders, safe haven. Integration with diversity in modern Britain' (London: The Stationery Office, 2002)

'Statement of intent: family migration' (London: Home Office, 2012)

Honkatukia, J., Ahokas, J. and Marttila, K., 'Työvoiman tarve Suomen taloudessa vuosina 2010–2025', VATT Tutkimukset 154 (2010)

House of Commons, 'Preventing violent extremism, sixth report of session 2009–10' (London: The Stationery Office, 2010)

House of Lords, 'Ready for ageing', Select Committee on Public Service and Demographic Change, 2013

Hugo, G., Rudd, D. and Harris, K., 'Emigration from Australia. Economic implications', CEDA Information Paper No. 77 (2001)

Istat, 'Il future demografico' (2011), available at: www.istat.it/it/files/2011/12/futuro-demografico.pdf

'Indicatori demografici. Stime per l'anno 2014', 12 February 2015

Kangasniemi, M. and Kauhanen, M., 'Who leaves and who stays? Outmigration of Estonian immigrants from Finland and its impact on economic assimilation of Estonian immigrants in Finland', NORFACE Migration Discussion Paper No. 2013-01

Kehusmaa S., 'Hoidon menoja hillitsemässä. Heikkokuntoisten kotona asuvien ikäihmisten palvelujen käyttö, omaishoito ja kuntoutus' Kela, Sosiaali- ja terveysturvan tutkimuksia 131 (2014)

Khoo, S., McDonald, P. and Edgar, B., 'Contribution of family migration to Australia', Department of Immigration and Border Protection (2014)

Kiander, J. 'Laman opetukset. Suomen 1990-luvun kriisin syyt ja seuraukset', VATT-julkaisuja, 27(5) (2001)

Koivuniemi, S., 'Maahanmuuttajataustainen koulutettu hoitohenkilöstö sosiaali- ja terveydenhuollon työyhteisöissä', Tehy ry:n Julkaisusarja B: 1/2012

Koponen, E., Laiho, U. and Tuomaala, M., 'Mistä tekijät sosiaali- ja terveysalalle – työvoimatarpeen ja -tarjonnan kehitys vuoteen 2025', TEM-analyyseja 43/2012

Korhonen, K. and Ellonen, N., 'Maahanmuuttajanaiset väkivallan uhrina', Poliisiammattikorkeakoulun tiedotteita 60/2007

Kundnani, A., 'Spooked! How not to prevent violent extremism' (London: Institute of Race Relations, 2009)

Kyhä, H., 'Koulutetut maahanmuuttajat työmarkkinoilla. Tutkimus korkeakoulututkinnon suorittaneiden maahanmuuttajien työllistymisestä ja työurien alusta Suomessa', unpublished PhD thesis, University of Turku (2011)

Lassila, J., Määttänen, N. and Valkonen, T., 'Työeläkeuudistus 2017. Vaikutukset työuriin, tulonjakoon ja julkisen talouden kestävyyteen', Valtioneuvoston selvitys- ja tutkimustoiminnan julkaisusarja 1/2015

Lee, E., Clements, S., Ingham, R. and Stone, N., 'A matter of choice? Explaining national variation in teenage abortion and motherhood' (York: Joseph Rowntree Foundation, 2004)

Lee, H. and Kim, C., 'The dynamics of migration processes: the gender dimension in Asian-Australian migration', working paper for the Department of Immigration and Citizenship (2011)

Leitch Review of Skills, 'Prosperity for all in the global economy – world class skills' (Norwich: HMSO, 2006)

Luoma, K., Räty, T., Moisio, A., et al., 'Seniori-Suomi. Ikääntyvän väestön taloudelliset vaikutukset' (Suomen itsenäisyyden juhlarahasto Sitra, 2003)

Maahanmuuttovirasto, 'Turvapaikanhakijat. Yksintulleet alaikäiset', at www.migri.fi/download/57238_Tp-hakijat_alaikaiset_2014.pdf?8af65ab3d7f3d288

McDonald, P., 'The role of family migration in Australia's permanent migration program. Policy discussion paper', report to the Department of Immigration and Citizenship, April 2013

Markkanen, K. and Tammisto, S., 'Maahanmuuttajat hoitoalan työyhteisöissä', Tehyn selvitys monikulttuurisuudesta, Tehy ry:n Julkaisusarja B: Selvityksiä 3/2005

Merlino, M., 'The Italian (in)security package', CHALLENGE Research Paper No. 14 (2009)

Migrant Rights Network, 'Damian Green tells Newsnight that new language tests will reduce migration', http://www.migrantsrights.org.uk/blog/2010/11/damian-green-tells-newsnight-new-language-tests-will-reduce-migration

Migration Council Australia, 'More than temporary: Australia's 457 Visa Program' (Canberra, 2013)

Migration Observatory, 'Commentary. Off target: Government policies are not on track to reducing net-migration to the tens of thousands by 2015' (Oxford: Migration Observatory, 2011)

'Net migration', migrationobservatory.ox.ac.uk/commentary/net-migration-genie-and-bottle-where-next-net-migration-target

Minister for Immigration and Border Protection, 'Explanatory statement. Select legislative instrument no. 65, 2014, Migration Amendment (Repeal of Certain Visa Classes) Regulation 2014', https://www.legislation.gov.au/Details/F2014L00622/Explanatory%20Statement/Text

Ministerial Group on Public Order and Community Cohesion, 'Building cohesive communities' ('Denham report') (London: Home Office, 2001)

Mölsä, M., 'Tyttöjen ympärileikkauksen hoito ja ehkäisy Suomessa' (Helsinki: Stakes 1994)

'Ajat ovat muuttuneet: Selvitys tyttöjen ja naisten ympärileikkaukseen liittyvistä asenteista ja aikeista pääkaupunkiseudulla asuvien maahanmuuttajien keskuudessa' (Helsinki: Ihmisoikeusliitto, 2004)

Münz, R. 'Demography and migration: an outlook for the 21st century', Migratio Policy Institute Policy Brief, September 2013

Myrskylä, P., 'Nuoret työmarkkinoiden ja opiskelun ulkopuolella', TEM julkaisuja 12/2011

'Hukassa – Keitä ovat syrjäytyneet nuoret?', EVA analyysi No 19 (Elinkeinoelämän Valtuuskunta, 2012)

Myrskylä, P. and Pyykkönen, T., 'Tulevaisuuden Tekijät', EVA analyysi No. 42 (Elinkeinoelämän Valtuuskunta, 2015)

Nieminen, I., 'Selvitys edellytyksistä myöntää täysi-ikäisen Suomen kansalaisen ulkomaiselle vanhemmalle oleskelulupa Suomessa' (Helsinki: Erik Castrén -instituutti, Helsingin yliopisto 2010)

Niikko, M., 'Syntyvyyden lisääminen veroeduilla ja muilla kannustimilla', Toimenpidealoite 12/2014 vp

Noro, A., Mäkelä, M., Jussmäki, T. and Finne-Soveri, H., 'Ikäihmisten palvelujen kehityslinjoja 2000-luvulla' in A. Noro and H. Alastalo (eds), Vanhuspalvelulain 980/2012 toimeenpanon seuranta. Tilanne ennen lain voimaantuloa vuonna 2013, Raportti 13/2014 (Terveyden ja hyvinvoinnin laitos, 2014), 19–30

Nykänen, A., 'Hyöty vai haitta, uhka vai uhri? Argumentit maahanmuuton puolesta ja vastaan Suomessa vuosina 2003–2011' (Turku: Siirtolaisuusinstituutti, 2012)

OECD, 'Jobs for immigrants (Vol. 4): labour market integration in Italy' (OECD Publishing, 2014)

Office of National Statistics, 'Fertility summary, 2010' (2010), at: www.ons.gov.uk/ons/rel/fertility-analysis/fertility-summary/2010/uk-fertility-summary.html

'Population ageing in the United Kingdom, its constituent countries and the European Union', at: www.ons.gov.uk/ons/dcp171776_258607.pdf

'Birth summary tables, England and Wales 2014' (2014), at: http://www.ons.gov.uk/peoplepopulationandcommunity/birthsdeathsandmarriages/livebirths/bulletins/birthsummarytablesenglandandwales/2015-07-15

'Births in England and Wales by parents' country of birth: 2013' (2014), at: www.ons.gov.uk/peoplepopulationandcommunity/births deathsandmarriages/livebirths/bulletins/parentscountryofbirthengland andwales/2014-08-28

Open Society, 'Somalis in Helsinki' (New York: Open Society Foundations, 2013)

Parjanne, M., 'Väestön ikärakenteen muutoksen vaikutukset ja niihin varautuminen eri hallinnonaloilla', Sosiaali- ja terveysministeriön selvityksiä 2004:18

Parkkinen, P., 'Hoivapalvelut ja eläkemenot vuoteen 2050', VATT Tutkimukset 94 (2002)

'Väestön ikääntymisen vaikutukset kuntatalouteen', VATT Tutkimukset 154 (2007)

Paunio, R. and Linnakangas, A., 'Ympärivuorokautisessa hoidossa olevien vanhusten perus- ja ihmisoikeuksien turvaaminen', eoae 213/2009 (Parliamentary Ombudsman of Finland)

Phillips, J., Klapdor, M. and Simon-Davies, J., 'Migration to Australia since federation: a guide to the statistics', background note (Parliament of Australia: Parliamentary Library, 2010)

Piekkola, H., 'Active ageing policies in Finland', ETLA Discussion Paper No. 898 (2004)

'Demographic aspects of ageing, labour market and time use in a set of European countries', ETLA Discussion Papers No. 899 (2004)

Pohjanpää, K., Paananen, S. and Nieminen, M., 'Maahanmuuttajien elinolot. Venäläisten, virolaisten, somalialaisten ja vietnamilaisten elämää Suomessa 2002' (Helsinki: Tilastokeskus, 2003)

Productivity Commission, 'An ageing Australia: preparing for the future', Productivity Commission Research Paper (Canberra, 2013)

Rantala, J., 'Varhainen eläkkeelle siirtyminen', Eläketurvakeskuksen tutkimuksia 2008:1

Rantanen, P. and Valkonen J., 'Ulkomaalaiset metsämarjapoimijat Suomessa' (Lappea-instituutti, 2011)

Registrar General Northern Ireland, 'Annual report 2014' (The Northern Ireland Statistics and Research Agency, 2015)

Royal Commission on Long Term Care, 'With respect to old age', m 4192 (London: The Stationery Office, 1999)

Rumbaut, R. and Ima, K., 'The adaptation of Southeast Asian refugee youth: a comparative study. Final report to the Office of Resettlement' (Washington, DC: Office of Refugee Resettlement (DHHS), 1988)

Sainio, P., Koskinen, S., Sihvonen, A., Martelin, T. and Aromaa, A., 'Iäkkään väestön terveyden ja toimintakyvyn kehityslinjoja' in A. Noro and H. Alastalo (eds), Vanhuspalvelulain 980/2012 toimeenpanon seuranta.

Tilanne ennen lain voimaantuloa vuonna 2013, Raportti 13/2014 (Terveyden ja hyvinvoinnin laitos, 2014), 37–41

Salis, E., 'Labour migration governance in contemporary Europe. The case of Italy', FIERI working paper, LAB-MIG-GOV Project, 2012

Samad, Y. and Eade, J., 'Community perceptions of forced marriage' (London: Community Liaison Unit, FCO, 2002)

Sawyer, C. and Wray, H., 'Country report: United Kingdom' (EUDO Citizenship Observatory, EUI: Robert Schuman Centre for Advanced Studies, 2012)

Sciortino, G., 'Fortunes and miseries of Italian labour migration policy', CeSPI Country Paper 1/09 (2009)

Shaver, S., 'Gender, social policy regimes and the welfare state', Social Policy Research Centre Discussion Paper No. 26 (Sydney: University of New South Wales, 1990)

Sisäasiainministeriö, 'Työvoiman maahanmuuton toimenpideohjelman loppuraportti', SM053:01/2008 (2012)

Sisäministeriö, 'Valtioneuvoston periaatepäätös Maahanmuuton tulevaisuus 2020-Strategiasta' (2013)

'Maahanmuuton tulevaisuus 2020-strategia. Toimenpideohjelma' (2014)

Sonkin, L., Petäkoski-Hult, T., Rönkä, K. and Södergård, H., 'Seniori 2000. Ikääntyvä Suomi uudelle vuosituhannelle' (Suomen itsenäisyyden juhlarahasto Sitra, 1999)

Sosiaali- ja terveysministeriö, 'Kansallinen omaishoidon kehittämisohjelma. Työryhmän loppuraportti', Sosiaali- ja terveysministeriön raportteja ja muistioita, 2014: 2

Tilastokeskus, 'Väestöennuste 2009–2060' (2009), at: tilastokeskus.fi/til/vaenn/2009/vaenn_2009_2009-09-30_tie_001_fi.html

'Ulkomaalaiset ja siirtolaisuus 2012' (Helsinki: Tilastokeskus, 2012)

'Elinajanodote' (2013), at: www.stat.fi/org/tilastokeskus/elinajanodote.html

'Syntyneiden määrä väheni yhä' (2015), at: www.stat.fi/til/synt/2014/synt_2014_2015-04-14_tie_001_fi.html

'Väestö' (2015), at: www.tilastokeskus.fi/tup/suoluk/suoluk_vaesto.html

'Väestöennuste 2015' (2015), at: www.stat.fi/til/vaenn/2015/index.html

Tuomaala, M., and Torvi, K., 'Kohti työperusteista maahanmuuttoa: ulkomailta palkattavan työvoiman tarpeen arviointi', TEM analyyseja 9/2008

Työ- ja elinkeinoministeriö, 'Kotoutumisen kokonaiskatsaus 2013', TEM raportteja 38/2013

United Nations, 'World population ageing: 1950–2050' (NewYork: Department of Economic and Social Affairs, Population Division, 2001)

'World population prospects. 2015 revision' (Department of Economic and Social Affairs, 2015)

Valtioneuvoston kanslia, 'Hyvä yhteiskunta kaikenikäisille. Valtioneuvoston tulevaisuusselonteko väestökehityksestä, väestöpolitiikasta ja

ikärakenteen muutokseen varautumisesta' (Valtioneuvoston kanslian julkaisusarja 27/2004)
'Väestön ikärakenteen muutos ja siihen varautuminen. Tulevaisuusselonteon liiteraportti 1' (Valtioneuvoston kanslian julkaisusarja 29/2004)
'Väestökehitykseen vaikuttaminen – tulisiko syntyvyyttä ja maahanmuuttoa lisätä? Tulevaisuusselonteon liiteraportti 3' (Valtioneuvoston kanslian julkaisusarja 31/2004)
'Ikääntyminen voimavarana. Tulevaisuusselonteon liiteraportti 5' (Valtioneuvoston kanslian julkaisusarja 33/2004)
'Matti Vanhasen II hallituksen ohjelma' (19.4.2007)
'Ikääntymisraportti. Kokonaisarvio ikääntymisen vaikutuksista ja varautumisen riittävyydestä' (Valtioneuvoston kanslian julkaisusarja 1/2009)
'Pääministeri Jyrki Kataisen hallituksen ohjelma' (22.6.2011)
Väestöliitto, 'Väestöpoliittinen ohjelma' (Helsinki: Väestöliitto, 2004)
Väänänen, A., Toivanen, M., Aalto, A.-M., et al., 'Maahanmuuttajien integroituminen suomalaiseen yhteiskuntaan' (Helsinki: Sektoritutkimuksen neuvottelukunta, 2009)
van Aerschot, L., 'Vanhusten hoiva ja eriarvoisuus', unpublished PhD thesis, University Tampere (2014)
Vanstone, A., 'Federal government perspective' in 'Australia's population challenge: the National Population Summit' (Adelaide: Australian Population Institute, 2004), 33–9
Wanless, D., Forder, J., Fernandez, J.-L., et al., 'Securing good care for older people: taking a long-term view' (London: King's Fund, 2006)
Wright, C. F., 'Policy legacies and the politics of labour immigration selection and control: the processes and dynamics shaping national-level policy decisions during the recent wave of international migration', unpublished PhD thesis, University of Cambridge (2010)
Zincone, G. and Basili, M., 'Country report: Italy' (EUDO Citizenship Observatory, EUI: Robert Schuman Centre for Advanced Studies, 2013)

INDEX

Abbott, Tony, 10, 12
abortion, 39, 61–2
Active Ageing Index, 178–9
Adult Dependent Relative rule, 173
adulthood, definition of, 71–3
Afghanistan, asylum seekers from, 88
age of consent, 72
aged parent visas, in Australia, 176
ageism, 179
Aguilar, Amber (Jeffrey), 102
Aguilar Quila case, 82–3, 102
Aliens Act of 2004 (Finland), 136, 163–4
anchor children, 94. *See also* children of immigrants
Anderson, B., 143
Antonova, Irina, 164–5
Antonova case, 163–6
Asian immigration, 114–15
Asquith, N., 181
asylum seekers
　in Australia, 123–4
　boat people, 88, 108, 114–15
　fake, 17
　from Iraq and Afghanistan, 88
　in United Kingdom, 128
attendance allowance (*indennità di accompagnamento*), 169
Australia, 2, 110–25
　asylum seekers, 124–5
　baby bonus in, 53
　balance of family rule, 176
　below-replacement fertility in, 10, 45–6, 52–3, 113, 115
　birth rates, 45–6, 52–3
　care for older people in, 175–6
　children of immigrants in, 69
　concerns over white women's fertility, 51
　demographic ageing in, 111, 149, 174–7
　457 visa programme, 108, 118–21, 141
　human capital, 112–13, 117, 139–40
　immigration policies, 52
　　control of annual immigration, 10
　　economic liberalisation and, 114
　　economic policies and, 112–13
　　history, 111–12
　　migrants' contribution to the state and, 115–16
　　multiethnicity and, 54–5
　　points system, 112, 117
　　quantity versus quality of immigrants, 116–25
　　White Australia policy, 52, 86, 110
　labour force, 114
　labour migrants, 108
　　intake of, 116
　　low-skilled migrant workers in, 143
　　parents of, 176–7
　　shift from permanent to temporary migration, 117, 122–3
　　skilled migration in, 137, 140
　　women migrants, 123–4
　low birth rates in, 113
　multiculturalism in, 69, 86–7
　new integrationism in, 88
　over 65 age group in, 167
　pension reforms in, 174–5
　population, 111
　population policy, 51–5
　Sydney gang rapes, 87
　temporary visa programme, 144
　transitions to adulthood in, 85–9

baby bonus
　in Australia, 53
　in Italy, 40–1
　limitations of, 42–3
baby boomers, 30
　in Australia, 113
　birth rates and, 31
　in Finland, 153–4
　pressures of population ageing and, 125
　retirement, 125
　in United Kingdom, 71
badanti (paid carers), 169
Bali bombings in 2002, 87
Bangladeshi immigrants. *See also* South Asian immigrants
　forced marriage, 79
　in United Kingdom, 74, 84
Beck, U., 142

INDEX

below-replacement fertility
  in Australia, 10, 45–6, 52–3, 113, 115
  definition of, 7
  demographic ageing and, 28
  in Finland, 46, 60
  in Global North, 28, 45
  in Italy, 31
  second demographic transition and, 8–9
  in United Kingdom, 45–6
Bibi, Shakira, 102
Biggs, S., 179
Billari, F.C., 85
biopower
  demographic governance and, 14–15
  governmentalisation and, 15–17
  individualisation and, 15
  totalisation and, 15
birth rates, 189
  in Australia, 45–6
  baby bonuses and, 42–3
  of care workers in Italy, 38
  decline in, 6, 49
  family policies and, 34, 39–40
  in Finland, 45–6
  in Italy, 31–3, 35, 39
  low, 7, 31–3
  and making of new citizens, 28–66
  of migrants, 38
  trends around, 11–12
  in United Kingdom, 45–6, 49
Block, L., 80
boat people, 88, 108, 114–15. *See also* asylum seekers
bonus phase, 150
Bossi-Fini law, 92, 132, 170
Brazilianisation of the West, 142
breadwinner model, 61
British Muslims
  anti-terrorism programs and, 77–8
  economic activity levels of women, 75–6
  integration of second-generation, 68, 75–6
  marriage, 75–6
  of South Asian origin, 74, 100
  transitions to adulthood
    citizenship and, 96–105
    education and, 98–9
    marriage as event, 97
    new normative good transition, 97–8
  urban disturbances and, 68, 74
British Nationality Act (1981), 51
Brubaker, R., 13

care allowance (*indennità di accompagnamento*), 169
care workers
  attendance allowance (*indennità di accompagnamento*), 169
  in Australia, 175–6
  expansion of care sectors, 143–4
  in Finland, 156, 162–3
  gender care gap and, 131
  in Global North, 184–5, 190
  in Italy, 35–8
    birth rates, 38
    hiring of immigrants, 169
    paid carers (*badanti*), 169, 175–6
  in United Kingdom, 171–4
  women, 131, 155, 185
Catholicism, 34
Central Europe, free movement rights, 143
childbearing
  and birth rates in United Kingdom, 49–50
  early, 62, 73–4, 79
  in Finland, 47
  global trends in, 6
  ideals in late-modern states, 56
  of immigrant women, 64
  immigration and patterns in, 38
  men's behaviour towards, 59
  opportunity costs of, 32
  postponement of, 71
  skilled migrants, 140
  teenage pregnancy, 62, 73–4
  youthful, 62, 73–4
childhood poverty, 63
childless couples, 60
children of immigrants
  in Australia, 69
  citizenship of, 65, 67, 96–105
  in Finland, 69
  integration of, 68
  in Italy, 43–4, 69, 89–92
  media coverage of, 91
  problem groups, 100
  racial and ethnic background, 74–5
  role of structural factors, 73
  transitions into adulthood, 67–106
    citizenship and, 96–105
    education and, 98–9
    marriage as event, 97
    new normative good transition, 97–8
  in United Kingdom, 70–85
China
  immigrants from, 90, 97
  population, 6
citizenship, 1–2
  of children of immigrants, 43, 65, 67, 96–105
  demographic governance and, 18–23
  denial of equal citizenship, 101–3
  governance of labour migration and, 137–46
  governance of national reproduction and, 55–65

of labour migrants, 109–10
law and policy on, 15
and management of ageing populations, 177–86
of migrant workers, 109–10
quality of future citizenry and, 96–105
reproductive governance and, 55–65
rules, 101–2
of second-generation immigrants, 96–105
climate change, 7
Coalition Government (UK), 78, 84, 127, 129
cohabitation, 85
Coleman, D., 64
corporatisation, 16
cousin marriage, 76
Crick report, 76
criminals as suspect populations, 17
Cronulla riots in 2005 (Australia), 88
Cruikshank, B., 67

deaths, 189–90
deep old age, 181–2
demographic ageing, 28, 147–87
 in Australia, 111, 149, 174–7
 baby boomers and, 125
 below-replacement fertility in, 28
 definition of, 8–9
 dependency ratio and, 151
 economic consequences of, 28, 158
 European strategy to counter the effects of, 178–9
 in Finland, 148, 150–2, 167, 179–80
 in Global North, 1, 107, 138, 147, 188
 immigration as solution to, 54–5, 156–7
 in Italy, 29, 130, 149, 168
 labour migrants and, 107, 137
 states' approach to, 149–50
 in United Kingdom, 149, 171–4
 in welfare state, 150–7
 in workforce terms, 151
 young people's transition to work and, 99–100
demographic gift, 150
demographic governance, 3, 12–18
 anxieties, 17
 biopower and, 14–15
 citizenship and, 18–23
 definition of, 13
 immigration and, 14
 population policies and, 13–14
 suspect populations and, 17
 taking charge of life and, 18
demographic transformations, 4–12
demographic transition, 5, 28
 in Australia, 149, 174–7

bonus phase, 150
 in Finland, 148, 150–1, 167
 in Italy, 149, 168
 paradox of, 56
 third, 11, 64
 in United Kingdom, 149, 171–4
denatalità (lacking births), 29, 32, 35
Denmark, 81
dependency ratio
 demographic ageing and, 151
 in Finland, 47, 151
 in Italy, 168
deregulation, 16
Disability Discrimination Act 1992 (Australia), 115
divorce, 39, 59
Down syndrome, 115–16
dual citizen model, in Global North, 138

early retirement, 151
Eastern Europe
 free movement rights, 143
 immigrant workers from, 38
economic liberalisation, 16
education, 98–9
emerging adulthood, 72
England, birth rates in, 45–6
environment, 7
Estonian immigrants, 93, 136
ethnic background, 74–5
European Convention of Human Rights, 82
European Economic Area, 173
European Union
 freedom of movement of workers in, 126
 labour migration policies in, 109
 older immigrants, 165–6
European Union, migration, 128
extracomunitari, 91
extremism, 78, 100

Fadayel, Eveline, 164–5
Fadayel case, 163–6
familialism, 157–67
families
 as caregivers, 183–4
 reconstituted, 104
 reliance on, 90
 transnational, 101–2
family migration, 80, 92, 123–4
family policies
 baby bonus as, 40–1, 42–3, 53
 birth rates and, 34, 39–40
 in Finland, 46
 in Nordic countries, 60
family wage, 113
fascism, 34, 39
feminism, 39

249

INDEX

fertility rates
  in 1800s, 5
  below-replacement fertility, 7
  fall in, 125
  total fertility rate, 7, 29, 45–6
  white women's fertility in Australia, 51
Fine, M., 186
Finland, 2
  ageing population in, 133
  Aliens Act of 2004, 136, 163–4
  baby boomers, 153–4
  below-replacement fertility in, 46, 60
  birth rates, 45–6
  care for older people in, 152–3
    migrant care workers, recruitment of, 162–3
    state's role in, 161–2
    without full involvement of state, 160–1
  childbearing issues in, 47
  children of immigrants in, 69
  citizenship regime, 48
  demographic ageing in, 148
    dependency ratio, 47
    economic consequences of, 151–2
    pressures on private and public care, 154–5, 179–80
    structural adjustments, 151–2
    welfare system and, 150–67
    in workforce terms, 151
  demographic transition in, 150–1
  dependency ratio in, 47, 151
  familialism in, 157–67
  family policies, 46
  immigrant births in, 48
  immigrants, 93
  immigration policies, 134–5, 136–7
  knowledge factories in, 98
  labour market, 134–5
  labour migrants in, 109, 133–7
    Estonian immigrants, 136
    government policies on, 134–5, 136–7
    migrant care workers, 156, 162–3
    sustainability of welfare standards and, 135–6
    women migrants, 135, 140
  low birth rates in, 150–1, 167
  low-skilled migration, 143
  municipal services in, 154–5
  naturalisation law, 95
  parents of immigrant-citizens in, 165–6
  pension reforms, 158
  population policy, 46–8
  postponement of marriage and childbirth, 85
  proportion of young and older people, 150
  raising birth rates in, 48
  transitions to adulthood in, 92–6
  welfare system, 152–3, 154–5
forced marriage, 79, 89
Forced Marriage Unit (FMU), 79, 82
Foucault, Michel, 14
457 visa programme, 118–21, 141
fourth agers, 161, 178, 181–2. *See also* older people
Fraser, N., 60
Friuli Venezia Giulia (Italy), baby bonus in, 40–1

gender equity, 33, 57, 60, 138
gender relations
  in Italy, 39
  role of, 2
  Western attitudes to, 103
genital mutilation, 94
Global North, 1
  ageing of, 190
  below-replacement fertility in, 28, 45
  birth rates, 45
  care workers, 144
  collaboration with Global South, 191
  demographic ageing in, 1, 107, 138, 147, 188
  demographic governance in, 4, 18
  demographic transition in, 28, 188
  dual citizen model in, 138
  end of adolescence in, 72
  low birth rates in, 188
  migrant labour in, 107, 184
  migration rates in, 29
  migration to, 191
  population, 7–8
  population policies in, 3
  skilled jobs in, 139
Global South
  collaboration with Global North, 191
  labour migrants from, 64
  low-skilled migration from, 108
  population, 6
  population control in, 3
  population growth, 6
  women migrants from, 64, 144
globalisation, 12–13, 77
Governmental Report on the Future 2004 (Finland), 47
governmentalisation and biopower, 15–17
granny cases, 163–6
Groenendijk, K., 104

Hampshire, J., 13, 14, 15
Hanafin, P., 41–2
Hanson, Pauline, 88
Hochschild, A.R., 37
Höhn, C., 60

250

INDEX

home care
  allowance, 153, 159
  in Finland, 152, 159
honour crimes, 75
Howard Coalition government, 116
human capital, 109

illegal immigrants, 17, 54
immigrants
  Bangladeshi, 74, 79, 84
  children of. *See* children of immigrants
  Chinese, 90, 97
  Estonian, 93, 136
  extracomunitari, 91
  illegal, 17, 54
  Indian, 51, 97
  Pakistani, 51, 74, 79, 84
  parents of, 182–3
  Philippine, 38, 162
  Polish, 162
  Russian, 93, 162
  South Asian, 75
  United Kingdom, 64–5
immigration
  for care and domestic work, 35–8
  demographic changes and, 64
  demographic governance and, 14
  law and policy on, 15
  as solution to demographic ageing, 9–11, 54–5, 156–7
immigration laws, 101–2
  Aliens Act of 2004 (Finland), 136, 163–4
  Bossi-Fini law, 92, 132, 170
  citizenship laws and, 15
  Finland, 95
  Italy, 170–1
  Turco-Napolitano law, 170
immigration policies
  Australia, 52
    control of annual immigration, 10
    economic policies and, 112–13
    history, 111–12
    migrants' contribution to the state and, 115–16
    multiethnicity and, 54–5
    points system, 112, 117
    White Australia policy, 52, 86, 110
  Italy
    care services and, 35–8
    on families of migrant workers, 170–1
    labour migration and, 130–3
    and labour migration in Finland, 134–5, 136–7
  United Kingdom, 79–81
    entry of immigrants over 65, 173
    long-term ethnic change, 51
    on non-EU citizens, 79–81

India
  immigrants from, 51, 97
  population, 6
individualisation and biopower, 15
in vitro fertilisation, 41–2
institutional care, 152
intergenerational justice, 63
intermarriage, 75
international students, 122
intragenerational justice, 63
Iraq, asylum seekers from, 88
Islamophobia, 78
Italy, 2
  below-replacement fertility in, 31
  care workers in, 35–8
    birth rates, 38
    hiring of immigrants, 169
    paid carers (*badanti*), 169, 175–6
  children of immigrants
    citizenship rules for, 44–5
    issues, 43–4
    transitions to adulthood, 89–92
  children of immigrants in, 43–4, 69, 89–92
  demographic ageing in
    denatalità (lacking births) phenomenon and, 29
    evolution of, 31–8
    labour migration policies and, 130
    steep curve of, 149, 168
  dependency ratio in, 168
  extracomunitari, 91
  governance of national reproduction, 39–45
  immigration laws, 170–1
  immigration policies
    care services and, 35–8
    on families of migrant workers, 170–1
    labour migration and, 130–3
  in vitro fertilisation, 41–2
  labour market, 130
  labour migrants, 130–3
    for care and domestic work, 35–8
    entry through backdoor, 131–2
    low-skilled versus skilled migration, 132–3
  migrant care workers, 169
  late transition to adulthood in, 85
  low birth rates in, 29–30, 31, 33, 35, 39
  net migration in, 29–30
  over 65 age group in, 167
  pension reforms in, 168
  reliance on families in, 90
  social care system in, 169–70
  working age population in, 130

Japan, negative population growth in, 8
jus sanguinis, 43, 54, 65
jus soli, 43, 48, 54, 65

251

INDEX

knowledge factories, 98
knowledge-based economy, 139, 142
Kotkas, T., 160
Kowslowski, R., 14
Krause, E.L., 34–5, 42

Labour Government, 127
labour market, 99–100
 Australia, 114
 Brazilianisation of the West, 142
 Finland, 134–5
 highly skilled and low-skilled end of, 137
 Italy, 130
labour migrants, 107–46
 in care services, 184–5
  expansion of care sectors, 143–4
  in Finland, 156, 162–3
  gender care gap and, 131
  in Italy, 35–8, 169, 175–6
 children of. *See* children of immigrants
 citizenship and, 109
 in Finland, 109, 133–7
  Estonian immigrants, 136
  government policies on, 134–5, 136–7
  in health and social welfare sectors, 156, 162–3
  sustainability of welfare standards and, 135–6
  women migrants, 135, 140
 governance of, 137–46
 in Italy, 130–3
  entry through backdoor, 131–2
  low-skilled versus skilled migration, 132–3
  migrant care workers, 169
 justice and temporariness issues, 142
 parents of, 165–6, 170–1, 176–7, 182–3
 proportion of future population from, 64
 replacement of missing citizens of workforce age, 139
 in United Kingdom, 109, 126–30
labour supply, 138–9
lähihoitaja (practical nurse), 162
Laslett, P., 153
Lega Nord, 39, 132
Leitch report, 77
lesbians, 28
life expectancy, rise in, 125
London bombings 2005, 68, 75
low birth rates, 31–3
 in Australia, 113
 demographic transition and, 5
 in developed world, 7
 equal citizenship and, 61
 feminism and, 39
 in Finland, 150–1, 167

framing women as reproductive citizens and, 56–7
gender equity and, 33, 60, 138
in Global North, 188
in Italy, 29–30, 31, 35, 39
population ageing and, 8–9
in population panic of 1930s and 1940s, 49
in United Kingdom, 64–5
in women migrant workers, 38
workforce and, 114, 138–9
low-skilled migration, 138, 142
Lutz, W., 64

managed migration, 80, 127
Mares, P., 144
marriage, 71
 cousin, 76
 as event, 97
 forced, 79, 89
 intermarriage, 75
 Muslim, 75–6
marriage rorts, 88
maternity bonus, 53
McDonald, Peter (demographer), 33, 56
McNevin, A., 114
Meyers, D.T., 63
migrant care workers
 in Australia, 175–6
 expansion of care sectors, 143–4
 in Finland, 156, 162–3
 gender care gap and, 131
 in Global North, 184–5, 190
 in Italy, 35–8
  birth rates, 38
  hiring of immigrants, 169
  paid carers (*badanti*), 169, 175–6
 in United Kingdom, 171–4
 women, 131, 155, 185
migrant workers, 35–8, 64, 107–46
 children of. *See* children of immigrants
 citizenship of, 109–10, 137–46
 in Finland, 109, 133–7, 156, 162–3
  Estonian immigrants, 136
  government policies on, 134–5, 136–7
  sustainability of welfare standards and, 135–6
  women migrants, 135, 140
 governance of, 137–46
 in Italy, 130–3
  entry through backdoor, 131–2
  low-skilled versus skilled migration, 132–3
  migrant care workers, 169
 justice and temporariness issues, 142
 low-skilled, 143
 parents of, 165–6, 170–1, 176–7, 182–3

INDEX

replacement of missing citizens of workforce age, 139
  in United Kingdom, 109, 126–30
migration, 9–11, 190–1
  desirable, 110
  family, 80, 92, 123–4
  to Global North, 191
  low-skilled, 138, 142, 143
  managed, 80, 127
  skilled, 80, 123–4, 138, 140–1
  temporary, 144–5
  undesirable, 110
minorities, deficiencies of, 104
Mizen, P., 76
model minorities, 74
Mohammed, Suhyal, 102
Montevideo Convention on the Rights and Duties of States, 3
mortality, 5
motherhood, 34–5
multiculturalism, 77, 86–7
Muslims
  in Australia, 87
  birth rates, 42–3
  Islamophobia and, 78
  marriage, 75–6
  as a transnational risk category, 87
  in United Kingdom. *See* British Muslims

National Health Service (United Kingdom), 141
National Health System (Italy), 170
Nazi Germany, 3
Netherlands, 81
new capitalism, 32
New Labour, approach to youth problem, 76
Numerical Multifactor Assessment System (NUMAS), 112

older people
  care for, 152–3, 175–6
  categories as citizens, 178–9
  family caregiving of, 183–4
  fourth agers, 161, 181–2
  informal carers, 155
  management of ageing population and, 177–86
  over 65 age group, 150
  over 85 age group, 172
  parents of immigrant-citizens, 165–6, 182–3
  shouldering risk of old ages as active individuals, 179–80
  social security and welfare system for, 149
  state's role in care for, 161–2
  third agers, 178
  vulnerability of, 180–1
  women, 155

One Nation party, 88, 125
one-child couples, 60
over 65 age group, 178

paid carers
  attendance allowance (*indennità di accompagnamento*), 169
  in Australia, 175–6
  expansion of care sectors, 143–4
  in Finland, 156, 162–3
  gender care gap and, 131
  in Global North, 184–5, 190
  in Italy, 35–8, 169
    birth rates, 38
    hiring of immigrants, 169
    paid carers (*badanti*), 169, 175–6
  in United Kingdom, 171–4
Pakistani immigrants
  assimilation of, 74
  birth rates, 51
  forced marriage, 79
  immigrants, 84
parent visas, in Australia, 176
parents of migrant workers, 182–3
  in Finland, 165–6
  limiting the migration of, 182–3
  visas for, in Australia, 176
Pension Acts of 2007 and 2008 (United Kingdom), 171
pension reforms
  in Australia, 174–5
  in Finland, 158
  in Italy, 168
  in United Kingdom, 171
Peru, 90
Philippines, 90
  immigrant workers from, 38, 162
Points Based System (PBS), 127–8
Poland, 51
  immigrant workers from, 162
population, world, 5–6
population ageing. *See* demographic ageing
population control, neo-Malthusian, 3
population implosion, 29
population policies
  Australia, 51–5
  baby bonus, 40–1, 42–3, 53
  definition of, 3
  demographic governance and, 13–14
  Finland, 46–8
  in Global North, 3
  Italy, 39–45
  United Kingdom, 49–51
post study work visa, 122
practical nursing (*lähihoitaja*), 162
privatisation, 16
problem groups, 100

INDEX

pronatalism, 62
provisional citizens, 67

racial background, 74–5
real old age, 181–2
reconstituted families, 104
refugees, 191
reproductive efficiency, 5
reproductive governance
   citizenship and, 55–65
   problematic reproductive citizens and, 62–3
residential care, 159
retirement age, 151, 180–1
Roach report, 117–18
Romani minorities, 93
Ruhs, M., 143
Russia, immigrant workers from, 93, 162

same-sex partners, 104
Sassen, S., 140
Schaffner, L., 71
second demographic transition, 8–9, 70
Second World War, 28
second-generation immigrants, 67
   in Australia, 69
   citizenship of, 96–105
   in Finland, 69
   integration of, 68
   in Italy, 89–92
   media coverage of, 91
   problem groups, 100
   racial and ethnic background, 74–5
   role of structural factors, 73
   transitions into adulthood, 67–106
   in United Kingdom, 70–85
segmented assimilation, 74
September 11 attacks, 68, 87
serial sponsorship, 89
Shachar, A., 65
Shutes, I., 185
single mothers, 17
single parenthood, 62
skilled migration, 80, 123–4, 138, 140–1
Skirbekk, V., 63
social citizenship, feminist critiques of, 56
social emancipation, 34
social liberalisation, 32
Somali refugees, 93–4
South Asian immigrants, 100
   forced marriage, 79
   intermarriage, 75
   restriction of, 80
Southern Europe, 184
Soviet Union, collapse of, 134
Soysal, Y.N., 141
sponsorship of spouse, 81–2
state, definition of, 3

step-parenting, 59
superannuation benefits, 174
suspect populations, 17
sustainability, 7
Sydney gang rapes, 87

teenage pregnancy, 62, 73–4
temporary migration, 144–5
temporary visa programme, 108, 118–21, 141
terrorism, 78
third agers, 153, 160, 178. *See also* older people
third demographic transition, 11, 64
time dimension, role of, 2
total fertility rate (TFR), 7, 29, 45–6
totalisation and biopower, 15
transitions to adulthood. *See also* children of immigrants
   citizenship and, 96–105
   education and, 98–9
   marriage as event, 97
   new normative good transition, 97–8
transnational families, 101–2
Trans-Tasman Travel Arrangement (1973), 121
Treaty on the Functioning of European Union, 126
Tronto, J.C., 185
Turco-Napolitano law, 170
Turner, Bryan, 28

UK Independence Party, 130
unemployed women, 62
United Kingdom, 2
   below-replacement fertility in, 45–6
   birth rate decline in, 45–6, 49, 51
   care workers in, 144, 171–4
   children of immigrants in, 70–85
   demographic ageing in, 149, 171–4
   human capital, 127
   immigration
      control after Second World War, 49
      net migration in 2014, 130
      zero immigration in late 1990s, 126
   immigration policy
      entry of immigrants over 65, 173
      long-term ethnic change, 51
      on non-EU citizens, 79–81
   labour market, 128–9
   labour migrants in, 109, 126–30
   liberal welfare regime in, 49–50
   low birth rates in, 64–5
   multiculturalism, 77
   pension reforms in, 171
   population
      growth in 2015, 64–5
      over 65 age group in, 167

panic in 1930s, 49
projected population by 2030, 51
population policy, 49–51
second-generation immigrants
  governance of, 76–85
  transitions to adulthood, 70–85
social care system in, 172–3
unmarried couples, 104

Vallin, Jacques, 3
Vanhanen, Matti, 47
victims of violence, 84
visa
  aged parent visas in Australia, 176
  457 visa programme in Australia, 108, 118–21, 141
  post study work, 122
  spousal, 81
  temporary visa programme, 108, 118–21, 141
  working holidaymaker, 121

Wales, birth rates, 45–6
welfare recipients, 17
welfare state
  demographic ageing in, 150–7
  social-democratic model, 154–5
  sustainability of standards in, 135–6
White Australia policy, 52, 86, 110–16
women
  childbearing
    and birth rates in United Kingdom, 49–50
    early, 62, 73–4, 79
    in Finland, 47
    global trends in, 6
    ideals in late-modern states, 56
    of immigrant women, 64
    immigration and patterns in, 38
    in late-modern states, 56
    men's behaviour towards, 59
    opportunity costs of, 32
    postponement of, 71
    skilled migrants, 140
    teenage pregnancy, 62, 73–4
    youthful, 62, 73–4
  fertility concerns
    in Australia, 45–6, 51
    in Finland, 45–6, 48

  in Global North, 7
  in Italy, 29
  in United Kingdom, 45–6, 49, 51
  in Finland's labour market, 135
  as reproductive citizens, 56–7
  reproductive rights, 61–2
  single mothers, 17
  unemployed, 62
  voluntary childlessness, 58
women migrants
  in Australia, 123–4
  for care and domestic work, 35–8
  in Finland, 135, 140
  from Global South, 144
  skilled, 140
women's citizenship
  feminist arguments, 57–8
  reproduction issues and, 58
women's rights
  biopolitical focus on, 59
  multiculturalism and, 87
  reproductive rights, 61–2
  violence against women and, 87
worker-citizens, 141
working holidaymaker visa, 121
world population, 5–6

youth, immigrant
  in Australia, 69
  citizenship of, 65, 67, 96–105
  education of, 98–9
  in Finland, 69
  governing misguided, 76–85
  integration of, 68
  in Italy, 43–4, 69, 89–92
  labour market, 99–100
  media coverage of, 91
  problem groups, 100
  racial and ethnic background, 74–5
  role of structural factors, 73
  transitions into adulthood, 67–106
    citizenship and, 96–105
    education and, 98–9
    marriage as event, 97
    new normative good transition, 97–8
  in United Kingdom, 70–85
Yugoslavia, 90
Yuval-Davis, N., 16

CAMBRIDGE STUDIES IN LAW AND SOCIETY

Books in the Series

China and Islam:
The Prophet, the Party, and Law
Matthew S. Erie

Diversity in Practice:
Race, Gender, and Class in Legal and Professional Careers
Edited by Spencer Headworth and Robert Nelson

Diseases of the Will
Mariana Valverde

The Politics of Truth and Reconciliation in South Africa:
Legitimizing the Post-Apartheid State
Richard A. Wilson

Modernism and the Grounds of Law
Peter Fitzpatrick

Unemployment and Government:
Genealogies of the Social
William Walters

Autonomy and Ethnicity:
Negotiating Competing Claims in Multi-Ethnic States
Yash Ghai

Constituting Democracy:
Law, Globalism and South Africa's Political Reconstruction
Heinz Klug

The Ritual of Rights in Japan:
Law, Society, and Health Policy
Eric A. Feldman

The Invention of the Passport:
Surveillance, Citizenship and the State
John Torpey

Governing Morals:
A Social History of Moral Regulation
Alan Hunt

The Colonies of Law:
Colonialism, Zionism and Law in Early Mandate Palestine
Ronen Shamir

Law and Nature
David Delaney

Social Citizenship and Workfare in the United States and Western Europe:
The Paradox of Inclusion
Joel F. Handler

Law, Anthropology and the Constitution of the Social:
Making Persons and Things
Edited by Alain Pottage and Martha Mundy

Judicial Review and Bureaucratic Impact:
International and Interdisciplinary Perspectives
Edited by Marc Hertogh and Simon Halliday

Immigrants at the Margins:
Law, Race, and Exclusion in Southern Europe
Kitty Calavita

Lawyers and Regulation:
The Politics of the Administrative Process
Patrick Schmidt

Law and Globalization from Below:
Toward a Cosmopolitan Legality
Edited by Boaventura de Sousa Santos and Cesar A. Rodriguez-Garavito

Public Accountability:
Designs, Dilemmas and Experiences
Edited by Michael W. Dowdle

Law, Violence and Sovereignty among West Bank Palestinians
Tobias Kelly

Legal Reform and Administrative Detention Powers in China
Sarah Biddulph

The Practice of Human Rights:
Tracking Law Between the Global and the Local
Edited by Mark Goodale and Sally Engle Merry

Judges Beyond Politics in Democracy and Dictatorship:
Lessons from Chile
Lisa Hilbink

Paths to International Justice:
Social and Legal Perspectives
Edited by Marie-Bénédicte Dembour and Tobias Kelly

Law and Society in Vietnam:
The Transition from Socialism in Comparative Perspective
Mark Sidel

Constitutionalizing Economic Globalization:
Investment Rules and Democracy's Promise
David Schneiderman

The New World Trade Organization Knowledge Agreements:
2nd Edition
Christopher Arup

Justice and Reconciliation in Post-Apartheid South Africa
Edited by François du Bois and Antje du Bois-Pedain

Militarization and Violence against Women in Conflict Zones in the Middle East:
A Palestinian Case-Study
Nadera Shalhoub-Kevorkian

Child Pornography and Sexual Grooming:
Legal and Societal Responses
Suzanne Ost

Darfur and the Crime of Genocide
John Hagan and Wenona Rymond-Richmond

Fictions of Justice:
The International Criminal Court and the Challenge of Legal Pluralism in Sub-Saharan Africa
Kamari Maxine Clarke

Conducting Law and Society Research:
Reflections on Methods and Practices
Simon Halliday and Patrick Schmidt

Planted Flags:
Trees, Land, and Law in Israel/Palestine
Irus Braverman

Culture under Cross-Examination:
International Justice and the Special Court for Sierra Leone
Tim Kelsall

Cultures of Legality:
Judicialization and Political Activism in Latin America
Javier Couso, Alexandra Huneeus, Rachel Sieder

Courting Democracy in Bosnia and Herzegovina:
The Hague Tribunal's Impact in a Postwar State
Lara J. Nettelfield

The Gacaca Courts and Post-Genocide Justice and
Reconciliation in Rwanda:
Justice without Lawyers
Phil Clark

Law, Society, and History:
Themes in the Legal Sociology and Legal History of Lawrence M. Friedman
Robert W. Gordon and Morton J. Horwitz

After Abu Ghraib:
Exploring Human Rights in America and the Middle East
Shadi Mokhtari

Adjudication in Religious Family Laws:
Cultural Accommodation: Legal Pluralism, and Gender Equality in India
Gopika Solanki

Water On Tap:
Rights and Regulation in the Transnational Governance of Urban Water Services
Bronwen Morgan

Elements of Moral Cognition:
Rawls' Linguistic Analogy and the Cognitive Science of Moral and Legal Judgment
John Mikhail

A Sociology of Constitutions:
Constitutions and State Legitimacy in Historical-Sociological Perspective
Chris Thornhill

Mitigation and Aggravation at Sentencing
Edited by Julian Roberts

Institutional Inequality and the Mobilization of the Family and
Medical Leave Act:
Rights on Leave
Catherine R. Albiston

Authoritarian Rule of Law:
Legislation, Discourse and Legitimacy in Singapore
Jothie Rajah

Law and Development and the Global Discourses of Legal Transfers
Edited by John Gillespie and Pip Nicholson

Law against the State:
Ethnographic Forays into Law's Transformations
Edited by Julia Eckert, Brian Donahoe, Christian Strümpell
and Zerrin Özlem Biner

Transnational Legal Process and State Change
Edited by Gregory C. Shaffer

Legal Mobilization under Authoritarianism:
The Case of Post-Colonial Hong Kong
Edited by Waikeung Tam

Complementarity in the Line of Fire:
The Catalysing Effect of the International Criminal Court in Uganda and Sudan
Sarah M. H. Nouwen

Political and Legal Transformations of an Indonesian Polity:
The Nagari from Colonisation to Decentralisation
Franz von Benda-Beckmann and Keebet von Benda-Beckmann

Pakistan's Experience with Formal Law:
An Alien Justice
Osama Siddique

Human Rights under State-Enforced Religious Family Laws in Israel, Egypt, and India
Yüksel Sezgin

Why Prison?
Edited by David Scott

Law's Fragile State:
Colonial, Authoritarian, and Humanitarian Legacies in Sudan
Mark Fathi Massoud

Rights for Others:
The Slow Home-Coming of Human Rights in the Netherlands
Barbara Oomen

European States and their Muslim Citizens:
The Impact of Institutions on Perceptions and Boundaries
Edited by John R. Bowen, Christophe Bertossi, Jan Willem Duyvendak
and Mona Lena Krook

Environmental Litigation in China
Rachel E. Stern

Indigeneity and Legal Pluralism in India:
Claims, Histories, Meanings
Pooja Parmar

Paper Tiger:
Law, Bureaucracy and the Developmental State in Himalayan India
Nayanika Mathur

Contractual Knowledge:
One Hundred Years of Legal Experimentation in Global Markets
Edited by Grégoire Mallard and Jérôme Sgard

Religion, Law and Society
Russell Sandberg

The Experiences of Face Veil Wearers in Europe and the Law
Edited by Eva Brems

The Contentious History of the International Bill of Human Rights
Christopher N. J. Roberts

Transnational Legal Orders
Edited by Terence C. Halliday and Gregory Shaffer

Lost in China?, Law, Culture and Society in Post-1997 Hong Kong
Carol A. G. Jones

Security Theology, Surveillance and the Politics of Fear
Nadera Shalhoub-Kevorkian

Opposing the Rule of Law:
How Myanmar's Courts Make Law and Order
Nick Cheesman

The Ironies of Colonial Governance:
Law, Custom and Justice in Colonial India
James Jaffe

The Clinic and the Court:
Law, Medicine and Anthropology
Edited by Tobias Kelly, Ian Harper and Akshay Khanna

A World of Indicators:
The Making of Government Knowledge Through Quantification
Edited by Richard Rottenburg, Sally E. Merry, Sung-Joon Park and Johanna Mugler

Contesting Immigration Policy in Court:
Legal Activism and its Radiating Effects in the United States and France
Leila Kawar

The Quiet Power of Indicators:
Measuring Governance, Corruption, and Rule of Law
Edited by Sally Engle Merry, Kevin Davis, and Benedict Kingsbury

Investing in Authoritarian Rule:
Punishment and Patronage in Rwanda's Gacaca Courts for Genocide Crimes
Anuradha Chakravarty

Iraq and the Crimes of Aggressive War:
The Legal Cynicism of Criminal Militarism
John Hagan, Joshua Kaiser, and Anna Hanson

Culture in the Domains of Law
Edited by René Provost

A Sociology of Transnational Constitutions:
Social Foundations of the Post-National Legal Structure
Chris Thornhill

Shifting Legal Visions:
Judicial Change and Human Rights Trials in Latin America
Ezequiel A. González Ocantos

The Demographic Transformations of Citizenship
Heli Askola

Criminal Defense in China:
The Politics of Lawyers at Work
Sida Liu and Terence C. Halliday

Contesting Economic and Social Rights in Ireland:
Constitution, State and Society, 1848–2016
Thomas Murray

Buried in the Heart:
Women, Complex Victimhood and the War in Northern Uganda
Erin Baines

Palaces of Hope:
The Anthropology of Global Organizations
Edited by Ronald Niezen and Maria Sapignoli